The Handbook of
Victim Offender Mediation

Mark S. Umbreit

Foreword by Marlene A. Young

The Handbook
of
Victim Offender
Mediation

**An Essential Guide to
Practice and Research**

Sponsored by the
Center for Restorative Justice & Peacemaking
University of Minnesota, School of Social Work

 JOSSEY-BASS
A Wiley Company
San Francisco

Jossey-Bass books and products are available through most bookstores. To contact Jossey-Bass directly, call (888) 378-2537, fax to (800) 605-2665, or visit our website at www.josseybass.com.
Substantial discounts on bulk quantities of Jossey-Bass books are available to corporations, professional associations, and other organizations. For details and discount information, contact the special sales department at Jossey-Bass.

 Manufactured in the United States of America on Lyons Falls Turin Book. This paper is acid-free and 100 percent totally chlorine-free.

Library of Congress Cataloging-in-Publication Data

Umbreit, Mark S., date.
   The handbook of victim offender mediation: an essential guide to practice and research/ Mark S. Umbreit; sponsored by the Center for Restorative Justice & Peacemaking.—1st ed.
      p. cm.
   Includes bibliographical references and index.
   ISBN 0-7879-5491-8 (alk. paper)
   1. Restorative justice. 2. Victims of crimes. 3. Mediation. 4. Criminals—Rehabilitation.
I. Center for Restorative Justice & Peacemaking. II. Title.
   HV8688 .U52 2000
   364.6'5—dc21   00-063928

FIRST EDITION
HB Printing   10 9 8 7 6 5 4 3 2 1

Contents

Part One: Philosophy, Practice, and Context

Part Two: What We Are Learning from Research

Part Three: Emerging Issues

Appendixes

Tables and Exhibits

Tables

Exhibits

This book is dedicated to the courage and strength of the thousands of crime victims, offenders, family members, and community activists and volunteers throughout the world who have breathed life into the notion of restorative justice through their participation in victim offender mediation and dialogue in one form or another.

All royalties from this book are being donated to the Umbreit Scholarship Fund for Restorative Justice & Peacemaking at the University of Minnesota School of Social Work to support the development of a new generation of restorative justice practitioners and scholars.

Foreword

Over the past twenty-five years, the victims' movement in the United States has made revolutionary change in the criminal justice system. Victims have been given more and more privileges that allow them to receive accurate and timely information and notification about their cases, to participate in plea bargains and sentencing decisions, to receive restitution from the offender, and to be present at critical stages in prosecution.

Despite these changes, victims often remain dissatisfied with the traditional processes of justice. The reasons are several: First, though many of these privileges are entitled "rights" through state or federal statutes, they in fact remain privileges that may or may not be extended in every case. Second, a critical question for many victims as they seek to understand what happened to them is why it happened to them. Since the adversarial process is not designed necessarily to elicit truth and of necessity precludes dialogue between victim and offender, there is little opportunity for victims to hear explanations from the accused—even from the great majority who plead guilty to one or more of the charges. Third, the adversarial system has not been particularly oriented toward altering patterns of criminal behavior—those concerns are handed off to correctional authorities. A common theme for many victims and survivors as they attempt to reconstruct their lives is their determination to prevent what happened to them from happening to others. Yet recidivism rates remain high, and despite the recent reduction in overall crime, violent crimes continue to take place in the United States with much greater frequency than in most other countries of the world. And fourth, the "accountability model" of corrections, championed by James Rowland and others, has not taken hold enough to satisfy many victims. Rowland's contribution to the model, the victim impact statement, is now a widespread tool of sentencing and parole decision makers, but all too often its submission does not lead to any acknowledgment or deeds of contrition from the offender.

It was in this environment that the National Organization for Victim Assistance (NOVA) began to explore alternative schemes of justice over a decade ago. That exploration evolved into the development of a concept of "restorative community justice"—a system that would be centered on the victim's restoration through practical assistance, crisis intervention, counseling, advocacy, and opportunities for involvement in the justice process when the victim desired it; driven by community involvement in preventing crime, responding to the criminal behavior, supporting the victim, and encouraging the reformation of offenders; and focused on holding the offender accountable for his or her behavior through restitution, reintegrative shame, and remorse.

These ideas were all drawn from the heritage of indigenous populations such as the Maori in New Zealand, Indian nations in Canada and the United States, and the Aborigines in Australia and were modified to reflect modern knowledge and experience.

Victim offender mediation is one process of striving for restorative justice and, by far, the most widespread in North America. It has most often been used to address property crimes and minor assaults, and it is most prominently used in juvenile justice systems. However, it has also been used with victims and offenders in serious and violent crimes.

One of its positive features for *victim* restoration, other than promoting restitution, is the opportunity for victims to talk to their offenders and understand the motivations behind the crime. It is a chance for them to master certain aspects of their own story of trauma by learning details that only the offender would know. A positive feature for *offender* restoration is the opportunity for offenders to learn of the impact of their actions on their victims and to begin to make amends.

Although studies of victim offender mediation have generally indicated satisfaction with the results, there remains considerable resistance to the idea among many in the victims' community. Much of this resistance seems to be based on fears and misperceptions of the process of victim offender mediation because it is confused with other types of mediation that view parties in mediation as equally culpable. Some of the resistance has arisen out of situations where uninformed criminal justice professionals have attempted victim offender mediation without proper training or without following clear guidelines governing its application. A third element of resistance is that many people believe that if restorative justice or victim offender mediation is offered, it would be applied to all cases, when it is generally recognized that the most "restorative" of these approaches succeeds only when participation by both victim and offender is voluntary.

The Handbook of Victim Offender Mediation: An Essential Guide to Practice and Research is a major contribution to the growing field of victim offender mediation and to the discussion of its efficacy for restoring victims to a new life. It both succinctly clarifies the philosophical basis for using a restorative justice approach and outlines specific guidelines for implementation. It provides a well-researched summary of the results of evaluations of victim offender mediation programs that can be of great value to public policy and criminal justice officials seeking to integrate victim offender mediation into systems of justice. It describes the process with simplicity so that both victims and victim advocates can make a determination whether they want to participate in such a proceeding. It also looks at new developments in the field so that the future implications of victim offender mediation programs can be assessed.

Whether readers are newcomers to the concept, experienced practitioners, or researchers in the area, this book is a practical exegesis of the state of the art in victim offender mediation today. It is an important and timely contribution in the worldwide victims' movement's advancement toward justice and healing.

Washington, D.C.   Marlene A. Young, Ph.D., J.D.
September 2000   Executive Director
                        National Organization for Victim Assistance

Preface

The presence of crime and victimization in our communities continues to cause enormous harm, frustration, anger, disruption, and trauma. A movement that offers a very different way of understanding and responding to crime—by empowering the people most affected by its impact and directly involving them in the process of doing justice—is gathering strength throughout North America, Europe, the South Pacific, and other parts of the world. Restorative justice moves far beyond the traditional liberal and conservative policies of the past. A victim-centered approach, restorative justice provides practical opportunities for crime victims and community members to work with offenders, holding them accountable for the harm they have caused while at the same time assisting with their reintegration into the community. The heart of restorative justice is engaging the participation of crime victims and communities to the greatest extent possible in the process of holding offenders accountable for repairing the harm they have caused. The opportunities it provides for dialogue among and between crime victims, offenders, families, and other members of the community bring the theory of restorative justice to life.

Twenty five years ago, the early experiments with restorative justice practices, such as victim offender reconciliation, were often met with tremendous skepticism and even hostility. Today, many former doubters and critics are active stakeholders in this growing international social reform movement. Both the American Bar Association, which has fully endorsed victim offender mediation, and the National Organization for Victim Assistance, which is actively involved in the movement, are the clearest examples of this turnabout in attitudes.

Restorative justice theory is most clearly exemplified in the emerging field of victim offender mediation (VOM), which now has more than thirteen hundred programs in North America and Europe. Meeting face to face in the presence of a trained mediator, victims, offenders, and often family members are able to talk with each other about how the crime has affected them, receive answers to questions they may have, and negotiate a plan for the offender to compensate the victim for losses and harm. This effort, developed extensively in recent years, serves as one of the most creative ways to further offender accountability and healthy youth development, promote victim assistance and active involvement in the justice system, and strengthen public safety and community connectedness.

As the field of restorative justice and victim offender mediation grows, there is a pressing need to keep the movement grounded in its core values and the empirical research and practice wisdom that has accumulated over a quarter of a century yet is still not widely known.

This book offers a practical state-of-the-art perspective on VOM for practitioners and researchers. It reflects material developed over a period of years by myself and my colleagues at the Center for Restorative Justice & Peacemaking (formerly the Center for Restorative Justice & Mediation) at the University of Minnesota School of Social Work. We have organized the book in an easy-to-access format that can serve as a primary reference for people just entering the field as well as a resource of substance for practitioners, policymakers, and researchers who are already involved in the restorative justice movement.

Part One focuses on the underlying philosophy, practices, and context of victim offender mediation. Chapter One describes the characteristics of humanistic mediation and its focus on premediation preparation of victims, offenders, and family members in order to provide an opportunity in a safe setting for direct dialogue between the parties, with minimal intervention by the mediator. Humanistic "dialogue-driven" mediation is quite different from the more common "settlement-driven" mediation, which features active intervention by the mediator and little, if any, premediation preparation of the parties. Humanistic mediation is at the heart of restorative justice through victim offender mediation. Chapters Two and Three offer specific guidelines for victim-sensitive mediation and dialogue with offenders and present the entire mediation process through its various phases and tasks. Chapter Four addresses important multicultural implications that are central to effective practice. Three case studies based on experience in the field—involving home burglary, auto theft, and damage to property—are presented in Chapter Five. Moving from the specifics of program philosophy, practice guidelines and phases, and case studies to a broader perspective, Chapters Six and Seven present details of the first large national survey of VOM programs throughout the United States, including important characteristics in terms of program sponsorship, referrals, mediator training and numerous other process and outcome data, and extensive material related to program development issues to be faced by anyone interested in initiating or strengthening programs in the community.

Part Two focuses on what we have learned from research. Chapter Eight summarizes the dominant themes that emerge from forty studies in the field of victim offender mediation performed over a twenty-year period. Chapter Nine reports on the first cross-national study of victim offender mediation, which I and my colleagues conducted at several sites in the United States, Canada, and England. Chapters Ten through Twelve provide more details of the specific studies in four states in the United States, four provinces of Canada, and two cities in England. Similarities and differences between sites are highlighted, and specific process and outcome data for each national context are presented.

The two chapters in Part Three confront important emerging issues in the VOM field. Chapter Thirteen addresses the emerging practice of advanced mediation and dialogue in crimes of severe violence such as sexual assault, attempted homicide, and first-degree murder. In the early years of the movement, no one would have thought this was likely to occur. However, in response to the requests of a small but growing number of victims and family survivors of some of the most heinous crimes imaginable, victim offender mediation is entering new territory that has enormous potential to deepen the impact of restorative justice, accountability, and peacemaking. At the same time, however, without advanced training and mentorship, this development could also lead to numerous unintended negative consequences. These and other critical issues are addressed in Chapter Thirteen. Chapter Fourteen identifies a number of potential hazards that could threaten the integrity and impact of restorative justice practice through mediation sessions with victims, offenders, and family members, as well as promising opportunities arising in the field.

Six appendixes place a wide variety of information at your disposal: sources of written and video resources and training, a directory of VOM programs in the United States, program profiles, an outline of promising practices, a table summarizing the forty VOM studies discussed in Part Two, and information on a recently developed victim satisfaction scale with VOM and plans for creation of an offender satisfaction scale for use by local programs to obtain practical consumer feedback.

St. Paul, Minnesota   Mark S. Umbreit
September 2000

Acknowledgments

This manuscript is based on the collective experience and contributions of numerous practitioners and scholars. The coauthors of selected chapters—William Bradshaw, Robert Coates, Jean Greenwood, Terri Grob, and Annie Roberts—have contributed enormously to the overall quality of this book. It has been an honor to work with such talented and gifted colleagues.

Special thanks also goes to the practitioners throughout North America and Europe whose wisdom has contributed in many ways to the material presented. Numerous discussions with members of the board of directors of the international Victim Offender Mediation Association have also led to important observations and contributions.

Many other staff and student assistants who have been affiliated with the Center for Restorative Justice & Peacemaking at the University of Minnesota over the years and made their own unique contributions deserve thanks. The assistance provided by Heather Burns, graduate research assistant, in editing the chapter on program development was particularly helpful. I would also like to acknowledge the valuable contribution of Robert Schug, former administrative aide at the Center for Restorative Justice & Peacemaking, to the production of many of the early documents that evolved into this manuscript. Grants from the Hewlett Foundation and the Office for Victims of Crime of the U.S. Department of Justice supported the initial development of many materials on which this book is based.

Preparation of this manuscript would never have been possible without the consistent support, patience, and talent of Betty Vos, who served as senior editor.

Last but not least, I owe my ability to engage in practice, training, research, and writing for the past thirty years almost entirely to the devotion and loving forbearance of my wife, Alexa, and my two daughters, Jenni and Laura.

M.S.U.

Introduction:
Restorative Justice Through Victim
Offender Mediation

One of the significant international developments in our current thinking about crime is the growing interest in restorative justice. At a time when the public debate around issues of crime and punishment is driven largely by political leaders embracing the conservative or liberal solutions of the past, restorative justice offers a fundamentally different framework for understanding and responding to crime and victimization in society. Restorative justice emphasizes the importance of elevating the role of crime victims and community members, holding offenders directly accountable to the people they have violated, restoring the emotional and material losses of victims, and providing a range of opportunities for dialogue, negotiation, and problem solving, whenever possible, that can lead to a greater sense of community safety, conflict resolution, and closure for all involved.

In contrast to the offender-driven nature of our current system of justice, restorative justice focuses on three client groups: crime victims, offenders, and community members. It represents a growing international movement with a relatively clear set of values, principles, and guidelines for practice, though at this point in its development still lacking a comprehensive plan for broad implementation as a new paradigm that might fully replace our current systems of juvenile and criminal justice.

Unresolved Issues Facing the Justice System

Restorative justice policies and practices have emerged in direct response to unresolved issues facing juvenile and criminal justice systems throughout the free Western world. In the United States, these unresolved issues have had an enormous impact on public policy, individual and community attitudes, and the quality of justice experienced by the individuals most directly affected by crime.

At a time when the emphasis on retribution is increasing, contradictory impulses between punishment and rehabilitation persist among correctional policymakers and practitioners. One such contradiction reflects a lack of clarity regarding the basic purpose of sentencing. Is it meant to rehabilitate and change offender behavior? Are criminal sentences meant to deter others from committing crimes? Or should the purpose of sentencing be to incapacitate criminals or remove them from circulation in society for a set period of time? These and other conflicting goals contribute to confusion about what courts are trying to achieve.

Victims of crime feel increasingly frustrated and alienated by our current system of justice. Even though the justice system exists precisely because individual citizens have been violated by criminal behavior, crime victims have virtually no legal standing in American courts. The crime is against "the state," and state interests drive the process of meting out justice. Individual crime victims and representatives of victimized communities are left on the sidelines, with little, if any, opportunity for input. Crime victims frequently feel twice victimized—first by the offender and then by the criminal justice system that their tax dollars are paying for. For many crime victims, their encounter with the justice system leads to increasing frustration and anger as they realize that they are being largely ignored and are often not even provided with information about the process, court date changes, or the final disposition of the case. Rarely do criminal justice professionals take the time to listen to the fears and concerns of crime victims and then seek their input and invite their participation in holding the offender accountable.

The failure of ever-harsher punishments to change criminal behavior is another problem facing our nation's juvenile and criminal justice systems. If severe punishment and incarceration were effective, America should be one of the safest societies in the world. Despite the common perception among many citizens that the United States is too lenient on criminals, the fact is that more Americans are locked up in prisons, per capita, than in any other developed nation in the world except Russia. Furthermore, sentences in the United States are far in excess of those in other democratic Western nations, and it is the only developed nation that still routinely employs capital punishment.

Finally, the skyrocketing cost of corrections—and incarceration specifically—is driving a growing number of legislatures and policymakers to reconsider the wisdom of the current retributive system of justice, which relies heavily on incarceration of offenders while largely ignoring the needs of crime victims.

What Is Restorative Justice?

Restorative justice is a victim-centered response to crime that gives the individuals most directly affected by a criminal act— the victim, the offender, their families, and representatives of the community—the opportunity to be directly involved in responding to the harm caused by the crime. Restorative justice is based on values that emphasize the importance of providing more active support and assistance to crime victims; holding offenders directly accountable to the people and communities they have violated; restoring the emotional and material losses of victims as much as possible; providing a range of opportunities for dialogue and problem solving among interested crime victims, offenders, families, and other support persons; offering offenders opportunities for competency development and reintegration into productive community life; and strengthening public safety through community building.

Restorative justice provides an entirely different way of thinking about crime and victimization (Van Ness & Strong, 1999). The prevailing retributive justice paradigm regards the state as the primary victim of criminal acts and casts victims and offenders in passive roles; restorative justice, by contrast, recognizes crime as first and foremost an activity directed against individuals. It assumes that the persons most affected by crime should have the opportunity to become involved in resolving the conflict. The goals of restoring losses, allowing offenders to take direct responsibility for their actions, and helping victims move beyond their sense of vulnerability and achieve some measure of closure stand in sharp contrast to the conventional focus on past criminal behavior and increasing levels of punishment. Restorative justice attempts to draw on the strengths of both offenders and victims, rather than dwelling on their deficits. While denouncing criminal behavior, restorative justice emphasizes the need to treat offenders with respect and to reintegrate them into the larger community in ways that can lead them to engage in lawful behavior. It represents a truly different paradigm based on the following values:

1. Restorative justice is concerned far more about restoration of the victim and the victimized community than about the ever more costly punishment of the offender.

2. Restorative justice elevates the importance of the victim in the criminal justice process through increased involvement, input, and services.

3. Restorative justice requires that offenders be held directly accountable to the person or community that they victimized.

4. Restorative justice encourages the entire community to be involved in holding the offender accountable and promoting a healing response to the needs of victims and offenders.

5. Restorative justice places greater emphasis on having offenders accept responsibility for their behavior and make amends, whenever possible, than on the severity of punishment.

6. Restorative justice recognizes a community responsibility for social conditions that contribute to offender behavior.

In a very real sense, the theory of restorative justice provides a blueprint for the future by drawing on the wisdom of the past. Following the Norman invasion of Britain in the eleventh century, a major shift occurred as people turned away from the prevailing understanding of crime as a victim offender conflict. William the Conqueror's son, Henry I, issued a decree securing royal jurisdiction over certain offenses (robbery, arson, murder, theft, and other violent crimes) against the "king's peace." Prior to this decree, crime had been viewed as a matter between individuals, and an emphasis on repairing the damage by making amends to the victim was well established.

Restorative justice also draws on the rich heritage of many recent justice reform movements, including community corrections, victim advocacy, and community policing. The principles of restorative justice are consistent with those of many indigenous traditions, including the Native American, Hawaiian, Canadian First Nation, and Maori cultures. These principles are also consistent with values emphasized by nearly all of the world religions.

Many of these principles can also be seen in the pioneering work of the Australian scholar John Braithwaite, who addresses the issues of crime, shame, and reintegration. Braithwaite (1989) argues for "reintegrative shaming," a type of social control based on informal community condemnation of wrongdoing, but with opportunities for the reintegration of the wrongdoer back into the community. He notes that in societies with low crime rates, people do *not* mind their own business, there are clearly understood limits to toleration of deviance, and communities have a preference for handling their own problems. Braithwaite argues for principles of justice that emphasize the personal accountability of offenders, active community involvement, and offender reconciliation and reaffirmation—principles that are deeply embedded in the restorative justice paradigm, with its emphasis on mediation and dialogue whenever possible.

The distinction between the old paradigm of retributive justice and the new paradigm of restorative justice has been most clearly articulated through the pioneering work of Howard Zehr at the Conflict Transformation Program of Eastern Mennonite University in Virginia, as summarized in Exhibit I.1. Whereas retributive justice focuses on punishment, the restorative paradigm emphasizes accountability, engagement of the parties most affected by the crime in responding to its impact, and repair of the emotional and physical harm caused, to the greatest extent possible.

How Widespread Is Restorative Justice?

The initial conceptualization of restorative justice began in the late 1970s and was first clearly articulated by Zehr (1985, 1990). At that time, the discussion of this new paradigm was based largely in North America, with a small additional network of academicians and practitioners in Europe. But at the time, restorative justice was not being considered seriously by the mainstream of criminal and juvenile justice policymakers and practitioners.

Governmental and Organizational Support

By 1990, an international conference supported by NATO funds was convened in Italy to examine the growing interest in restorative justice throughout the world. Academicians and practitioners from a dozen countries (Austria, Belgium, Canada, Finland, France, Germany, Greece, Italy, the Netherlands, Norway, Turkey, and the United Kingdom) presented papers related to the development and impact of restorative justice policies and practice.

Exhibit I.1 Paradigms of Justice

Retributive	Restorative
1. Crime defined as violation of the state	1. Crime defined as violation of one person by another
2. Focus on establishing blame, on guilt, on past (did he/she do it?)	2. Focus on problem solving, on liabilities and obligations, on future (what should be done?)
3. Adversarial relationship and process normative	3. Dialogue & negotiation normative
4. Imposition of pain to punish and deter/prevent	4. Restitution as a means of restoring both parties' goal of reconciliation/restoration
5. Justice defined by intent & process: right rules	5. Justice defined as right relationships and outcomes
6. Interpersonal, conflictual nature of crime obscured, repressed; conflict seen as individual vs. the state	6. Crime recognized as interpersonal conflict; value of conflict is recognized
7. One social injury replaced by another	7. Focus on repair of social injury
8. Community on sideline, represented abstractly by state	8. Community as facilitator in restorative process
9. Encouragement of competitive, individualistic values	9. Encouragement of mutuality
10. Action directed from state to offender • victim ignored • offender passive	10. Victim & offender engaged in the process • victim rights/needs recognized • offender encouraged to take responsibility
11. Offender accountability defined as taking punishment	11. Offender accountability defined as understanding impact of action and helping decide how to make things right
12. Offense defined in purely legal terms, devoid of moral social, economic and political dimensions	12. Offense understood in whole context—moral, social, economic, political dimensions

(Continued)

Exhibit I.1 Paradigms of Justice, cont'd.

Retributive	Restorative
13. "Debt" owed to state and society in the abstract	13. Debt/liability to victim recognized
14. Response focused on offender's past behavior	14. Response focused on harmful consequences of offender's behavior
15. Stigma of crime irreparable	15. Stigma of crime reparable through restorative action
16. No encouragement for repentance & forgiveness	16. Possibilities for repentance & forgiveness
17. Dependence upon proxy professionals	17. Direct involvement by participants

Source: Zehr, 1985, p. 18. Used with permission.

International interest in restorative justice has continued to grow. In 1995, the New Zealand Ministry of Justice issued a working paper on restorative justice for serious consideration as a federal policy. During 1996 and 1997, a group of scholars in North America, Europe, and the South Pacific (Australia and New Zealand) interested in restorative justice met in the United States and Belgium to examine this emerging theory further. Increasingly large international restorative justice conferences have been convened in subsequent years.

In the United States, the pace of interest in restorative justice has picked up in recent years. The restorative justice practice of victim offender mediation (VOM), which began in the late 1970s, is now quite widespread. The American Bar Association (ABA) has played a major leadership role in the area of civil court mediation for more than two decades. After many years of little interest in criminal mediation, the ABA in the summer of 1994 fully endorsed the practice of victim offender mediation and recommended its development in courts throughout the country.

In January 1996, the U.S. Department of Justice convened its first national conference on restorative justice, bringing together policymakers and practitioners from all over the country. This was followed by five Department of Justice–sponsored regional restorative justice conferences during 1997 and 1998. Thousands of restorative justice information packets have been sent out by the Center for Restorative Justice & Peacemaking at the University of Minnesota, the Community Justice Institute at Florida Atlantic University, and related organizations in response to requests from correctional officials, policymakers, and practitioners.

Perhaps one of the clearest expressions of the growing support for restorative justice is the National Organization for Victim Assistance's monograph endorsing "restorative community justice" (Young, 1995). During the early years of this movement, most victim advocacy groups were skeptical. Many still are; however, growing numbers of victim support organizations now actively participate in the restorative justice movement.

Public Opinion and Interest

Despite growing governmental and organizational support for restorative justice theory and practice, the question remains, Is the larger public really interested? Is there evidence of public support for the principles of restorative justice? The strong "law and order" and "get tough" rhetoric that dominates most political campaigns would suggest not. After all, how often have we heard ambitious politicians or criminal justice officials state that "the public demands that we get tougher with criminals"? This perception— or, some would argue, misperception—fuels the engine that drives the nation toward ever-increasing and ever more costly criminal punishments.

There is, however, a growing body of evidence to suggest that the general public is far less vindictive than often portrayed and far more supportive of the basic principles of restorative justice than many observers might think, particularly when applied to property offenders. Studies in Alabama, Delaware, Maryland, Michigan, Minnesota, North Carolina, Oregon, and Vermont have consistently found a public deeply concerned with holding offenders accountable while being supportive of community-based sanctions that allow for more restorative outcomes.

A study from Minnesota is particularly illustrative. The results of a statewide public opinion survey, conducted by the University of Minnesota (Pranis & Umbreit, 1992) using a large probability sample, challenges conventional wisdom about public feelings related to crime and punishment. A sample of 825 Minnesota adults, demographically and geographically balanced to reflect the state's total population, were asked three questions with implications for restorative justice as part of a larger omnibus survey. A sampling of this size has a sampling error of plus or minus 3.5 percentage points.

The first question was, "Suppose that while you are away, your home is burglarized and $1,200 worth of property is stolen. The burglar has one previous conviction for a similar offense. In addition to four years on probation, would you prefer the sentence include repayment of $1,200 to you or four months in jail?" Nearly three out of four Minnesotans indicated that having the offender pay restitution was more important than a jail sentence for the burglary.

To examine public support for policies that address some of the underlying social problems that often cause crime, a concern that is closely related to restorative justice, the following question was asked: "For the greatest impact on reducing crime, should additional money be spent on more prisons or on education, job training, and community programs?" Spending on education, job training, and community programs rather than on prisons to reduce crime was favored by four out of five Minnesotans.

The third and final question related to restorative justice addressed the issue of interest in victim offender mediation. This question was presented in the following manner: "Minnesota has several programs that allow crime victims to meet with the person who committed the crime, in the presence of a trained mediator, to let this person know how the crime affected them, and to work out a plan for repayment of losses. Suppose you were the victim of a nonviolent property crime committed by a juvenile or a young adult. How likely would you be to participate in a program like this?" More than four of five Minnesotans expressed an interest in participating in a face-to-face mediation session with the offender. This finding is particularly significant in that criminal justice officials and program staff who are unfamiliar with mediation often make such comments as "There is no way in the world that victims in my community would ever want to confront the offender" or "Only a small portion of victims would ever be interested." The finding is further noteworthy because the vast majority of crime is committed by either juveniles or young adults. Some theorists suggest that the victim offender mediation process is likely to be supported only for crimes involving juvenile offenders. This is certainly not the case in Minnesota. Fully 82 percent of respondents indicated that they would be likely to participate in a program that would allow them to meet the juvenile or young adult who victimized them.

A picture of a far less vindictive public than is often portrayed emerges from this statewide survey. Respondents indicated greater concern for restitution and prevention strategies that address underlying issues of social injustice than for costly retribution. Holding offenders personally accountable to their victim is more important than incarceration. Public safety is understood to be more directly related to investing in job training, education, and other community programs than in imprisonment.

While it might be tempting to suggest that this public opinion survey simply reflects the liberal social policy tradition of Minnesota, its findings are consistent with a growing body of public opinion research (Bae, 1992; Galaway, 1984; Gottfredson & Taylor, 1983; Public Agenda Foundation, 1987; Public Opinion Research, 1986; Thomson & Ragona, 1987). These earlier studies found broad public support for payment of restitution by the offender to the victim instead of incarceration for property crimes and for crime prevention strategies instead of prison strategies to control crime. The studies did not explicitly ask respondents if they supported "restorative justice." The questions asked, however, addressed important underlying principles that are fundamental to the theory of restorative justice, which places far more value on crime prevention and restoration of physical and emotional losses than on retribution and blame for past behavior.

Implementation of Restorative Justice Programs

In contrast to many previous reform movements, the restorative justice movement has major implications for systemwide change in how justice is done in American society. As a result of the Balanced and Restorative Justice (BARJ) project supported by the Office of Juvenile Justice and Delinquency Prevention of the U.S. Department of Justice, numerous county and state jurisdictions throughout the country are examining the merits of restorative justice. Eighteen states have adopted legislation promoting a more balanced and restorative juvenile justice system, and restorative justice programs are being developed in the thirty-two other states. The BARJ project has been working extensively with six juvenile justice systems (Deschutes and Lane Counties in Oregon, Travis County in Texas, Dakota County in Minnesota, Allegheny County in Pennsylvania, and Palm Beach County in Florida) that are actively involved in implementing restorative justice polices and practices. Mission statements are being reexamined and rewritten, job descriptions are being changed, policies are being revised to include more victim and community involvement, resources are being redeployed, new restorative interventions are being initiated, and a far greater awareness of victim needs for involvement and services is being developed.

In 1994, the Vermont Department of Corrections embarked on one of the most ambitious systemwide restorative justice initiatives in the United States. Following a public opinion poll that indicated broad dissatisfaction with the criminal justice system and openness to more restorative and community-based responses to nonviolent crime, the department abolished a hundred-year-old correctional system built on the options of either prison or probation. Officials determined that up to 50 percent of the current probation caseload could be held accountable by Reparative Probation Community Boards made up of citizen volunteers. Instead of being subjected to traditional probation supervision, property offenders would be referred directly to appear before a Reparative Probation Community Board. In dialogue with the offender, the board would determine a community-based restorative sanction, often including victim offender mediation, community service, or meeting with a victim panel. The department is now encouraging crime victims to be represented on each Reparative Probation Community Board. No other known current restorative justice initiative represents such a major structural change, which clearly elevates the role of community volunteers and crime victims in the process of holding offenders accountable to the community they violated.

In comparison to such systemwide initiatives, individual restorative program initiatives are much more widely dispersed throughout the country. In addition to the more than three hundred victim offender mediation programs throughout the United States, numerous other programs (including creative community service, neighborhood dispute resolution, financial restitution with victim input, and victim offender dialogue groups or panels) incorporate many or all of the principles of restorative justice. Although hard figures are difficult to obtain, a conservative estimate would be that well over a thousand of these programs are in place in urban and rural communities in virtually every state.

Restorative Justice Through Victim Offender Mediation

Victim offender mediation is but one of the wide range of restorative justice policies and practices directed toward offenders and crime victims. Others include community policing, family group conferencing, peacemaking circles, sentencing circles, community reparative boards that meet with offenders to determine appropriate sanctions, victim impact panels, restitution programs, offender competency development programs, victim empathy classes for offenders, victim-directed and citizen-involved community service by the offender, community-based support groups for crime victims, victim advocacy programs, and community-based support groups for offenders.

What Is Victim Offender Mediation?

Victim offender mediation is a process that gives victims of property crimes or minor assaults the opportunity to meet the perpetrators of these crimes in a safe and structured setting, with the goal of holding the offenders directly accountable while providing important assistance and compensation to the victims. Assisted by a trained mediator, the victim is able to let the offender know how the crime affected him or her, receive answers to questions, and be directly involved in developing a restitution plan for the offender to be accountable for the loss or damage caused. The offenders are able to take direct responsibility for their behavior, understand the full impact of what they did, and develop a plan for making amends. An offender's failure to complete the restitution results in further court-imposed consequences. Some victim offender mediation programs are called victim offender meetings, victim offender reconciliation, or victim offender conferencing.

People who have been victimized by crime have been able to play an active role in the justice process, receive direct information about the crime, express their concerns about the full impact of the criminal behavior on their lives, and negotiate with the offender a mutually acceptable plan for restoring losses to the greatest extent possible. Individuals who have committed criminal acts have been able to gain a far better understanding of the real human impact of their actions, "own up" to their behavior, and have the opportunity for making amends directly to the person they harmed. Family members or other support persons who are often present also have an opportunity to become involved and to express their concerns. Both victim and offender can gain a greater sense of closure and the ability to move on with their lives.

In some programs, cases are primarily referred to victim offender mediation as a diversion from prosecution, assuming that the agreement is successfully completed. In other programs, cases are referred primarily after a formal admission of guilt has been accepted by the court, with the mediation being a condition of probation (if the victim so desires). Some programs receive case referrals at both the diversion and postadjudication levels. Most cases are referred by officials involved in the juvenile justice system, although some programs also receive referrals from the adult criminal justice system. Judges, probation officers, victim advocates, prosecutors, defense attorneys, or police can make referrals to victim offender mediation programs. In general, programs in the United States receive approximately one-third of their referrals at the diversion level, one-third at the postadjudication but predisposition level, and one-third at the postdisposition level.

In most instances, referral into mediation is initiated by persons connected with offenders or with the criminal justice system. Occasionally, however, it happens that a victim will wish to pursue mediation without having received any such contact. Victims typically enter the process through local victim services programs, contacting their local probation department, or directly contacting the specific criminal justice agency that is handling the offender's case.

In none of the wide range of programs offering victim offender mediation is there any financial cost to crime victims who choose to participate. In most programs, there is also no cost for the offenders. In some programs, offenders are required to pay a program participation fee to the court to help offset some of the cost of the local VOM program.

How Does VOM Differ from Other Mediation?

Mediation is being used in an increasing number of conflict situations, such as divorce and custody cases, community disputes, commercial disputes, and other civil court conflicts. In such settings, the parties are called "disputants," the assumption being that both are contributing to the conflict and therefore both must compromise to reach a settlement. Often mediation in these settings is focused heavily on reaching a settlement, with a lesser emphasis on a discussion of the full impact of the conflict on participants' lives.

In victim offender mediation, the involved parties are not "disputants." Generally, one has clearly committed a criminal offense and has admitted doing so, and the other has clearly been victimized. Therefore, the issue of guilt or innocence is not mediated. Nor is there an expectation that crime victims compromise or request less than what they need to address their losses. While many other types of mediation are largely "settlement-driven," victim offender mediation is primarily "dialogue-driven," with the emphasis on victim healing, offender accountability, and restoration of losses. Most victim offender mediation sessions (commonly more than 95 percent) do in fact result in a signed restitution agreement. This agreement, however, is secondary to the importance of the initial dialogue between the parties. This dialogue addresses emotional and informational needs of victims that are central both to their healing and to development of victim empathy in the offender, which can lead to less criminal behavior in the future. Research has consistently found that the restitution agreement is less important to crime victims than the opportunity to talk directly with the offender about how they felt about the crime. A restorative impact is strongly correlated with the creation of a safe place for dialogue between victim and offender. Characteristics of victim offender mediation that have the most restorative impact are summarized in Exhibit I.2.

Exhibit I.2 Victim Offender Mediation Continuum: From Least to Most Restorative Impact

Least Restorative Impact:
Agreement-Driven, Offender-Focused

1. Entire focus is on determining the amount of financial restitution to be paid, with no opportunity to talk directly about the full impact of the crime on the victim, community, or offender

2. Victims not given choice of where they would feel the most comfortable and safe to meet or whom they would like to have present

3. Victims given only written notice to appear for mediation session at preset time, with no preparation

4. No separate preparation meetings with victim and offender prior to bringing the parties together

Most Restorative Impact:
Dialogue-Driven, Victim-Sensitive

1. Primary focus on providing an opportunity for victims and offenders to talk directly to each other, to allow victims to express the full impact of the crime on their lives and to receive answers to important questions they have, and to allow offenders to learn the real human impact of their behavior and take direct responsibility for seeking to make things right

2. Victims continually given choices throughout the process: where to meet, whom they would like to have present, and so on

3. Restitution important, but secondary to the dialogue about the impact of the crime

4. Separate preparation meetings with victim and offender prior to bringing them together, with emphasis on listening to how the crime has affected them, identifying their needs, and preparing them for the mediation or conference session

(Continued)

**Exhibit I.2 Victim Offender Mediation Continuum:
From Least to Most Restorative Impact, cont'd.**

Least Restorative Impact: *Agreement-Driven, Offender-Focused*	Most Restorative Impact: *Dialogue-Driven, Victim-Sensitive*
5. Mediator or facilitator describes the offense and offender then speaks, with the victim simply asking a few questions or responding to questions of the mediator; low tolerance of moments of silence or expression of feelings	5. Nondirective style of mediation or facilitation, with the parties talking most of the time, high tolerance for silence, and use of a humanistic or transformative mediation model
6. Highly directive style of mediation or facilitation with the mediator talking most of the time, continually asking both the victim and offender questions, with little, if any, direct dialogue between the involved parties	6. High tolerance for expression of feelings and full impact of crime, with emphasis on direct dialogue between the involved parties and with the mediator saying little
7. Correctional staff serve as mediators	7. Trained community volunteers serve as mediators independently or assisted by agency staff
8. Voluntary for victim but required of offender whether or not offender takes responsibility	8. Voluntary for victim and offender
9. Settlement-driven and very brief (10–15 minutes)	9. Dialogue-driven and typically at least an hour long

History and Development of
Victim Offender Mediation

The origin of what is today known as victim offender mediation (referred to as criminal court mediation by some) began in Canada many years ago in the province of Ontario. In May 1974, an experiment began in Elmira, a few miles north of Kitchener, Ontario, that would later trigger the international development of a new justice reform. Two young men pleaded guilty to twenty-two counts of property damage. Their probation officer and a colleague of his with the Mennonite Central Committee in Canada had the vision and courage to try some basic peacemaking principles in resolving the conflict between these young men and the twenty-two people they had victimized.

A recommendation was made to the court that these two offenders go back and meet every single person they had victimized and assess how much loss occurred. The judge ordered a one-month remand in order to allow these two young men to meet their victims, with the help of their probation officer and his colleague from the Mennonite Central Committee. After the offenders had met with their victims and gained a more human understanding of the impact of their criminal behavior, the judge sentenced them to probation and required them to pay restitution to the victims. Three months later, the offenders again visited each victim and handed each a check for the amount of his or her loss. The Kitchener experiment led to the initiation of the Victim Offender Reconciliation Project (VORP) in North America. Victim offender mediation and reconciliation projects have now spread to more than twenty other jurisdictions throughout Canada, largely as "alternative measures" programs pursuant to the provisions of the Canadian Young Offenders Act of 1984.

Development of similar programs in the Untied States followed fairly rapidly. The first replication of VORP in the United States occurred in 1978 when the Mennonite Central Committee, probation staff, and a local judge in Elkhart, Indiana, began accepting cases. By the mid-1990s, a network of approximately 150 victim offender mediation or reconciliation programs existed in the United States, in addition to the 26 programs in Canada, and awareness of such programs and their replication began to spread across the globe.

How Many VOM Programs Exist?

More than thirteen hundred victim offender mediation programs are known to exist throughout the world, primarily in North America and Europe. Undoubtedly there are many other programs in existence that have not yet been listed in directories. The current extent of VOM programs worldwide is summarized in Table I.1. A 1996 survey of the VOM field in the United States, more fully reported in Chapter Six, found a total of 291 VOM programs; the number now exceeds 300. Community-based agencies operated 44 percent of the 117 programs interviewed, 11 percent were sponsored by probation departments, 10 percent were church-based programs, 4 percent were based in victim services agencies, and 3 percent were operated by prosecuting attorneys' offices. In these 117 programs, 74 percent of the cases handled were in the juvenile court and 26 percent were criminal court cases involving adult offenders. Programs most frequently identified their primary source of funding as either state or local government. Foundations were the third most frequent source of funding.

After twenty years of development and many thousands of cases (primarily property crimes and minor assaults) in more than one thousand communities in North America and Europe, victim offender mediation is finally beginning to move from the margins toward the mainstream of criminal justice. Some programs are still quite small, with a very limited number of case referrals. Many other programs are receiving several hundred referrals a year. A few programs in recent years have been asked to divert a thousand or more cases a year from the court system, and county governments have provided hundreds of thousands of dollars to fund them. Although the need for more research in this field remains, we now have far more empirical data on VOM, based on multisite assessments in Canada, the United States, and England, than on many more widespread correctional interventions. The central findings that have emerged from a review of forty studies of VOM are presented in Chapter Eight.

It is clear that the field of victim offender mediation has grown extensively since its unassuming 1974 beginnings in Kitchener, Ontario. A recent statewide survey of victim service providers in Minnesota found that 91 percent believed that victim offender mediation should be offered as an option to crime victims in every judicial district.

Table I.1 Victim Offender Mediation Programs
Around the World

Country	Number of Programs
Australia	5
Austria	17
Belgium	31
Canada	26
Denmark	5
Finland	175
France	159
Germany	450
Italy	4
Netherlands	2
New Zealand	Available in all jurisdictions
Norway	41
Poland	5
South Africa	1
Sweden	50
United Kingdom	46
United States	302
Total	1,319

Sources: Umbreit and Greenwood (1999); author's own data.

What Have We Learned About VOM from Research?

As noted, during the past decade, empirical data have accumulated
from studies in Canada, the United States, and England; much of
this material will be taken up in greater detail in Part Two. Studies
conducted in Europe and North America report high levels of satisfaction with the mediation process and outcome on the part of
victims and offenders (Coates & Gehm, 1989; Collins, 1984;
Dignan, 1990; Gehm, 1990; Marshall & Merry, 1990; Perry,
Lajeunesse, & Woods, 1987; Umbreit, 1994, 1995b). Some
studies found higher restitution completion rates (Umbreit, 1994),

reduced fear among victims (Umbreit & Coates, 1993; Umbreit, 1994), and reduced future criminal behavior (Nugent & Paddock, 1995; Nugent, Umbreit, Wiinamaki, & Paddock, in press; Schneider, 1986; Umbreit, 1994). Multisite studies in England (Marshall & Merry, 1990; Umbreit & Roberts, 1996), the United States (Coates & Gehm, 1989; Umbreit, 1994), and Canada (Umbreit, 1995b) have confirmed most of these findings. A large multisite study in the United States (Umbreit, 1994) found that victims of crime who meet with the offender are far more likely to be satisfied with the justice system's response to their case than similar victims who go through the normal court process.

During the early 1980s, many people questioned whether crime victims would even want to meet with their offender face to face. Today it is very clear, from empirical data and practice experience, that the majority of crime victims presented with the opportunity of mediation and dialogue chose to engage in the process, with victim participation rates often ranging between 60 and 70 percent in many programs.

It is becoming increasingly clear that the victim offender mediation process humanizes the criminal justice experience for both victim and offender; holds offenders directly accountable to the people they victimized; allows for more active involvement of crime victims, family members of victims and offenders, and community members (as volunteer mediators and support persons) in the justice process; and reduces further criminal behavior in offenders.

The balance of this book brings together the most current available knowledge base undergirding the development and practice of victim offender mediation, including philosophy and values, practical guidelines, impact, and future directions. Part One is designed to provide an inside look at the establishment and practice of victim offender mediation, Part Two focuses on what is currently known about the outcomes of victim offender mediation programs, and Part Three explores future directions as this powerful intervention continues to move from the margins toward the mainstream of juvenile and criminal justice systems around the world.

The Handbook of
Victim Offender Mediation

Part One

Philosophy, Practice, and Context

Part One provides a detailed look at the practice of victim offender mediation at both the micro and macro levels. Chapter One explores the implications of a humanistic approach to mediation and conflict resolution, a process that is central to the practice of victim offender mediation. This is followed in Chapter Two with specific guidelines for the practice of victim-sensitive VOM. Chapter Three offers step-by-step instructions for conducting such mediation, and Chapter Four introduces multicultural issues that mediators need to consider. Case examples illustrating the application of these steps and principles are presented in Chapter Five. The last two chapters of the part focus on program development issues. Chapter Six provides information about the variety of program contexts and formats across the United States, and Chapter Seven gives an overview of the issues to be considered in establishing or expanding VOM programs.

Chapter One

Humanistic Mediation

A Transformative Journey of Peacemaking

The use of mediation practices to resolve a wide variety of disputes, disagreements, and conflicts across a broad range of settings is well documented. The application of mediation consistently results in high levels of client satisfaction and perceptions of fairness, within families, among coworkers, in neighborhoods, and in the criminal justice system.

This chapter explores the philosophy, assumptions, values, and practices that constitute a humanistic model of mediation (Umbreit, 1997). Such a model intentionally taps into the full potential of mediation to offer a genuine transformative journey of peacemaking that is grounded in compassion, strength, and the common humanity of all participants. Humanistic mediation as presented in this chapter is appropriate for use in a wide variety of conflictual situations. Its more specific application in victim offender mediation will be developed further in subsequent chapters.

Although some conflicts, such as complex commercial disputes, clearly require a primary focus on reaching an acceptable settlement, most conflicts develop within a larger emotional and relational context characterized by powerful feelings of disrespect, betrayal, and abuse. When these feelings about the past and current state of the relationship are not allowed to be aired in a healthy manner, an agreement might be reached, but the underlying emotional conflict remains. Little healing of the emotional

---

Note: This chapter is based on Umbreit (1997). Copyright ©1997, Jossey-Bass, Inc., a subsidiary of John Wiley & Sons, Inc. Adapted with permission.

wound is likely to occur without an opening of the heart through genuine dialogue, empowerment, and a recognition of each other's humanity despite the conflict. This requires moving far beyond the well-known techniques of "active listening" or "reflective listening," with their emphasis on paraphrasing, summarizing, and related skills. Clearly, these techniques, when used by disputants or mediators, can be very helpful in the resolution of conflict. However, listening techniques can also get in the way of genuine dialogue, particularly when their use prevents the mediator from being able to honor and feel comfortable with silence, reflect deeply on what is being said, and discern what he or she is feeling and experiencing in the present moment. An example of a technically accurate application of reflective listening skills that nevertheless inhibits genuine communication would be a mediator's paraphrasing of every bite-sized chunk of verbal conversation in such a way that the disputant experiences it as intrusive and insensitive or even obnoxious.

After many years of being applied in diverse settings, mediation now faces a wonderful opportunity to build on the many reports that mediation often constitutes far more than simply working out a settlement. By moving toward a humanistic approach, the practice of mediation can intentionally and more consistently tap into its transformative and healing powers. These healing powers are intrinsic to the process of mediating conflict between individuals but need to be consciously drawn out and utilized.

Principles of Humanistic Mediation

The model of humanistic mediation being proposed in this chapter rests on a set of assumptions about the nature of human existence, conflict, and the search for healing, as summarized in Exhibit 1.1. These beliefs and values are not subject to empirical testing. They derive from a variety of sources and are shared across a range of cultures.

Exhibit 1.1 Values and Beliefs Underlying the Humanistic Mediation Model

1. Belief in the connectedness of all things and our common humanity

2. Belief in the importance of the mediator's presence and connectedness with the involved parties in facilitating effective conflict resolution

3. Belief in the healing power of mediation through a process of the involved parties helping each other through the sharing of their feelings (dialogue, mutual aid)

4. Belief in the desire of most people to live peacefully

5. Belief in the desire of most people to grow through life experiences

6. Belief in the capacity of all people to draw on inner reservoirs of strength to overcome adversity, to grow, and to help others in similar circumstances

7. Belief in the inherent dignity and self-determination that arise from embracing conflict directly

The potential of effective conflict resolution to promote healing of relationships within communities, rather than just immediate resolution of problems between individuals, is particularly well grounded in the traditions of many indigenous peoples throughout the world. The practice of *ho'oponopono* by native Hawaiians, family group conferencing by Maori people in New Zealand, and healing circles and other practices among First Nation people in Canada and Native Americans in the United States all provide beautiful examples of spiritually grounded forms of resolving conflicts through a journey of healing and peacemaking. As Diane Le Resche (1993) points out, "At its core, Native American peacemaking is inherently spiritual; it speaks to the connectedness of all things; it focuses on unity, on harmony, on balancing the spiritual, intellectual, emotional and physical dimensions of a community of people" (p. 321). These principles of balance have also been adapted by tribal leadership in Canada (Huber, 1993) for use in urban tribal settings, using the traditional symbol of the medicine wheel.

In Western culture, the transformative dimensions of mediation have been eloquently described by Bush and Folger (1994) in
their widely acclaimed book *The Promise of Mediation*. They
emphasize the importance of genuine empowerment and mutual
recognition of each other's humanity, in addition to the value of
compassionate strength among parties in conflict. Bush and Folger
emphasize that through empowerment, "the parties grow calmer,
clearer, more confident, more organized, [and] more decisive,
regaining a sense of strength, being able to act and handle life's
problems" (p. 85). Through recognition, "the parties voluntarily
choose to become more open, attentive, [and] responsive to the situation of another, thereby expanding their perspective to include
an appreciation for another's situation" (p. 89). Whether an actual
settlement occurs is quite secondary to the process of transformation and healing that occurs in their relationship.

The elements of a humanistic model are grounded in the experience of many mediators over the years and have been applied in
areas ranging from family conflict to criminal conflict involving
such offenses as burglary, theft, and minor assaults. Instead of the
highly directive "settlement-driven" model practiced widely in civil
court settings, a humanistic mediation model is very nondirective
 and "dialogue-driven." It prepares the parties, through separate premediation sessions with the mediator, so that they feel safe enough
to have an opportunity to engage in a genuine conversation about
the conflict, experience their own sense of empowerment, and
express what Bush and Folger (1994) call "compassionate strength"
(p. 83), including empathy for the other party in the conflict. The
emphasis is on the mediator's facilitating a dialogue that allows the
 parties to discuss the full impact of the conflict; assist each other in
determining the most suitable resolution, which may or may not
include a written agreement; and recognize each other's common
humanity, despite the conflict.

A humanistic model of mediation in some respects parallels a
humanistic style of psychotherapy or teaching, which emphasizes
the importance of the relationship between the therapist and client

or teacher and student while embracing a strong belief in each person's capacity for growth, change, and transformation. Carl Rogers (1961), a pioneer in humanistic psychology, emphasized the importance of empathic understanding, unconditional positive regard, and genuineness. Although his theories were developed in the context of psychotherapy, they have enormous implications for mediation practice and life in general.

Parties in conflict may be likely to experience emotional benefits from the practice of humanistic mediation, through healing that often occurs in the relationship encounter in the present. It is important to note, however, that such a process is not psychotherapy, nor does it require a mediator to have training in psychotherapy. Acknowledgment of brokenness or hurt is intrinsic to humanistic mediation. Working on that brokenness and dealing with past emotional issues contributing to these feelings, however, is the domain of therapists, not mediators.

A humanistic dialogue-driven model of mediation is further grounded in what Lois Gold (1993), former chair of the Academy of Family Mediators, describes as a paradigm of healing. She identifies twelve characteristics that differentiate the paradigm of healing from the more deeply entrenched paradigm of problem solving, with its settlement-driven emphasis, as summarized in Exhibit 1.2.

Although this conceptual framework has grown out of Gold's extensive experience as a family therapist and family mediator, the paradigm of healing has enormous implications for humanistic mediation practice in any context in which the nature of the conflict relates to broken relationships. This is particularly so in those cases in which one or both parties are grieving the loss of the relationship that once existed, whether among colleagues at work, friends, spouses, partners, parents and children, or neighbors. It is also highly relevant in response to the needs of many crime victims and offenders who had no prior interaction but now find themselves in a relationship (certainly not by the victim's choice) because of the nature of the criminal act and its effect on their lives. Crime victims, particularly victims of more serious offenses,

Exhibit 1.2 Paradigm of Healing

1. Caring, nonjudgmental acceptance of the person's humanity
2. Building rapport and emotional connection—"being there"
3. Helping people listen to their innate wisdom, their preference for peace
4. Generating hope—"with support, you can do it"
5. Tapping into the universal desire for wellness
6. Speaking from the heart
7. Thinking of clients in their woundedness, not their defensive posture
8. Being real and congruent
9. Creating safe space for dialogue
10. Creating a sacred space
11. Recognizing that a healing presence does not "fix it"
12. Understanding that a healing presence acknowledges brokenness and shares the journey

Source: Gold, 1993, pp. 56–58. Used with permission.

often experience grief at their loss of a sense of safety or invulnerability that has been shattered by the crime.

Understanding and practicing humanistic mediation in the context of the paradigm of healing offered by Gold is ultimately grounded in a profound recognition of the precious gift of human existence, relationships, community, and the deeper spiritual connectedness among all of us in our collective journey through this life, regardless of religious, cultural, political, and lifestyle differences. Gold notes that the language of healing is not the language of problem solving but rather the language of the soul.

One of the most powerful and perhaps most controversial expressions of the transformative qualities of empowerment and recognition has been consistently observed in the small but growing application of mediation and dialogue between parents of murdered children and the murderer (Umbreit, Bradshaw, & Coates, 1999; Umbreit & Vos, 2000). After lengthy preparation by the mediator, involving several individual meetings, the parties frequently, through a genuine dialogue about what happened and its impact on all involved, get beyond the evil, trauma, and inconsistencies surrounding the event to achieve an acknowledgment of each other's humanity and a greater sense of closure.

Implications for Practice

To embrace a more humanistic model of mediation, a number of significant changes in the dominant Western European model of mediation are required. Though clearly not capturing the full spiritual richness of many traditional practices of indigenous people, these changes will lead to a more transformative and healing experience of mediation. Each change in the practice of mediation to bring it more in line with the humanistic model will be discussed in greater detail. The changes are outlined in Exhibit 1.3.

Exhibit 1.3 Practice Implications of the Humanistic Mediation Model

1. Continual centering of the mediator—clearing the mind of clutter and focusing on the important peacemaking task at hand

2. Reframing of the mediator's role, from directing a settlement-driven process to facilitating a process of dialogue and mutual aid

3. Premediation sessions with each party—listening to each party's story, providing information, obtaining voluntary participation, assessing the case, clarifying expectations, preparing for the mediation

4. Connecting with the parties by building rapport and trust (beginning in the premediation phase)

5. Identifying and tapping into parties' strengths (beginning in the premediation phase)

6. Coaching on communication, if required (during premediation sessions)

7. Nondirective style of mediation

8. Face-to-face seating of victim and offender (unless inappropriate because of the parties' culture or individual request)

9. Recognition and use of the power of silence

10. Follow-up sessions

Centering of the Mediator

The humanistic mediation model emphasizes the importance of the mediator's clearing away the clutter in his or her own life so that he or she can focus intensely on the needs of the involved parties. Prior to initiating contact between people in conflict, mediators are encouraged to take a few moments of silence to reflect on the deeper meaning of their peacemaking work and the needs of the people in conflict. The centering of the mediator throughout the entire process of preparation and mediation also helps the parties in conflict experience it as a safe journey toward genuine dialogue and healing. Through the practice of being centered, the humanistic mediator is more likely to stay grounded in a deeper sense of spirituality that recognizes the interconnectedness of all people, regardless of our many differences, as well as the sacred gift of human existence.

Reframing of the Mediator's Role

Tapping into the full power of mediation in resolving important interpersonal conflict reframes the mediator's role. Instead of actively and efficiently guiding the parties toward a settlement, the mediator helps the parties enter a dialogue with each other, to experience each other as fellow human beings, despite their conflict, and to seek ways to help them come to understand and respect their differences and arrive at a mutually acceptable way to deal with those differences. This may or may not involve a formal written settlement agreement. Once the parties are engaged in a face-to-face conversation, the mediator intentionally gets out of the way. For example, mediators might pull their chair back farther away from the table and cross their legs, displaying a more informal posture. It should be noted that rarely does the mediator get out of the way entirely; if nothing else, the mediator will intervene now and then to comment or to redirect communication. This is especially true during the later stages of mediation when the parties in conflict may need help in constructing a formal settlement agreement if one is needed. It is also important in all cases for the mediator to provide a brief closing statement, thanking the parties for their work and scheduling a follow-up meeting if necessary.

Premediation Sessions

Routine use of separate premediation sessions with the involved parties should become a standard practice. These individual sessions should occur at least a week or more before the mediation session. Collection of information, assessment of the conflict, description of the mediation program, and clarification of expectations are important tasks to complete. The first and most important task, however, is establishing trust and rapport with the involved parties. The development of trust and rapport enhances any dialogue process but is particularly beneficial in intense interpersonal conflicts. For this reason, the mediator would need to get into listening mode as quickly as possible during the initial meeting, inviting the involved parties to tell their stories of the conflict and how it has affected them. Clearly explaining how the mediation process works and what they might expect to experience will help put the involved parties at ease.

Connecting with the Parties

A far greater emphasis needs to be placed on the mediator's establishing a connection with the parties in the conflict. Instead of viewing mediators as technicians who are emotionally distant and uninvolved, with no prior contact with the involved parties, emphasis would be placed on mediators' establishing trust and rapport with the involved parties before bringing them to a joint session. A mediator does not need to lose his or her impartiality to connect effectively with the involved parties before bringing them together. The art of mediation, much like teaching, nursing, therapy, and social work, is founded on connecting with people on a human level through the expression of empathy, warmth, and authenticity.

The late Virginia Satir, a renowned family therapist, teacher, and trainer, recognized the supreme importance of the "presence" of the therapist. Satir regarded authentic human connection as fundamental to change processes. Making contact with people on a basic human level requires "congruence," the condition of being emotionally honest with yourself so that there is consistency in your words, feelings, body and facial expressions, and actions. Authentic connection with others, through therapy or mediation, first requires looking inward. According to Satir (1976), there are four significant areas, each characterized by key questions.

1. Self-esteem: How do I feel about myself?
2. Communication: How do I get my meaning across to others?
3. Rules: How do I treat my feelings? Do I accept them or blame them on someone else? Do I act as though I have feelings that I don't or that I don't have feelings that I really do?
4. Risk taking: How do I react to doing things that are new and different?

The process of connecting with individuals involved in mediation takes energy. As Satir (1976) points out, "Making real contact means that we make ourselves responsible for what comes out of us" (p. 18). Although Satir developed her concepts of making contact and congruence in the context of family therapy, her material is relevant to a humanistic model of mediation. Humanistic mediators can have a powerful presence with their clients, as Satir did, through a more spiritual understanding of life that embraces the connectedness of all people, along with the connectedness of the mediator's actions and belief system with the core of his or her being.

Building on Satir's work, Lois Gold (1993) identifies four specific elements of presence that can increase the effectiveness of mediators: (1) being centered, (2) being connected to one's governing values and beliefs and highest purpose, (3) making contact with the humanity of the clients, and (4) being congruent.

Tapping into Individual Strengths

When people become embroiled in conflict, it is common for them to communicate and interact in dysfunctional ways. The careless expression of intense anger and bitterness, along with the inability to listen to the other party or effectively communicate their own needs, can mask many strengths that they may have. It is the mediator's task, during separate premediation sessions, to learn the communication style of each party and identify specific strengths that may directly assist in the mediation or dialogue process and to encourage the expression of those strengths in mediation. An example would be a mediator discovering that an individual has a difficult time responding to questions of a global or abstract nature, such as "How are you feeling about all of this?" When asked more concrete questions related to the individual's specific experience, however, the same individual may feel quite comfortable responding. Tapping into the strengths of individuals and coaching them in how to communicate their feelings effectively can contribute greatly to the mediator's ability to use a nondirective style of mediation.

Coaching of Communication

The open expression of feelings related to the conflict is central to a humanistic mediation model. Because of the extreme intensity of those feelings, it may become necessary during the separate premediation session for the mediator to coach the disputant on helpful ways of communicating those feelings so that they can be heard by the other party. Coaching one or both parties on the communication of intense and potentially hurtful feelings may be required. This coaching focuses on how to acknowledge and accept one's feelings rather than projecting them on the other party. Projecting intense feelings through aggressive communications will often

trigger defensiveness in one or both parties and shut down honest dialogue. To avoid this, speakers need to acknowledge their feelings and communicate them as an "I" statement, rather than attacking the other party. Furthermore, through coaching, the mediator works to help identify and tap into the strengths of each of the parties in conflict, despite any emotional baggage. In the process of coaching, however, the mediator is careful not to suggest what specifically should be said.

Nondirective Style of Mediation

The practice of humanistic mediation requires a nondirective style. The mediator assists the involved parties in a process of dialogue and mutual aid in which they help each other through the direct sharing of feelings and information about the conflict with minimal interruption. The mediator opens the session and sets a tone that will encourage the parties in conflict to feel safe, understand the process, and talk directly to each other. The mediator's ability to fade into the background is directly related to connecting with the parties before the joint session and having secured their trust. Without separate premediation meetings with the parties in conflict, it is unlikely that a truly nondirective style of mediation can be employed. The process of dialogue and mutual aid cannot succeed unless all parties trust the mediator, are prepared for the process with clear expectations, and feel safe and reasonably comfortable and the mediator stays in the background until needed.

Do not confuse a nondirective style with a passive style, in which the mediator provides little direction, leadership, or assistance. In the nondirective approach, the mediator remains in control of the process and, though saying little, is actively involved in the encounter and is able to respond or intervene at any point, particularly when people get stuck and indicate a need for assistance. By setting a clear and comfortable tone, the mediator puts the parties at ease so that they can talk directly to each other, and a far more empowering and mutually expressive form of mediation results. This style of mediation, effective only if the mediator has conducted separate premediation sessions, often requires that the mediator needs to say very little after the opening statement.

Face-to-Face Seating of the Parties

Seating arrangements during a mediation session are important. Seating the involved parties across from each other allows for natural eye contact and is central to the process of direct communication and dialogue. If a table is required, the mediator would be at the end and the parties in conflict would sit across from each other. Mediator-assisted dialogue and mutual aid are far more difficult when the involved parties are seated next to each other, facing the mediator across the table. (Of course, if any of the parties would be uncomfortable or offended seated face to face because of their cultural tradition, alternative arrangements should be made.)

Recognizing and Using the Power of Silence

Moments of silence in the process of dialogue and conflict resolution are inherent to a nondirective style of mediation. Recognizing, using, and feeling comfortable with the power of silence (qualities that are often more common in non-Western cultures) are important to the humanistic mediation process. By honoring silence and resisting the urge to jump in with guidance or questions (slowly and silently counting to ten before speaking is a handy technique), the mediator is more consistently able to promote the process of dialogue and mutual aid—a journey of the heart in harmony with the head.

Follow-Up Sessions

The importance of joint follow-up sessions between the parties in conflict is recognized as central to the humanistic mediation model. Because of the nature of conflict and human behavior, problems may not be resolved in only one session, particularly when the conflict involves an important relationship or the issues are complex. And even if the conflict is resolved in one session, a follow-up session several months later to assess how the agreement is holding up or to resolve any new issues that may have emerged can be important in the overall process of healing and closure.

The dominant model of settlement-driven mediation in Western culture is clearly beneficial to many people in conflict and superior to the adversarial legal process and court system in most cases. Moving to a higher plane, which embraces the importance of spirituality, compassionate strength, and our common humanity, holds even greater potential. As an expression of the transformative power of conflict resolution, the humanistic mediation model, as noted in Exhibit 1.4, can lay the foundation for a greater sense of community and social harmony. With its focus on the intrinsic healing power of mediation and dialogue, this model can bring a more complete resolution to the conflict. Through a process of dialogue and mutual aid between the involved parties, humanistic mediation practice facilitates the achievement of outer peace by addressing and often resolving the presenting conflict while also facilitating a journey of the heart to find inner peace, which brings forth the true goal of humanistic mediation—real peace.

Exhibit 1.4 Comparison of Problem-Solving and Humanistic Mediation

	Classic Problem-Solving Mediation	Humanistic or Transformative Mediation
Primary focus	Problem and settlement.	Dialogue and relationship.
Preparation of parties in conflict	No separate mediator contact with involved parties prior to mediation. Intake staff collect information.	At least one one face-to-face meeting between mediator and each party prior to joint mediation session. Focus is on listening to their story, building rapport, explaining the process, and clarifying expectations.
Role of mediator	To direct and guide the communication of the involved parties toward a mutually acceptable settlement of the conflict.	To prepare the involved parties prior to bringing them together so that they have realistic expectations and feel safe enough to engage later in a direct conversation or dialogue with each other facilitated by the mediator.
Style of mediation	Active and often very directive, speaking frequently during the mediation session and asking many questions.	Very nondirective during the mediation session. After making opening statement, mediator fades into the background and is reluctant to interrupt conversation between the parties except when clearly necessary.
Dealing with the emotional context of conflict	Low tolerance for expression of feelings and "storytelling" related to the history and context of the conflict.	Encouragement of open expression of feelings and discussion of the context and history of the conflict; recognition of the intrinsic healing quality of storytelling when speaking and listening from the heart.
Moments of silence	Few moments of silence.	Many prolonged moments of silence. Mediator honors silence as integral to genuine empowerment and healing.
Written agreements	Primary goal and most likely outcome of mediation; focused on clear, tangible elements.	Secondary to the primary goal of dialogue and mutual aid (the parties helping each other through the sharing of information and expression of feelings). Agreements may focus on symbolic gestures, personal growth tasks, or affirmations of the new relationship between the parties.

Chapter Two

Guidelines for Victim-Sensitive Mediation and Dialogue with Offenders

Chapter One presented the philosophy and practice implications of a general model of humanistic mediation. This chapter provides greater detail about the application of this model in victim offender mediation. An overview of the guidelines for victim-sensitive VOM is provided in Exhibit 2.1. Each of these guidelines will be taken up in turn.

Basic Guidelines

The underlying principles outlined in Chapter One give rise to basic guidelines regarding victim safety, victim choice, victim-sensitive language, and careful screening of cases. These guidelines have developed over time to prevent revictimization of crime victims and to encourage their involvement and participation in mediation. Although extra deference is shown to victims because of the context of what has happened to them, it is important to note that from a humanistic perspective, offenders are also in need of safety, choice, and respectful language.

Note: Material in this chapter is based on a monograph (Umbreit & Greenwood, 1997) produced and distributed by the Center for Restorative Justice & Peacemaking, School of Social Work, University of Minnesota, and made possible through a grant from the Office for Victims of Crime, U.S. Department of Justice.

Exhibit 2.1 Overview of the Guidelines for
Victim-Sensitive Mediation

I. Basic Guidelines
   A. Victim Safety
   B. Victim Choice
      1. Participation
      2. Support
      3. Schedule for mediation session
      4. Mediation site
      5. Seating
      6. First speaker
      7. Termination of session
      8. Restitution
   C. Use of Victim-Sensitive Language
   D. Careful Screening of Cases

II. Premediation with Offender
   A. Offender Choice to Participate
   B. Careful, Extensive Offender Preparation
      1. Reality testing
      2. Restitution possibilities
      3. Offender support

III. Premediation with Victim
   A. Providing Information
      1. About the mediation program
      2. About oneself as mediator
      3. About the mediation process
      4. About the judicial system
      5. About victims' rights
      6. About available resources
      7. About the offender
      8. About possible risks and benefits
   B. Careful, Extensive Victim Preparation
      1. Reality-testing victim expectations
      2. Assessment of losses and needs
      3. Restitution possibilities
      4. Victim support

IV. Conducting the Mediation Session
   A. Perspective of the Mediator
   B. Relaxed, Positive Atmosphere
   C. Dialogue Focus
   D. Guidelines
   E. Feedback from Participants
   F. Follow-Up Option

V. Follow-Up
   A. Completion of Agreement
   B. Notification of Victim Regarding Status of Agreement
   C. Scheduling Additional Sessions If Needed
   D. Phone Contact with Parties
   E. Evaluation

VI. Mediator Training in Victim Sensitivity

Victim Safety

A fundamental guideline for victim offender mediation programs is the safety of the victim. The mediator must do everything possible to ensure that the victim will not be harmed in any way. At every point in the mediation process, the mediator needs to ask, "Does this pose a physical or emotional threat to the safety and well-being of the victim?" Maintaining rapport with the victim is essential for the mediator, as well as attending to verbal and nonverbal communication and requesting feedback from the victim as the process unfolds. If the victim feels unsafe, the mediator needs to be prepared to act immediately—to provide options, to terminate mediation, or to provide an escort for the victim leaving mediation. If the victim appears agitated or vulnerable in the mediation session, the mediator should call for a break and check in with the involved parties. The mediator should ask how the victim is feeling and what he or she may need and then present various options for proceeding.

To ensure the safety of the victim, the mediation should be conducted in a location that feels safe to the victim, and the victim should be encouraged to bring along a support person or two if so desired (for example, a family member, friend, minister, or victim advocate). The mediator may also wish to bring in an additional mediator, if co-mediation is not generally practiced by the program. In addition, victims may find it reassuring to have input on the arrangement of the room and the seating of the parties and to have the freedom to introduce themselves in the manner they choose—for example, using first name only.

An important safeguard for victims is knowing that the victim offender mediation program has credibility. That credibility needs to be reinforced in writing, with an informative letter of introduction and a program brochure. Victims may also need reassurance that the program is not offender-focused. In programs that use volunteers, victims need to be assured that staff work closely with the volunteers, that victims may contact staff if they have questions or concerns, and that referrals are screened by staff with safety issues in mind.

Victim Choice

Following a crime, many victims experience feelings of vulnerability and powerlessness. Added to that is the victim's experience with the criminal justice system, which is focused on the offender. Victims are excluded from the process, rarely being offered an opportunity to tell of their experiences or express their needs. It is not surprising that in the wake of a crime, victims often experience a lack of control in their lives, which can intensify their fear and anxiety. The presence of choices and options for the victim in the mediation process can restore a sense of power. Empowerment is conducive to healing, expanding the capacity to move through and integrate difficult and painful experiences. The mediator provides information and support for the victim engaged in decision making but is careful not to apply any pressure or impose expectations on the victim. It is also important that victims have sufficient time to make decisions, without the pressure of arbitrary time constraints. Choices should be presented to victims throughout the mediation process as various decisions need to be made.

The victim must always have the right to say no to mediation, refusing to participate, and to have that decision honored and respected. The victim did not choose to be a victim of a crime. It is crucial then that victims be given the choice to participate in the mediation process or not. Victims must be invited and even encouraged to participate but never pressured. The mediator should give accurate information about mediation, describing the process itself and the range of responses for victims who have participated in mediation, along with research findings on client satisfaction. The mediator then encourages the victim to consider the possible benefits and risks of mediation before a decision is made. Victims may also wish to consult with a respected friend, relative, member of the clergy, or victim advocate before making a final decision. It is important that the victim participate on the basis of informed consent.

Another important option for victims is the choice of support persons to accompany them to the mediation session. The presence of a friend or relative can enhance the victim's sense of comfort and safety, even though the support person will typically have little or no speaking role. It is helpful for the mediator to meet or phone support persons as well, to prepare them for the mediation session.

The mediation session should be scheduled at a time that is convenient for the victim. The victim's schedule needs to be a priority, again, so that the victim can retain a sense of power in the situation and find comfort in the deference extended, even as the needs of others are not ignored.

Site selection is an important ingredient in the mediation process. Victims need to know the range of possibilities available in the situation (for example, private room in a community center, library, church, office building, city hall) and to be asked what they prefer. What setting would feel safe, neutral, comfortable, and convenient? Occasionally, a victim chooses a more personal setting, such as a home, or an institutional setting, such as a detention center where the offender is being held. Victims should be encouraged to consider the advantages and disadvantages of particular settings. The final decision, however, should be the victim's.

Generally, the parties are seated across from each other, allowing them to establish direct eye contact as dialogue between them develops. The use of a table may increase the victim's sense of safety and add decorum. Mediators are then typically seated at the ends of the table, and support persons sit off to the side of each party. Although this arrangement is usually acceptable, if victims find it uncomfortable, their wishes should be given serious consideration. Occasionally, a victim will choose to sit closest to the door, will seek greater distance from the offender, or will request that support persons sit on the other side of the table, so as to be visible to the victim. Various cultural traditions may also suggest a different arrangement. Whatever the seating, it should be conducive to dialogue and comfortable for all parties.

Victims should have the opportunity to choose whether they speak first during the *initial* narrative portion of the mediation session or whether they speak last. This displays a bit of deference to their position as victims of crime, largely ignored by the justice system once the complaint has been filed. Often victims will find it empowering to begin, telling offenders first what they experienced and the effect it has had on them. At times, however, victims feel "put on the spot" and request that the offender go first, initiating the story and accepting accountability. Some victims find it healing to hear an offender's spontaneous words of regret or remorse, not elicited by the victim's story. The mediator must make sure, however, that whatever the order, both parties' complete stories are heard, that the victim's emotional content is not compromised by any remorse the offender may express, and that the offender does not retreat into silence in the face of the victim's emotional intensity.

In some cases, a judgment call may be required by the mediator as to who should speak first, based on the age, needs, and communication styles of the parties. The mediator may find that it is most helpful to the dialogue process in a particular case if the victim or the offender initiates the conversation. In such cases, it is important that the mediator discuss the decision and the rationale privately with both parties, prior to the mediation session. Creating a safe place where both parties feel comfortable enough to engage in a genuine dialogue to the extent of their abilities is ultimately the most important principle, regardless of who speaks first.

An extension of the victim's choice to participate in mediation is the right also to exit at any point. The victim should be informed that mediation remains a voluntary process to the end. If the victim feels uncomfortable or unsafe, the mediator may caucus first with both parties and then halt the mediation session for the time being or terminate the process altogether.

Victims have the right to select what kind of restitution would most fit their needs. In addition to out-of-pocket expenses, victims may request community service (a public service of their choice), personal service, a letter of apology, offender treatment, or other options. Although the final restitution plan will be negotiated with the offender, it is important that victims understand that they can request the compensation they choose, within any legal limitations that may exist.

Use of Victim-Sensitive Language

Mediators need to be careful in their use of language. Certain words and phrases can imply judgment or convey expectation. For example, if a mediator says or implies "you should," neutrality is lost, rapport and credibility may be damaged, and a victim may feel pressured and experience a diminished sense of power. The mediator must provide information, present the options, and then encourage victims to make the best decision for themselves. Most people are accustomed to seeing professionals or trained volunteers as experts with answers. Mediators must be vigilant in guarding the choices and thus the autonomy of the parties.

It is also important that mediators avoid the use of words such as *forgiveness* or *reconciliation*. Again, such words pressure and prescribe behavior for victims. In addition, it is vital that mediators try to avoid raising expectations that cannot be fulfilled in a particular case. For example, using words such as *healing, restoration,* or *being made whole* to describe possible outcomes for mediation may elevate victims' hopes unrealistically. Some victims may experience something of reconciliation, but it must occur spontaneously, without a directive from the mediator. In fact, it is more likely to occur if the mediator avoids directives. Forgiveness may also be expressed during the mediation session, but if the mediator so much as uses the word *forgiveness,* it may be destructive to the victim. Victims may, for instance, feel guilty if they fail to feel very forgiving. They may resent the suggestion and shut down to the point that they miss the opportunity to express fully how the crime has affected them, typically a major component in a victim's journey toward healing.

Careful Screening of Cases

Each mediation program will have its set of criteria for case selection, including type of crime, age of offender (juvenile or adult), and history of offenses. In addition to program criteria, staff and mediators will also exercise discretion as each case is developed and at each step in the process, asking themselves if this case is appropriate and should proceed to mediation.

In general, it is important in the mediation process that offenders take responsibility for their participation in the crime and proceed willingly to mediation. If mediators have any doubts about moving ahead with the process, they should talk with the victim, explaining the situation, sharing information about the offender (with the offender's permission), and inquire about the victim's desire to proceed. Victims may choose to proceed even if the offender is inarticulate or less than remorseful, simply because they wish to be heard, or victims may decide not to mediate in such a situation.

It is important also that mediators consider the readiness of both parties to participate in mediation, noting particularly victims' ability to represent their interests and express their needs.

Premediation Meeting with the Offender

Mediators will generally need to meet first with the offender, prior to contacting the victim. If the offender is willing to participate in mediation, the victim can then be contacted and a meeting arranged as desired. If the mediator meets first with the victim, however, gaining consent to participate, and then later discovers that the offender will not participate, the victim may feel revictimized, having had hopes raised for some resolution to the crime only to be denied that opportunity. If, however, contacting the offender results in a significant delay for the victim, the mediator needs to talk to the victim about the situation, explaining the importance of voluntary participation on the part of the offender.

Offender Choice to Participate

It is important that offenders participate voluntarily in mediation throughout the entire process. It must be made clear that even when under pressure from the court system to participate, offenders may decline. Forcing offenders into mediation against their will is not appropriate and likely to be counterproductive. The offender's attitude or insincerity may constitute an additional offense in the eyes of the victim.

Careful, Extensive Preparation of the Offender

In the initial meeting with the offender, the mediator seeks to establish credibility and rapport, as well as to accomplish three additional tasks: to hear the offender's experiences, to offer information and answer questions, and to assist the offender in considering mediation as an option. The mediator, as an attentive listener, gains an understanding of the offender's experiences and feelings relative to the crime, provides information, and responds to the offender's questions. Offenders need to know about the mediation program and the mediator, about the process itself and its relationship to the judicial system, about their rights, and about resources available to them. They may also have questions about the victim. Again, the mediator needs to gain permission before reporting what the victim has said. With all the information in hand, the mediator assists the offender in making a decision about participating in mediation. It is important that offenders consider the risks and benefits of the process in their particular situation. Having a well-informed, willing participant increases the chances that the mediation session will be beneficial for all parties involved.

After the offender has decided to go ahead with mediation, the mediator will need to prepare the offender for the session. It is important that offenders feel ready to proceed before the mediation session is scheduled. They need a chance to reflect on the crime and their feelings about it, a chance to work through the kinds of things they may wish to say to the victim. To help offenders understand the victim's experience, the mediator may invite offenders to recall their own experiences of being a victim and then consider what the victim of their crime might be feeling and might want from them. Mediators may ask offenders what they would like to do for the victim as well as what they wish to accomplish for themselves.

Reality-Testing Offender Expectations. Offenders may need assistance in maintaining realistic expectations of mediation. Some offenders may expect that an apology will automatically diffuse the intensity of the victim's emotions or that one mediation session will erase the harm caused by the crime. The offender's disappointment if such expectations are not met can be detrimental to the victim, who may experience guilt or anger as a result.

Assessment of Losses and Restitution Possibilities. Mediators should assist offenders in thinking about the victim's needs and the possible losses a victim may have experienced, both tangible and intangible, and then engage offenders in preliminary brainstorming about the ways the needs and losses might be addressed— for example, what would it take to repair the harm done? The mediator should discuss with the offender resources that might be used in addressing the losses, including present income, potential additional jobs that might be available, and other types of skills that might be offered to the victim. Offenders should be encouraged to continue thinking of restitution ideas and resources, in preparation for the mediation session.

Offender Support. Offenders may choose to have a friend or relative accompany them to the mediation session. The presence of support people can reinforce the seriousness of the mediation process. In addition, these supporters may in the future serve as reminders to the offender of the commitments made and as "coaches" who can encourage the offender in the completion of the agreement. Creating a humane environment for the offender also makes for a better mediation, which benefits victims, offenders, and communities.

Premediation Session with the Victim

The mediator visits with the victim face to face, at a time and place most convenient to the victim. Mediators will usually offer to come to the home, at the same time offering alternatives if the victim prefers another setting. The purpose of the visit is to establish credibility and rapport with the victim and to accomplish these tasks: to hear the victim's experiences, to offer information and answer questions, and to assist the victim in considering mediation as an option. The mediator should ask victims whether they would rather begin by telling their story or whether they would prefer to learn first about the mediation program.

A critical task for the mediator is to attend to the victim, listening carefully, patiently, and empathetically out of a genuine desire to hear the victim's experience. Effective listening will give the victim a chance to vent and experience the validation of feelings. Attentive listening on the part of the mediator will also help build trust with the victim and send the message that the victim is a priority. Occasional informal paraphrasing or summarizing by the mediator will assure the victim that the mediator is indeed paying attention and valuing what is being said.

Providing Information and Answering Questions

The mediator will need to provide the following kinds of information:

- *About the mediation program:* The mediator needs to give thorough and accurate information about the program itself (orally and in writing), its goals, its history, the population it serves, and costs involved, if any, for participants.

- *About oneself as mediator:* Mediators should offer a few brief words about their work as mediator, about their training and experience, and about themselves personally, as deemed appropriate. Giving information about oneself helps build rapport and trust with the victim.

- *About the mediation process and its purpose:* The victim will also need to know, in some detail, what the mediation process is like, the role of participants, and overall purposes.

- *About the judicial system:* Victims will typically want to know what has happened so far to the offender and what might occur if they proceed with mediation or if they decline. Mediators need to be attentive to ongoing questions that may arise, even after mediation has been completed.

- *About victims' rights:* Helpful information to leave with the victim is a summary of the rights granted to victims in that state.

- *About available resources:* Mediators must be attentive to needs expressed by victims and will need to contact staff members, offer resources, or make referrals as requested to local, state, and national organizations or agencies.

- *About the offender:* As victims begin to consider their decision about mediation, they may find it helpful to know something about the offender's state of mind and circumstances. Mediators must first get permission from the offender before sharing this kind of information.

Having given victims the necessary information, the mediator now needs to assist the victim in considering the risks and benefits of mediation in the particular situation.

Careful, Extensive Preparation of the Victim

After victims have made a decision to proceed with mediation, mediators will need to prepare them for what lies ahead. This can be done in the initial meeting or in additional sessions. It is important that the mediation session not be scheduled until victims feel ready.

Reality-Testing Victim Expectations. Reality testing is an important component of preparation at this stage. At times, victims may develop inflated expectations of the mediation process—for example, reconciliation with the offender, complete healing or peace of mind for themselves, rehabilitation of the offender, or total repair of the damage done. Although victims generally experience very positive outcomes, as do offenders, these cannot be guaranteed. Mediators themselves need to be realistic with victims, providing accurate information about possible outcomes and the kinds of results that are most typical, with the strong caution that each mediation is unique and cannot be predicted.

Assessment of Losses and Needs. Victims may appreciate assistance in identifying losses experienced in the crime and present needs related to the crime. This can include material and out-of-pocket monetary losses, as well as less tangible losses, such as a sense of safety and feelings of connection and community.

Restitution Possibilities. Mediators should engage victims in preliminary brainstorming about the ways their losses and needs might be addressed—for instance, what would it take to repair the harm done? This is intended to spark the victim's ideas about possibilities for restitution, which culminates in the victim's decisions during the actual mediation session when an agreement is negotiated. Victims should also be informed of any public funds dedicated to reimbursing victim losses and any legal limitations on what may be included in restitution agreements.

Victim Support. Victims may choose to invite a family member, friend, relative, victim advocate, or other person who might serve in a supportive role. The primary focus of the dialogue, however, remains on the victim and offender. Having a support person present for the victim can greatly assist with debriefing after the mediation session and can help provide follow-up support.

Conducting the Session Using Humanistic Mediation Principles

The mediation session itself will be guided by a humanistic approach to the mediation process as described in Chapter One. The mediator brings a nonjudgmental attitude and a positive and hopeful demeanor and conveys a sense of personal integrity and sensitivity to the needs of the parties. The mediator needs to put the parties at ease as much as possible, renew the connection developed earlier, and establish an informal yet dignified atmosphere that will be conducive to dialogue, constructive problem solving, and mutual benefit. It is the mediator's responsibility to be present in a calm, centered manner.

As the session proceeds, it is important that plenty of time be allowed, not just for personal narratives, but for interaction as well. Silence must be honored. Time pressures or a focus on reaching agreement can detract from the benefits of thorough dialogue, questions, and answers.

The mediator will need to discuss with participants guidelines that will shape the process. These guidelines help establish a safe, structured setting and respectful conversation that encourages acknowledgment and recognition of the other and elicits the strengths of the participants. Each party is assured the opportunity to speak without interruption, after which the mediator assumes a more nondirective role as guardian of the process.

The mediator needs to maintain continued attentiveness to the parties, watching for nonverbal cues and listening for unacknowledged feelings, as well as directly requesting feedback and caucusing with the parties as needed to get further information in private. It is helpful for the mediator to check in with each party before and after the mediation session.

The mediator needs to mention the possibility of an additional session. Some parties find it useful to meet again, for example, to conclude the conversation, allowing for additional thoughts, feelings, or questions to arise, to negotiate further details regarding restitution, or to acknowledge fulfillment of the agreement.

Follow-Up After the Mediation Session

It is vital that the mediator follow through with commitments and details arising out of the mediation session. Dependability is of utmost importance to victims and offenders. The agreement needs to be carefully monitored. It is helpful for the mediator to check in with the offender periodically to reinforce what was accomplished in the mediation session and to assist with any problems that may arise. The victim should be notified when the agreement has been fulfilled or if circumstances have changed that may suggest alterations in the agreement. If another meeting is desired by either victim or offender, the mediator should contact the parties and negotiate an additional session.

It is helpful if the mediator maintains phone contact with both parties for a period of time following the mediation session, whether or not the agreement has already been completed. A brief check-in is all that may be required. The mediator can serve as a continuing source of information and referral. If the case is not mediated, it may be beneficial nonetheless for the mediator or victim support staff to maintain phone contact with the victim for a period of up to six months.

It is important for victim offender mediation programs to establish procedures for evaluation of all mediations. Victims and offenders need to be surveyed regarding their satisfaction with the mediation process and the outcomes.

Mediator Training in Victim Sensitivity

The initial training of mediators, as well as continuing education, should contain information on the experiences of victims of crime, referral sources, appropriate communication skills for mediators, victims' rights, and guidelines for victim-sensitive mediation. It is helpful for trainees to hear from victim advocates and victims themselves. The training of mediators will be taken up in greater detail in Chapter Seven.

Chapter Three

The Mediation Process

Phases and Tasks

This chapter provides a detailed description of the phases and tasks necessary to carry out humanistic victim offender mediation. The chapter will cover the phases of intake, preparation, mediation, and follow-up. Discussion of each phase will include its purpose, its component tasks or activities, various options for carrying out those tasks, and where applicable, benefits or liabilities of these options. The chapter concludes with the presentation of several dos and don'ts designed to help prevent some of the more common pitfalls encountered by new mediators and new programs.

Phase One: Intake

The purpose of the intake phase is to obtain from the criminal justice system cases that are appropriate for mediation.

Determining Case Selection Criteria

Criteria need to fit the context of mediation—for example, the needs of the program or the nature of the referral source. Typically, the director of the program will work with the referral source to determine appropriate cases to refer. Suitability usually depends on

---

Note: This chapter is based on material initially drafted by Jean Greenwood for a training manual (Umbreit, Greenwood, & Lipkin, 1996) produced and distributed by the Center for Restorative Justice & Peacemaking, School of Social Work, University of Minnesota.

the following criteria: property offense or minor assault, identifiable victim, admission of guilt by the offender, no more than two or three prior convictions, no major mental health problems with the offender, and no major chemical abuse problems, which must first be addressed before mediation.

Establishing an Effective Referral System

Some mediation programs use a passive case referral procedure. The program provides the referral source with a list of criteria for referral of cases and then waits for referrals to be made. Often this method produces few referrals. Other mediation programs have found that a more proactive and assertive case referral process is more effective. Rather than waiting for referrals to come, mediation program staff can negotiate with the referral source to arrive at a process by which the staff can visit the office of the referral source on a regular basis and select cases for mediation. Then the referral source does not need to struggle to decide whether or not a given case is suitable for mediation. The source simply needs to identify a pool of cases that are likely to benefit from mediation. The mediation program staff then review these cases in detail, select the ones most appropriate for mediation, and complete the necessary paperwork. This makes the referral process much easier and less time-consuming for the referral source.

Securing the Necessary Data

The mediator will need background information regarding the offense, the offender, and the victim in order to begin the case. It will also be important to obtain sufficient data on the parties so that they can be contacted by mail or by phone.

Assigning the Case to an Appropriate Mediator

It is important to consider which mediator would be the most effective in a particular case. Sometimes gender, age, racial, or ethnic factors affect a mediator's success. Other factors may include mediation style, value orientation, and level of skill.

Introductory Letter

A letter should be sent to all involved parties, indicating that the case has been referred to the program, naming the referral source. It should include a brief description of the mediation process, in simple, jargon-free, nonthreatening language—for example, "Mediation is a process that allows participants to talk about what happened and its impact on their lives and to develop a plan to make things right." It should state that both parties will be invited to participate in mediation if they so choose and that a mediator will be phoning within a week to set up a meeting time to talk with each party individually about the offense and about mediation. The letter should also contain the name and number of a staff person who can answer questions while the parties await contact with the mediator.

Phase Two: Preparation for Mediation

There are two important subphases in preparing participants for mediation. The first is the initial telephone contact with each of the involved parties to arrange to meet with them. The second, more extensive, consists of the actual in-person meetings with both the victim and the offender.

First Telephone Contact with Offender and Victim

The purpose of the first telephone contact is to follow up on the letter sent regarding mediation and arrange for separate premediation interviews with victim and offender. The first contact is critical. Mediators need to be assertive and persuasive, yet sensitive and cooperative, in attempting to schedule a visit. Meeting in person is crucial because it encourages victims and offenders to build trust in the mediator and the process. If too much information is given over the phone, clients may feel no need for a visit. If clients feel pressured to make a decision about mediation over the phone, they will be inclined to say no. If the mediator isn't able to set a time to meet face to face for the premediation interview during that first contact, it is less likely that the case will go to mediation. Tasks for mediators include the following:

Calling All Parties. Within one week of receiving the mediation letter, the involved parties should be called. The general rule is to begin with the offender because victims may feel revictimized if their expectations are raised by the thought of a mediation session and then they learn that the offender has refused to participate. If the mediator has difficulty contacting the offender within a week, it is advisable to inform the victim of this and that the mediator is working on the case.

If the victim or offender is a juvenile, mediators must first speak with a parent or guardian to explain the program briefly, secure approval to talk with the son or daughter, and arrange a time convenient to all. If the parent or guardian is unavailable and it proves necessary to meet with the juvenile alone, it is important to do so in a public place rather than at the home.

Explaining the Purpose of the Call. Mediators need to introduce themselves and the organization and indicate the source of referral. They will then need to explain their purpose, which is to set up a meeting to learn more about the incident and to explain mediation in detail.

Explaining Briefly About Mediation. The mediator should explain that mediation allows victims and offenders to meet and talk about what happened and to work out a resolution to the situation, including restitution. The point should also be made that participation in mediation is voluntary for both victim and offender. Victims should be encouraged to wait with their decision until the mediator can visit in person, when they will have the opportunity to learn more about how mediation works and how it might be beneficial for them.

Making Arrangements to Meet. This can be done by asking if there is a convenient time to meet and inquiring about other persons whom participants may wish to have present at the meeting for support.

Offering Additional Information as Needed. The mediator should supply, within reason, whatever additional information is necessary to secure an appointment. This may mean emphasizing that the mediator's role is neutral and facilitative and that mediators do not have decision-making authority; that the parties themselves determine how to resolve the situation; or that all parties will have ample opportunity to ask questions, explain what happened, and describe their feelings about the incident.

Reiterating the Appointment and Providing Contact Information. Before closing the conversation, mediators should repeat the date and time of the meeting and also leave a phone number where they can be reached in case the participant has further questions. It is not advisable for the mediator to give out a home phone number. The mediator may wish to make a reminder call several days before the scheduled visit.

Premediation Interviews with Victim and Offender

The purpose of the individual premediation interviews with victim and offender is to learn their experience of the crime, explain the mediation process in detail, and assist the parties in deciding whether or not to participate in mediation. To accomplish this, the mediator needs, first of all, to allow adequate time for the interview. It is important not to rush the visit. Usually at least one hour should be allowed for meeting with each party.

Second, the mediator needs to shift to a focused listening mode, inquiring about what happened from the perspective of both parties and how it affected them. The interview provides an opportunity for the mediator to gather background information, to assess the client's readiness and appropriateness for mediation, to coach individuals in preparation for the mediation experience (in terms of expectations, process, and communication skills, if necessary), and to develop rapport with clients by exhibiting genuine interest and concern and adopting an empathic listening style. If the pre-mediation interview is done well, the participants will understand the mediation process, trust the mediator, and make an informed decision about their own participation. Tasks for mediators include the following:

Opening the Meeting. Mediators begin by introducing them-selves and the sponsoring organization and expressing appreciation that participants have taken time to get together. They strive to create a relaxed atmosphere by generating informal conversation, encouraging clients to share a bit about themselves (for example, asking how long they have lived in the area, where they are from, how old their children are), and sharing similar information about themselves, as appropriate.

Gathering Information. Important first steps include asking victim and offender to tell what happened, how they felt about it, and how they were affected by it. It is vital that the mediator assume a fully attentive listening mode.

It is extremely important at this stage to explain confidential-ity and its limits. Mediators should assure the parties that what is said will be held in confidence. The exception to the confidential-ity rule is mandated reporting. If the mediator is told of child abuse, abuse of a vulnerable adult, intended suicide, or a planned homi-cide, it is crucial to let participants know that it must be reported.

In addition to such mandated reporting, there may be times when it would be helpful to share information between the parties prior to mediation. In such a case, mediators must secure permis-sion from the party to share a specific piece of information. Occa-sionally, the parties may base their decision to participate in mediation on the attitude of the other party, and it is important for the participants to have realistic expectations about the process. At the end of the premediation session, it is often good to ask the person for permission to share any information with the other party. This can be done by saying the following: "Sometimes the other party is interested in learning about your general attitude about what happened and even your appearance. Would it be OK to share this information?" Also, if there is any information from premediation interviews that mediators wish to bring up in the mediation session, they must get permission to share it if permission has not already been secured.

Explaining Mediation. The first component of this phase involves presenting the basics of the mediation process, including a brief description of how the mediator came to hold that position and what his or her experience has been. Using ordinary language, the mediator should then describe the mediation process, in chronological order, with sufficient detail. Clients need a clear sense of what happens in mediation and what would be expected of them. The explanation should include the following points:

- After participants introduce themselves, the mediator makes an opening statement that explains the mediation process, the mediator's neutral role and commitment to confidentiality, and possible ground rules—for example, allowing each person to speak without interruption and speaking and listening respectfully.

- After ground rules are agreed on, each person has the opportunity to tell what happened from his or her perspective, without interruption, expressing reactions and feelings about the incident then and now. The victim will be permitted to choose whether to speak first or second.

- Following the telling of stories, participants have a chance to ask questions of each other and make additional comments.

- Both parties then propose options to resolve the situation and repair the damage as much as possible.

- Once the participants have agreed on a mutually acceptable resolution, they fill out an agreement form, which is then read aloud and signed by both parties.

Most mediators find it useful to provide a summary overview of the components of mediation:

THE VICTIM will have the opportunity to meet the person who victimized him or her, let the offender know how the crime affected his or her life, ask questions and get answers, resolve issues, and have a more direct say about consequences.

THE OFFENDER will have the opportunity to meet with the victim and directly express any thoughts or feelings, respond to questions and concerns, ask questions and get answers, make a bad situation better, make amends for wrongdoing, and have a say in determining restitution.

It is important to discuss in detail with both victim and offender various options they may want to include in an agreement. In cases involving juvenile offenders, it is important to explain that the parents will also need to approve the terms of an agreement, affirming the juvenile's ability to meet the obligation. It is often useful to describe the kinds of solutions other victims and offenders have found helpful:

- Monetary restitution, amount not to exceed victim's out-of-pocket loss.

- Community service, site and hours to be determined by both parties, unless the victim chooses to allow the offender choice of site (a value may be established for the unpaid work—for example, $5 per hour—as a way of partly or completely fulfilling what would have been a monetary obligation).

- Personal service—for example, mowing the lawn, painting a fence, cleaning (unpaid work done by the offender for the victim, which may be similarly valued at $5 per hour).

- Charitable contribution, amount not to exceed victim's out-of-pocket loss.
- Apology, verbal or written.
- Class, training, counseling, or treatment program for the offender.
- Creative restitution designed by the victim and the offender, building on the interests of the victim and the abilities and interests of the offender—for example, creating a work of art or maintaining lines on the Little League field.
- Combinations of these that are mutually agreed on as fair, safe, and reasonable.

In considering what options might be appropriate, it is crucial to ask the offender to consider what he or she would be able to do in terms of monetary restitution, community service, and personal service and asking victims to consider what they would like to request of the offender. Victims should describe the actual losses they incurred, if that information has not already been given. Documentation of losses should be provided, to the extent possible. Estimates for repair of damages need to be obtained prior to the mediation and brought to the session.

As the meeting comes to a conclusion, mediators need to elicit any further questions participants may have about the mediation process and remind them that participation in mediation is voluntary. As the client considers participating in mediation, mediators can encourage them to reflect on questions such as these, depending on what might be appropriate:

- What would it be like to sit across the table from the other party and hear his or her story?
- How do you think the other party might feel, meeting with you face to face?
- What might you like to say to the other party?
- What are the risks and benefits of mediation for you?

• Have you [the offender] ever experienced being a victim? What was that like?

Mediators can mention that many victims and offenders find it helpful to meet and work things out, but mediation is not for everyone—it is an individual choice. It is appropriate to encourage participation but not to pressure or coerce, and judgmental language, such as *should* or *ought,* should be avoided. It is important also not to oversell the program.

Throughout the meeting, mediators need to provide appropriate information about the status of the case relative to the justice system.

Obtaining a Decision. Mediators will need to assess readiness for mediation. An initial consideration is the stance of the offender. Most programs require that the offender acknowledge guilt by taking personal responsibility for the crime or at least some portion of the crime. It is of course desirable for remorse to be present as well. Often remorse is elicited through the mediation process, though that result cannot be predicted. A lack of remorse on the part of the offender may be important information for the victim to have in making a decision about proceeding with mediation. Even if the offender does not reach a remorseful state, there still may be benefits to the victim in addressing the offender. That is a decision that the victim needs to make. The mediator's responsibility is to provide accurate information, gaining permission for any sharing of information with the other party.

Other considerations include the capacity of both victim and offender to communicate their perspectives and to refrain from destructive behavior. Anger in and of itself is not destructive to the mediation process, particularly if it is "owned," using "I" messages. Rage and vindictiveness expressed through attacking language is usually counterproductive.

Once the mediator has assessed readiness, it is appropriate to ask participants whether they wish to proceed with mediation or if they need additional information or time to make the decision. If the participants are not ready to decide, a time to call back must be scheduled.

One frequent obstacle that may surface in this phase is the possibility that one or the other participant may say no to mediation. While the mediator's efforts during the first contact are very important, some cases referred to mediation do not get to the table for reasons that are beyond the control of the mediator. The victim or offender may be too frightened to meet. Occasionally, a mediator will be unable to locate one or more of the parties. Sometimes one party may agree to mediate but the other does not. Some victims may believe they were unaffected by the crime or may not want or need anything from the offender. The parties may feel that the situation has already been resolved.

Whatever the reasons, it is important to remember that the decision to mediate is in the hands of the clients. It is the mediator's responsibility to explain mediation clearly and invite each person to decide whether it is desirable. Failure to get people to agree to mediation does not mean that the mediator has failed. In fact, the premediation interview can often be helpful to victims even if they decide not to participate in mediation, particularly if they are able to vent their feelings and tell their story to an interested and concerned person. The mediator is very often the first person in any way connected with the criminal justice system who has taken the time to listen attentively to the victim's story about the impact of the crime.

Options for the mediator if participants have decided not to mediation include the following:

- If victims are reluctant to participate, mediators can ask if they might want to designate someone else—relative, friend, or minister—to represent them at the mediation in their absence. In this case, mediation can be done with secondary victims or surrogate victims.

- Indirect mediation can be offered as an option. In this case, the mediator serves as a go-between to reach an agreement that both sides believe is fair and reasonable, even though the parties never meet face to face. This type of "shuttle diplomacy" mediation can be done either by phone or through additional in-person meetings with each party. The agreement must be signed by all parties, which can be done by mail. Signed copies of the agreement are then mailed to the victim, the offender, the offender's parents, and the referral source or other court personnel. The offender may choose to write a letter of apology to be forwarded to the victim.

• If the parties refuse these options, the mediator can inquire about the victim's losses and ask if the victim wishes to complete a loss claim form in order to request restitution through the court system or a board of reparations, if such services are available. This needs to be clearly coordinated with the local court system's procedures.

Making Arrangements for the Mediation Session. At this point, it is appropriate to explore possible dates, times, and locations for the mediation if the participants have decided to proceed. Any court-imposed deadlines need to be clarified, and the importance of resolving issues quickly should be emphasized. Victims need to have priority in determining the place. The setting should feel neutral, safe, and comfortable. Appropriate venues include public libraries, community centers, churches, a conference room located in the building housing the mediation program, or even a home if it is mutually agreeable.

Both parties should be asked whether there is anyone they wish to have present at the mediation in a supporting role (for example, a family member, friend, neighbor, community leader, minister, teacher, probation officer). In most programs, support persons must be at least eighteen years of age. It is important to clarify that the support person is not a participant in the dialogue but will be allowed to make a brief statement after the telling of the stories and to comment on the terms of the agreement prior to signing. If parents are allowed to dominate the discussion in mediation sessions involving juveniles, the focus of accountability is shifted away from the youth, and the message about taking responsibility for one's own actions gets diluted.

On rare occasions, an offender or victim may request to have a lawyer present in the mediation session. The lawyer must agree to a nonparticipatory role identical to that of support persons. In all cases, participants should be encouraged to inform their attorneys of their decision to proceed with mediation.

Concluding the Interview. Mediators should thank the clients for their time and their willingness to talk about their experiences. Plans for the mediation should be reviewed, and participants should be encouraged to call if they have questions. Leaving a flyer listing other available victim services in the community is a particularly helpful way of ending the premediation interview.

Phase Three: Mediation

The purpose of the mediation session is for victim and offender to have the opportunity to learn from each other the events surrounding the crime and how it affected their lives, to get answers to their questions, to express their feelings, to gain a greater sense of closure, and to develop a mutually acceptable plan that addresses the harm caused by the crime.

An important consideration in planning for the actual mediation session is deciding whether or not to use co-mediators. Mediating alone makes scheduling much simpler and rapport building less complex. However, being the only mediator means risking not seeing or hearing everything that takes place during a mediation session. Choosing to co-mediate means another pair of eyes and ears to help facilitate discussion of feelings, needs, and issues. A co-mediator can be an effective resource when confronting an impasse in the process. Mediating alone means missing out on feedback provided by another mediator after the session. The decision to co-mediate or not may depend on the nature of the case.

When preparing to co-mediate a case, it is important to determine how much participation each mediator expects of the other. In most cases of co-mediation, one mediator conducts the entire premediation phase and the second mediator participates in the actual mediation session, usually in a secondary role. Is the mediation to be a team effort or a mediator-and-observer situation?

Mediators must decide roles in advance so that expectations are clear, the process runs smoothly, and participants feel confident in the skills and leadership arrangement demonstrated by mediators. There are many ways of dividing responsibilities. For example, one may give the introductory statement while the other initiates and monitors the telling of the stories. When victim and offender are generating options, both mediators may facilitate the discussion. Verbal cues may be helpful—for example, "Mary, do you want to take it from here?" or "John, may I suggest something?" It is crucial to be aware that victims and offenders may look for an alliance with one of the mediators. Both mediators need to be careful to maintain absolute neutrality.

Trust in the mediators is a key ingredient for a successful mediation. Lack of cooperation between the mediators will result in lack of trust in the mediation process. If tension develops, the mediators may need to confer with each other.

The mediation session consists of six subphases: preparation, beginning the session, storytelling and dialogue, discussion of losses and generating options, developing an agreement, and closure.

Preparation

Mediators need to arrive early in order to arrange the room in a manner most conducive to mediation. The space needs to be quiet and private, small enough to create a feeling of intimacy and facilitate ease of hearing, yet large enough to avoid a sense of confinement. It is possible to use a corner of a large room, set up in such a way as to define a smaller space.

The physical seating arrangement is very important and can greatly affect how the session proceeds. The seating arrangement should be determined by the mediator, except in special circumstances when it might make a victim feel more comfortable to have a say in the setup. If the participants enter and seat themselves, mediators should consider moving them. Most people perceive this as an indication that everything is under control, which increases their sense of safety in the mediation. If a particular arrangement isn't working, participants can be invited to change seating. Sometimes such a change can help reduce tension, suggesting that each person's needs are important and that everyone is working together for mutual benefit.

In general, seating should be arranged so that victim and offender have the opportunity to face each other directly across the table, unless such an arrangement would inhibit one of the parties. Mediators need to be alert to differing cultural values that may discourage direct eye contact, in which case participants can be seated facing the mediator. However, it is important to seat victim and offender where they will be able to look at one another if they so choose, perhaps becoming more at ease as the mediation proceeds. Parents or support people should be seated behind and to one side of the person they are supporting. This arrangement keeps the focus on the actual victim and offender, rather than on the parent or support person.

Sitting at a table is often helpful, and it creates safe boundaries. In many cases, it is also possible to sit in a circle, with no table, but with the victim and offender across from each other to allow for direct eye contact.

In addition to preparation of the physical space, mediators need to prepare themselves by reviewing the case briefly. This includes refreshing their memory about strategies that may have come to mind during the premediation interviews, as a way to tailor the mediation to the unique factors of the case, and taking a few moments of silence to clear their minds and quiet themselves in preparation for giving full attention to the parties.

Beginning the Session

The introductory statement should be clear and concise. Participants are often tense and may not be able to concentrate on a lengthy introduction. Mediators will want to welcome everyone to the mediation session and then introduce themselves and ask the parties to introduce themselves. It is wise to allow individuals to do their own introducing, as some occasionally wish to use only their first names, out of a concern for their own safety. At this time, those present who are not directly involved in the incident may also be invited to identify their connection.

To set the proper tone, mediators use their voice, body language, and affect to communicate calm, purpose, seriousness, and empathy. They build in moments of silence and act comfortable during quiet times. It is important to affirm the willingness of all parties to participate in mediation, which is a challenging experience to face, to share hope and expectation that everyone present will benefit from the mediation experience, and to encourage everyone to be as open and honest as possible in a spirit of mutual problem solving.

Following the introductions, it is wise to spend some time orienting participants to the mediation session, even though much of the orientation material may already have been covered in the individual meetings.

One important component is to describe the purpose of coming together—that is, to deal directly with an event that has affected many people, to seek to come to terms with the incident as much as possible, and to try to make things better. The mediator needs to choose language appropriate to the context. In some cases, the mediation process may be described as a way of resolving issues or of helping the parties move on. However, in crimes of greater severity or cases of more intense emotional involvement, resolving issues and moving on may not be realistic goals, and certainly not ones that a mediator should impose on the process. In such cases, the goal may be simply to help participants deal with the crime as one step in a long-term process of coming to grips with a painful and tragic event. In cases where the parties had a connection prior to the crime or anticipate future contact, it is important for the mediator to mention both past and future aspects to be considered when identifying desired outcomes.

Also important is describing briefly how the mediation session will proceed:

- Each person will have the opportunity to tell what happened from his or her perspective, without interruption, expressing reactions and feelings about the incident then and now.

- Participants will have a chance to ask questions of each other and make additional comments; support persons will be invited to make a brief statement.

- Both parties will then discuss ways to resolve the situation and repair the damage as much as possible.

- Once the participants have agreed on a mutually-acceptable resolution, an agreement form will be completed and signed by both parties.

Mediators must make it absolutely clear that the mediated dialogue is between the victim and the offender. Support persons need to refrain from participating beyond making a brief statement as indicated.

The mediator should announce that anyone can request a short break, not to exceed two to three minutes, or a brief caucus with the mediator or someone else present. In the event that one party wishes to caucus with the mediator, it is important to give equal time to the other party. The mediator may also initiate a caucus with each party separately.

It is indispensable to define the mediator's role clearly, stating that the mediator is neutral, working for the benefit of both parties; the mediator maintains confidentiality, except for mandated reporting (any notes the mediator makes during the mediation are for use in developing an agreement); and the mediator does not make determinations or require the parties to agree to anything but rather assists the parties in developing their own solution by guiding and facilitating the process.

It is also wise to discuss ground rules and list guidelines that others have found useful. Commonly used guidelines include the following:

- Allowing each party to speak without interruption. It may be helpful to provide paper for the participants, to be used to note thoughts that come to mind as the other party is speaking.
- Listening and speaking respectfully to each other.

Participants may also be invited to suggest any additional ground rules they feel are important. The parties are then asked if they will agree to the ground rules.

Finally, the mediator should ask both parties individually if they are ready to proceed with the mediation.

Storytelling and Dialogue

This step may be introduced by reviewing instructions given earlier: each party will be asked, one at a time, to tell what happened, what was going on at the time, how he or she felt about what happened then and how each feels now, and how the crime affected each person's life. Participants can be reminded that the focus will be on each person's experience; mediation is not a fact-finding mission. In cases where the parties do not agree on all the facts, it may be important to acknowledge that reality, as by saying, "Even though we may not find agreement on all the facts of this case, it is still our task to come to terms with this incident and find a way to resolve the issues."

Usually, the victim is invited first to begin telling the story, unless the victim has indicated a preference for the offender to go first. The danger in having the offender begin is that the offender's story and possible apology may "soften up" the victim, making it difficult for the victim to be forthright about the impact of the crime. This is particularly true if the offender is young. It is also possible that the offender may not reveal as much after hearing the victim speak, realizing that the victim may not have known the full extent of the crime. At times, however, the victim may insist that the offender go first, desiring to see the offender venture first into vulnerable territory, while the victim then has the opportunity to gauge his or her responses to the tone and content of the offender's words. It is possible that hearing the victim's story may move the offender to greater empathy and remorse.

Even during the storytelling part of the mediation phase, it is appropriate to initiate direct communication between victim and offender, unless that might inhibit a participant. For example, "Mr. Smith, could you tell Jane what happened from your perspective and how you felt about it?" Mediators are intensely involved in monitoring the process throughout this subphase. While devoting full attention to the speaker, mediators maintain an awareness of the other participants, assessing their level of stress or agitation. It is crucial to be cautious about intervening. Participants will benefit from the opportunity to tell their stories uninterrupted. If one of the parties omits information about feelings or impact, the person may be gently coached—for example, "What were some thoughts and feelings you had at the time?" Respect for silences is one of the hallmarks of this subphase.

When both parties have had a turn to speak, they should be asked whether they have anything further to add to their stories, any comments, or any questions that they would like to ask the other party.

Once the storytelling appears to be complete, support persons may be asked if they wish to speak briefly about what they experienced and its impact on them. Enough time needs to be allowed for additional questions and comments after the initial storytelling and for additional silences. It is important not to move too quickly to a discussion of losses and development of a restitution plan.

The transition from storytelling to discussion of losses can be facilitated by summarizing or acknowledging what has been said and by identifying any common ground that may exist.

Discussion of Losses and Generating Options

This subphase may be introduced by asking the parties to consider what it would take for them to feel that things have been resolved as best they can be, the damage has been repaired, and things have been made better.

Discussion about options can be encouraged by identifying what is important to each party (positions) and why it is important (interests), by summarizing the losses that have been mentioned and asking if there is anything that needs to be added, and by asking both parties for ideas on possible ways of addressing the losses.

If the parties are finding it difficult to come up with resolution options, mediators may want to remind them of possibilities discussed during the premediation interview or some that other victims and offenders have found appropriate. Implications of the various proposals can be explored by asking, is it practical, workable, reasonable? Does it address the needs of the parties?

As the discussion of options nears a close, support persons may be invited to offer additional ideas they may have. Before moving to negotiating the actual agreement, first the victim and then the offender should be asked if there are any further questions for the other party.

Developing an Agreement

There are a number of general guidelines for writing an agreement:

- The introduction should indicate that "both parties have discussed the issue and have decided to resolve it in this manner."
- Entries should be brief but detailed and clear. Agreements should be specific, attainable, and measurable. "John agrees to

build a fence for Mr. Jones" is too vague. A better agreement would be "John agrees to construct a fence around Mr. Jones's deck. Mr. Jones will provide the materials and will supervise the work. John will be responsible to call Mr. Jones on May 25 to make final arrangements to do the work. Mr. Jones will give John his phone number. The work is to be completed by June 15, 2002."

- The victim's losses need to be determined and verified, as far as possible (victims are not allowed to recover more than the amount of the actual loss).

- If an apology has been made and accepted, the agreement needs to reflect it.

- The final date of completion for the agreement needs to be stated.

- If the agreement resolves the issue satisfactorily for both parties, the conclusion to the agreement needs to convey this—for example, "Both parties agree that the issue is resolved."

- Each offender must have his or her own separate agreement with each victim. Mediators must not include information about companion offenders in a contract; this would constitute a breach of confidentiality in cases involving juvenile offenders.

- The parties need to be informed, prior to signing, who will get copies of the agreement (victim, offender, offender's parents, referring agent, probation officer, court).

Both parties should be reminded that the agreement is based on mutual consent and that both parties must feel it is fair and workable. The mediator's use of discretion is important here. If there are some serious concerns about the appropriateness of the agreement, mediators should consult with staff.

In the actual negotiation process, it is often helpful to begin with the easiest issue. Mediators carry out this process by finding a mutually agreeable solution, drafting the specifics (who does what, when, where), and then proceeding to work through the remaining issues.

During the negotiations, it is important to explore the offender's ability to keep the agreement in a balanced and nonjudgmental manner. In cases involving juveniles, the offender's parents should be asked if the agreement sounds realistic for their child.

As drafts of the agreement are developed, they should be reviewed with both parties, clause by clause, to verify that it reflects their wishes. Participants should be encouraged to amend or delete any clauses or words that do not fit and to add any points that seem relevant. Sometimes victims seek to include words of encouragement for the offender, which is very appropriate if both parties agree. Mediators may wish to remind the parties of any additional ideas for restitution that were discussed earlier but are not in the agreement.

When the draft is finished, it is extremely important to read the draft aloud. Occasionally, a participant is not able to read very well. Reading the agreement aloud keeps everyone a full participant without embarrassment. This plan should be indicated during the premediation interview so that someone who has trouble reading will know not to decline to participate out of fear of exposure.

Any changes resulting from the read-through need to be written into the final version of the agreement, if the parties approve. Then the agreement should be read aloud once more, and both parties need to sign it. In the case of juveniles, parents or guardians should initial the agreement as well.

Occasionally, not all the issues can be dealt with in one session. Participants may become stuck or simply be unable to sustain their attention to the task. Also, parties may need to get estimates for damage done or wish to consult with family or legal counsel before continuing. One or more additional sessions may be scheduled if necessary.

After the agreement has been signed, it is important to explain carefully what happens next:

- Copies of the agreement go to the victim, offender, offender's parents, and court officials. Copies should be provided at the time of mediation whenever possible.

- Parties need to be informed about who will be monitoring compliance with the agreement—for example, the mediator, program staff, probation officer, restitution worker.

- Participants should be reassured that the offender will be given proper credit for payments and that the correct amount of money will be forwarded to the victim. It is important to reconfirm the victim's address (in private), as well as current information for the offender.

- The consequences of noncompliance with the agreement should be reiterated—for example, the case will be returned to the referral agency and may go to court. Any state regulations affecting the handling of juvenile cases need to be outlined at this point.

Closing the Mediation Session

This is the time to mention that a brief follow-up meeting is often helpful. Some participants wish to meet again to review progress on the agreement, to deal with minor issues that may arise, to reinforce the impact of mediation, to make direct payment of restitution, to celebrate completion of the agreement, or simply to achieve greater closure for themselves. Participants should be asked whether they want to schedule a follow-up session.

The mediator concludes the session by asking if anyone has anything more to say, thanking the participants for coming, and commending them for the good work they have done. Mediators often wish participants well and shake hands with them as they leave. It is important not to suggest that the parties shake hands. This must be genuinely initiated by the parties. Mediators may wish to check with each party as they leave, asking such questions as "How are you doing?" or "How was the mediation experience for you?"

After the session, mediator debriefing is crucial. This may be done individually, with a co-mediator, or with a staff member, answering such question as "What did you as mediator do that was helpful?" or "What might you have done differently to be more effective?" Debriefing allows mediators to process what happened and then leave the session behind, letting go of feelings and thoughts that may continue to churn inside. Co-mediators can give each other feedback on how well they worked together, how their styles blend or complement. They may also choose to discuss strengths and growth areas of each mediator, thus facilitating the development of new skills.

Phase Four: Follow-Up

The purpose of the follow-up phase is to monitor the agreement, to renegotiate the terms as needed, to reinforce and enhance the impact of the mediation, to humanize the process further, and to provide closure.

Sending Copies of the Agreement

Depending on the procedures and policies of individual programs, copies of the agreement need to be mailed out to all relevant parties in a timely manner.

Convening Follow-Up Meetings

Follow-up meetings are typically shorter and less formal than the initial mediation session. Mediators should figure that a scheduled follow-up meeting will be brief; many last no longer than thirty minutes. They will need to be explicit about the purpose of the meeting—for example, to check in with each other and review progress on the agreement, to deal with unresolved issues, to renegotiate the terms of the agreement, to acknowledge completion of the agreement, or to make a direct payment of restitution. The informality may be increased by encouraging less structured, more spontaneous dialogue by participants, which enhances a sense of closure, mutual acceptance, personal accountability, and a spirit of reconciliation.

Monitoring Progress and Completion of the Agreement

If no follow-up meetings are held, mediators will need to keep in contact with the offender while the agreement is being fulfilled to see how things are going, especially tracking whether there are any problems that might affect completion of the agreement. If problems do arise, mediators will need to schedule another mediation session to renegotiate terms, or they may renegotiate by phone. Victims will need to be periodically informed about the progress being made. When the agreement is fulfilled, mediators should contact both parties to notify them of completion and offer congratulations to the offender.

Tips for Mediators

The following list of dos and don'ts has been developed out of the experience of many mediators and is a useful checklist to review before beginning a new mediation case.

Dos

DO remember that participation is voluntary. Regardless how beneficial the mediator believes mediation will be for the victim and offender, the choice to mediate must be theirs. Resist the "hard sell." It is appropriate to be gently persuasive and encouraging, but mediators must guard against manipulating people to agree to mediate. Laying a guilt trip on a victim to get the person to meet with the offender runs the risk of revictimizing the victim.

DO call for a causus when unsure. When the mediation process reaches an impasse; when participants are shutting down, arguing, stuck, belligerent; or if the process is simply not moving ahead productively, mediators should confer with each other, the victim, or the offender as needed. They may also suggest that the participants confer with their support persons if that seems appropriate. In general, these caucuses should be limited in number and should be relatively brief.

DO summarize when stuck. A brief summary of what has been said, or simple repetition, can help participants think of other things they can say to get the discussion flowing. Don't overdo summarizing. Don't interrupt to summarize if discussion is flowing freely and participants appear to understand each other. Do interrupt to check understanding of what was said if there appears to be a misunderstanding.

DO ask if participants would like suggestions. If they say yes, refrain from giving a specific solution. Instead, suggest that they brainstorm, trade places ("If I were you, I might want . . ." or "I'd offer to . . ."), or make a list of possibilities including pros and cons. If that doesn't help them generate ideas for solutions, mediators might ask if they'd like explanations about common options again: monetary restitution, community service, personal service, treatment or counseling, donation to charity, school grade improvement, or other creative solutions.

DO encourage participants to talk directly to each other. Participants will know they need to speak to each other because of information shared by the mediator at the premediation interview and at the beginning of the session. At first, it may be difficult for them to do this. They may be more comfortable looking at the mediator. Mediators can help them overcome their reluctance to look at each other by directing their focus to the listener and away from the speaker. If this fails, the mediator may ask the speaker to direct comments to the other party or may move back from the table slightly and look down at a note pad for an extended time, thus avoiding eye contact with the speaker. Also be alert to and respectful of cultural traditions that may prohibit eye contact in situations such as mediation.

DO clarify when someone seems puzzled. Paraphrasing what has been said in the form of a question to the speaker is a good clarification technique. The mediator might say, "Do you mean . . . ?" or simply ask, "Could you explain what you meant a little further?" If by observing body language or intonation the mediator senses that a participant is unable to express directly what he or she wants or is feeling, mirroring or reflecting may be helpful—for example, "I hear that you are agreeing to the plan, but I sense that you are feeling a little uneasy about it. Is that correct?"

DO reframe to temper heated discussion. Neutral rephrasing of facts and issues helps remove value-laden language and balance intense emotions. If one participant made a statement that angered the other, the mediator might restate the message without the "attack." Reframing can help a speaker convey information without the listener's getting defensive—for instance, "What I hear you saying is this: . . . Is that accurate?" Reframing the statement shifts the focus away from the position toward the underlying needs and interests of the speaker.

DO end the mediation if ground rules aren't followed. Give participants a chance when ground rules are broken, but if rules continue to be ignored, and this is interfering with the process, remind participants of the ground rules and terminate the session if the rules continue to be broken. All participants at the table must be treated respectfully and fairly.

DO contact staff when stuck. Staff or fellow mediators are vital resources. Mediators are working in difficult situations with people who are themselves in a challenging situation. Each mediation has its own unique set of twists and turns. Mediators may need to get more information before the mediation can continue. It is perfectly acceptable to delay completing the mediation until staff can be contacted. If staff can't be reached at the time, schedule an additional meeting.

Don'ts

DON'T solve problems for participants. Both victims and offenders need to be in charge of their discussion and negotiations. It is their mediation. Mediators can assist with suggestions if the participants are truly stuck, but only with their permission.

DON'T get into fact finding. Although it is important to review the event during the storytelling subphase, it is not beneficial to cross-examine anyone or to retry the case. A victim who does not understand mediation may start to interrogate the offender. If that happens, the mediator needs to call a timeout and explain that interrogation is not a part of mediation. It is also not essential that all the facts agree. Even when there is no consensus about all the details, it may still be the desire of the parties to resolve the situation. Always ask the participants if they wish to proceed.

DON'T allow participants to argue. Arguing is unproductive and is usually a form of fact finding. Interrupt the process and reiterate the task at hand—for example, to describe what happened and its impact. If arguing continues, summarize and suggest that to continue arguing is unproductive. Point out that the participants may need to agree to disagree. Confer with each party separately, reiterating the process, the purpose of mediation, and the ground rules. Encourage the parties to be open and proceed in a cooperative problem-solving mode. If arguing continues, end the mediation, giving participants the option to try again at a later date. If both parties wish to meet again, schedule the next mediation session before leaving the table. If they are undecided, set a time within a day or two for a phone conversation with each party. It may be helpful to ask one party to wait at the table while the other leaves. Instruct both participants not to attempt to resolve the issue in the parking lot. Notify staff of the situation.

DON'T philosophize, patronize, or preach. The mediation is the participants' time. Mediators are there to model mediation techniques and facilitate discussion, not lecture or teach. Mediators must demonstrate the respectful communication skills and behaviors expected of the participants. Avoid being judgmental and using words such as *should* and *ought*.

DON'T allow nonparticipants to take over. The mediation is between the victim and the offender. Going over the rules at the beginning of the mediation helps people follow them. Stating each person's role constitutes a promise to the victim and the offender that they are the only ones who will be resolving the problem. Allowing others (for example, parents) to take over is violating the commitment made with the victim and offender. Consequently, neither may feel safe in the mediation session. Nonparticipants have carefully defined times to give input. Beyond those times, they may speak only with the permission of both participants.

DON'T use jargon or technical terms. When jargon is used, people feel excluded and communication breaks down. Encourage participants to ask questions if anyone uses language they do not understand. For example, the term *restitution* may be unclear, particularly to juveniles. The mediator's task is to explain it.

DON'T write an agreement compensating for pain and suffering. Only out-of-pocket losses may be paid to victims. The courts do not allow payment for pain and suffering.

DON'T fill the silences. The mediator's most effective skill is listening attentively. Participants often need time to collect their thoughts before speaking or responding to questions. Do not rush the process.

DON'T intervene too frequently. Be cautious about interrupting speakers. Do so only with good cause. Too much involvement by the mediator will detract from the conversation between victim and offender.

DON'T use language that pressures participants. Words like *forgiveness* and *reconciliation* may place undue pressure on participants to achieve a particular outcome. Although the mediation process often results in a sense of reconciliation, and forgiveness may occur, no one can predict or prescribe such an outcome, and seeking to force it may revictimize the victim. Victims are entitled to their anger and entitled to receive restitution. Victims may decide to forgive, but it must be on their own initiative.

Similarly, do not suggest that the offender apologize. A forced apology is not helpful to either party. If the victim requests an apology, the mediator may urge the offender to give thought to the request before responding, to make sure what is said is genuine. If the victim has shared his or her perspective and the offender has made no acknowledgment, the mediator may consider respectfully prompting—for example, "Is there anything you would like to say in response?" Parents often instruct their children to apologize. Mediators may not.

This chapter has covered in great detail the specific steps mediators must carry out when conducting humanistic and victim-sensitive mediation sessions between crime victims and offenders. Each of the phases and tasks presented here stems directly from the beliefs, values, and principles of humanistic mediation presented in Chapter One. The purpose, as always, is to empower, to provide safety, and to create a context and an environment in which the healing potential of a genuine human encounter can flourish. The training needed to enable mediators to carry out the tasks presented here is extensive and will be explored more fully in Chapter Seven.

Chapter Four

Multicultural Implications of
Victim Offender Mediation

"The hell you say! I won't stand for it!" Banging the table with his fist, the black store owner shouted, "You're not gonna get off that easy!" The Native American teen shoplifter cowered in silence. She worked hard at keeping her lips from trembling and her stare fixed on an old picture hanging on the wall to the right of the black man. With churning stomach, the Anglo mediator believed the entire mediation was torpedoed by the store owner's angry outburst. He tried to think of a way of aborting the session with some semblance of civility. Frustrated, the black man looked with disgust at the two others at the table. He expected and wanted a response. But both individuals looked barely alive. How could justice ever come out of this mishmash?

The purpose of this chapter is to share with practitioners of restorative justice concerns regarding the implementation of such frameworks when working with persons of differing cross-cultural perspectives. Worldviews, perceptions of justice, and communication styles are greatly influenced by one's cultural milieu (Myers & Filner, 1993). Working with persons of different cultures, particularly in attempts at conflict resolution, can be a challenge replete with potential dangers and pitfalls. Even when all parties are well intentioned, natural ways of speaking and behaving, when misunderstood, can destroy the best efforts and hopes of restoring and repairing relationships.

Note: This chapter is based on an early version of Umbreit and Coates (1999).

We will begin by considering various pitfalls and dangers that may hamper restorative justice efforts carried out in cross-cultural contexts. We will then turn to looking at ways of increasing the likelihood of positive interactions when working with persons of differing cultural backgrounds.

Potential Cross-Cultural Pitfalls and Dangers

The continuing movement toward adaptation of restorative justice frameworks can be enhanced only if practitioners, advocates, and policymakers become increasingly sensitive to and knowledgeable about cross-cultural issues and dynamics that impinge on the practice of such programs and on the very notion of justice. The cultural background of victim, offender, and program staff member are often different; this carries a risk of miscommunication, misunderstanding, or worst of all, revictimization. The narrative that opened this chapter demonstrates an exchange between people of differing cultural backgrounds that left each person feeling dissatisfied and used. Each would walk away from such an experience turned off to efforts to "humanize" the justice system.

A great danger when speaking of things cross-cultural is that of overgeneralization. There are likely as many differences within cultures as between cultures. For example, significant customs, communication styles, and shared values distinguish the rural white from the urban white, the upper-class black from the lower-class black, the Mexican Latino from the Puerto Rican Latino, the reservation Native American and the nonreservation Native American, and so on. We will return to this question of intracultural differences later. It suffices for the moment to note that such differences do exist as we begin to consider variations across cultures.

Differences between persons raised or living in varying cultures will likely be reflected in communication styles. Those differences will typically be as evident in the way points of view are communicated as in the message being relayed. Let us take a moment to consider some possible pitfalls in understanding one another's nonverbal statements. The following discussion draws considerably from research-based findings reported by Sue and Sue in *Counseling the Culturally Different* (1990).

Proximity

Depending on one's cultural experience, one may be most comfortable talking face to face or at a distance. Generally, Latin Americans, African Americans, Africans, Indonesians, Arabs, and the French are more comfortable speaking with less distance between conversants than Anglos are. In mediation or conversation, the Anglo staff person may back away, as if feeling confronted or attacked. The Latin American victim will appear to be chasing the mediator across the room, believing the mediator to be aloof, thinking "he believes he's too good for me." Both participants are misreading cues and taking actions that only reinforce misunderstandings. Another example of the use of space is the frequent desire by many white Americans to keep a desk between themselves and the person they are trying to help. In contrast, some Eskimos prefer to sit side by side when talking of intimate matters rather than across from each other.

Body Movements

Body movements often speak louder than words. Posture, smiling, eye contact, laughing, gestures, and many other movements communicate. How we interpret what we hear and see may vary greatly from culture to culture. Asians may be puzzled and offended by a white mediator who wants to express herself—her likes and her dislikes—with facial grimaces and smiles. The white mediator may interpret the Asian who has been taught to keep a tight rein on his emotions tightly as having no feelings. It is inappropriate to expect an individual raised to value emotional control to shed tears of remorse for having burgled a home, despite feeling remorseful.

How many times have mental health professionals interpreted avoidance of eye contact to mean avoidance of an issue, poor self-confidence, submissiveness, or guilt and shame? In many traditional Native American cultures, it is disrespectful to look an elder in the eye. In the classroom, Native American students often fail to look at the professor when speaking; many prefer not to speak at all. Blacks make more frequent eye contact when speaking than when listening. The lack of eye contact when listening leads some practitioners to describe their black clients as resistant and disinterested. Whites, by contrast, tend to hold eye contact more when listening than when speaking. One must wonder how these contrasting ways of eye contact contribute to misunderstandings that may impinge on the process of justice-making.

Paralanguage

Vocal cues such as hesitations, inflections, silences, loudness of voice, and pace of speaking also provide ample opportunity for misinterpretation across cultures. Rural Americans tend to talk more slowly than their urban counterparts. Put a northern Minnesota farmer in the same room with a New York City cab driver, and they may find it difficult to converse—not because they don't have anything in common or are not curious about each other but because they don't have the patience to work at communicating with each other. The New Yorker would feel that an eternity had gone by before the Minnesotan had completed a thought. The latter would have difficulty straining to listen to the fast-paced patter of the former.

In Native American culture, silence is valued as sacred. Each person must have the opportunity to reflect, to translate thoughts into words, to shape the words not only before speaking but also while speaking. White Americans often feel uncomfortable with silence. A Frenchman might regard silence as a sign of agreement. To an Asian, silence may be considered a token of respect or politeness.

Related somewhat to pace and silence is hesitation. For persons who speak rapidly and feel uncomfortable with silence, hesitation on the part of another is a cue to begin speaking. To the one who hesitates, such an action might be taken not as an interruption but as an intentional, grievous insult.

Asians are given to speaking softly as if not to be overheard; many find Anglo American speakers to be brash and loud. Arabs, by contrast, may find Anglo American speakers to be soft-spoken. The Arab prefers volume.

Similarly, persons of Asian descent may find Anglo Americans to be too direct, blunt, and frank. The former will go to great lengths to not hurt feelings; the latter are often unaware when feelings are being hurt.

Density of Language

Density of language also differentiates among speakers from different cultural backgrounds. Blacks tend to be sparse and concise. They often employ shared codes that require little further information. Even a simple "uh-huh" is loaded with meaning, depending on the social situation. To outsiders, blacks may seem terse or disinterested.

Asians and Native Americans will often use many more words to say the same thing as their white colleagues. The poetry of the story may be more important than the content and may actually be the entire point. Much patience is required of blacks and whites to hear what is being said when conversing with Native Americans or Asians. One can readily see potential problems for doing mediation work across groups that possess such contrasting communication patterns.

Looking at these communication styles through a somewhat different lens, Sue and Sue (1990) regard Native American, Asian

American, and Hispanic manners of expression as low-keyed and indirect, whites' as objective and task-oriented, and blacks' as affective, emotional, and interpersonal. Blacks will interrupt or act on a cue to speak when they can. Whites will nod to indicate listening or agreement. Native American and Asians seldom provide cues to encourage the speaker; they listen without a lot of nonverbal engagement.

In addition to these potential pitfalls of misunderstanding based on different communication styles, other metafactors loom over attempts at restorative justice with persons of differing cultures. For example, the emphasis on individualism, competition, action, rational linear thinking, "Christian principles," and the "Protestant work ethic" may to a large extent reflect values of the dominant U.S. white culture but not values particularly shared by all whites, let alone persons raised in other cultures. Asians, Hispanics, and Native Americans are likely to place more emphasis on community and kinship networks than on reifying the individual. Some Native Americans and others take that community value a step further by cherishing the place of the individual in the context of the entire natural world. Without nature, the individual has no value.

Persons from religious perspectives other than Christianity, which emphasizes individual "salvation," may see the individual as equal to all living things, as on a journey toward individual fulfillment, or even as insignificant in the total scheme of things.

We are not suggesting that any one worldview is the correct one to have. We are simply noting that differing worldviews may clash (too often literally in the course of wars) and may very well threaten to undermine attempts at repairing wrongs experienced as a result of crime.

Though beyond the scope of this work, it might be worthwhile to examine how the concept of justice itself varies across cultures. It is not difficult, for example, to imagine that in traditional Native American culture, what must be restored after commission of a crime is more than the personal relationship that has been damaged. More important is that the communal or tribal relationship be repaired, and perhaps even the relationship of the individual with the universe, for violations in the tribal context may be regarded as a ripping of the fabric that holds everything together. How, in the end, is justice to be promoted without knowing how the various parties to a given conflict understand and value justice?

Differences Within Cultures

As noted, a significant danger involved in discussing cross-cultural differences is overgeneralizing intercultural differences and overlooking intracultural differences. Another way of viewing this is to recognize subcultures existing within larger cultures. There may be some cultural characteristics shared by most whites, yet whites raised in poor, rural Appalachia may vary considerably as to values, mannerisms, and communication patterns from whites raised in San Francisco. Likewise, middle- and upper-class blacks of Los Angeles will share certain characteristics with blacks raised in the blighted areas of south Los Angeles yet vary considerably regarding values, mannerisms, and communication patterns. The same can be said of Asians raised in dense inner-city enclaves versus those who grew up in small-town America or of the Ute who is raised on a reservation far from the urban world compared with the Ute raised in the fast pace of a metropolis.

Race, socioeconomic status, ethnicity, gender, religion, sexual orientation, degree of urbanization, and many other characteristics will shape an individual's views of the world and his or her place and chances in it. These factors will also influence whether the person tends to blame the offender, the victim, or the community for crime. They will color whether participants come to a justice program seeking revenge or seeking repair, wanting to act or wanting be acted on, expecting success or expecting defeat.

Chances for restoring justice can only be enhanced when the individuals who work in justice programs make the time, expend the energy, and take the risks of coming to understand themselves better regarding cultural understanding and misunderstandings.

Racism as a Subset of Cultural Conflict ·

Although race and culture are intertwined, they are not the same thing. As we have indicated, speech patterns, intensity of communication, interpretation of nonverbal cues, and many other nuances of interaction are influenced by the mix of race and culture. While it would be a mistake, for example, to assume that blacks from different social classes and different regions of the culture communicate and handle conflict in the same ways, the fact of being black is likely one, if not the only, key determining factor in how they perceive the world and how others perceive them.

The extent to which they are aware of being overtly or covertly subjected to prejudice and discrimination because of the pigmentation of their skin, the more likely this awareness will influence communication and conflict resolution with persons of other races. Being on guard, lack of openness, being passive or aggressive, and choosing what role to play in an interaction will be affected by each person's experiences of individual or institutional racism.

The impact of racism is always a contextual variable in restorative justice programs where participants are of different races. Where an imbalance of political power is associated with race, one may expect to find resources for schools, recreation, police, and other civic causes to be weighted in favor of the group with the most political clout. In the United States, this often means that whites have more resources, as representatives of their racial group are most often in positions of political power. However, it would be erroneous to assume that there are no consequences of racism felt in localities where, for example, blacks have more political power than Hispanics or Hispanics have more political power than Native Americans or Asian Americans have more political power than whites. Racism is not the prerogative of persons of any particular skin color.

Staff—paid or volunteer—will need to analyze closely their own behaviors to determine what residual elements of racism may be subtly apparent in their nonverbal behaviors or assumptions about the worlds of the victim and the offender. For example, do nonverbal actions such as folding the arms, scooting a chair backward, or shuffling papers indicate feeling ill at ease and wanting to be somewhere else? Such behaviors may be acceptable in the context of the flow of communication, or they may be suggestive of prejudice. Do we assume that the Native American youth offender sitting before us comes from a broken family of alcoholics, doesn't want to work, and has no goals? These descriptors may indeed describe a particular youth. But if they are assumed simply because of the youngster's ethnicity, they betray a racist attitude. And when actions are taken based on those assumptions, such as withholding educational services because the youth is lazy, or failure to acknowledge the strengths of the existing family structure because "it's not normal," we have discrimination resulting from erroneous prejudicial assumptions based on race.

Program staff must not only examine their own beliefs and actions but also be alert to the imbedded racial biases of offender and victim. Racism may be a justification used by the offender for committing the crime. Racism may play into why the victim wants not an "ounce of flesh" but a "pound of flesh." Where racist assumptions or accusations are likely between offender and victim, the mediator will need to be prepared to act as interpreter or buffer during early meetings and during any actual face-to-face encounters, be they in the form of mediation, community boards, or other restorative justice programs.

In short, although race cannot be equated with culture, it can be such a powerful determining factor of communication and interaction patterns that it should not be ignored as we are sorting out cultural differences.

Cultural Skills for the Restorative Justice Practitioner

In *Counseling the Culturally Different*, Sue and Sue (1990) identify five characteristics of culturally skilled counselors. We believe they are just as necessary for restorative justice practitioners. The characteristics are summarized in Exhibit 4.1, in which "restorative justice practitioner" has been substituted for "counselor."

Avoiding Dangers and Pitfalls

Whatever we do to reduce the consequences of cross-cultural misunderstandings, be they subtle snubs and miscommunications or explicit prejudicial actions, we will not be able to remove all misunderstandings and consequences. Attempts to avoid the pitfalls and dangers of cross-cultural differences may serve at best only to reduce the probability of further conflict or disrepair. In human interaction, even when awareness has been increased and behavior modified, there is plenty of room for matters to go awry. For example, in situations where the antagonists are embittered by age-old conflicts passed on from generation to generation, our short-term efforts at understanding and amelioration are not likely to overcome such insurmountable odds. Such extreme cases, however, should not deter us from taking steps to learn, to inform, to model, and to seek supportive roles in helping others restore themselves to more harmonious relationships.

We believe that particularly those of us who work in the justice field must take every step we can to reduce the likelihood of such bias and discrimination. The following is a simple list of suggested steps. We encourage you to add freely to the list.

Know Yourself Well

We begin with ourselves. We need to reflect on and study our own behaviors and communication styles. Are we comfortable with silence? Do we interrupt frequently? Can we stand closer to someone or farther away than we usually do when speaking? And can we do this comfortably? Do we overinterpret straying eye contact? Can we talk to someone without staring them directly in the eye if it appears to be offensive? Do we carry imbedded, learned prejudices toward persons of different skin color than our own? Or toward per-

Exhibit 4.1 Characteristics of Culturally Skilled Restorative Justice Practitioners

1. The culturally skilled restorative justice practitioner is one who has moved from being culturally unaware to being aware and sensitive to his or her own cultural heritage and to valuing and respecting differences.

2. Culturally skilled restorative justice practitioners are aware of their own values and biases.

3. Culturally skilled restorative justice practitioners are comfortable with differences that exist between themselves and their clients in terms of race and beliefs.

4. The culturally skilled restorative justice practitioner is sensitive to circumstances (personal biases, stage of ethnic identity, sociopolitical influences, etc.) that may dictate referral of the minority client to a member of his or her own race or culture, or to another practitioner.

5. Culturally skilled restorative justice practitioners acknowledge and are aware of their own racist attitudes, beliefs, and feelings.

Source: Adapted from Sue and Sue, 1990, pp. 167–168. Copyright ©1990, John Wiley & Sons, Inc. Reprinted by permission of John Wiley & Sons, Inc.

sons of the same skin color who are less educated or better educated than ourselves? Do we expect persons who live in certain parts of the city to be law violators?

It might be helpful to keep a journal of our interactions with persons, recording our speech patterns and theirs, things which make us uncomfortable and those that make us comfortable, our use of and response to gestures and to intensity of conversation, and our overall assessment of the extent to which clear, mutual communication took place. Do patterns vary over time, depending on whether we are speaking with someone of our own culture or of a different culture?

We might consider taking pencil-and-paper inventories designed to identify hidden biases. Bias is part of human life and will likely always be. Some people like rock music, some like blues, some like rap, some like classical, some like country, and so on. Having biases—likes and dislikes—is not the problem (Duryea,

1994). The problem is when those biases, intentionally or unintentionally, lead to discriminatory practices. It behooves each of us to be open to discovering our own biases so that they won't end up hurting others or ourselves.

Get to Know the Participants

Don't make quick assumptions about others. It is difficult enough to know ourselves well; it is impossible to know everything there is to know about another person. A tatter-clad young woman with bright pink spiked hair shows up for a mediation session to meet with an elderly, conservatively dressed couple about theft of property from an unlocked car. As mediator, do we say, "Oh, no, why didn't I stay home today?" Or do we move ahead assuming that we can help these folks, who appear very different and who have already experienced conflict due to the stolen property, find some common ground from which to communicate and possibly even reach understanding, and achieve restitution and some semblance of justice?

If we were to take this case cold without talking to the participants previously, we might be surprised by any number of possibilities. The young woman may be quite cooperative. After all, she is certainly aware that her appearance may affect others. Perhaps it is the elderly woman who is turned off by someone of her gender "not caring how she looks." Or perhaps the elderly man finds the young woman attractive and flirts with her. Or perhaps things just progress smoothly (it does happen occasionally). In any case, to make assumptions based on appearances without any prior information or contact with a person will likely result in unreliable stereotypical assessments and outcomes.

Look at the World Through the Other Person's Eyes

Every participant is unique. Cultural influences may be quite evident, yet each individual will reflect his or her cultural heritage somewhat differently. We must understand the client as an individual within the cultural context (Ridley, 1995). If we are going to work with clients within a restorative justice framework, we will need to take the time to meet with the clients to listen and learn how they see their world. What meaning did the burglary have for the single mom: loss of mementos, invasion of privacy, erosion of a sense of community, planting seeds of fear? How does she view the offender: as vermin, as someone gone astray, as someone with potential? What does she think of as justice: getting her pound of flesh from the offender, having her possessions returned or replaced, the offender making restitution to the community, the offender being helped so that future criminal acts are less likely, something else?

We can ask similar questions of the offender: view of victim, remorse, sense of justice, motivation to change, willingness to repair the community fabric, blame or placement of responsibility.

Likewise, if other community members will be involved, as in peacemaking circles (a process deeply rooted in Native American and Canadian First Nation traditions), we will want to know how these persons see themselves vis-à-vis the victims and the offender, their notions of justice and restoration, and their willingness to accept or reject possible resolutions to the conflict, which has embroiled individuals and the community as a whole.

In the process of seeking answers to these kinds of questions, we will also want to pay attention to communication styles. Does the victim speak slowly and haltingly, taking time to form thoughts and sentences? Does the offender speak in staccato fashion, using few words? Does the elder speak in story forms, letting each listener discern meaning? Does the offender avoid eye contact? If so, is this a possible sign of shame, or is it characteristic of his or her culture to defer to persons of authority by not looking at them directly? It is important to remember that we will be perceived by many as persons of some authority. Will the participants be comfortable sitting around a table or more willing to communicate with open space between them? Does the fact that the victim speaks loudly and even seems to shout at times mean that she's angry, or is this communication style representative of her culture? Will her loudness intimidate other participants?

In the course of human interaction where the stakes are as high as they are when matters of justice are being decided, we must know the key participants as well as we can so that the process leading toward a just resolution is not derailed by what may appear initially to be incompatible points of view and communication styles. To gain such knowledge will require spending ample time with each participant, asking appropriate questions, listening thoroughly, and adapting one's own communication style to whatever is encountered. For example, if silence is a significant part of the victim's mode of communication, we will have to learn to tolerate silence if we are to achieve a satisfactory resolution.

It is difficult to imagine how we can help persons repair relationships and restore a sense of justice if we fail to understand or are insensitive to their points of view and their culturally learned ways of communicating, both nonverbal and verbal. To gain some awareness and sensitivity, we will need to devote time and energy to that purpose. Like so many other processes, the desired result—in this instance, a sense of restoration—begins with the beginning. A restored sense of justice is enhanced by our ways of interacting as well as that of the offender and the victim. After all, one of the driving forces of restorative justice is the humanizing of the justice system. In these programs, we are the justice system to a large extent. Our actions not only shape and influence specific outcomes but also serve to promote (or diminish) the sense of the system's being responsive, considerate, fair, and just.

Listen to Key Informants

It is often helpful to nurture relationships with individuals in a community or culture unfamiliar to us in order to check out our assumptions about how persons work out conflicts and communicate with one another in that particular community or culture. This has been a common practice of cultural anthropologists and sociologists involved in qualitative field studies. Key informants can provide rich information that may prevent us from making foolish errors or causing injury. These key informants are often not in the professional justice community. They may include the black mother who manages an informal delinquency prevention agency out of her apartment, the Asian elder who wants to help his grandchildren make their way in the larger culture while appreciating and holding on to traditional ways, or the Latino teenager who is curious about our presence and at least willing to test our sincerity.

One advantage we have with these persons is that we know each individual has stories to share. If we are genuinely willing to listen, we may surprise ourselves with what we will learn. Very few persons take the time to listen to their stories—or to our stories for that matter. Being willing to listen to another person's story initiates a bond of mutuality.

But mutuality can only go so far. We are not naive enough to assume that even by genuine, respectful listening we will be admitted into a fully mutual relationship. Nor do we assume that it is ever possible to understand another person or another culture entirely.

Likewise, while these key informants provide a potential wealth of information as to culture values and mores, such individuals may at times be so ingrained in their ways of doing things that they are unable to step back and see, and therefore share, how values are actually shaped and imposed or how the nuances of communication style play out in day-to-day living. Still they offer much potential to the outsider seeking to have a positive impact on their community.

Prepare the Participants

As noted, so much of the work involving bringing persons together to interact around issues of conflict needs to be done before that encounter happens. As we get to know the values and ways of the various potential participants, we may be able to foresee possible difficulties in their interaction that could easily abort any movement toward restoration.

If so, it will be necessary for us to try to help participants understand the viewpoints and different communication styles that they will be exposed to when they meet each other. Sharing this awareness and nurturing such sensitivity may have little impact; then again, it might make a lot of difference. At least the participants are given some information that may help them prepare for the encounter and not be thrown off by what they would normally regard as insulting or disrespectful behaviors. Also, each participant might be moved to some self-awareness and thereby temper some behaviors that might be interpreted as offensive by others.

We recognize that we are perhaps being overly optimistic. It is easier to expect persons to increase their awareness of how others speak and behave than actually to change their own behaviors, particularly in situations that might become tense and conflictual. Any increased awareness or sensitivity to other cultural values or communication styles by our working with the participants is a gain; any positive change on the part of participant behavior is an added bonus.

Case Study

To illustrate some possibilities of preparing the participants to be aware of how others may think and speak, let us return to our brief opening scenario involving a black male store owner, a female Native American shoplifter, and an Anglo mediator. In that illustration, the mediator had done no homework on himself or with others.

Now, let us assume, he has spent a fair amount of time with the store owner. He has learned of the businessman's sense of invasion and loss. He knows that the man wants to work with the teen so that there is no repetition of the shoplifting, but neither does he want to see her dealt with harshly. The man volunteers that he grew up on the streets and knows how difficult it is. His casual conversation is punctuated by gestures. His voice booms, particularly as he speaks of how the system generally rips off kids and people of color in general. The man wants his economic loss recovered and the girl to be helped. Essentially, he is quite sympathetic to meeting with the teenager for his benefit as well as hers, or "I wouldn't be taking the time out of my busy schedule."

When our mediator meets with the Ute teenager, he discovers a very different way of communicating. She is more subservient than he is comfortable with. She will answer only direct questions. There is much space between her sentences. Sometimes he thinks she is done speaking when she adds still another thought. Rarely does she make eye contact with him. The mediator leaves the young woman perplexed, feeling that he is not yet ready for these two to meet face to face.

Through a mutual friend, the mediator is able to identify and connect with an elder of the band to which the teen belongs. He asks questions. He listens, seldom to direct answers, but he gets the information he needs. The mediator comes to understand that the girl was not being surly or uncooperative. She had been showing him signs of respect by not looking him in the eye. She did not ask questions because such an insult would have suggested that he had not been thorough in his work with her. Her slow speech pattern was quite consistent with her upbringing and cultural background. The silences he experienced demonstrated how important it was to her to answer his questions as well as she could.

Now having the kind of appreciation for the participants that he needed, he was ready to proceed. He went back to each participant in turn. He told the girl that she might perceive the black man as coming on quite strong. The man would speak rapidly to her, seeking to make direct eye contact, and he would probably raise his voice, but his doing these things did not mean he was angry with her or trying to put her down. They were simply his ways of conversing about things of importance to him.

The mediator informed the girl that he did not expect the store owner to change his ways, so she should listen to the content of what the man was saying rather than focus on the mannerisms and style, which might make her want to recoil.

To the black store owner, the mediator pointed out that he should not expect the Ute girl to look him in the eye, but interpreting that as weakness, disinterest, or rebellion would be wrong. In her culture, it was a sign of respect, of deference to authority. The mediator encouraged the man to refrain from interrupting the girl until she had worked through her thoughts and spoken her mind. Again, the slowness of speech did not indicate a learning disability or any other weakness; it simply reflected the speech patterns of her culture.

While moving back and forth between the victim and the offender, the mediator has also been working on his own awareness of how cross-cultural differences might affect his efforts with these two individuals. With new information, he is also exploring his own reactions: his initial discomfort with the black man's seeming abrasiveness, with the Ute teen's excessive meekness and seeming inability to articulate, with his wonderings about his own ability to work with two people so diametrically opposed in style and worldview.

Relieved and enlightened by what he had discovered, the mediator was now ready to bring the two participants together. Having done his homework, he was comfortable and better prepared for the usual unpredictable directions that such encounters take, and he was hopeful that positive resolution would be agreed on between persons who had very little in common other than being on opposing sides of a situation.

To repair or restore relationships, personal or communal, damaged by criminal or delinquent acts is a challenging goal in any circumstances. When participants—victims, offenders, support persons, program staff—are of differing cultures, typical patterns of communicating and expressing values can lead to confusion, if not complete disruption of the process. To arrive at justice, it seems reasonable that the views of all parties need to be considered. It is our belief that the likelihood of repair and restoration of relationships is increased by the extent to which we take the time to know and understand the differing communication styles and worldviews of the participating individuals. It is hoped not only that the restorative justice–oriented programs will be enhanced by such awareness and sensitivity to cultural differences but also that openness to diversity will enrich the lives of all who choose to participate.

Chapter Five

Case Studies

This chapter presents three case examples illustrating the application of the humanistic model of victim offender mediation in a variety of situations. The offender in case one is an adult; in the other cases, they are juveniles. One case is a diversion from court, and two are postadjudication. Presentation of the particulars of each case will be followed by discussion of common themes and individual variation among the three cases.

Case One: Residential Burglary

Bob and Anne Northrup had worked hard all their lives; in their mid-forties, they were finally beginning to get just a little ahead of the game when their home was burglarized. It had taken more time than they felt they could spare to document the items that had been stolen and coordinate with the various personnel involved in the investigation. In spite of their efforts, the culprit had never been found, and they developed a jaundiced opinion of the criminal justice system in general and their local police department in particular.

Since they had no insurance, it took them nearly a year to set aside enough money to replace their stolen belongings. They had just celebrated these accomplishments and Bob's new promotion

---

Note: The first case in this chapter is based on one in which Mark Umbreit served as co-mediator. Cases two and three were initially drafted by their lead mediator, Terri Grob. All names and identifying data have been altered to protect the participants.

with a weekend away at a nearby resort hotel. As they pulled into their garage upon their return, they could hardly believe their eyes. Their back door stood open, hanging half off its hinges: they had been struck again!

They were furious. Both of them felt violated, as though they had been personally assaulted. Many questions went through their minds. Why was their house chosen? Was it the same criminal who had broken in before? Were their movements being watched? Did someone have a personal vendetta against them? They went through the now familiar movements of identifying what had been taken, speaking with police, repairing the damage to their home, and putting their daily lives back together all over again.

Referral

Jim Albright was picked up within several weeks of this second burglary. He was twenty years old and had had several minor brushes with the law as a juvenile but no prior adult convictions. Two months previously, Jim had lost his production-line job at a nearby factory. He pleaded guilty to the burglary charge. During the sentencing hearing in court, as a condition of probation, he was referred to the local victim offender mediation program.

Preliminary Meeting with the Offender

When first approached about the mediation program, Jim was not enthusiastic. During an individual meeting with Jim, the lead mediator listened attentively to his story about the burglary. She then explained to him that confronting his victims might be helpful for several reasons. First, he would have an opportunity to discuss what happened with the victims. Second, he would be able to negotiate a restitution agreement that was considered fair to both parties. Third, by taking such direct responsibility for his criminal behavior, he would also be able to have input into a portion of his court-ordered punishment.

The mediator explained that although the court would prefer that he participate in this mediation program, he was not obligated to do so. If he felt that it was simply not appropriate for him, his case could be sent back to court to arrange for restitution through the normal procedures. Jim finally indicated that he would be willing to meet the victims and work out a way of paying them back. The mediator then went on to describe how the actual process would work when offender and victims met.

Preliminary Meeting with the Victims

After having secured Jim's consent to the mediation process, the mediator then met separately with Bob and Anne at their home. She first listened to their story about what happened. Both Bob and Anne expressed a great need simply to talk about how outraged they were about the incident. In addition to feeling angry at the criminal who violated them, both expressed anger at the criminal justice system, which seemed to treat them like pieces of evidence. The system's seeming disdain for their concerns and needs only intensified their sense of victimization.

When it came time to explain the mediation program, Bob and Anne were not interested initially. They couldn't see any value in confronting the offender. The mediator pointed out some possible benefits. They could let the offender know how angry they were and how this crime affected them. Many of the questions that Bob and Anne had asked the mediator could be answered directly by the only person who really knew, the offender. Also, rather than sitting on the sidelines of the justice process, like most victims, Bob and Anne could get directly involved and help shape part of the penalty that would be imposed on their offender by the court. Finally, both Bob and Anne would have the opportunity to negotiate a mutually acceptable restitution agreement that was considered fair to all parties.

After further thought, Bob and Anne agreed to try the mediation process. Both said that they were not certain of the value of such a confrontation, but they relished the opportunity to "let that punk know" how angry they were. The mediator provided specific information about what typically happens in the mediation session—how the session opens, the role of the mediator, and the general flow of the session.

The Joint Session

Because of the high level of anger in this case, two mediators, both trained social workers, were assigned. The mediation session was held at a neutral community center.

The lead mediator made introductory comments. She thanked participants for coming and trying the process. She clearly identified the purpose of the session: first, to provide time to talk about the burglary and how the people involved felt about it, and second, to talk about losses and the possibility of negotiating a restitution agreement. The role of the mediators was explained. They were not official representatives of the court, nor could they impose any settlement on either party. Rather, their role was to provide an opportunity for both parties to talk about what happened and to see if a settlement could be reached. Whatever was agreed on, they emphasized, must be perceived as fair to both parties. The parties would first have some uninterrupted time to tell their stories.

The lead mediator asked Bob to begin the dialogue process by first telling Jim about what happened from his perspective and how it affected him. The mediator indicated by hand movements that Bob was to talk directly to Jim. At this point, Bob had both arms rigidly crossed on his chest. He quickly began talking about how he was furious about this kind of "crap." He said he was fed up with kids who violated other people's property. Anne chose not to speak at this point.

Because of the level of anger Bob was expressing, the mediators were about to intervene to prevent any direct verbal attacks on Jim. Just before they intervened, however, something atypical occurred. Jim jumped out of his chair and said, "I'm not taking this crap any longer—I've had it. I'm leaving." At that point, the co-mediator intervened by saying directly to Jim, "I'm sure it has been difficult listening to the anger expressed by Bob, but I know that he is interested in working out some kind of settlement. Could you just give it another ten minutes? If you can, I think we might be able to work something out tonight. If you want to leave after ten minutes, it's up to you." Jim paused and then sat down.

The co-mediator's comment appeared to have validated some of Jim's concern that he was being "dumped on." The interaction between the mediator and Jim also evidently had a positive impact on Bob. From this point on, Bob's communication to Jim was far less emotional, and his body language slowly began to loosen up.

When it became evident that Bob had completed his initial statement and Anne still did not wish to speak, the mediator turned to Jim and asked him if he could tell them what happened from his perspective. Jim explained that he had been out drinking with some buddies and they needed extra money. They were cruising around in the neighborhood and saw what appeared to be an empty house, since no lights were on. They knocked on the front door and, when no one responded, walked around the house and broke in through the back door. Once in the house, they took a television, VCR, stereo set, and $100 in cash. Jim explained that they had not initially intended to burglarize Bob and Anne's home. When they did break in, he was quite nervous and anxious to get out of the home as quickly as possible. Jim admitted that he took the items he mentioned.

After Jim completed his version of what happened, Bob and Anne asked Jim numerous questions. Why us? Were you watching our movements? Jim again indicated that he had not been watching them. Anne then asked Jim if he knew their daughter Carol. Jim said he did. She mentioned that Carol had been living on the streets for the past year, ever since she had left a drug treatment center. Jim said he knew that. Bob asked Jim when he saw Carol again if he would mention that her mom and dad loved her and would welcome her home if she would be willing to come back.

It was clear at this time that the conflict had been reframed; rather than interacting in stereotypical roles of victim and offender, the participants now interacted on a more human level, with concern about issues beyond the criminal event.

Discussion of what happened that evening and how all parties felt about it lasted for nearly one hour. Before the co-mediator suggested discussing restitution, a short silence was allowed to give both parties an opportunity to think things over and raise any additional questions.

The co-mediator then stated that it was now time to review the losses that Bob and Anne had suffered and to begin the process of negotiating a restitution agreement if that was possible. The mediator turned to Anne and asked her to identify their losses, providing any documentation she could. Anne presented a long list of items. Jim was then asked to review this list and comment.

Jim had a number of questions about several items and particularly their replacement value. After discussing this further with Anne and Bob, he indicated that he now understood the full impact of what he had done and was ready to talk about a plan to "make things right."

Bob, Anne, and Jim worked out a restitution plan that required Jim to pay $50 a month over a ten-month period, beginning the following month. The terms of the restitution agreement were read back to both parties and then written up in a formal agreement. Both parties then signed it, and copies were given to each. A copy would also be forwarded to Jim's probation officer.

The co-mediator then stated that "in cases like this when an agreement is reached, we prefer that both parties meet briefly several months from now to check out how the agreement is working out. What do you think about doing this?" Jim turned to Bob and Anne and said, "I'd really like to do that. Could we have it at my house?" He added, "I would like you to meet my wife and my baby. . . . I'm not a criminal." The meeting was scheduled two months later at Jim's home, with a mediator present. Jim offered to cook lasagna. Bob and Anne quickly indicated their interest.

Case Two: Auto Theft

Late one October evening, Tom Hall had fallen asleep on the living room couch in his half-basement apartment. He was rudely awakened just before 3:00 A.M. by a crash against his living room window. Shaking out of his daze, he could see flashing red, white, and blue lights dimly through the drapes, and he heard shouting and the barking of dogs.

Slowly he rose and walked to the window, which looked out at ground level. Pulling the drapes aside, he found himself mere inches from a surreal scene: a police officer pinned a teenage boy flat on his belly on the ground with the boy's right arm pulled firmly behind his back. The boy must have hit the side of the apartment and the window as the officer wrestled him to the ground. Tom remembered thinking that the boy was fortunate not to have hit the window with his full weight. The back of the boy's head was against the window, so he didn't see Tom and Tom couldn't get a look at his face. When the officer slapped the cuffs on the boy's wrists, Tom heard the boy cry out, "OK, OK, I'm sorry, don't hurt me officer, I'm not gonna try anything, please, please don't hurt me!" Looking further into the distance, Tom was shocked to see police officers rummaging through his brand new truck, taking pictures!

Pulling on jeans and a T-shirt, Tom ran out the door and asked the officer what was going on. "Are you Mr. Thomas Randolph Hall?" the officer asked. "Yes, I am, sir. What's the problem here? Why are the police in and around my truck?" "Well, Mr. Hall, it seems that the young man over there was attempting to hot-wire your vehicle. A minute more and he would have succeeded. We received a call from your neighbor, who arrived home and noticed the truck door open and inside lights on. Looks like there's been a little damage—the kid removed part of the dash and steering column to get at your wires. Too bad—nice truck." Then he briefly flashed a smile and added, "Not exactly a professional job."

As Tom warily approached the truck, he could see that the seat held a mess of plastic parts, screws, and small tools. The dash had been ripped open, and wires were visibly protruding. Tom felt sick to his stomach. For four years he had scrimped and saved for this truck. He had ordered it special from the factory, waited five months to get it, and had been driving it for only two weeks.

Looking over his shoulder, Tom watched as two police officers escorted the boy to the cruiser to take him to the station. And one thought popped into his head: "Why, this kid doesn't even look old enough to have a driver's license!"

Referral

County Department of Corrections probation staff referred the case to Mediation Services, a small private nonprofit agency that offered, in addition to its VOM program, a menu of services to county residents and courts to assist in resolving most types of community disputes, as well as postdivorce visitation issues, at little or no charge to participants. Corrections sent, on the average, two hundred cases a year to the VOM program at either the diversion (first-time offenses) or postadjudication level to address victims' needs and determine restitution if necessary.

The referral was received four months after the crime occurred. The boy, Joshua Ryan Jenkins, age sixteen, had been charged, adjudicated, and placed in long-term lockup (about nine months) in the county's juvenile detention center. During an investigation, the police were able to provide enough evidence to charge Josh with three separate car thefts. (Later Josh would admit to stealing forty-one vehicles over the course of about three years.)

While in the detention center, Josh had participated in various programs, group and individual, designed to help kids become sensitized to the short- and long-term impact of their crimes on others as well as themselves. Josh understood what had led him to do what he did, but he'd never had to face any of his victims and so had a difficult time understanding how his behavior had hurt them. It was *his* idea, in a counseling session, to see if it would be at all possible to meet with any of his victims face to face.

Mediation Services accepted the case. Staff sent out letters to all three victims, to Josh at the detention center, and to his mother at her home address.

Preliminary Meeting with the Offender

The program manager assigned herself and one other facilitator to the case and made an appointment to meet with Josh at the detention center. The staff there were immensely helpful and worked with the mediators throughout the process. The meeting took place in a small booth inside of a larger main room within the detention center. Though the booth was soundproof, it had glass windows all around it, making it easily observable from any vantage point in the outer room, which was bustling with activity at the time.

Though shy at first, Josh was very open with the mediators and willing to talk. He discussed his past up to this arrest. A close adult male family member, he said, had "taught me how to steal cars and sell dope" from a very early age. His parents had been divorced for many years; he lived with his mom and very seldom saw his dad. Since he always felt different from other kids, he had been something of a loner in school and began skipping classes and acting up. Early in high school, he was initiated into a neighborhood gang. The gang members carried guns, sold drugs, and stole cars; his early training had prepared him well! He had been in and out of trouble most of his young life, his crimes gradually escalating.

He revealed that just weeks before the meeting, his best friend, Allen, was killed in a high-speed chase with police while attempting to evade arrest in the stolen vehicle he was driving. Josh pulled a newspaper clipping detailing the accident out of his pocket. He was visibly shaken as he spoke: "I would have been with Allen that night if I wasn't in detention. . . . That would have been *me*." He told the mediators he wanted his friend's death to *mean* something and that he definitely did not want to end up like him.

The mediators were impressed with his candor, his intelligence, and what seemed a very sincere desire to turn his life around in spite of many obstacles. He told them that he hoped meeting with one or more of the people he'd ripped off would somehow help him resist slipping back into old habits. It was clear that he had been unsupervised most of the time and had always just "gotten away with stuff." It was also obvious that he doubted his ability to make the changes he needed to make on his own and that this frightened him.

Preliminary Meeting with the Victims

During the initial phone contact with the three victims of the crimes for which Josh had been adjudicated, all expressed interest in meeting with each other prior to any encounter with the offender. The mediators therefore arranged to meet with them all together in a conference room at Mediation Services. One of the three did not show up at the meeting even though initially he had been very willing to meet. When staff called him later, he apologized and said, "After much thought about this, I've come to realize I just don't have the time or patience to deal with this situation. First, I'm out a car for two weeks while it's in the shop being fixed, then I have to take the time to come and meet with you, and then later with this kid. I'm real sorry, but I just can't do it." Staff thanked him for his time and assured him there was nothing to apologize for.

The first to arrive for the meeting was Tammy Erickson and her live-in boyfriend, Fred; they were soon joined by the other victim in this case, Tom Hall. With everyone seated and introductions made, the mediators began the meeting by discussing the process of the conference and answering questions. Once everyone understood the process—their role as central to the conference and the purpose of the dialogue as restorative—they felt comfortable telling their stories. Tammy went first.

Tammy was still very upset over the incident. As she described the morning of the theft, she was running late getting ready for work. She ran down her apartment steps, out the door, and into the parking lot. She looked where she thought she had parked her car. It wasn't there. "No," she assured herself, "the car has to be here somewhere. I must have simply forgotten where I parked it." She walked back and forth looking for it again and again. Finally there was no avoiding the obvious: her car had been stolen. She remembers the shock and then the anger. The car wasn't new, and it hadn't even been expensive, but it was the one thing she owned outright, and it was her only means to get to work. It was probably just some kids out for a joyride, she thought; surely the police would find it within blocks of the apartment.

Tammy was unable to get to work that day. As it would happen, the police did not locate Tammy's vehicle for an entire month. She would lose pay for many other days she had to miss as a result.

When her car was finally was returned to her, Tammy said, "it was trashed. It looked like there had been kids living in there for months. There were empty fast-food bags, blankets, clothes, pop and beer cans, cigarette butts, candy and condom wrappers—and the starter had been torn off. Since I haven't been able to afford to get the starter fixed, I still have to start my car with a screwdriver every time I get in it. It is a constant daily reminder to me of what happened. I'm never able to forget it. I vacuumed and scrubbed the car when I got it back, but every time I get in it, it feels dirty to me. I feel so violated! I also want the $700 it will cost to fix my starter. I don't care how he gets it; he's got to pay!"

The mediators listened as Tammy vented. She recognized that she was still very angry, as well as nervous about meeting Josh. She was concerned that she would become too angry with him sitting right across from her, yet she had many unanswered questions and wanted to see him face to face. The mediators helped her brainstorm what she might do if, during the session, she felt that she might lose control. Fred would be present as a support for her. He agreed to help her if he saw her getting agitated. The mediators also agreed to check in with her again prior to the conference date to see how she was doing. This all seemed to help her, and she felt she could go ahead with the meeting.

Tom Hall told what had happened to him and how he felt about it at the time. He admitted that although he had been angry at first after having seen what had been done to his truck, the sight of the boy on the ground had really stuck with him, and he "sort of felt sorry for the kid." His insurance had paid for the damage, other than a small deductible. It wasn't so much the money he was after; he was more interested in doing this for the boy. If he could say something that would somehow help this boy, it would be worth meeting with him.

The Joint Session

At the time of the joint session, Josh was still being held in deten-tion. The victims did not wish to meet at the detention center, so the meeting was scheduled for the mediation center, and proba-tion staff arranged to transport Josh to and from the center for the meeting.

Tom, Tammy, and Fred arrived first and were seated in the con-ference room. At check-in they all admitted to a little nervousness, especially Tammy. Though she said she was OK, she seemed quite tense. The lead mediator waited for Josh while her cofacilitator sat in with the others. In the preliminary meeting, Josh had indicated he wanted to face his victims alone, so he planned to arrive with-out family or any other support such as his therapist or probation officer. This was not typical, but it was what he had wanted.

When he arrived, he and the mediator entered the conference room together. Tammy looked at Josh and in an instant her shoul-ders dropped about two inches. Just seeing Josh in person as a young, frightened, vulnerable boy went a long way toward easing her initial tension before any words were spoken.

After a brief opening statement by the lead mediator, Tom and Tammy began by telling Josh what their experience had been. Though they gave details, they were surprisingly subdued. Tammy in particular was far less angry than she had been during the initial meeting. They shared their feelings and the impact of the crime in an honest and heartfelt but gentle manner.

As Josh spoke, the victims learned more of his past and the circumstances leading up to the crime. Josh explained what it had been like to have been incarcerated and what he had learned. He hung his head when he spoke of his remorse. And he told them about the death of his friend.

As the dialogue began to flow, they all talked about how Josh might avoid temptation to return to the gang. He indicated that although his resolve was strong now, he knew it was going to be really tough when he left the protective environment of the detention center. Tammy, Fred, and Tom were all very concerned for Josh. Tom gave Josh his home telephone number and told Josh he would be available any time of the day or night if Josh needed to talk, needed support, or for any reason at all. Josh's eyes filled with tears as he thanked each one of them. He said he couldn't believe that they could care so much for him after what he had done to them.

Someone asked Josh about his mother and why she didn't come with him. There was much interest in how much support Josh would have once he got home. Through discussion, it was mutually agreed to meet again, with Josh and his mom, once he had been released and was back home. The date was set before they all left. Tammy chose not to pursue monetary restitution.

Session Debriefing

In debriefing, Tom said, "On a scale of one to ten, I would rate the session a nine and a half! What was interesting too is that I expected you [the facilitators] to be more on our side, but you weren't." Tammy thought the session went well and commented, "I expected myself to be meaner to him, but I guess my human compassion kicked in." Fred said he was very proud of Tammy. Josh said he thought they would all be much harder on him and was surprised they were such "nice people," considering how his actions had affected them.

The Second Joint Session

As planned, after Josh was released, the mediators held a second session, attended by Josh; his mother, Marsha Jenkins; and Tom Hall. Tammy and Fred were in the process of moving and felt that the previous meeting had brought them sufficient closure. Marsha did much of the talking this time. She talked about the trials of single-parenting and financial difficulties. The neighborhood they had been living in was "not a good environment for the kids," so she was making every attempt to sell her home and move into an area that would be a better place for Josh and his younger sibling. Tom listened quietly and with great concern.

Josh shared some of the difficulties he had been having since his release. The gang members were not going to give up their hold on him without a fight, and resisting them was becoming very challenging for him. His mom and Tom worked with him and brainstormed ways he could avoid the gang and keep himself safe. It was clear that Josh's mother was very grateful for additional support.

At the end of the session, Marsha thanked Tom several times for his efforts with her son. She said that most of their experiences with people outside of their family had been quite negative. She was very touched that someone, particularly a stranger, would go so far out of his way and care so much. Tom reminded Josh to call him anytime. They all parted on very positive terms.

Case Three: Damage to Property

From the accounts given by the offenders after they were picked up, it is easy to reconstruct the scene. On a warm Friday evening near the end of the school year, Doyle Underwood, age fourteen;

Ricky Anderson, twelve; Noah Long, eleven; and Amber Jessup, twelve, had met at their usual hangout, a small, one-room wooden fort they'd built under the trees out on Amber's family's ten-acre hobby farm. They were bored, and Doyle suggested that they hike to a nearby construction site and see if "that old guy" was around.

They did and he wasn't. Doyle got brave and started climbing on one of the bulldozers: "Hey, look at this—there's *lots* of cool machinery out here!" Someone else picked up a brick, threw it through one of the windows, and climbed in. "C'mon," he said, imitating the sound of shifting gears and loud engine noises—"this is fun!" "You guys!" Amber called, "let's get outta here. We're gonna get caught!" "Naaaa," laughed Ricky as he jumped up and down on the hood of a large Caterpillar, "even if that old guy saw us, he's so slow he'd *never* catch us." Things quickly snowballed, and soon the kids were grabbing anything they could find to smash, dent, scratch, and tear at the construction equipment, inside and out. Amber came around the far side of a backhoe with a lead pipe she'd found on the ground. "Drop it, young lady!" boomed a man's voice from the shadows. "Drop it right now!" The man was a police officer. After a half-hour spree that caused $4,000 worth of damage, the four children were headed in police cars to the police station.

Referral

This referral came to the victim offender program from the county corrections diversion department. Due to the children's ages and the fact that this was a first offense for all of them, the county attorney's office felt that the case could best be handled in a conference with the victims if they were willing. Even though it was a felony-level offense, officials hoped that facing the victims would have a greater impact on these kids at this point in their lives and help the families work out restitution arrangements.

Preliminary Meeting with the Offenders

Mediation staff met with the offenders and their families all together. Everyone was pretty somber, except for Noah and Doyle. Doyle, the oldest, seemed the least affected by the incident; he had all the airs of a "cool" teenager and seemed more upset about having gotten caught than about what he'd done. His mom lived out of state, so his dad, George Underwood, attended with him. George's attitude was basically that "boys will be boys," and he seemed eager to get the meeting over with. Noah, for his part, looked up to Doyle, three years his elder. Noah hung on Doyle's words, laughed nervously, and looked to him before answering any questions.

The meeting progressed unremarkably, and the kids took responsibility for the incident but seemed to have short memories regarding who did what. It was disturbing to hear them joke about the slow, elderly gentleman who owned the company. Several of the parents indicated their displeasure with these and other comments, and the tone became somber again.

Preliminary Meeting with the Victims

Staff initially had much difficulty reaching the owners of the construction company, Ned and Eileen Ramsey. Their daughter, Barbara Manskey, finally responded to the phone calls and arranged to meet with the mediators in place of her parents. They met at a nearby coffee shop during a time when it was relatively quiet. Barbara explained that her father, Ned, eighty-four years old, was dying of cancer. Her mother, Eileen, was caring for him and couldn't get away to meet with us. Just two days after the damage was done to Ned's equipment, his business was to have been sold at auction. Months and months had gone into painstaking preparation for the sale. Now it was postponed indefinitely because the insurance company was having a difficult time finding replacement parts for machines that dated back thirty-five to forty years or more. Her dad had wanted to see the place, which he had built with his father, sold before he died so that he'd know his wife would be well taken care of. Now Barbara and the rest of the family feared that he would not live to see that day.

This crime, she said, had taken more out of the family than her dad's illness because the satisfaction of seeing the business sold had meant so much to him. She told the mediators that after the vandalism happened, he'd laid in bed and cried like a baby. The mediators spent much of their time simply listening as Barbara told her story. Clearly, she appreciated having someone to talk to. It had been a very difficult time for everyone in her family, she said, and none of them were "raised to talk about their feelings much."

She had mixed feelings about meeting with the culprits. Her emotions were very raw at the moment, and she was not sure how she would hold up, but it was important to her to do this for her family, so she resolved to see it through. She said she "would like them to pay the insurance deductible" and was interested in thinking about what she might request they do to repay the community for the offense. She wanted whatever they did to be meaningful for her family, so she wanted the opportunity to discuss and decide this with them. The conference meeting was scheduled two weeks later to allow her time to think things through.

The Joint Session

The day for the mediation session was hot and humid, with thunderstorms threatening. The children and their families arrived at the mediation center on time and were ushered into the far conference room, a very comfortable, informal space. They all seemed surprisingly animated. Time came and went for the conference to begin with no word from Barbara. The mediators called her home and got no answer. The youngsters were getting antsy, getting up, going to the bathroom, getting cans of soda.

Finally Barbara arrived breathless, red-faced, and spattered with raindrops. The mediators quickly met with her in private to check in. She shared the details of her distressing day, and the mediators offered her the choice of either canceling or rescheduling the session. However, she was resolved more than ever to get on with the meeting, so they entered the conference room together.

The boys and Amber were all seated on one side of the rectangular conference table, with their parents seated behind them. Since Barbara had come alone, the mediators asked her if she would like one of them to sit with her on the other side of the table, but she responded, "No, thank you. I'm OK." So the mediators sat at each end and began with introductions and opening statements. These statements simply reiterated what the participants had already heard in preparation and read in program literature and letters: the mediators' volunteer status, a description of the mediator role and the process, a reminder of mediator neutrality, confidentiality of the meeting, the right to call for a timeout at any time or to leave at any time, and the two standard ground rules: only one person speaks at a time, and treat every participant with respect. After confirming that everyone understood, the mediators began the actual mediation session. Barbara wanted the young people to begin; Doyle volunteered to go first.

One at a time, the children discussed what happened that night from their own perspective and how they felt at the time and now that they'd had time to think about it. Barbara chose to keep asking them questions before taking her turn to talk about the impact on her and her family. Her questions served to draw the kids out and get to the heart of the matter without giving them a lot of "wiggle room."

Barbara asked them, "Whose idea was it to go the construction site that night?" While the three boys nervously eyed each other, Amber piped up with "Well, it was Doyle's idea." "Hmmm, Doyle," Barbara responded. "It looks like you're a lot older than the other kids. How old are you all?" The children gave their ages, and Barbara continued: "My, that *is* quite an age difference. So what are you doing hanging around the younger ones, Doyle? Why aren't you out playing with young men your own age?" This question sparked comments from Doyle and his father about their home life.

The year before, Doyle's mother had left the city with another man—abandoning Doyle. Perhaps to mask his intense hurt and pain, he had taken out some of his hostility on others at school. Therefore, he had very few friends at the moment. Doyle looked down at his hands as he talked about this; it was very difficult for him to discuss.

Barbara was visibly moved as she watched Doyle struggle. "So in a sense, you know what it's like to have lost a parent too." Doyle nodded. There was a long, thoughtful pause. "Please tell me, each one of you, because I cannot understand, why weren't you afraid you'd get caught?" Noah chimed in, "Because the old guy, the owner—well, we'd seen him before, ya know?—and he walks so slow, we knew we could outrun him if he heard us out there making noise."

"Well, let me tell you about that 'old man,'" she began softly. "That person happens to be my dear, sweet father, Ned, and those 'funny machines' you destroyed without a thought helped pay my way through college and then some. That man you say was slow is in the hospital today fighting for his life. . . ." She began to cry. "I'm sorry, I wasn't going to do this. . . . Kids, my dad has had cancer for the last four years, and now it's going to take his life, . . . and that's *not your fault.* I'm especially sad today because he went in to the hospital this afternoon and I don't think he's going to come out again. That's why I was late getting here. I was with my family and him at the hospital. I'm not trying to make you feel bad; it's just that I want you to understand that it wasn't that he was slow—why, my dad could've outrun *me* three years ago—it's just that he was very, very sick. And the fact that he's been sick has been really, really hard on those of us who love him so much. Can you understand that?"

Amber and Ricky were crying, Noah's head was buried in his arms, and Doyle looked flushed and red-eyed. They all nodded to her. Amber then took a Kleenex off the table and slowly slid the box over to Barbara. "I'm so sorry about your dad," she said through sobs. "Thank you," said Barbara as she reached for the box. The parents were passing Kleenex in the back; even Doyle's dad needed one. The atmosphere in the room had become transformed.

As Barbara went on, she talked about the auction, the problems fixing the equipment, and all the other things she had discussed with the mediators in addition to what her family had asked her to share. Toward the end of the discussion, to everyone's surprise, Doyle raised his hand. "I just wanna say I'm sorry for what I did," he said. "I won't ever do something that stupid again." Immediately there was a chorus of "I'm sorry's" from the others; the parents, too, offered their apologies and shared feelings of remorse and shock that their children would have been involved in such a thing. "Thank you all," Barbara said, wiping her eyes. "That will mean a lot to my family."

The discussion turned to talk of repairing the harm. Barbara indicated that the biggest thing the family wanted was for the kids to commit to themselves that they would never participate in any activity like this again and that they would talk to other kids and discourage them from this kind of behavior as well. All four youngsters readily agreed. She added that her family wanted any out-of-pocket expenses to be covered, which she anticipated to be the insurance deductible, and that they wanted the children to work off the money themselves. Last, tears returning as she spoke, she said her family had asked that each child attempt to do some volunteer work for the cancer society and earn a sum, determined by the child, to contribute on behalf of her father. All the kids felt this was very fair and agreed to help in this way. The parents were also grateful and willing to help their children follow through on the agreement. As the mediators closed the session, most of the parents and young people came over to hug Barbara and offer words of encouragement.

Session Follow-Up

The mediators were unable to debrief each participant immediately after the meeting but did so within a couple of days. The kids said they felt sorry for the victims and guilty about what they'd done but also glad that they could do something to make Barbara feel better. The parents were grateful that their children were given this opportunity instead of court and were convinced it would be an experience that would "stick with them for life."

Barbara told the mediators she felt much better after the meeting. She said, "I'm so glad I was able to do this for my family, difficult though it was. Maybe I was able to help bring some peace to them in all of this. I feel good about that." Then she added, "I don't know how to explain this exactly, but I feel a little lighter on my feet, kind of like I'm walking on my tiptoes."

All restitution was eventually paid. Two of the four children completed the community service, but the other two fell through, in part because the cancer society had just completed its door-to-door campaign for the year and so needed few volunteers.

Reflections on the Case Studies

Each of these cases is in many ways typical of humanistic victim offender mediation. The voluntary nature of participation, the process of careful preparation of both victims and offenders, the low-key role of the mediator, the interplay of the themes of restitution and rehabilitation, and the transformation of victim offender interaction from one based on role and conflict to one based on shared human qualities are all common features across the wide variety of ways in which VOM is carried out.

Context

In some ways, it is the differences in detail in spite of these common features that highlight the power of VOM as an intervention. In case one, both the offender and the victims live in a small working-class community where many residents struggle hard, feel disenfranchised, and are often at odds with one another. The participants' relative isolation and experience of being disconnected is shattered during the mediation when Bob and Anne discover that Jim has contact with the daughter who is lost to them.

Although this level of specific interconnectedness between victim and offender is quite unusual, it underscores the common humanity that is so often the bedrock of the VOM process.

The compelling components of context in case two derive from the offender's life history. Auto theft is not inherently a life-threatening crime, but for Josh at sixteen it was already embedded in a pattern learned from his immediate family and reinforced by his teenage gang connections. The lethal potential of this pattern was starkly and dramatically revealed to him through the sudden death of his best friend, and he desperately wished to find another way to live. The victims who chose to meet with him following his request were touched by his situation and his vulnerability, a common human experience deriving from the most basic desire for life itself.

The mediators in case three were struck by the impact of context on what at first seemed a routine case of property damage. One commented, "What never ceases to amaze those of us that do this work is the fact that the cases are as individual as people are individual. Each case has its own particular set of unique dynamics. One can never ascertain on paper the context of people's lives within which a crime occurs. The crime always has effects, but many times what we don't see is what has happened in that life prior to and leading up to the crime. For a victim, this can make the difference between a merely hurtful event and a trauma or crisis."

Referral

Referral sources and procedures were within normal parameters in case one: the adult offender who had admitted guilt was referred as a condition of probation but had the option of deciding not to participate and thereby allowing the court to set his restitution amount and payment schedule. The four children in case three were also fairly typical, being diverted from court proceedings largely because of their young age and first-offense status.

Case two is more unusual in that the mediation was initially sought by the offender. Offender-initiated mediation requests need to be handled with special care to avoid potential revictimization of the victims. The process in this particular case was presented to the victims as entirely optional and voluntary, and in fact one of the three victims chose not to participate and was supported in that decision by program staff.

Choice and Reasons for Participation

These three cases are fairly typical in the terms of reasons participants chose to come to mediation. Among victims, restitution, making offenders aware of the impact of their crime, holding offenders accountable, and in many cases hoping to prevent future criminal activity are frequently encountered reasons. Investment in rehabilitation of the offender was most pronounced in case two; it was Tom's major reason for agreeing to participate and quickly also became a central focus for Tammy once she began to hear Josh's story, even though initially she had sought restitution.

Sometimes it proves difficult to differentiate between the threads of restitution and rehabilitation, as in case three. Clearly, the business insurance would take care of most of the financial impact of the damage to the construction equipment. Yet the owners and their daughter felt it was important that the young offenders be held accountable for what they had done and be made to feel and understand the impact of their actions. That the daughter took time away from the more compelling family crisis of her father's hospitalization to meet with the children and request their participation in making amends attests to the importance the family placed on making a difference in these young lives.

Mediator Role

In all three mediation sessions, the mediator role was characteristically low-key once the initial introductions, explanations, and ground rules were completed. In case one, the mediators were more verbally active at three additional points in the process. They responded quickly when Bob's angry outburst provoked the offender into trying to bolt. Without requiring that Jim stay, the mediators interpreted Bob's positive intent and urged Jim to give it some more time. Though this intervention was most specifically directed at Jim, it also served indirectly as a reminder to Bob about his stated intent and resulted in moderation of his level of expressed anger. Midway into the session, a clear transition point was required to move from talking about what happened and how everyone felt to discussing the need for restitution. The mediators then again faded into the background. Finally, when efforts were being made to work out a written agreement, the mediators needed to be more active in presenting various options and helping the parties structure the agreement in a workable way.

Outcomes

Substantive outcomes in terms of restitution agreements and their completion were fairly typical; two of the three cases resulted in a negotiated restitution agreement, and both these agreements were fulfilled. As noted, the community service component of the agreement in case three was only partly fulfilled.

As is often the case, the "process" outcomes of VOM, though typical, are never routine. The potential for individual variation on the themes and links of human connectedness appears nearly infinite. In cases one and two, the initial anger and hostility of the victims toward the offender was later transformed into a human understanding of each other and a specific plan for "making things right." This transformation had little to do with the amount of information and advice provided by the mediators (which was minimal) during the mediation session. Rather, the process of reconciliation had far more to do with the safe structure provided by the mediators that allowed the parties to deal directly with each other and provided room for common human connectedness to surface.

In case one, Bob commented in a later conversation that after several victimizations, "this was the first time that I ever felt any sense of fairness. The courts always ignored me before. They didn't care about my concerns. And Jim wasn't such a bad kid after all, was he?" Jim also indicated that he felt better after the mediation and more aware of the impact the burglary had had on Bob and Anne.

Humanistic, dialogue-driven principles played out in three distinct ways in these three cases, with somewhat varying outcomes in terms of actual settlement; yet all three mediations resulted in high levels of satisfaction for both the victims and the offenders who participated.

Chapter Six

National Survey of
Victim Offender Mediation Programs

Previous chapters in Part One have presented the general principles of humanistic victim offender mediation and provided details about how to conduct such mediation in a victim-sensitive manner. Our consideration of the context in which such mediation takes place will begin in this chapter with the presentation of results from an extensive national survey conducted to determine the number and the characteristics of victim offender mediation programs developing in communities throughout the United States. Information about existing services, their context, and the various programs and solutions being implemented across the country will provide an empirical grounding for the discussion of program development issues in Chapter Seven.

The survey was initiated in 1996 by the Center for Restorative Justice & Peacemaking at the University of Minnesota's School of Social Work and was made possible by a grant from the Office for Victims of Crime (OVC), U.S. Department of Justice. OVC has become increasingly interested in the development of victim offender mediation and its potential for serving a wider range of crime victims through development of more victim-sensitive procedures and policies.

Note: This chapter is based in part on Umbreit and Greenwood (1999). Reprinted with permission of John Wiley & Sons, Inc.

Methodology

The methodology for conducting the survey involved securing lists of actual or potential programs from such organizations as the international Victim Offender Mediation Association, the Mennonite Central Committee, and the National Association for Community Mediation. In what is known as "snowball sampling," existing program staff and other resource people were asked if they knew of new programs in their area that were unlikely to appear as yet on any organizational lists. A total of 289 victim offender mediation programs were identified. These ranged from large, well-established programs that had been in operation for many years to entirely new programs that had yet to receive their first case referral. Of the total 289 programs identified in the survey, 35 had not yet developed enough experience to be interviewed. Extensive phone surveys were conducted with 116 programs throughout the country.

The quantitative findings of the survey will first be introduced by highlighting each specific variable. A number of themes that developed from the open-ended questions and occasionally lengthy conversations will then be discussed.

Type of Agency

The vast majority of programs participating in the survey were non-public agencies. The largest single category of programs (43 percent) consisted of private community-based agencies. The second largest category (23 percent) was church-based programs. As Table 6.1 indicates, victim offender mediation programs are now developing in probation departments, victim service agencies, prosecuting attorneys' offices, and correctional facilities.

Programs most frequently identified their primary source of funding as either state or local government. Foundations were the third most frequent source of funding. Churches, individual contributions, and the federal government were the next most frequently identified sources.

Table 6.1 Types of Agencies Sponsoring Victim Offender
Mediation Programs

Type of Agency	Number of Programs	Percentage of All Programs
Private community-based	49	43
Church-based	26	23
Probation	18	16
Correctional facility	9	8
Prosecuting attorney's office	5	4
Victim services	4	3
Police	2	2
Residential facility	2	2
Other	1	0
Total	116	100[a]

[a]Figures do not add up to precisely 100 percent due to rounding.

The average program budget of the 116 programs participating in the phone interview was $55,077, with a range from $1 (totally voluntary effort) to $413,671. The average number of staff in the programs was 2.3 full-time equivalent (FTE), with a range of 1 to 13. The average number of volunteers working with the program was 37.

Case Referrals

The actual number of cases referred to victim offender mediation programs varied a great deal. The average annual number of juvenile cases referred to programs was 136, with a range from 1 to 900. The average number of adult cases referred to programs was 74, with a range from 1 to 1,672. Of the total cases referred to programs in the survey, approximately two-thirds involved misdemeanors and one-third felonies. The primary referral sources were probation officers, judges, and prosecutors.

Ninety-four programs, representing 81 percent of the total number of programs in the survey, reported working with juvenile offenders and their victims. Fifty-seven programs reported working with adults, representing 49 percent of the total programs. These figures are not mutually exclusive, since a number of programs work with both juveniles and adults. Of the 103 programs that responded on this variable, 46 (45 percent) work only with juvenile offenders and their victims; 9 (9 percent) work only with adult offenders and their victims; and 48 (46 percent) work with both.

The three most common offenses referred to the victim offender mediation programs in the survey, in order of frequency, were vandalism, minor assaults, and theft. These were followed in frequency by burglary. These four offenses together accounted for the vast majority of offenses referred, with a small number of other property-related offenses and a few severely violent offenses being identified.

When asked if programs ever conducted mediation sessions in cases of more severe violence, a surprising number of respondents stated that they occasionally handle such cases as assault with a deadly weapon, assault with bodily damage, sexual assault, domestic violence, negligent homicide, attempted murder, and murder.

Of the total cases referred annually to the programs in the survey, an average of 106 cases per program, or approximately half of those referred, participated in an actual mediation session, with a range of per-program mediation sessions from 1 to 771 mediations. Of these cases that were mediated, an average of 92 cases per program (87 percent) resulted in a written agreement, with a range per program of 1 to 720 written agreements. Fully 99 percent of these agreements were successfully completed.

All programs in the survey indicated that victim participation in the mediation program was voluntary, and all but one indicated that victims could back out of the mediation program at any time. Offender participation in mediation, however, was not entirely voluntary in all programs. For 79 percent of programs, offenders voluntarily entered the mediation process with the victim. In the remaining 21 percent, the offender was required to meet with the victim if the victim was interested. In 65 percent of the programs surveyed, offenders are required to admit their guilt for the specific offense that led to their referral into the victim offender mediation program as a condition for participation in mediation.

Mediation Process

Throughout the twenty-year development of victim offender mediation in the United States, a great deal of emphasis has been placed on preparing the parties for the mediation. This has usually involved the mediator's conducting an in-person meeting with the victim and with the offender separately prior to bringing them together, as described in earlier chapters. Nearly all (99 percent) of the programs in the survey contact both the victim and the offender by telephone prior to the mediation session; calls are placed by the mediator (51 percent of programs) or program staff (49 percent). Separate meetings are held with the victim and offender prior to the joint mediation session in 78 percent of the programs; 80 percent of these preparatory meetings are with the mediator and 20 percent with intake staff.

The most frequent point in the justice process at which the victim offender mediation session occurred (34 percent) was identified as diversion, prior to any formal finding of guilt. Mediation that occurred at a postadjudication but predisposition level or postdisposition were both identified by 28 percent of the programs in the survey. Ten percent of the programs stated that mediation occurred at various points or, for a smaller number of programs, prior to any court involvement.

The most frequently identified locations for mediation sessions were program offices; neighborhood or community centers; conference rooms in libraries; and houses of worship. In 94 percent of the programs in the survey, the victim and offender sit across from each other during the mediation session, allowing for direct eye contact.

With regard to specific tasks of the mediator, the three most important were identified, in order of frequency, as facilitating a dialogue between victim and offender, making the parties feel comfortable and safe, and helping the parties negotiate a mutually acceptable plan for restitution for the victim. A number of other important mediator tasks were also identified, as indicated in Table 6.2.

Co-mediation is widely used in the field of victim offender mediation. Participants in the survey identified many benefits of co-mediation, including: greater opportunity for involvement of community volunteers, quality control, responding to issues of diversity unique to a specific case, case processing and debriefing, safety, and teamwork. Ninety-three percent of the programs either routinely or occasionally use co-mediators.

Following a brief opening statement by the mediators, typical victim offender mediation sessions begin with the parties "telling their stories," describing what happened and its impact on their lives. In the majority of programs in the survey (53 percent), the mediator determined which party begins the storytelling phase of the mediation, while in other programs this decision was determined by either the program staff, the victim, or the victim and offender mutually. In more than half of programs (53 percent), the victim spoke first. The offender was first in a third of the programs, and in 14 percent of the programs it varied, depending on the specific case.

When working with juveniles, only a small number (8 percent) of victim offender mediation programs never have parents of the offender present during the mediation session. The majority of programs in the survey (52 percent) always have the parents present, and another 27 percent sometimes have parents present.

Mediator Training

Victim offender mediation programs frequently train community volunteers to serve as mediators. The average number of hours of training for staff or volunteer mediators is 31 hours, with some programs in the survey indicating more lengthy training, up to 89

Table 6.2 Most Important Mediator Tasks

Mediator Tasks	Number of Responses	Percentage of All Responses
Facilitating a dialogue between victim and offender	90	28
Making the parties feel comfortable and safe	75	24
Helping the parties negotiate a restitution plan	39	12
Actively listening to both parties	36	11
Getting out of the way so that the parties can talk directly to each other	20	6
Moving the parties toward a written agreement	19	6
Reframing the parties' statements	14	4
Providing leadership	12	4
Paraphrasing comments made by the parties	6	2
Other	9	3
Total	320[a]	100

[a]Based on interviews with the directors of 116 programs, who were permitted to give multiple responses.

hours. The average amount of time spent role-playing the mediation process during training was 11 hours. In addition to the classroom training, the average number of cases in which trainees were required to participate with an experienced mediator, as a period of apprenticeship prior to completing their initial training, was four cases.

When asked if victim offender mediators should be required to become certified in the completion of a legislatively mandated number of hours for VOM training, the vast majority of respondents to the survey (61 percent) indicated no. For the 39 percent that indicated certification of mediators should be required, the average number of hours for such training was 35. Yet when asked if advanced training should be required in applying the VOM process in cases of severe violence, all indicated that such advanced training is necessary. The most frequently identified components of training were mediation skills, communication skills, victim offender mediation concept and process, understanding conflict, preparing the victim and offender for mediation skills, risks and benefits of mediation, and restorative justice concepts and principles.

Themes That Emerged from Interviews with Program Staff

A number of important themes emerged from the interviews with staff. (Several will be taken up again in Chapter Seven, which focuses on related program development issues.)

The Impact of Program Context

In victim offender mediation programs, procedures, practices, program design, and viability are all significantly affected by the community context. General attitudes among the populace and receptivity among victim service providers and juvenile and criminal justice system personnel influence the procurement of funding, access to mediation, and the availability of volunteers to serve as mediators. Many interviewees commented on local retributive, "conservative" attitudes and their negative impact on the growth and effectiveness of the victim offender program. They bemoan the difficulty of working with unsympathetic judges, attorneys, and victim service personnel and the challenge of cultivating a cadre of mediators who are sensitive and empathic.

Without support at the top, interviewees note, it is hard to develop a viable program. When court personnel do not understand the principles of restorative justice and the nature of the victim offender process, they may be prone to pressure for particular outcomes or simply for a "quick fix." "A huge mind change is needed!" commented one interviewee. When volunteer mediators lack sufficient commitment, programs may abbreviate mediation training and even curtail the process by omitting the in-person preparation phase. According to other programs, lack of funding may lead to elimination of the preparation phase, which takes time. Organizers may then limit the severity of the crime when screening cases for admission to the program.

Some programs encounter difficulties because of a highly transient population. Volunteer mediators, as well as victims and offenders, are constantly on the move, restricting the program's ability to provide services and to ensure quality and continuity. Other programs, operating in rural areas, have found that the closeness of the community may shape the goals of the mediation session. In a locale where "everyone runs into everyone" all the time, issues of confidentiality can be particularly important and challenging, and when "wrongs last a lifetime," reconciliation may become compelling to participants.

As the needs of the local community change, along with the availability of funding and referrals, many programs make major adaptations, carving out, for example, a new use for the victim offender process to match the changing needs. One program works primarily with shoplifting cases, while others specialize in providing mediation for runaway juveniles and their parents or for juveniles returning home after treatment.

Program and Staff Isolation

Victim offender mediation programs frequently operate in relative isolation from other programs, and mediators often have minimal contact with other mediators or staff personnel. A number of survey respondents expressed concern about isolation. Many program directors noted that they have no idea what other programs are doing and no peers with whom to discuss critical issues in the field, strategies for program development, procedures, or best practices. Interviewees attribute this isolation to geographical distance in some cases or to lack of resources, primarily staff time. For some, the survey interview represented the first opportunity to discuss, in depth, concerns about their programs, accomplishments, and issues of interest in the VOM field.

This isolation is echoed in the relative autonomy with which mediators handle cases. "I wish I had others to talk to before a mediation," lamented one program director who also mediates cases. The outstanding—and far too rare—program provides the mediator with brainstorming and coaching with staff prior to the mediation session and full case debriefing with staff afterward. While some programs conduct quarterly case review sessions for all volunteer mediators, most programs offer only informal debriefing as requested by mediators.

Mediation with More Violent Crimes

Victim offender mediation programs are being asked to mediate crimes of increasing severity and complexity. Many programs report a trend in referrals toward a "higher level of crime," as they see it. Courts are referring cases that are more serious and more involved. They entail greater violence, committed by offenders with significant prior convictions. Cases may also involve more parties or some degree of ambiguity regarding the victim and offender role, as when several involved parties have both committed offenses and been victimized.

Program directors are wondering at what point the current process or the training of mediators will prove inadequate to meet the needs of these more serious cases. Further, if they question the appropriateness of mediation in these cases, will that diminish the flow of referrals and threaten their funding base?

Questions Regarding Preparation Phase Procedures

The preparation phase of the victim offender mediation process, a fundamental element for most programs, continues to be problematic for some. Program directors who see in-person preparation as central to the effectiveness of the victim offender process cite the importance of spending adequate quality time with all parties in order to lay the groundwork for an effective mediation session. Seriously "working the case," with commitment, is essential, according to many participants. Some interviewees suggest that even if the parties do not proceed to mediation, the premediation session itself is a highly valuable service, tantamount to an intervention.

Several program directors indicated that with victims of property crimes, particularly lower-level offenses, it doesn't seem necessary to conduct a premediation interview because little, if any, personal trauma is involved. Other directors disagree, noting that many people feel personally violated by property crimes.

The differences between victim offender mediation and more generic mediation is evident in the concerns of a few interviewees who represented community mediation programs newly adding a victim offender component. They voiced concern about mediator neutrality, positing that preparation of the parties for the mediation session crosses the line of neutrality, as the mediator presents the benefits of mediation and eases the parties' concerns. One director comments that any type of preparation by the mediator threatens that mediator's ability to be neutral.

In several programs that do not hold premediation sessions, program directors express concern about the emotional intensity of the victim and the consequent need for the mediator to assume a more aggressive and more intervening style. Others worry that without face-to-face preparation, victims may be volatile in the mediation session, and mediators may be forced into the role of referee or arbitrator.

Perception of the Strong Positive Impact of Mediation

Program staff in victim offender mediation programs typically express strong convictions about the positive impact mediation has on participants and communities. Zeal and enthusiasm for mediation are evident among the vast majority of program directors. The more involved in the practice and administration of victim offender mediation they are, the more they believe in it. Program directors report high levels of participant satisfaction, gleaned from evaluation instruments and informal comments. Interviewees add that communities benefit as well, because mediation works to reduce community isolation and fragmentation.

Here are some examples of comments made by program directors:

> When they walk into the mediation session, these are people who don't trust each other or recognize any importance or commonality in each other. Then an hour and a half later, they walk out recognizing their commonality. . . . It's sort of a soul-purging for something that had happened to them—they get it off their minds, and it's really a revelation for them. They get it out and get on with their lives. . . . It is a wonderful thing to be able to say you're sorry.

> When offenders are done with probation, the probation officer asks them what it is that will most help them not reoffend. Those who have experienced mediation often remark, "Mediation was the hardest thing to do, but I get it now—it made me think about the victim."

> Even just contacting the parties and acknowledging that they've been through an experience that's different [from everyday life]. . . . They don't have this opportunity elsewhere in their lives to have a third person assist them through a recognition process. They come out saying, "This is really nice—everyone should have a chance to do this."

> If we truly follow the process, people will be changed even if we don't see it. . . . We can't undo the damage or take pain away, but we can help them put it into perspective, set it aside a bit or use it, and move ahead so that they don't have to define themselves only as a victim.

The personal dedication of program staff is noteworthy. A number of programs are run virtually on a shoestring—even, in one instance, solely on the personal pension of the director. The enthusiasm and dedication of mediators and program staff has no doubt contributed to the growing interest in restorative justice measures evident in many judicial systems. Interviewees report, for example, that victim offender mediation is in fact finding its way into the penal codes in a number of states.

Similarity of Goals Across Diverse Practices

Victim offender mediation programs may incorporate different practices in different areas, but the goals espoused and achieved are relatively similar, typically articulated more as transformation than settlement. Some programs, for instance, seeking a process that addresses the needs of both victims and offenders, encourage parents of juvenile offenders to attend the mediation session in order to provide helpful support to their child and later encouragement in the fulfillment of the agreement. Other programs, asserting also the importance of a dialogue meaningful to both parties, discourage the presence of parents, who may be intrusive and controlling and may detract from the juvenile's experience. Certain programs may seek to limit the number of people in attendance at a mediation session, wishing to preserve the personal, private quality of the face-to-face dialogue, while other programs seek to expand the number of supporters, believing that extensive ongoing emotional support for the victim and accountability and support for the offender will enhance the mediation session and the effectiveness of the follow-up phase.

A range of perspectives exists also in regard to the first speaker in the mediation session. According to some programs, victims need to be encouraged to go first because they should have the right to be heard fully, their story undiminished by any remorse or apology offered by the offender. For other programs, the offender should be urged to start, sparing the victim the discomfort and risk of speaking first. Still others ask the parties to decide, ensuring equality of opportunity for both parties. One interviewee comments that victims are often moved that the offender spoke voluntarily, offering words of remorse not elicited by the victim's remarks.

Similar variations exist regarding seating. Some programs use rectangular tables, others round tables, and still others no table at all. One interviewee commented that the round table eliminates any power angle or "head of table" status. What all agree is that the parties should be seated in a way that enhances their comfort and allows for direct dialogue between them, at such time as they feel ready.

A number of programs feel it is important to decide the particulars on a case-by-case basis, rather than setting rules that apply to all cases, while other programs establish set practices as a way to standardize quality of service and simplify responsibilities for mediators.

But even if the actual procedures may vary among programs, the underlying intentions are relatively congruent. Victim sensitivity, for instance, a concern of virtually all programs, is manifested in a range of practices. And so, though it may be argued that certain structures or procedures are more sensitive to victims than others, it must also be granted that any particular practices can be made more victim-sensitive and that the most important elements of victim sensitivity are the style and attitude of the mediator—for example, listening patiently, empathizing, not pressuring or pushing, and allowing sufficient time.

Consensus on Training Issues

Considerable agreement exists among victim offender mediation programs regarding the training format, the importance of role playing, and challenging issues for mediators that need to be addressed during training. There is relative consensus among victim offender programs that training will be most effective when it is interactive, participatory, and experiential, with a varied format allowing for different learning styles. Training thus typically involves the use of videos, written material, brief presentations, discussion, stories of cases, exercises, skill practice, and modeling of skills and processes. Many programs also encourage trainees to draw on their own personal experience in order to understand the nature of conflict or the experience of victims and offenders.

Apprenticeship with an experienced mediator is indispensable in mediator training. This experiential mode permits training to be customized to the needs of particular trainees. It lets novices observe experienced mediators in action, test out newly acquired skills, and receive one-on-one coaching.

Role playing is essential to the effectiveness of mediation training. Many programs, to customize role playing to the needs of trainees, craft role-plays to elicit specific problems or issues, such as cross-cultural challenges or common sources of impasse. Other adaptations are made to enhance the efficacy of role-plays, including the use of experienced mediators to play the roles of victims and offenders or simply to serve as coaches, videotaping of trainees as mediators, or inviting actual offenders and victims to play the appropriate roles.

Commonly incorporated into mediation training are such issues as maintaining neutrality, appreciating diversity and working effectively with diverse participants, dealing with difficult people, and becoming comfortable with conflict and the expression of intense emotions, particularly anger. Working with juveniles and cultivating empathy for the offender are other concerns mentioned by a number of program directors. "How can we help trainees relate to the experience of offenders, humiliated in court? All of us fear being weak and not in control," comments one interviewee.

Concerns About Follow-Up

Follow-up on the mediation session, often given little more than routine attention, is an area ripe for substantive and creative enhancement of victim offender mediation programming. Program directors often lament the inadequacy of their follow-up procedures. More could be done, they suggest, to evaluate the mediation session, for example, or to support the victim and the offender following the mediation and to monitor and encourage the completion of the agreement. Several interviewees expressed regret that once the agreements are signed, other agencies then monitor completion. At that point, compliance may founder for lack of support, and even when agreements are fulfilled, the results may not be communicated to the mediation program or to the victims themselves.

A number of programs are experimenting with the follow-up phase in a variety of ways. Some are exploring new ways of gaining helpful information about the mediation session from participants, for example, by using volunteers to conduct in-person interviews with the parties several months after the mediation. Other programs are asking mediators to debrief mediations routinely with co-mediators, staff, and other volunteer mediators at regular debriefing sessions.

Continued contact with victims is a standard feature in a number of programs. Most often this service is provided by staff members. Victims are contacted repeatedly by phone and encouraged to stay in touch. Referrals are made as needs arise. Occasionally, visits are made to the victim's home, or victim advocates provide ongoing support and services or referrals.

In some programs, compliance with the agreement is monitored by the mediator, who then provides ongoing contact with all parties and arranges additional mediation sessions if the terms of the agreement need to be renegotiated.

Support for the offender is mustered in a variety of ways. Several programs provide juvenile offenders, and occasionally their parents, with training in conflict resolution, anger management, and life skills. Some mediators become mentors for offenders, helping them find a job so that they can make restitution payments and offering job coaching. Several programs train selected offenders as mediators, who then co-mediate actual cases, or as trainers, who teach conflict resolution skills to juveniles in treatment. One program assigns a worker to groups of juvenile offenders. The worker then oversees community service for the group, develops relationships with the youth, and occasionally organizes recreational activities. This program is currently developing plans to build a residential facility for youth unable to return home following treatment. Now and then, a victim will choose to maintain contact with the offender, who may be a neighborhood acquaintance. Victims may see themselves as potential mentors or surrogate parents or grandparents, able, perhaps, to influence the life of another person and in this way giving some meaning to their own painful experience as a victim.

Common Challenges

Many victim offender mediation programs report facing the same challenges: securing funding and referrals, building support in the community and in the justice system, and eliciting victim participation.

A frequent complaint is the general paucity of resources for victim offender mediation. Despite the overall effectiveness of the process and high levels of satisfaction on the part of participants, funds may be difficult to secure, from both private and public sources.

Another concern is ensuring a regular supply of appropriate referrals. Programs report considerable fluctuation in the flow of VOM candidates. Sometimes a drop in referrals seems to correspond to an influx of new personnel at the referring agencies, who may be unfamiliar with victim offender mediation and consequently hesitant to refer cases. At times, referral sources seem to need fresh reminders about the availability and efficacy of the mediation program.

The concerns voiced about referrals and funding suggest that mediation programs would do well to invest in the development of these external relationships. Such an investment will also contribute to changing attitudes in the community and in the justice system toward a more restorative approach.

An additional concern is victim participation. "How can we help victims be open to mediation?" ask several interviewees. A number of program directors lament that it is distressing to encounter so much resistance to mediation among victims, to the point that it is difficult to overcome. Some express discomfort with the level of victims' anger and their occasional "self-righteousness," as it seems to some. One interviewee tells of a high school principal who refuses to participate in mediation because "I want to be mad at that punk for the rest of my life—I am so angry!" and goes on to ask, "How do we work with victims who seem to be resistant or stuck? How do we legitimize their position and still help them get back to larger interests, especially when the culture legitimizes staying angry and blaming others?"

Longer Range Issues

Practitioners in the field of victim offender mediation continue to wrestle with a variety of issues and to raise questions about the long-range implications of procedures and practices. Interviewees voiced numerous concerns, which may be suggestive of growth areas for the field of victim offender mediation. The following represent lingering questions that emerged from the interviews:

Certification of Mediators.   If certification for victim offender mediators becomes legislatively mandated, will the field move in the direction of professionalism and away from volunteerism? Will we then shift away from a "grassroots movement" paradigm and lose the rich resource of citizen participation or community involvement that undergirds the goals of restorative justice and the efficacy of the mediation process itself? Would certification of mediators lead to higher-quality mediations? How do we maintain quality standards in the field?

Mediation Process. How can we balance the needs of victims and offenders? Is preparation of the parties, in separate face-to-face sessions, essential in order to maximize the potential of victim offender mediation? Is it possible for offenders to be victimized by a victim offender process that is strongly punitive and shaming?

Presence of Parents and Other Supporters at the Mediation Session. Is it helpful to have multiple supporters attend the mediation session with the victim and the offender? Can the presence of too many others detract from the mediation, shifting what was intended to be a personal meeting between two people into a "show and tell" session? What is an appropriate and helpful role for parents of juvenile offenders in the mediation session? Are parents inherently problematic in that setting, or are they essential as potential supporters of compliance with the agreement?

Program Procedures. Under what circumstances should co-mediation be practiced? Is it a preferable model to be used always, unless limited resources dictate otherwise, or is it appropriate primarily for cases involving multiple parties? How can we provide for mediator safety and avert other types of liability suits without establishing practices that will compromise the effectiveness of mediation? If victim offender mediation is sponsored by victim services or by an arm of probation or corrections, will the neutrality of the program be jeopardized in the eyes of participants? Is victim offender mediation most useful as an alternative to adjudication, treatment, or incarceration or as a supplement to the normal court process?

Relationships with the Judicial System and Other Service Providers. How can our program establish a healthy, collegial, nonadversarial working relationship with victim service providers? How can we, in good conscience, deal with pressure from the court system for particular outcomes, such as quick settlement? Can we maintain positive relationships with our referral sources while maintaining the integrity of the victim offender process? How can we help our sources understand the labor-intensive nature of victim offender mediation and perhaps reframe for ourselves what constitutes a successful mediation and a successful program, one that provides important services even in cases where agreement is not reached?

Screening of Cases. At what point in a victim's process, following the crime, is it most beneficial for mediation to occur—after the anger has peaked and before neglect or resignation sets in? Do we absolutely need an unequivocal confession of guilt by the offender before proceeding with the mediation process? Is the victim offender process potentially effective even if the offender takes some responsibility for the crime or for a portion of the crime? Should it simply be the victim's decision whether or not, in these particular circumstances, to move forward with mediation, even if the offender does not admit guilt?

Training. What should be taught in the classroom, and what is better taught through apprenticeship or continuing education? How useful is it to teach communication techniques when they seem to work against a natural flow and an authentic, spontaneous communication style? Are mediation role-plays realistic enough to be genuinely helpful to trainees? How can we train our mediators to have empathy for the unique experiences of both offender and victim while countering the danger of labeling, which identifies a person solely as "victim" or "offender"? Does training need to be geared to the victim offender model of mediation, or can training be focused on a more generic model? How does the victim offender model differ from other models of mediation? Is it advisable for mediators to have experience mediating other kinds of cases, such as community conflicts, prior to tackling victim offender cases?

Summary

A far larger number of victim offender mediation programs exist in the United States than was previously known. It is clear that the process of mediating victim offender conflict, after twenty years of development, is moving toward the mainstream of justice in a growing number of communities while remaining fairly marginal to the justice system in many other communities. A more diverse range of practice was found in this national survey than previously understood. As the field of victim offender mediation continues to expand throughout the United States, it will be important for practitioners to network with each other, learn from one another's successes and failures, provide high-quality mediation training and technical assistance to new program initiatives, and continue to make the process more accessible to a wide range of crime victims and offenders in juvenile and adult courts throughout the country.

Chapter Seven

Program Development Issues

A variety of issues must be addressed when establishing new victim offender mediation programs or expanding existing programs. These issues include goal clarification, the community and justice system support, funding, the target population, program design, program evaluation, program development, the management information system, and the training of mediators.

Goal Clarification

Precisely because the mediation process has clear benefits for both the offender and the victim, as well as for the larger community, it is important for local program organizers to be clear about the goals toward which their efforts are directed. The victim offender mediation process, by definition, is grounded in the primary goal of providing a restorative conflict resolution process that is perceived as fair to both victim and offender, as well as family members or other support people involved in the process. Each local program, however, needs to identify which secondary goals are important for its community.

The victim offender mediation process involves a variety of potential benefits. Victims can become directly involved in the

---

Note: This chapter draws on Umbreit and Greenwood (1999) and Umbreit (1994), ch. 10. Reprinted with permission of John Wiley & Sons, Inc., and Criminal Justice Press.

justice process. They can let the offender know of the impact that the crime has had on their life and can receive answers to any lingering questions. Victims can directly influence the manner in which the offender is held accountable, through negotiation of a mutually acceptable restitution agreement.

Through mediation, offenders are allowed to be held accountable in a very personal fashion. They have the opportunity to repair the damage they caused, to accept responsibility for their behavior, and to display the more human dimension of their character. The opportunity for offering a direct apology to the person they victimized is also present. Offenders who participate in mediation may avoid a harsher penalty.

Family members or other support persons who may be involved in the mediation also have the opportunity to learn more about the full impact of the crime on all involved. They, too, can express their concerns and get answers to questions.

The community at large also benefits from the increased practice of nonviolent conflict resolution skills that results from the presence of a local victim offender mediation program. Community members can serve as volunteer mediators and become directly involved in the process of building a safer and more caring community. Many offenders who participate in a mediation session with their victim are far less likely to commit additional crimes. Through diversion of certain cases from the court system to mediation, scarce tax dollars can also be saved.

In addition, there are a number of different possible secondary goals of the victim offender mediation process, including crime prevention, offender rehabilitation, victim assistance, community conflict resolution, victim empowerment, victim offender reconciliation, or serving as an alternative to expensive incarceration in certain cases. These secondary goals are not mutually exclusive; however, to develop an effective program design, local organizers must first clarify which goals are the most important for their specific jurisdiction.

Community and Justice System Support

A crucial component of any victim offender mediation program is the cultivation of connections with stakeholders in the community. Stakeholders might include judges and others who may make referrals to the program, prosecuting attorneys and public defenders who have an interest in the outcome of the case, defense attorneys, correctional staff, victim services personnel who may refer cases or work with clients prior to or after mediation, directors of victim services agencies, probation officers who may follow-up with offenders, city or county political leaders, clergy, neighborhood leaders, community organizers and activists, community-based agencies, and civic and corporate leaders. All possible stakeholders in the development of a local victim offender mediation program should be considered. Establishing these relationships is vital to the continuing flow of appropriate referrals and the overall success of the program.

An analysis of potential stakeholders should focus on assessing the degree to which each individual could either significantly influence the development of a new program or could offer resistance. It might be helpful to develop a chart in which the stakeholder names and positions are listed along the left margin and the following four columns are to be filled out for each person: (1) rate the person's influence or power, (2) rate the person's probable support or nonsupport, (3) identify who can influence the person, and (4) develop a strategy either to gain the person's support or to neutralize the person's active opposition.

Building local support for a new victim offender mediation program will also require the development of a plan for presenting the concept and program to the public in a clear and understandable fashion—what some would call a marketing strategy. This might entail the preparation of a clear and brief presentation about the program, scheduling many presentations before a wide range of community organizations and justice system agencies, and inviting

Exhibit 7.1   Crucial Components for a VOM Marketing Plan

The outcome of the planning stage should allow you to do all of the following:

- State the purpose of the program in one sentence.
- State the human interest aspect of the program in one sentence.
- State the public policy or criminal justice system relevance of the program in one sentence.
- Summarize the benefits of the program.
- Identify briefly any possible self-interest the following key actors might have in supporting your program: judge, prosecutor, defense attorney, probation officer, police, local politicians, community activists and leaders.
- Based on the foregoing, develop a general outline for presenting your program to local officials and the public; this should include purchasing at least one of the short victim offender mediation videos that are now available.
- Identify a strategy for using the local print and broadcast media.

the active involvement of stakeholders and others in the actual process of developing and managing the new VOM program. Exhibit 7.1 lists the goal clarification components that should be accomplished by the end of this phase of the planning stage.

Because mediation represents a serious departure from the way crimes are traditionally handled, a concerted effort needs to be made to educate the community and court-related personnel on the victim offender mediation process. They need information on the benefits and risks of mediation, the types of cases suitable for referral, specific outcomes of cases, research done on the short- and long-term impact of mediation, safeguards, and quality control procedures. Stakeholders will also want assurance about the credibility of the program itself and the training and competency of the mediators.

Staff play a vital role in establishing and maintaining these networks as ongoing relationships, involving frequent personal contact. In addition to providing information to stakeholders, program personnel may seek to strengthen the partnership by exploring avenues for collaboration. The training of mediators is a natural opportunity for collaboration. Victim service providers can present a training segment on the experience of victims. Portions of the training can be held in the office of victim services. Probation officers can provide a parallel segment on the experience of offenders. A judge can describe what happens to victims and offenders in the courtroom and offer information about what typically may happen to a case that is not mediated. The presence of representatives of the judicial system also informs trainees that the system appreciates and supports mediation and values their contributions as volunteer mediators. A variety of service providers may role-play how a case progresses through the system from beginning to end. Such collaboration not only provides trainees with needed information but also builds relationships within the system that can help ensure the success of a mediation program.

Another opportunity for collaboration emerges out of the necessity of seeking resources and support for victims and offenders. A victim services worker may, for instance, provide the victim with support throughout the entire mediation process and beyond, even attending the mediation session with the victim, if requested, in the role of support person rather than active participant. Such support may assist victims in understanding and articulating their experiences and needs. Similarly, a social worker or probation officer may be helpful to the offender, encouraging the development of understanding and empathy for the victim, and assisting the offender in preparing for dialogue with the victim.

Building connections within the larger community is also essential. The community is a stakeholder in the victim offender mediation process. Crime has an impact that reaches far beyond the immediate parties involved. The community is also a potential source of financial support for a mediation program. Many programs are also dependent on the community as a source of volunteers to serve as mediators. When the public is educated about victim offender mediation and becomes invested in it, victims and offenders, family members of both, and support persons may be more willing to participate in the process, and other community members are more likely to volunteer to be mediators. In addition to general public education about mediation, specific ties should be made to community agencies, houses of worship, religious organizations, business organizations, and local and state government, including those that influence legislation and public policy. Program leaders, in particular, need to have a thorough understanding of the community's structure and resources.

Volunteers may serve as a bridge to the wider community. They can be highly effective in representing or promoting a mediation program, in both the community and the court system. Volunteers may at times be more convincing about the positive impact of mediation than a staff person may be. Community members who serve as volunteer mediators, for instance, may speak enthusiastically about their experiences with the process, and victims and offenders who have found the mediation experience useful can serve as eloquent promoters of the program, including giving presentations during the training of mediators.

Victim offender mediation programs should maintain close ties with other VOM programs and other agencies providing mediation services to the community. These connections can offer much needed ongoing support, resources, and consultation. In addition, programs may wish to share materials and trainers and to collaborate in areas of common concern, such as legislative initiatives. All local victim offender mediation programs should join the international Victim Offender Mediation Association (VOMA) and benefit from its annual conference, training, newsletter, and broader networking in the field.

Funding

Securing sufficient funds to support the operation of a new victim offender mediation program is one of the most difficult tasks to be faced during the initial program development process. Fortunately, victim offender mediation programs do not require huge budgets. The average budget of the 116 VOM programs in the survey presented in Chapter Six was $55,077. Operating budgets ranged from zero for programs run exclusively by volunteer efforts to more than $400,000 a year in a large urban area.

Many programs begun with relatively small amounts of money, often from private foundations and churches, later secure larger amounts of public funding as the program develops. Although a small amount of federal funds is available to support victim offender mediation programs, the most likely source of funding is to be found within the state and, particularly, local private and public sources.

The task of securing local funds should not be postponed until the plans for the new program are finalized. Rather, potential funding sources should be identified and researched during the initial planning phase. When the initial plans for the new program are worked out, including a tentative budget, it is often helpful to develop a brief concept paper that can be distributed to potential funding sources. A more thorough proposal will eventually have to be prepared.

A strategy of developing a multiple-source funding base is often helpful. Having several sources provide funding for the program can often be more prudent than making the entire project dependent on one grant. If that single grant is lost, the project's existence is immediately threatened. Public agencies, such as probation departments, are in a position to consider reassigning responsibilities and existing resources in such a manner that only a marginal amount of additional funding may be required. By contrast, departments that are overburdened with high and growing caseloads will certainly not be in a position to develop a new victim offender mediation program without a significant amount of new resources. In such situations, the department should try to secure new funding for a position that focuses entirely on the development and management of the VOM program, with no traditional probation caseload or supervision responsibilities.

Target Population

In the planning of a new victim offender mediation program, it is important to identify the target population for referrals to the program. Will the program focus on juvenile or adult court cases? Will it accept any referrals, regardless of age, type of offense, or prior convictions? Will it focus on only the most minor property offenses, or will it attempt to receive referrals of more serious property offenses and some violent offenses? These are important questions to address early in the planning process. Depending on the choices made, the program can become stereotyped as an alternative for lightweight cases (many of which would have been essentially ignored by the system) or as an important new effort to deal with more serious offenses.

Within the field of victim offender mediation, there are two schools of thought on this important issue. Some experts argue that since the primary goal of the mediation process is to resolve conflict between victim and offender, nearly any case referred is appropriate. From this perspective, there is little concern about the seriousness of the offenses, age or circumstances of the offender, or possible impact of the mediation on the justice system (for example, widening the net of social control or serving as an alternative to incarceration). Many programs that embrace such a wide definition of their target population tend to receive a high volume of minor misdemeanor offenses (lightweight cases).

Others in the field would argue that given the limited resources available to all programs and the relative needs of the individual victims and offenders, as well as the justice system, a more serious range of case referrals should be identified. It is less likely that a program will be marginalized if it chooses to work with more serious cases. The impact of the mediation program in truly diverting certain cases from the justice system or from a penalty of costly incarceration would likely be greater. Victims and offenders involved in more serious cases usually have greater emotional and material needs that could be resolved through mediation and dialogue.

Although working with any and all cases seems logical in the abstract, it is simply not possible. By focusing primarily on the least serious offenses, many observers would argue that such a policy results in a tremendous underutilization of the full power and potential of the mediation intervention to create a greater sense of healing and accountability among the involved parties. This is particularly so given the fact that it is becoming increasingly clear that mediation can be very effective in working with cases involving severe trauma and loss, including homicides and attempted homicides, although this requires far more advanced training and supervision. The mediation process in such cases also requires a number of modifications and a far more intense case management process. The fact that mediation can be effective in such severely violent offenses bodes well for those in the field who advocate both the importance of targeting more serious offenses and the need to limit the negative effects of increased social control through net widening and strengthening. (The actual process of working with crimes of severe violence is described in Chapter Thirteen, along with three case studies.)

Identifying an appropriate target population for case referrals ultimately involves a balance between the desires of the program advocates and the willingness of the criminal justice system to support the new program and experiment through taking some risks. A negotiated process is required between representatives of the referral sources and program staff. Keeping the principles of restorative justice and the expressed goals of the program in the forefront of such negotiations is critical. Without such focus, it will become far too easy for the new program to be seduced into taking cases that have little relationship to the ultimate goals of the program.

Identifying an appropriate target population also requires recognition of the tremendous capacity of the criminal justice system to co-opt true reforms. Many "diversion" programs and "alternatives" that were developed over the past decades were found to have little real impact in either truly diverting cases from the courts or reducing the use of incarceration. The good intentions of reformers did not often lead to the desired changes. Local organizers are encouraged to avoid repeating the errors of the past by choosing not to support the creation of "wider and stronger nets of social control" that remain entirely offender-focused, offer little, if any, assistance to crime victims, and often reinforce deeply embedded patterns of injustice based on race and socioeconomic status.

Program Design

The most crucial yet difficult task of initiating a new victim offender mediation program is designing the local program to maximize the achievement of its primary goal, with direct impact on the desired target population. Clarification of goals and identification of a target population can easily become abstract and irrelevant exercises if they are not directly formulated as clear strategies stipulating how a local program will actually operate. For this reason, the task of effective program design is the most demanding and critical step in any local replication effort. Experience in the field of victim offender mediation has shown that many local organizers underestimate the importance of program design and are often too quick to initiate the training of mediators.

There is no simple or perfect way of designing a local victim offender mediation program, but in all cases, a handful of key issues need to be addressed. These include creation of an advisory board, determining program sponsorship, staffing, use of volunteers, point of referral in the system, referral criteria and procedures, and use of co-mediators.

Creation of an Advisory Board

The establishment of an advisory board can contribute significantly to the effectiveness of a victim offender mediation program. The board's role is usually consultative, without decision-making authority. The board can assist in program development, in maintaining quality in program procedures and practices, in fundraising, and in building support for the program within the judicial system and in the community at large.

The composition of the advisory board may vary, depending on program context and needs. The board may include a victim who has participated in victim offender mediation, an offender who has participated in victim offender mediation, youth workers from the community representatives from the judiciary or court administration, representatives from probation or parole, police officers or diversion workers, representatives from victim services, social workers, counselors, health care workers, community activists, or other community representatives from the media, schools, or houses of worship.

Determining Program Sponsorship

Identifying the appropriate agency to sponsor a new victim offender mediation program is extremely important. Agencies that are already identified as strong advocates for either victims or offenders are unlikely to be able to offer a mediation service that requires the use of impartial third parties unless they can clearly and consistently step out of their advocate role for these cases. It is preferable to hire a new person who works exclusively on the VOM program, with no traditional caseload responsibilities. In some communities, the establishment of an entirely new nonprofit organization may be appropriate. In other communities, a collaborative effort between a local probation department and a victim services agency or a community agency might be the best option. The victim offender mediation programs in Albuquerque and Austin are particularly good examples of collaborative efforts between private and public agencies. In Albuquerque, the juvenile probation department and the New Mexico Center for Dispute Resolution (a private community-based organization) sponsor the program. In Austin, the juvenile probation department directly sponsors the program but relies on the local dispute resolution center to provide the volunteer mediators to handle the cases.

Staffing

The number of staff required to manage a new victim offender mediation program can vary a great deal, depending on the type of organization sponsoring the program, the level of new funding secured, and the projected caseload. In existing well-established nonprofit community agencies or in some probation departments, it may be possible to initiate a program with a very limited number of staff. Some programs have begun with a half-time staff person and a pool of volunteers. It is usually preferable to have at least one full-time staff person, perhaps assisted by another working half time, to initiate the program and coordinate volunteers. Programs that are not able to receive supportive services from a larger organization (such as free office space, phone access, and secretarial services) are likely to need more staff. As programs expand over time, more staff will be required to manage the program.

Use of Volunteers

The use of trained community volunteers needs to be addressed early in the planning process because it has a direct impact on the budget and staff required to initiate the program. The benefits of using volunteers include increased citizen participation in the justice process, broader community exposure to nonviolent conflict resolution skills, and reduced costs for the program. Volunteers often add a level of enthusiasm and commitment to a program, both valuable assets.

Nevertheless, using volunteers in a new mediation program requires a good deal of planning and effort devoted to recruitment, training, and monitoring. Periodic in-service training is important, along with various events to provide recognition and support. The benefits must be examined in the context of the energy and resources that must be expended. Most victim offender mediation programs have chosen to use community volunteers as mediators.

Point of Referral

The point at which cases are referred to mediation by the justice system is a critical strategic issue to consider. There are at least four points at which cases are referred to victim offender mediation programs. Some programs receive referrals directly from the police prior to a formal charge being made. Many programs receive cases after the police have filed a report but prior to a trial, as a diversion from prosecution. Other programs have cases referred after an admission or finding of guilt but prior to the sentencing or disposition hearing. Still others receive referrals of cases after the sentencing hearing. Some programs would accept referrals at any of these points.

There are benefits and drawbacks related to each referral point. Whereas mediation is more likely to be an alternative to the court process if cases are received prior to trial, it is also more likely that only relatively minor offenses will be referred. If more serious cases, including some violent offenses, are meant to be referred to mediation, it is more likely that the point of referral would be after conviction or adjudication. Some programs find it desirable to have cases referred after an admission of guilt but prior to sentencing. This allows victims to have direct input into the penalty required of their offender and represents a time of high motivation for the offender to make amends.

Referral Criteria and Procedures

The importance of developing clear referral criteria and effective referral procedures cannot be overstated. Failure to address these issues will likely result in both few referrals and inappropriate cases, both of which can marginalize the program. Experience has shown that clear referral criteria and proactive referral procedures work best. Rather than providing the referral source with a list of criteria and then waiting for referrals to be made, it is far more effective to have program staff directly review and select cases at the offices of the referral source. A sample set of clear and concise criteria and procedures is offered in Exhibit 7.2. Actual referral criteria and procedures developed for specific programs are likely to be more detailed. Time frames for completion of certain procedures can be helpful if they are understood as targets and not rigid goals.

Use of Co-Mediators

In designing the program and preparing for mediation of cases, it will be important to determine if single mediators or co-mediators will be used. There are advantages to both approaches. On the one hand, it is easier to schedule mediation sessions when single mediators are used, and a smaller pool of volunteers is required. On the other hand, use of mediator pairs can increase quality control through peer support and critiquing, provide greater support and assistance during the mediation session and subsequent debriefing, allow for more flexibility in addressing cross-cultural issues present in the conflict (if one or both co-mediators share the cultural backgrounds of the participants), and promote broader volunteer involvement in mediation.

Co-mediation can involve having one person serve as the lead mediator with the other in a secondary role, clarifying or assisting with difficult issues that may arise. It can also involve having the mediators both take the lead in different parts of the session. For example, one mediator could handle the opening of the session and the discussion of the facts and feelings related to the case. The other mediator could then take the lead in reviewing the losses and helping the parties negotiate a mutually acceptable restitution agreement.

Program Evaluation

Procedures for program evaluation need to be established from the outset. Such information is crucial to quality control. Evaluations provide the program staff with feedback on the mediation process

Exhibit 7.2 Referral Criteria and Procedures

Referral Criteria

- Adult felony offenders convicted of burglary or theft, regardless of prior offenses
- Identifiable loss by victim and need for restitution
- Absence of intense hostility that could lead to violence
- Admission by the offender of complicity in the offense

Referral and Case Management Procedures

1. Probation staff temporarily place all burglary and theft case files in VOM program in-basket at probation office immediately following conviction.
2. Program staff visit the probation office daily to review all burglary and theft cases within twenty-four hours of conviction.
3. Program staff select appropriate cases to be referred to mediation, subject to final review by the probation staff.
4. Program staff transfer case information from the file to the VOM program case referral form.

itself and the effectiveness of program procedures. Evaluations also offer information about specific cases and the competency of the mediators. As a result, staff may suggest further training or consultation for a mediator or follow-up work with the participants in a particular case. In general, evaluations should be anonymous to encourage honest responses. A coding system can be used so that staff can identify the particular case and mediator involved.

One model for participant evaluation has two phases. The first phase gathers information at the time of the mediation session. A simple evaluation instrument is distributed to all participants, including parents. The participants are asked to complete the evaluation as soon as possible and mail it back in a postpaid envelope, or they may complete the form at the time of the mediation session if they prefer.

The second phase of this evaluation process occurs later, three to six months following the mediation session. It may be conducted in several ways: another written instrument may be mailed out to all participants with a postpaid return envelope, or a telephone survey or face-to-face interview may be used to gather the information. The person conducting the survey or interview may be a volunteer or a staff person but should not be the person who mediated the case. An additional method for gathering information from victims is to sponsor focus groups made up of victims who are willing to discuss their experiences in mediation and offer input regarding the program and its practices.

Mediators also need to be asked to evaluate the mediation. A feedback instrument can be completed immediately following the mediation session. Such a procedure can enhance learning for the mediator, encouraging skill development through observation, analysis, and self-reflection. It can also alert program staff to any issues or problems that may need further attention or suggest revisions in program procedures. In addition, feedback needs to be gathered form probation officers and victim service personnel who work with the parties following mediation. This may be accomplished through formal evaluation or informal feedback.

Program Development

Once the groundwork for a sound mediation program has been laid, the organization can begin to explore opportunities for broadening the scope of services provided. The following are some ideas that a number of programs are pursuing to strengthen the core victim offender mediation program:

- Develop a course for offenders and their parents, covering such topics as conflict management, empathy development, communication skills, life skills, building esteem, anger management, and building peer support.
- Train mediators to maintain a connection with victims and offenders for a period of time following the mediation, as support for the victim, mentor to the offender. Mediators may

monitor agreements, accompany offenders on job search excursions, and offer encouragement and reminders about restitution obligations.

- Train selected victims and ex-offenders to be mediators who co-facilitate actual cases or to be trainers, providing conflict resolution training in detention centers or correctional facilities.

- Establish a public works program, which can serve as an arena for community service responsibilities, and provide opportunities for staff to develop relationships with offenders, as well as monitor restitution.

- Provide offenders with job search assistance and actual job training. Establish a work-study program for offenders.

- Develop victim impact panels for use in cases where the victim chooses not to participate in mediation.

- Use mediation with parents and children when juvenile offenders leave a correctional facility, return home, or run away.

- Train young people, including those involved in peer mediation in high schools, to be victim offender mediators who cofacilitate actual cases.

Management Information System

When planning a new VOM program, a management information system (MIS) can be an effective mechanism for collecting, storing, and retrieving important information about the program. Management information systems have several uses. These include to assist in the delivery of mediation services; to document accurately what is done; to facilitate supervision of staff and volunteers; to provide a basis for program evaluation that can inform planning, program development, and policy formulation; and to provide a basis for presenting the program to potential users, funders, and other interested groups.

The concept of a management information system may call up visions of an endless stream of paperwork and hassle. A good MIS, however, should actually increase efficiency, streamline paperwork, and systematically provide helpful information to both supervisors and line staff. To develop an MIS, the program staff need to determine what data are required to meet the desired uses of the system; how and in what form the data will be collected; how the data will be managed; and how the MIS can be used for evaluation, feedback, and reporting purposes.

The various forms used in the management information system of many victim offender mediation programs are identified in Exhibit 7.3. Some programs have streamlined the number of forms used, while others might have additional forms. A growing number of programs are using computer software for their MIS, significantly reducing the volume of paperwork.

Training of Mediators

A final issue that needs to be addressed as local communities replicate the victim offender mediation model is that of recruiting and training volunteer mediators. A number of basic characteristics are important to keep in mind as individuals are considered to serve as mediators. These include good communication skills, particularly deep listening skills, which require patience and a high tolerance for silence; problem-solving and negotiation skills; the ability to exercise appropriate leadership; good organizational skills; commitment to the philosophy of restorative justice and techniques of nonviolent conflict resolution; and the ability to understand and work within the criminal justice system.

The length of mediation training provided in the victim offender mediation field can vary from twelve to forty hours. We recommend thirty-two to forty hours of training, including case apprenticeship. Training should introduce volunteers to restorative justice principles and the victim offender mediation concept, clarify how it operates within the local justice system, and convey the procedures of the local program. A major portion of the training should focus on communication skills, problem solving and nego-

**Exhibit 7.3 Forms Used in a Typical Victim Offender Mediation
Program Management Information System**

VOM program case record form

VOM program case referral form

Letter to victim

Letter to offender

Mediator narrative report form

Progress report form

Agreement form

Case referral input log

Case referral output log

Monthly statistical summary form

tiation, and conducting the various elements of the process, including calling the victim and the offender, meeting with the participants separately, and then conducting the joint mediation session. Maximum time should be allowed for small group practice of skills and processing. Volunteers should be trained in humanistic dialogue-driven mediation, as described in Chapter One, rather than the more common legalistic settlement-driven mediation.

New programs do not have to "reinvent the wheel" of mediation training. A number of excellent training curricula and videotapes are available; many of these are listed in Appendix A. Here are some guidelines to keep in mind.

• *Maintain high quality standards for mediators*. Most VOM programs have developed extensive reliance on the use of volunteers, making it especially vital that a variety of quality control mechanisms be in place. There are several strategies programs can use to support the quality level of their mediators.

• *Screen applicants seeking mediator training*. The first step in creating a team of effective, competent mediators is an effective application process. A prospective mediator should complete a form that elicits, among other things, professional and volunteer history, reasons for choosing to become a mediator, and some aspects of personal style and values. Upon completion of the form, an interview may be conducted to screen further. Because attitude and perspective are vital to effectiveness as a mediator, the interview serves as a natural tool for assessing suitability.

• *Use mediation training as an additional tool for screening mediators.* Be intentional about observing all trainees during role-plays. Note the nature of their skills and their styles as mediators. Follow up with any concerns that arise, by co-mediating cases with trainees and discussing pertinent issues. Also solicit input from coaches.

• *Maintain quality control through a meaningful staff-mediator relationship.* To ensure the effectiveness of mediators, it is important to consider not only the quality of training but also the ongoing relationship between staff and mediators. Program staff need to be in close contact with mediators actively involved in cases. Procedures need to be established that provide for this supervisory and consultative relationship. Relatively inexperienced mediators, in particular, may be expected to contact staff after each client contact and to meet with staff both prior to and immediately following the mediation session.

Staff also need to be available for consultation on any case, as requested by the mediator. With more complex cases, it is helpful to arrange at the outset for brainstorming or consultation sessions involving the mediator, program staff, and perhaps more experienced mediators. To provide adequate supervision and support, it is advisable for program staff to co-mediate at least one case annually with each mediator.

In the interest of quality, it is helpful for training size to be limited to a group of twelve to twenty, depending on the likely number of case referrals. This gives the trainees more individual attention and provides critical information to the trainer about the learning process for each individual. It is also important to provide trainees with ample and excellent opportunities for apprenticeship, co-mediating with experienced mediators and staff before taking on their own cases. Following apprenticeship, trainees will gain the most by having frequent opportunities to mediate cases. Much that is gained through training and apprenticeship can be lost if it is not reinforced by repeated experience with actual cases. Also, mediators who are not used may lose interest. It is generally a better strategy to train fewer mediators and use them more, maintain closer contact with them, provide them with all the resources they need, and establish firm expectations about communication and collaboration with staff, evaluation, and reporting requirements, timely case management, quality procedures, continuing education, and time commitment (cases handled diligently may typically take ten to fifteen hours or more). Some programs find that a smaller cohort of mediators working on more cases is likely to increase commitment and promptness among the mediators.

• *Establish regular continuing education as a mechanism for strengthening skills.* Continuing education for mediators should be built around issues in the field, advanced skill development, needs expressed by mediators, and staff assessment of needs. Case review can be a vital component in skill development and quality control. Mediators may meet quarterly, for example, along with staff, prepared to present to the group a case scenario, along with questions and concerns that emerged from the case.

• *Maximize experiential learning through role playing.* When conducted carefully and realistically, role playing can be one of the most effective mechanisms for immersing trainees in the mediation experience and for continuing to screen for quality.

Role-plays must be performed realistically. Trainees need to visualize what is expected of them. In a role-play, the trainer might take the mediator role and experienced mediators or actual victims and offenders the other roles. The scenario should be planned out in terms of basic information and perhaps an issue or two that could arise, but it should not be scripted. Role players should seek authenticity and spontaneity. There are also some excellent videotapes that realistically portray the preparation and mediation process.

Arrange the role-play schedule so that each trainee experiences each of the roles. It is important that trainees try out the mediator role, of course, but they may learn just as much by playing the victim and offender roles and reflecting on mediator techniques and strategies from the perspective of the participants.

Coach trainees in their roles. The full value of the role-play exercise may be lost if trainees overplay or overdramatize the roles and the experience bears no resemblance to reality. Instruct trainees to use what they have learned about the victim and offender experiences to play the roles: Try to take on the actual feelings of the role you are playing. Feel what it is like to be a victim—how would you respond? Don't script the role for yourself; play it authentically and see what happens.

You should also guide trainees in debriefing the role-play. Structure the debriefing to encourage peer review. Allow the trainee playing the mediator to begin by commenting on what worked, what didn't work, and questions that arose. Then instruct the trainee in the victim or offender role to comment next, in a similar fashion, on aspects that worked for them and others that didn't and to give the mediator feedback on the amount and kind of interventions used and their impact. Allow the other trainee to debrief as well. Also invite the victim and offender role players to answer questions such as "Did you feel that you were heard—did you have the chance to tell the full story?" "Did you feel respected?" and "Did you feel that you had the power to make decisions?"

Use experienced mediators to coach role-plays. A coach can provide a useful perspective as a person experienced with the victim offender mediation process. If need be, the coach can rotate between two groups. Clear instructions should be given regarding the coach's role. In general, it is best if coaches not intervene unless requested to do so by the trainees, for example, in a moment of impasse. Following the role-play, the participants themselves should debrief the experience first before the coach comments. Effective coaches will seek to elicit information by asking questions of the participants and then, if necessary, frame their comments in terms of positives and possibilities for other ways of proceeding, as opposed to "right" and "wrong" methods. The participants will learn more if they reflect on the process and its effects and brainstorm possibilities than if they are told explicitly what should have been done.

Videotape role-plays involving trainees. Trainees may find videos of themselves in the mediator role to be quite useful. Videos may be checked out by participants for their own observation and reflection. Videos may also be used in a one-on-one coaching situation. In addition, clips of exemplary practices by trainees may be shown to the entire training group.

Design role-plays to address specific problem areas. As trainees advance toward more complex role-play scenarios, build in issues known to be a challenge to many mediators—for example, cross-cultural tensions, agreements deemed unfair or unrealistic by the mediator, or controlling or out-of-control parents.

Use input from actual victims and offenders when creating role-plays. Have them critique role-play scenarios, or ask them to create a role-play. A juvenile offender may augment a scenario with realistic features of adolescent culture.

Turn to current cases for inspiration. For example, you might consider designing individualized role-plays to reflect, unbeknown to the trainees, the actual first case they will be assigned.

Don't forget to role-play typical parts of the mediation process. For example, invite trainees into the hallway one by one to role-play greeting the participants as they arrive for the mediation session.

• *Use a multidimensional format to enhance learning.* New knowledge is better apprehended and retained when presented in a variety of ways that arouse interest and decrease boredom while allowing for important repetition of critical content.

Incorporate the personal experiences, perspectives, and knowledge of trainees into their training. Always seek to build in interactive opportunities. Ask trainees what they know about the judicial system and what they might do differently if they were designing a system. Encourage self-reflection about personal responses to conflict. Ask trainees to consider their own experiences of victimization, how they felt, what responses of others they found helpful, and what they needed and wanted in order to move on. Similarly, invite trainees to reflect on their experiences of offending or having a hurtful impact on others.

Arrange for trainees to observe the court process firsthand, including the role of victims and offenders in that setting. Consider also having trainees witness an actual mediation before they attend training, in the middle of training, splitting the training into two segments, or immediately following training. A visit to a jail or a correctional facility might also be relevant.

Make training as realistic as possible. Invite actual victims and offenders, who have participated in mediation, to speak to trainees. Representatives of victim services, probation, and the judiciary can contribute important and accurate information. A panel of adolescents can educate trainees in adolescent culture and strategies for working with youth. Illustrate important points by describing actual cases, and similarly, use material for exercises drawn directly from real cases.

Vary the training format. For each skill or process segment addressed, for example, present the material briefly; demonstrate the skill or process; distribute a worksheet, if relevant; allow for individual, dyadic, and group practice and then role-play; debrief as a group; debrief with a coach; and interact with the trainer and trainees. Use stories, written exercises, case studies, guest speakers, individual reflection, modeling, videos, overheads, charts, and other visuals.

Vary the pace as well. Alternate quiet, reflective modules with interactive or active modules. Provide generous opportunities for questions, at certain points in the schedule, and at other times make it clear that a move to the next topic is necessary.

Incorporate experiential learning whenever possible. In addition to role-plays and practice exercises targeting specific skills, allow trainees to experience other dimensions of the mediation process. For example, trainees may pair up to experiment with "zingers"—inappropriate, hurtful responses—discovering for themselves how it feels to be ignored, interrupted, judged. A brief demonstration or role-play scripted to be mishandled can be a useful tool as trainees directly experience the impact of destructive practices. Trainees may also explore "quick decisions"—for instance, what would you do if the offender's parent threatens to leave? If the offender won't talk? If the victim is willing to forgo any monetary restitution?

Make the training manual user-friendly. Consider building the manual with handouts distributed as you go. Manuals should seem accessible and helpful to trainees.

Be current and creative; fresh and interesting; engaging. Training sessions should be dynamic. Be alert to repetitious patterns that become tedious for you as a trainer. Use material that excites and challenges you. Let trainees know your own journey with mediation, how your life has been affected by the work. Always be on the lookout for new material; for example, consider using movie clips or newspaper articles portraying conflict scenarios that can be reshaped using conflict resolution skills.

• *Assist trainees in enhancing the potential of the preparation phase.* It is important that training materials and experiences be oriented toward producing something trainees will actually use in their practice of mediation. A number of components of training can enhance this potential.

Encourage trainees to consider the use of outside support persons to help prepare the participants for mediation. A victim services worker may assist the victim in determining issues and interests. A probation officer may help the offender understand the victim's perspective and prepare a tentative script reflecting ideas the offender may wish to express.

Develop materials that are useful to victims and offenders preparing for mediation. A video describing the mediation process or the experiences of the participants may be helpful for participants prior to the mediation. A self-guided workbook may be developed for use by victims and offenders that assists them in thinking about their experiences and the impact on themselves and others and in determining what they wish to express or ask for in the mediation session.

Explore with trainees methods for seeking to deepen participant interaction. Victims and offenders need to be encouraged to discover and sort out thoughts, feelings, and questions that arise in conjunction with the mediation process. Mediators may offer to role-play aspects of the mediation session with victims or offenders to help them anticipate reactions, needs, or ideas that may be evoked. It may be useful, in advance of the mediation session, for mediators to provide offenders with questions typically asked by victims or actual questions raised by the victim in that particular case so that the offender can be prepared to address the needs of the victim.

Guide trainees in understanding strategies for eliciting the goals of the participants. The parties need direct guidance when considering what they want to happen during the mediation session. Again, a walk-through of the session or a role-play may be useful in establishing personal goals for the mediation.

The ideas presented in this chapter represent only a brief overview of several important issues that need to be addressed as new communities attempt to replicate the victim offender mediation program model in their jurisdiction. Resources for more extensive program development material are included in the appendixes.

Part Two

What We Are Learning from Research

Victim offender mediation has been a focus of inquiry almost since its inception, although like most interventions, its practice has consistently outstripped both theory and research. This part opens with a summary of what has been learned from two decades of exploratory research. The summary is followed by a report on a study comparing program implementation and outcomes in the United States, Canada, and England. Finally, chapters on each of these three international studies offer a more detailed look at the variety of program auspices, formats, and practices across national boundaries.

Chapter Eight

The Impact of Victim Offender Mediation

Two Decades of Research

Innovation is often used in criminal justice as a code word for *reform*. From *jail* to *penitentiary* (theoretically inspiring penitence) to *reformatory* to *corrections center* to *halfway house* to *therapeutic community* to *community corrections* to *boot camp* to whatever the next catchphrase might be, reform has too often meant changing the name without radically changing program content. And far too often, the latest judicial "innovation" captures the imagination and zeal of a vocal following without the slightest scrutiny. Thus policies and supporting dollars outdistance the needed empirical research to determine impact and to help shape programming. Frequently, the result of enthusiasm without a critical eye is flash-in-the-pan programming, frustrated policymakers, disheartened workers, and ill-treated victims and offenders.

Victim offender mediation, too, has attracted, at times, more zeal than substance. Certain enthusiasts regard VOM as the solution for an entire juvenile court jurisdiction's "less serious offenders" or the means to handle all restitution cases more efficiently or to mollify victims while staff get on with what really needs to be done. Some have said, "This is what we have been waiting for. We will assign one probation officer to manage the thousand cases that we expect will involve restitution." Others ask, "How do we fold VOM into what we already do without it costing more or changing how we handle youth?"

Fortunately, many experts have tried to keep the expectations of VOM reasonable while assuring officials and policymakers that it is not a single program panacea. And there have been numerous efforts to evaluate and assess the working of the programs in a variety of settings during the past twenty years or so.

Though modest in proportion to many larger-scale reforms, victim offender mediation is one of the most empirically grounded justice interventions to emerge. This chapter's overview of empirical studies designed to assess the growth, implementation, and impact of VOM programs is based on a review of forty evaluation reports. The studies were conducted in fourteen states, the District of Columbia, and four Canadian provinces, as well as in England, Scotland, and New Zealand. Included are simple but informative post facto studies along with twelve that incorporate comparison groups. Five of the studies consist of in-depth secondary analysis, which is often the mark of a field of inquiry moving beyond immediate programmatic and policy questions to longer-range questions of causality. Most of the studies are quasi-experimental designs. Several studies offer more rigorous experimental designs with random assignment of subjects and higher-level statistical analysis. The outcomes of the forty studies are presented in Appendix E.

Although certain studies focus on particular sets of questions germane to local interest, overall they address questions of consumer satisfaction with the program and the criminal justice system, victim offender mediation as a means for determining and obtaining restitution, victim offender mediation as diversion from further penetration into the system, and the relationship of victim offender mediation to further delinquency or criminality.

The remainder of this chapter is devoted to considering the consequences of victim offender mediation as revealed by the studies into its implementation and impact over the past twenty years. Consequences are analyzed in seven areas: client satisfaction, client perception of fairness, restitution, diversion, recidivism, costs, and use with violent offenders.

Some topics, such as client satisfaction, client perception of fairness, and restitution, are examined in most of the studies under review, and we provide a sense of the overall findings while offering illustrations from a few specific studies. Other topics, such as recidivism and costs, are addressed by a handful of studies, and we are able to provide a bit more detailed information regarding these.

As one might expect, victim offender mediation programs are called by many names and share an array of acronyms reflecting philosophical, regional, and cultural characteristics. To reduce confusion in the following discussion of a large number of studies, programs will simply be referred to as victim offender mediation, or VOM.

Client Satisfaction

Victim offender mediation proponents often speak of their efforts as ways of humanizing the justice system. Traditionally, victims were left out of the justice process. Neither victims nor offenders had the opportunity to tell their stories and to be heard. The state stood in for the victim, and the offender seldom noticed that his or her actions affected real, live people. Victims, too, were left with stereotypes to fill their thoughts about offenders. VOM, reformers believed, offered opportunities for both parties to come together in a controlled setting to share the pain of being victimized and to answer questions of why and how. This personalizing of the consequences of crime, it was thought, would enhance satisfaction levels with the entire judicial process.

The vast majority of studies reviewed reported in some way on victims' and offenders' satisfaction with victim offender mediation and its outcomes. Regardless of program site, type of offender, type of victim, and culture, high levels of participant satisfaction were found.

Before exploring the nature of this satisfaction further, it should be noted that in all these studies, 40 to 60 percent of persons offered the opportunity to participate in VOM refused, making it evident that participation is a self-selective process. Typically, these refusals came from victims who believed the crime to be too trivial to merit the time required, feared meeting the offender, or wanted the offender to have a harsher punishment (Coates & Gehm, 1989; Umbreit, 1995a). Gehm (1990), in a study of 555 eligible cases, found 47 percent of the victims willing to participate. In this study, the primarily white victims were more likely to participate if the offender was white, if the offense was a misdemeanor, and if the victim was representing an institution.

Offenders were sometimes advised by lawyers not to participate (Schneider, 1986). And some simply didn't want to be bothered (Coates & Gehm, 1989).

The voluntary nature of participating in VOM is a self-selection factor overlaying these findings. The high levels of satisfaction may have something to do with the opportunity to choose. Perhaps those who are able to choose among justice options are more satisfied with their experiences.

Several studies noted that victim willingness to participate was driven by a desire to receive restitution, to hold the offender accountable, to learn more about the wherefores of the crime, to share the victim's pain with the offender, to avoid court processing, to help the offender change behavior, or to see the offender adequately punished. Offenders choosing to participate often wanted to "do the right thing" and to "get the whole experience behind them" (Coates & Gehm, 1989; Perry, Lajeunesse, & Woods, 1987; Umbreit, 1989a, 1995a; T. Roberts, 1995; Niemeyer & Shichor, 1996).

Expressions of satisfaction with VOM is consistently high for both victims and offenders regardless of site, culture, and seriousness of offense. Typically, eight or nine out of ten participants report being satisfied with the process and with the resulting agreement (Davis, Tichane, & Grayson, 1980; Perry et al., 1987; Coates & Gehm, 1989; Marshall, 1990; Umbreit, 1991, 1994, 1995a; Warner, 1992; Umbreit & Coates, 1993; T. Roberts, 1995; Carr, 1998; L. Roberts, 1998).

Participants in one British study (Umbreit & Roberts, 1996, discussed in more detail in Chapter Twelve) yielded some of the lowest satisfaction scores among the studies reviewed. Although 84 percent of the victims who engaged in face-to-face mediation were satisfied with the outcome, most victims did not meet face to face with an offender. These victims undertook indirect mediation, depending on "shuttle diplomacy" between the parties without face-to-face meetings; only 74 percent were satisfied with the experience. These findings were consistent with an earlier study done in England in which a small subsample of participants were interviewed, indicating that 62 percent of individual victims and 71 percent of corporate victims were satisfied (Dignan, 1990). About half of the offenders responding reported being satisfied. Participants involved in face-to-face mediation were more satisfied than those who worked with a go-between who facilitated indirect mediation.

Victims often reported being satisfied with the opportunity to share their stories and their pain resulting from the crime event. A victim stated she had wanted to "let the kid know he hurt me personally. [It was] not just the money. . . . I felt raped." Some expressed satisfaction with their role in the process. One victim said, "We were both allowed to speak. . . . [The mediator] didn't put words into anybody's mouth" (Umbreit, 1988, p. 988).

Another female victim indicated, "I felt a little better that I've a stake in the punishment" (Coates & Gehm, 1989, p. 255). Another indicated that "it was important to find out what happened, to hear his story, and why he did it and how" (Umbreit & Coates, 1992, p. 106). Numerous victims were in serious need of closure. A victim of violent crime indicated that prior to mediation, "I was consumed with hate and rage and was worried what I would do when he got out" (Flaten, 1996, p. 398).

Of course, not all victims were so enamored with the process. A small but vocal minority of victims was not pleased with the program. A male victim complained, "It's like being hit by a car and having to get out and help the other driver when all you were doing was minding your own business" (Coates & Gehm, 1989, p. 254). A Canadian stated, "The mediation process was not satisfactory, especially the outcome. I was not repaid for damages or given compensation one year later. The offender has not been adequately dealt with. I don't feel I was properly compensated" (Umbreit, 1995b, p. 162).

Offenders generally report surprise at having positive experiences. As one youth said, "He understood the mistake I made, and I really did appreciate him for it" (Umbreit, 1991, p. 195). Some reported changes: "to understand how the victim feels makes me different" (Umbreit & Coates, 1992, p. 18) and "most satisfying was the self-responsibility" (Umbreit, 1995b, p. 173). One Canadian offender stated his pleasure quite succinctly: "Without mediation I would have been convicted" (Umbreit, 1995b, p. 144).

The following comment reflects the feelings of a relatively small number of offenders who felt that victims at least occasionally abused the process: "We didn't take half the stuff she said we did; she either didn't have the stuff or someone else broke in too" (Coates & Gehm, 1985, p. 12). An offender in Albuquerque also believed that the process allowed the victim too much power: "The guy was trying to cheat me—he was coming up with all these lists of items he claimed I took" (Umbreit & Coates, 1992, p. 110). Some offenders felt powerless to refute the accusations of victims.

Secondary analysis of satisfaction data from a U.S. study and a Canadian study yielded remarkably similar results (Bradshaw & Umbreit, 1998; Umbreit & Bradshaw, in press). Using stepwise multiple regression procedures to determine the variables most associated with victim satisfaction, three variables emerged to explaining over 40 percent of the variance. In each study, the key variables associated with victim satisfaction were that the victim felt good about the mediator, perceived the resulting restitution agreement as fair, and had, for whatever reason, a strong initial desire to meet the offender. This third variable supports the notion that self-selection and choice are involved in longer-run satisfaction. These findings also underscore the important role of the mediator and, of course, the actual outcome or agreement resulting from mediation.

These high levels of satisfaction with victim offender mediation also translated into relatively high levels of satisfaction with the criminal justice system. Where comparison groups were studied, victims and offenders going through mediation reported being far more satisfied with the criminal justice system than those going through traditional court prosecution (Davis et al., 1980; Umbreit & Coates, 1993; Umbreit, 1995a). For example, a multisite U.S. study of VOM in four states (Umbreit & Coates, 1993; Umbreit, 1994; discussed in more detail in Chapter Nine) found that victims of juvenile crime were significantly more likely to be satisfied (79 percent) with the manner in which the justice system dealt with their case than similar victims (57 percent) who went through the regular court process.

Fairness

Related to satisfaction is the question of fairness. Many of the studies asked participants about the fairness of the mediation process and of the resulting agreement (Davis et al., 1980; Coates & Gehm, 1989; Umbreit, 1988, 1989a, 1991, 1995b; Umbreit & Coates, 1992).

Not surprisingly, given the high levels of satisfaction, the vast majority of VOM participants (typically over 80 percent), regardless of setting, culture, or type of offense, reported believing that the process was fair to both sides and that the resulting agreement was fair. Again, these experiences led to feelings that the overall criminal justice system was fair. Where comparison groups were employed, individuals exposed to mediation were more likely to feel that they had been treated fairly than those going through the traditional court proceedings. One study of burglary victims in Minneapolis (Umbreit, 1989a) found that 80 percent of those who went through VOM indicated that they felt the criminal justice system was fair, compared to only 37 percent of burglary victims who did not participate in VOM.

Statements from victims and offenders about fairness bore out the statistical assessment. Typical comments were along the lines of "The mediator was not biased; she was not judgmental" and "He listened to everyone during the meeting" (Umbreit & Coates, 1993; Umbreit, 1994). A few participants, however, did not feel the same way. Comments like "He seemed more like an advocate for the kid" and "She seemed kind of one-sided" in favor of the victim (Umbreit & Coates, 1993) reflected perceptions of unbalance and unfairness in the mediation process. Although positive comments far outweighed negative ones, the negative statements provided insight into unintended consequences the mediation process may have on participants.

The overall positive satisfaction and fairness experiences, however, have generated support for VOM as a criminal justice option. When asked, typically nine out of ten participants would recommend a VOM program to others (Coates & Gehm, 1989; Umbreit, 1991).

Restitution

Early on, program advocates regarded restitution as a by-product of bringing offender and victim together in a face-to-face meeting. It was considered secondary to the meeting, which afforded each party the opportunity to talk about what happened. The current emphasis on humanistic "dialogue-driven" mediation reflects this traditional view of restitution's secondary importance. But a few jurisdictions are beginning to regard VOM as a promising major vehicle for achieving restitution for the victim. These jurisdictions view the meeting as necessary to establish appropriate compensation for the victim and obtain the offender's commitment to honor a restitution contract. Victims frequently report that even though restitution was what initially motivated their participation in VOM, what they appreciated most about the program was the opportunity to talk with the offender (Coates & Gehm, 1989; Umbreit & Coates, 1993).

In many settings, restitution is inextricably linked with victim offender mediation. About half the studies under review looked at restitution as an outcome of mediation (Collins, 1984; Coates & Gehm, 1989, Perry et al., 1987; Umbreit, 1988, 1991, 1994; Galaway, 1989; Warner, 1992; Roy, 1993; Umbreit & Coates, 1993). Of those cases that led to a meeting, typically 90 percent or more generated agreements. Restitution of one form or another (monetary, community service, or direct service to the victim) was part of the vast majority of these agreements. Looking across the studies, approximately 80 to 90 percent of the contracts are reported as completed. In some instances, the length of the contract exceeded the length of the study.

One study was able to compare restitution completion between young offenders who participated in VOM with a matched group who did not (Umbreit & Coates, 1993). In that instance, 81 percent of participating youth completed their contracts, contrasted with 57 percent of those not in the VOM program, a statistically significant finding. In another study comparing an Indiana county whose restitution was integrated into victim offender mediation with a Michigan county with court-imposed restitution, no difference in completion rates was found (Roy, 1993). Each was just shy of 80 percent completion.

Diversion

Many VOM programs are nominally established to divert youthful offenders into less costly, less time-consuming, and, according to some observers, less severe options. Just as diversion was a goal lauded by many, others expressed concern about the unintended consequence of widening the net, that is, ushering in youth and adults to experience a sanction more severe than they would have if VOM did not exist. While much talk continues on this topic, little study has been devoted to it. Only a handful of the studies reviewed here address this question.

One of the broadest studies considering the diversion question was that conducted over a three-year period in Kettering, Northamptonshire, England (Dignan, 1990). Offenders participating in the VOM program were matched with similar nonparticipating offenders from a neighboring jurisdiction. The author concludes that at least 60 percent of the offenders participating in the Kettering program were true diversions from court prosecution. Jurisdictional comparisons also led him to conclude that there was a 13 percent widening of the net effect, much less than local observers would have predicted.

In a Glasgow, Scotland–based agency where numbers were sufficiently large to allow randomly assignment of individuals between the VOM program and a comparison group going through the traditional process, it was discovered that 43 percent of the latter group were not prosecuted (Warner, 1992). However, most of them pleaded guilty and were fined. This would suggest that VOM in this instance was a more severe sanction and indeed widened the net of government control.

In a very large three-county study of mediation in North Carolina (Clarke, Valente, & Mace, 1992), results on diversion were mixed. In two counties, mediation had no impact on diverting offenders from court. In the third, Henderson County, however, the results were dramatically different. The authors concluded, "The Henderson program's effect on trials was impressive; it may have reduced trials by as much as two-thirds" (p. 45).

Mediation impact on incarceration was explored in an Indiana-Ohio study by comparing consequences for seventy-three youth and adults going through VOM programs with those for a matched sample of individuals who were processed in the traditional manner (Coates & Gehm, 1989). VOM offenders spent less time incarcerated than their counterparts did. And when incarcerated, they did county jail time rather than state time. The length and place of incarceration also had substantial implications for costs.

Recidivism

Although recidivism may best be regarded as an indicator of society's overall response to juvenile and adult offenders, it is a traditional measure used to evaluate the long-term impact of justice programs. Accordingly, a number of studies designed to assess VOM have incorporated measures of recidivism.

Some simply report rearrest or reconviction rates for offenders going through the VOM program under study (Carr, 1998; L. Roberts, 1998). Since no comparison group or before-and-after outcomes are reported, these recidivism reports have local value but very little meaning for readers unfamiliar with typical rates for that particular region.

One of the first studies to report recidivism in connection with VOM was part of a much larger research project involving restitution programs (Schneider, 1986). Youth randomly assigned to a Washington, D.C., VOM program were less likely to have subsequent offenses resulting in referral to a juvenile or adult court than youth in a comparison probation group. These youth were tracked for more than thirty months. The recidivism results were 53 percent for the first group and 63 percent for the second, a statistically significant difference. A third group, those referred to mediation but who refused to participate, also did better than the probation group. This group's recidivism rate was 55 percent.

Marshall and Merry (1990) report recidivism on two programs handling adult offenders in Coventry and Wolverhampton, England. The results are tentative but encouraging. At both sites, the offenders were divided into four groups: those who did not participate in mediation at all, those who were involved in discussions with staff even though their victims were unwilling to participate, those who were involved in indirect mediation, and those who met their victims face to face. Offender records were analyzed to determine criminal behavior for comparable periods before referral to program and after program intervention.

In Coventry, while there was no statistically significant difference between the no-work or no-participation group and the others, offenders who went through direct mediation and those who received individual attention even though their victims were unwilling to meet did better—they either committed fewer crimes or committed less serious offenses.

In Wolverhampton, the indirect-mediation group fared best, with 74 percent of offenders improving their behavior, compared to 55 percent for offenders in direct mediation, 45 percent for individuals receiving staff attention only, and 36 percent for those not involved in the program. The authors regard these findings as highly tentative and remain puzzled about why at one site indirect mediation fared so much better than direct while the reverse was noted at the other.

The study based in Kettering (Dignan, 1990) compared recidivism data between VOM offenders who went through face-to-face mediation and those who were exposed only to "shuttle mediation." The former group did somewhat better than the latter: 15.4 percent versus 21.6 percent. As with satisfaction measures reported earlier, face-to-face mediation seems to generate better results than the less personal indirect mediation both in the short run and the longer run.

In a study of youth participating in VOM programs in four states, youth in mediation had lower recidivism rates after a year than a matched comparison group of youth who did not go through mediation (Umbreit & Coates, 1993). Overall, across sites, 18 percent of the program youth reoffended, compared to 27 percent for the comparison youth. Program youth also tended to reappear in court for less serious charges than their comparison counterparts did.

The study conducted in Elkhart and Kalamazoo Counties (Roy, 1993) found little difference in recidivism between youth going through the VOM program and the court-imposed restitution program. VOM youth had a slightly higher rate, 29 percent versus 27 percent. The author noted that the VOM cohort included more felons than the court-imposed restitution cohort did.

A study of 125 youth in a Tennessee VOM program (Nugent & Paddock, 1995) reported that these youth were less likely to reoffend than a randomly selected comparison group: 19.8 percent versus 33.1 percent. The VOM youth who did reoffend did so with less serious charges than their comparison counterparts did.

A sizable cohort of nearly eight hundred youth going through mediation in Cobb County, Georgia, between 1993 and 1996 was followed, along with a comparison group from an earlier time period (Stone, Helms, & Edgeworth, 1998). No significant difference in return rates was found: 34.2 percent mediated versus 36.7 percent nonmediated. Three-quarters of the mediated youth who returned to court did so because of violation of the conditions of mediation agreements.

An article by Nugent, Umbreit, Wiinamaki, and Paddock (in press) features a rigorous reanalysis of recidivism data reported in four previous studies involving a total sample of 1,298 juvenile offenders, 619 who participated in VOM and 679 who did not. Using logistic regression procedures, the authors determined that VOM youth recidivated at a statistically significant 32 percent lower rate than non-VOM youth and that when they did reoffend, the VOM youth committed less serious offenses than the non-VOM youth.

All in all, recidivism findings across a fair number of sites and settings suggest that VOM is at least as effective as traditional approaches at reducing recidivism. And in a good number of instances, youth going through mediation programs fare considerably better.

Cost

The costs of correctional programs are difficult to compare. Several studies reviewed here addressed the issue of costs.

Cost per case is obviously influenced by the number of cases handled and the amount of time devoted to each case. The results of a detailed cost analysis in a Scottish study were mixed (Warner, 1992). Mediation was less costly than other options in some instances and more in others. The author notes that given the "marginal scope" of these programs, it remains difficult to evaluate their cost impact if implemented on a scale large enough to affect overall program administration.

Evaluation of a large-scale VOM program in California led authors to conclude that cost per case was reduced dramatically as the program expanded (Niemeyer & Shichor, 1996). Cost per case was $250.

An alternative way of evaluating the cost of VOM is to consider its broader system impact. Reduction of incarceration time served can yield considerable savings to a state or county (Coates & Gehm, 1989). Reduction of trials, as in Henderson County, North Carolina, where trials were reduced by two-thirds, would have a tremendous impact at the county level (Clarke et al., 1992). And researchers evaluating a VOM program in Cobb County, Georgia, point out that even though they did not do a cost analysis, time is money (Stone et al., 1998). The time required to process mediated cases was only a third of that needed for nonmediated cases.

The potential cost savings of VOM programs when they are employed as true alternatives rather than as showcase add-ons are significant. But caution is warranted: like any other program option, these programs can be swamped with cases to the point that quality is compromised. And in the quest for savings there is the temptation to expand the eligibility criteria to include individuals who would not otherwise penetrate the system or to take on serious cases that the program staff are ill equipped to manage. Staff and administrators must be prepared to ask, "Cost savings at what cost?"

VOM and Violent Offenders

In 1990, a survey of victim offender mediation programs in the juvenile justice system noted that most programs excluded violent offenders and sex offenders (Hughes & Schneider, 1990). Two-thirds of cases reported by VOM programs in a 1996–1997 survey (Umbreit & Greenwood, 1999) involved misdemeanor offenses. Forty-five percent of reporting programs worked only with juveniles, and 9 percent handled adults only; the remainder worked with both. These figures support the notion that VOM is typically used as a "front-end" diversionary option, reserved primarily for "lightweight" cases.

Many program staff contend that if they are to work with burglary and moderately serious assault cases, programs must also accept the less serious cases. Others would argue that these so-called less serious cases nevertheless involve human loss and tragedy. And still others claim that making crime a human problem for offenders at these less serious levels will prevent more serious crimes from occurring. As indicated in our discussion of recidivism, there is modest empirical support for these contentions.

Without disparaging the work of VOM programs with cases perceived and defined as "less serious," it should be noted that significant developments are occurring marking a subtle shift in the use of VOM. In the 1996–1997 survey, many program administrators indicated that programs "are being asked to mediate crimes of increasing severity and complexity." And "virtually all interviewees indicated that advanced training is necessary in working with cases of severe violence" (Umbreit & Greenwood, 1999, p. 243).

Unrelated to the general pressure to take on more severe and more complex cases, certain individuals and programs already specialize in working with the most violent kinds of crime. Studies involving murder, vehicular homicide, manslaughter, armed robbery, and sexual assault in such disparate locations as New York, Wisconsin, Alaska, Minnesota, Texas, Ohio, and British Columbia (Umbreit, 1989b; T. Roberts, 1995; Flaten, 1996; Umbreit, Bradshaw, & Coates, 1999; Umbreit & Brown, 1999; Umbreit & Vos, 2000) are yielding important data for shaping mediation work with violent offenders and victims of violent crime.

These very intense, time-consuming mediation efforts have shown promising, positive results. Victims who seek and choose this kind of encounter and dialogue with an individual who brought unspeakable tragedy to their lives report feelings of relief, a sense of closure, and gratefulness for not being forgotten, silenced, or ignored. In several states, the number of victims seeking to meet with violent offenders far exceeds the resources available to accommodate their desires.

Summary

Victim offender mediation has received considerable research attention, more than many other justice alternatives. With over twenty years of experience and research data, there is a solid basis for the following conclusions:

1. For persons who choose to participate—be they victims or offenders—victim offender mediation and dialogue engenders very high levels of satisfaction with the program and with the criminal justice system.

2. Participants typically regard the process and resulting agreements as fair.

3. Restitution comprises part of most agreements, and more than eight out of ten agreements are completed satisfactorily.

4. VOM can be an effective tool for diverting juvenile offenders from further penetration into the system, yet it may also become a means for widening the net of social control.

5. VOM is at least as effective as traditional probation options in reducing recidivism and some VOM programs are far more effective.

6. In instances where comparative costs have been considered, VOM offers considerable promise for reducing or containing costs.

7. There is growing interest in adopting mediation practices for working with victims and offenders involved in severely violent crime, and preliminary research indicates promising results, including the need for a far more lengthy and intensive process of preparing the parties.

For at least a significant minority of persons affected by the justice system, VOM is regarded as an effective means for holding offenders accountable for their actions. Although a fairly extensive base of research on victim offender mediation at numerous sites supports this contention, more work needs to be done. Most of the studies reported offer results that are at best suggestive because of the limitations of their research methodology. Far more rigorous studies, including random assignment, control groups, and longitudinal designs, are required. Yet in the real world of field research in the criminal justice system, the twenty-five-year experience of victim offender mediation has been shown to be one of the most promising and empirically grounded reform movements to emerge during the last quarter of the twentieth century.

Chapter Nine

Cross-National Assessment of Victim Offender Mediation

This chapter provides an overview and summary of a series of studies conducted at the University of Minnesota that focused on the outcome of victim offender mediation programs in the United States, Canada, and England. Chapters Ten, Eleven, and Twelve provide more details on each of these nations, including information about program development and processes.

The cross-national assessment was initiated as an effort to look at victim offender mediation as it is being developed in different contexts using, to the extent possible, common research questions, common methodology, and common instrumentation. It consists of three separate studies of the consequences of participating in victim offender mediation, covering programs in four states in the United States (Umbreit & Coates, 1993; Umbreit, 1994), four provinces of Canada (Umbreit, 1995b), and two cities in England (Umbreit & Roberts, 1996). The studies were conducted between 1990 and 1996, beginning with the four-site study in the United States, followed by the four-site study in Canada, and then the two-site study in England. VOM is implemented in different ways in different places, reflecting cultural norms and mores. An overarching question the research hoped to answer was, given the vast range of possible ways of doing victim offender mediation, are there common experiences shared among participants that can inform program delivery and justice policy?

Note: This chapter is based on Umbreit, Coates, and Roberts (2000). Reprinted with permission of John Wiley & Sons, Inc.

The Program Sites

The four sites in the United States consisted of three private non-profit community-based organizations, located in: Albuquerque, New Mexico; Minneapolis, Minnesota; and Oakland, California; and a county probation department located in Texas. All four programs work solely with juveniles, and nearly all the referrals came from juvenile court and probation staff.

The four programs in Canada were private nonprofit community-based organizations located in cities in different provinces: Langley, British Columbia; Calgary, Alberta; Winnipeg, Manitoba; and Ottawa-Carleton, Ontario. They provide a wide range of diversity in program design, caseload size, and case management procedures. The programs in Langley and Calgary worked primarily with juvenile offenders and received case referrals from probation staff and judges. The programs in Winnipeg and Ottawa worked primarily with adults; participants were referred by the prosecuting attorney's office.

The programs in England were located in Coventry and Leeds. Both were administered by the local probation service and worked primarily with adults. At the time of the study (1993), 15 percent of individuals going through mediation in England participated in direct face-to-face mediation as described in Part One of this book. The remainder participated in "indirect mediation," in which the mediator shuttled back and forth between victim and offender. This group is analyzed separately.

Samples and Data Collection

Each of the three studies was based on quasi-experimental designs with postmediation interviews and comparison groups of similar cases. At each program site, victims and offenders participating in the mediation efforts and willing to be part of the research studies were interviewed. At all except the Texas site, a comparison sample of individuals who were referred but did not participate in the mediation was also interviewed. In addition, in the United States, a second comparison group consisting of similar participants who were not referred to mediation and who were matched along several important variables was also used by all of the sites except Texas. Further details of the design in each of the three countries will be taken up in subsequent chapters.

At the United States sites, 280 victims and 252 offenders who went through mediation were interviewed along with 210 victims and 206 offenders who did not participate in mediation. In Canada, 183 participating victims and 159 offenders were interviewed, while the comparison group consisted of 140 victims and 128 offenders. The English experience was a bit different, given the nature of the programs operating there. Interviewed were 19 victims and 16 offenders who experienced direct face-to-face mediation, 25 victims and 14 offenders who participated in indirect mediation, and 26 victims and 23 offenders who did not participate in any type of mediation.

At each of the sites, participants who were willing to be interviewed were questioned two to four months after going through the mediation process. Interviews were conducted either face to face or by phone. Questions focused on participant satisfaction with the mediation process and with the overall criminal justice system response to the case.

Extensive observation work was also conducted at all the U.S. and Canadian sites, and portions of the resulting qualitative data will be cited here to provide a flavor of the mediation process and participant comments. Similar interview schedules were used at all sites, although the specific language and wording of the questions was adapted to the cultural context and program specifics of the three nations.

Who Participates?

Of candidates who were referred to mediation, 40 percent in the United States, 41 percent in Canada, and 7 percent in England actually participated in direct face-to-face mediation; an additional 39 percent in England participated in indirect mediation. It should be understood that in all programs, in order for a case to move forward to mediation, both the victim and the offender must agree to participate. Reasons that referred cases did not reach mediation were varied. Some offenders refused to become involved. Some victims changed their minds. Occasionally, the matter was resolved before getting to the point of mediation.

Clearly, the emphasis in most situations is to underscore the voluntary nature of participation for both victim and offender. Atypically, some, particularly offenders, felt that they had no choice but to participate. One Canadian offender put it quite succinctly: "It wasn't a choice—I didn't want a record." Of course, the offender made a choice that might result in his not receiving a record. If offenders were routinely required or coerced into participating, however, the percentage of cases referred resulting in mediation would be much higher. Such coerced participation, though, would undermine the very notion of victim offender mediation.

In the U.S. samples, the typical participating victim was a white male in his mid-thirties. The typical offender was a fifteen-year-old white or Hispanic male with no criminal record, charged with a property offense (most frequently reported was burglary), who was referred as a means of diverting the youngster from more formal system handling. There were no significant differences between those who chose to participate and those who did not.

Across the Canadian samples, the typical victim again was a Caucasian male in his early to mid-thirties. On average, the offenders were older than in the U.S. study, with an average age of twenty-four. Offenders were typically white males charged with assault. There were no significant differences between those who participated in mediation and those who did not. Referrals generally came from probation or the Crown's Prosecutor's Office.

In England, both victims and offenders were typically male. There were some age differences distinguishing the participants in direct mediation from those in indirect mediation. Victims who went through direct mediation averaged thirty-four years old, while those in the indirect mediation averaged forty-six. Offenders who went through direct mediation also tended to be younger, with a mean age of nineteen. Those who were involved in indirect mediation averaged twenty-seven. The most frequent offense charged was burglary. Most referrals were made by probation services.

Results

Key findings in the three studies are highlighted for areas covered by all three.

Participant Satisfaction with the Mediation Process

Both victims and offenders at all sites reported high levels of satisfaction with the mediation process (see Table 9.1). About nine out of ten victims and offenders in the United States and Canada were satisfied with the mediation outcome. In England, 84 percent of victims were satisfied with the outcome of face-to-face mediation, compared to 74 percent of those participating in indirect mediation. The comparable numbers for offenders were 100 percent and 79 percent.

Victim participants in the United States indicated that their satisfaction with the mediation process was determined by their attitude toward the mediator, the fairness of the restitution agreement, and the importance of meeting the offender.

An English woman commented that she felt like an "entirely different person" after having received information about the crime from the offender through an indirect mediation effort.

At a U.S. site, a juvenile offender noted that the co-mediators "were open minded and helped us to suggest a compromise to the victim when there was a stalemate."

A victim from the United States stated, "I feel good about it because it worked out well, because I think the kid finally realized the impact of what happened and that's not what he wants to do with himself."

Table 9.1 Participant Perceptions of the Victim Offender Mediation Experience

	United States		Canada		England Direct		England Indirect	
	Victim	Offender	Victim	Offender	Victim	Offender	Victim	Offender
Satisfied with mediation outcome	90% (204)	91% (181)	89% (117)	91% (152)	84% (19)	100% (15)	74% (19)	79% (14)
Satisfied with criminal justice system referral of case to mediation	79% (204)	87% (181)	78% (178)	74% (157)	68% (19)	73% (15)	57% (23)	86% (14)
Justice system processing of case by referral to mediation was fair	83% (204)	89% (178)	80% (174)	80% (156)	71% (14)	80% (15)	50% (20)	100% (12)
Mediated agreement was fair	89% (200)	88% (175)	92% (170)	92% (143)				
Telling of impact of crime was important	91% (166)	90% (137)	89% (181)	84% (140)	90% (41)	93% (29)		

An English victim documented her satisfaction with mediation in the following manner: "I have gained a sense of security from mediation. . . . It helped to see the offender's face."

An English offender gave an overview of the process while expressing satisfaction: "Mediation made me feel better. . . . I was able to apologize and reimburse the victim. . . . [That] helped me come to terms with it and put the crime behind me."

Meeting face to face was emphasized in comments at all three sites as the most satisfying aspect of participating in mediation.

Participant Satisfaction with the Criminal Justice System

Persons participating in mediation efforts reported fairly high levels of satisfaction with the larger criminal justice system for referring their case to mediation. In Canada and the United States, nearly eight out of ten victims were satisfied with having been referred. U.S. offenders were a little more pleased than their Canadian counterparts: 87 percent compared with 74 percent. When examined with comparison groups, victims in mediation in the U.S. sample were significantly more likely to have felt satisfied with the justice system's referral of their case to mediation than victims who did not meet with the offender. Both victims and offenders in the Canadian mediation samples were significantly more likely to have felt satisfied with the justice system's referral of their case to mediation than those who did not enter the mediation process.

The English were less certain overall that being referred was a good idea. Sixty-eight percent of victims in direct mediation and 57 percent of those in indirect mediation were satisfied. The offenders were more satisfied with the criminal justice system's referral of their case to mediation: 73 percent of those in direct mediation and 86 percent in indirect mediation reported being so. Differences between groups were not significant.

A number of victims were pleased that the justice system was able to give the offender a "last chance," and that had a significant part to play in their decision to participate in mediation.

A Canadian victim pointed out that "the justice system seems to be making an effort to personalize an essentially impersonal, inefficient, and ineffective system."

Another Canadian felt that the system had offered "a sense of control. It gave me a voice. I felt powerless before."

Participant Perception of Criminal or Juvenile Justice System Fairness

Another way of looking at the participants' view of the criminal or juvenile justice system is whether they believed they were dealt with fairly by the referral of their case to mediation. When taking fairness into consideration, responses are slightly higher. Eighty-three percent of the U.S. victims and 89 percent of offenders believed the system to be fair in referring their case to mediation. In Canada, eight out of ten victims and offenders agreed that the system had been fair. Again, the English were a bit more skeptical. Seventy-one percent of the victims participating in face-to-face mediation thought the system was fair, but only half of those involved in indirect mediation agreed. Offenders were more likely to rate the justice system as fair: 80 percent of those in direct mediation and 100 percent of those in indirect mediation perceived it to be fair.

In general, the criminal justice system and its response was viewed as more fair by individuals who went through mediation than those in the comparison groups who did not. In the United States, more than 80 percent of the victims and offenders in mediation believed the system to be fair. An equally high percentage of nonparticipating offenders thought the system was fair. However, barely half of the victims not participating in mediation experienced the system as fair. The findings are similar at the other sites, with 80 percent of participants in Canada reporting fair treatment, while only 43 percent of nonparticipating victims and 56 percent of nonparticipating offenders regarded the system's response to their case as fair. The differences between victims in mediation and the comparison group in the U.S. samples were significant, while in Canada both the victim and offender differences with the respective comparisons groups were not significant. The response in England was more subdued, with nearly 60 percent of victims in mediation versus 50 percent of those not in mediation regarding the system as fair. Among offenders, the numbers were 89 percent and 56 percent, respectively. None of the differences found in the English samples, however, were significant.

An English victim spoke to the question of system fairness in this way: "I experienced fairness—he paid up." A Canadian offender expressed his sense of the system's fairness in very personal terms: "It's way better than sitting in front of a judge. Incarceration doesn't do any good, and it's not the judge who was involved, it's the two people."

Participant View of Whether the Mediated Agreement Is Fair

More specifically, participants in the United States and Canada were asked whether they believed the particular agreement worked out between offender and victim was fair. The response was quite positive: about nine out of ten victims and offenders felt that their particular agreement was fair.

Fairness often becomes an issue for discussion in face-to-face mediation, as the following excerpt from one of the U.S. mediation sessions illustrates.

"I would like to get my $500 back," Alice, the victim, says. "I think it is only fair. After all, I had to suffer all the hassles besides the loss of the car itself."

"What about you, Edward?" the mediator asks the offender. "What's fair from your point of view?"

"You want to know what I think is fair?"

"Yeah." Alice is watching Edward intently.

"Sure, she deserves her money back," says Edward looking directly at Alice. "That's only fair." He turns and addresses the mediator. "Since there were four of us, can it be split four ways?"

Alice also turns to the mediator. "That's what I was expecting."

The Importance of Telling One's Story

One of the hoped-for outcomes of victim offender mediation programs is making the justice process more human, that is, recognizing that real people are hurt by crime and that real people commit crime. Conceptually, an important way of facilitating this notion that crime is a human event is getting the participants to tell their stories of the event. A victim may talk of coming home and finding the house in disarray, conveying how it felt and still feels to know that one's private space has been invaded. The offender may speak of sporadic occurrences that led up to the burglary, perhaps group pressures, alcohol, or drugs.

Two to four months after the mediation session, participants were asked how important this telling of their story or telling about the impact of the crime was for them. In each country, about 90 percent of the participants said it was important. The study design in the United States allows this response to be placed in perspective. In that sample, subjects who participated in mediation were interviewed again one week prior to their mediation session. In the premediation interviews, 79 percent thought telling of the impact was important, compared to 91 percent who so indicated in their interviews after the mediation was concluded, a finding that was statistically significant.

Not only was the telling of the impact or of the personal story important, but so was listening to the other person. As one U.S. victim stated, "It was important to find out what happened, to hear his story and why he did it and how." One Canadian offender said, "I was able to apologize and talk and have my story heard."

Fear Reduction

Face-to-face mediation reduces an individual's fear of being revictimized by the same offender. Such fears are frequently reported by crime victims after the initial crime incident through such comments as "Will they come back now that they know how to get in?" Prior to meeting the juvenile offender, 23 percent of the participating victims in the U.S. study feared they would be revictimized by the same offender. Only 10 percent expressed such fears after mediation; that is a 56 percent reduction in fear of revictimization, a finding that was statistically significant.

In the Canadian study, after the mediation session, 11 percent of participating victims expressed fear of being revictimized by the same offender, compared to 31 percent of similar victims who did not participate in a mediation session with the offender, a finding that was statistically significant. The findings in England were not significant but tended in the same direction. Victims who participated in mediation reported less fear of revictimization by the same offender than victims who did not participate (16 percent versus 33 percent), and victims in direct mediation were less fearful than victims in indirect mediation (11 percent versus 21 percent).

One Canadian victim expressed reassurance about not being victimized by the offender again. "It is very unlikely that he'll do another crime against me, but I would have never have known that if it hadn't been for mediation." Another Canadian indicated, "I've gotten some questions answered. [I] was assured and put at rest [the fear of the] offender wanting to victimize me personally."

Restitution

Restitution is an important by-product of victim offender mediation in both the United States and Canada, where over 90 percent of the mediated cases resulted in restitution agreements. Some kind of restitution was often of importance to the victim. Victims in the

United States reported, "Getting paid back was real important because I was in a very bad financial situation at the time." "The money was not important, but it was very important that the offender worked off the time and that she had done something that was of benefit to me." "He owes me that." Some Canadian victims were also clear that restitution, in some form, motivated their participation: "I chose mediation for getting paid back and for the inconvenience." "It was a chance to work out an agreement. The agreement was getting this resolved to my satisfaction." "I was compensated for my damages."

Data are available from two U.S. sites regarding restitution completion. At those sites (Albuquerque and Minneapolis), 81 percent of the agreements were successfully completed, compared to 58 percent completed by a matched comparison group that had restitution set by the court. This difference is statistically significant. One can at least speculate that face-to-face contact between offender and victim reinforces the importance of fulfilling restitution agreements. The agreement in those cases was made between two persons rather than imposed by an external authority.

Recidivism

One hundred sixty youth from three of the sites (Albuquerque, Minneapolis, and Oakland) in the United States were followed to determine if they committed a new criminal offense within a year after mediation. Eighteen percent of the youth in mediation committed a new offense within a year, compared to 27 percent of those in a matched comparison group. This finding of reduced recidivism was statistically significant.

Implications

A number of general implications arise from this overview of the three differing national applications of VOM.

Model Flexibility and Transportability

The practice of victim offender mediation varies from nation to nation and site to site. Depending on local situations and cultural conditions, these programs work with a wide range of offenders and victims, and often with their families as well. Some programs specialize in working with youth offenders, and others focus on adult offenders. Some are used for purposes of diversion before formal adjudication or official finding of guilt, and others occur after adjudication, often as part of the court disposition. Most of the programs studied were administered by the private sector; some were operated by local and provincial governments. Most emphasized the use of volunteer mediators; some relied on paid workers. Some operated in small localities and others in large cities. Some worked with a substantial number of minority offenders and victims, and others did not. On the one hand, the great diversity of programming makes research difficult. That is, it is nearly impossible to control for all the possible differences found in the operation of these programs. On the other hand, there is positive news to be learned from the diversity. The model itself—bringing victim and offender together, usually face-to-face—can be managed in many ways that achieve the purpose of humanizing the justice process and giving participants a role in that process as well as stake in the outcome.

The fact that we find victim offender mediation programs in different forms in divergent communities in three nations means that the basic concept is highly transportable. The structure of the programs may be somewhat different, yet the kernel of bringing victims and offenders together as a way of achieving justice remains constant.

High Satisfaction Levels in Various Settings

No matter what the population being worked with, whether the private or public sector is administering the program, where the program is being used within the justice process, whether mediators are volunteers or paid (as long as they are well trained), or what form the program takes, victims and offenders who have participated in VOM programs consistently indicate high levels of satisfaction with the process and with the outcome. It is remarkable to see a justice program have such high appeal anywhere. When it does occur, such appeal is often attributed to the personality of a particular leader, for example, a group home director. Yet in light of the number and diversity of sites in the VOM studies, as well as the research that preceded them, it seems reasonable to assume that satisfaction is not merely linked to the personalities of referral sources or mediators.

Satisfaction with the Criminal Justice System

It is rare indeed to see a wide range of victims and offenders favorably disposed toward the criminal justice system. More than eight out of ten of the participants in mediation were not only favorably disposed toward the program but also to the system that made it possible for them to participate. This satisfaction goes beyond "feeling OK" about things. It goes to the heart of the justice system: fairness. Is it possible that part of what is being heard here is the desire and gratification of genuinely participating in the justice process? Many victims feel lost in the traditional process. They complain of becoming mere bystanders even though the crime was committed against them. Beyond the scope of these studies, it would be interesting to know if similar cases handled traditionally yielded similar or greatly different outcomes (for example, in terms of restitution). It is quite likely that those outcomes are not radically different; what is different is that victims, in particular, but offenders too, feel that they played a significant role in the process of achieving justice. The criminal justice system is a primary beneficiary of the favorable attitudes engendered by individuals participating in victim offender mediation.

Empirical Grounding of Restorative Justice Theory

The theory of restorative justice is grounded in a number of core values and principles. These include elevating the role of crime victims and the community in responding to the harm caused by crime; holding offenders directly accountable to the people they have harmed; restoring losses incurred by victims to the greatest extent possible; providing opportunities for dialogue among interested crime victims, offenders, family members, and community members; and providing opportunities for offenders to take responsibility for their criminal behavior, to make amends, and to develop competencies and skills that will reintegrate them into the community. Restorative justice principles are expressed through a wide range of policies and practices in more than forty-five states in the United States. With the exception of a few studies on a closely related and newer intervention, family group conferencing (Fercello & Umbreit, 1998; McCold & Wachtel, 1998; Umbreit & Fercello, 1998), there is little empirical evidence, however, to support many restorative justice policies and practices. This study provides strong empirical grounding to the emerging practice theory of restorative justice as expressed through its oldest and most widely dispersed expression—victim offender mediation.

Chapter Ten

Victim Offender Mediation in the United States

A Multisite Assessment

This chapter reports on the first large cross-site analysis of victim offender mediation programs conducted in the United States, involving multiple data sets, research questions, comparison groups, and multiple quantitative and qualitative techniques of analysis. The programs examined worked closely with juvenile courts in Albuquerque, New Mexico; Austin, Texas; Minneapolis, Minnesota; and Oakland, California. Issues related to the mediation process and outcomes, client satisfaction, perceptions of fairness, restitution completion, and recidivism are examined.

Methodology

Random assignment of subjects into experimental and control groups was not possible because of ethical concerns of court officials and program staff. Therefore, a quasi-experimental design (Cook & Campbell, 1979) was employed, consisting of quantitative and qualitative data collection and analysis, involving multiple data sets, research questions, and comparison groups. A total of 1,153 interviews were conducted with crime victims and juvenile offenders: 304 premediation interviews, 432 postmediation interviews,

Note: Material in this chapter is drawn from Umbreit and Coates (1993) and Umbreit (1994). Reprinted by permission of Sage Publications, Inc., and Criminal Justice Press. Certain quotations are not attributed for reasons of confidentiality.

and 417 interviews with persons in two comparison groups. The study focused on the following research questions.

1. Who participates in mediation and why?
2. How does the mediation process work?
3. How do participants in mediation evaluate it?
4. What do court officials think about mediation?
5. What were the immediate outcomes of mediation?
6. What is the impact of mediation on restitution completion?
7. What is the impact of mediation on recidivism?

Attitudes of victims and offenders regarding a number of important issues in the mediation process were examined through the use of pre- and postmediation interviews. Client satisfaction and perceptions of fairness were examined through use of postmediation interviews and two comparison groups: (1) victims and offenders who were referred to the mediation program but did not participate in mediation ("referred, no mediation") and (2) victims and offenders from the same jurisdiction who had been matched with the mediation sample on the offender variables of age, race, sex, and offense but who were never referred to the mediation program ("nonreferred"). Premediation interviews were conducted over the phone up to a week before the mediation session. Postmediation research interviews were conducted with the subjects, usually at their home, approximately two months after mediation. Comparison group interviews were conducted over the phone approximately two months after the case disposition date.

Restitution completion by offenders in victim offender mediation programs, as well as recidivism rates, was analyzed though use of a (nonreferred) comparison group from the same jurisdiction; group members were matched on variables of age, race, sex, offense, and restitution amount. Offenders in this matched sample were ordered to pay restitution through the existing restitution program in the probation office.

All victims and offenders referred to the mediation programs in 1990 and 1991 were given the opportunity to participate in the study. Table 10.1 describes the subsamples for the mediation group and the two comparison groups.

Eleven data collection instruments for interviewing juvenile offenders and their victims were developed. The interview schedules consisted of both open-ended and closed-ended items, including Likert-type questions. Program monitoring, which consisted of reviews of program files, mediated restitution agreements, interviews with staff and volunteers, and observations of mediation sessions, indicated that the mediation intervention was consistent across all four sites.

Program Sites

The programs in Albuquerque, Minneapolis, and Oakland were the three primary sites; the fourth program, in Austin, was added later in the study and received a more limited range of analysis.

The three primary programs are operated by private nonprofit community-based organizations working closely with the juvenile court. Nearly all of the mediation cases were referred by the local juvenile court and probation staff. A relatively small number of cases were referred by the prosecuting attorney or police.

Several factors were considered in selecting these program sites. Private nonprofit organizations sponsor the majority of victim offender mediation programs throughout the country, and most programs focus on juvenile offenders (Hughes & Schneider, 1990; Umbreit, 1988). The three primary programs offered both regional and program development diversity. With a few notable exceptions, each victim offender mediation program employed a very similar case management process with juvenile offenders and their victims.

Table 10.1 Sample of Individuals Interviewed, 1990–1991

Program Site	Referred to Mediation, Participating	Referred to Mediation, Nonparticipating (Comparison Group 1)	Not Referred to Mediation (Comparison Group 2)	Total
Albuquerque				
Victims	73	33	25	131
Offenders	65	36	28	129
Austin				
Victims	50	50	72	219
Offenders	50	50	71	192
Minneapolis				
Victims	96	51	72	219
Offenders	81	40	71	192
Oakland				
Victims	61	19	10	90
Offenders	56	19	12	87
Totals	532	198	218	948

Note: Many of the participants were interviewed both before and after mediation, resulting in a total of 1,153 interviews.

Mediation Referrals

A total of 5,458 victims and offenders were referred by the juvenile court to the four victim offender mediation program sites during calendar years 1990 and 1991, representing 2,799 individual victims and 2,659 individual offenders. Eighty-three percent of these referrals involved a property crime such as vandalism, theft, or burglary, and 17 percent involved a crime of violence, primarily minor assaults.

Eighty-five percent of the cases were referred to the four programs prior to formal adjudication as a diversion effort. As Table 10.2 indicates, the remaining cases (15 percent) were referred following formal adjudication by the juvenile court. Although the proportion of postadjudication referrals at individual sites varied from 2 percent in Austin to 28 percent in Minneapolis, the vast majority of cases at all sites represented preadjudication or diversion referrals.

The average age of offenders referred to the four mediation programs was fifteen, with a range of seven to eighteen years of age. Of the referrals, 86 percent were male and 14 percent female. A very large proportion of case referrals (46 percent) represented minority youth, with Hispanics being the largest minority group referred. The vast majority of offenders referred to the mediation programs had no prior criminal convictions. The minority who did have prior convictions had two to six offenses. Table 10.3 indicates the characteristics of offenders at the four program sites.

Findings

The results reported here include participant perceptions on a number of variables, short- and longer-term outcome data, and information on justice system support across the four program sites.

Client Expectations of Mediation

Victims and offenders who participated in mediation had varied expectations. Victims were most likely to indicate that recovering their loss and helping the offender were equally important. These

Table 10.2 Referral Characteristics, 1990–1991

Variable	Albuquerque	Austin	Minneapolis	Oakland	Total
Cases referred	591	1,107	903	541	3,142
Preadjudication	76%	98%	72%	91%	85%
Postadjudication	24%	2%	28%	9%	15%
Individual victims	654	1,058	633	454	2,799
Individual offenders	604	1,087	658	310	2,659
Types of offenses					
Against property	73%	81%	89%	87%	83%
Against people	27%	19%	11%	13%	17%
Most frequent property offense	Burglary	Burglary	Vandalism	Vandalism	Burglary
Most frequent violent offense	Assault	Assault	Assault	Assault	Assault

Table 10.3 Offender Characteristics, 1990–1991

Variable	Albuquerque (N = 604)	Austin (N = 1,087)	Minneapolis (N = 658)	Oakland (N = 310)	Total (N = 2,659)
Average offender age	15	15	15	15	15
Offender age range	10–19	10–17	10–18	7–18	7–18
Offender gender					
Male	90%	87%	85%	82%	86%
Female	10%	13%	15%	18%	14%
Offender race					
Caucasian	30%	31%	70%	64%	54%
Black	2%	25%	23%	15%	14%
Hispanic	65%	42%	2%	15%	27%
Other minority	3%	2%	5%	6%	5%

expectations were followed in frequency by the opportunity to tell the offender the effect of the crime and the opportunity to get answers to questions they had about the crime. Whereas only one in four victims admitted being nervous about the pending mediation session with the offender, nine out of ten victims believed that the mediation session would probably be helpful.

Offenders indicated that "making things right" was their primary expectation, followed in frequency by having the opportunity to apologize to the victim and being able "to be done with it." Only one out of ten offenders indicated that they expected the mediation session to result in less punishment than they would have otherwise received. Nearly half of the offenders stated that they were nervous about the pending session. Six out of ten indicated that they cared about what the victims thought of them, and like the victims, nine out of ten offenders believed that the mediation session would be helpful.

Voluntary Participation in Mediation

The question of whether or not victims and offenders actually participate voluntarily in mediation is crucial to the integrity of the victim offender mediation process. It is important that young offenders particularly have a choice about participating in the mediation process and directly contribute to the outcome since coercion to participate would likely cause anger that would in turn be reflected in their behavior in the meeting with the victims.

A major concern of the victims' rights movement is the issue of choice, allowing victims various options to regain a sense of power and control in their lives. If the mediation process is imposed on victims of crime, that experience itself could be further victimizing.

Whereas a very high proportion of both victims (91 percent) and offenders (81 percent) in the current study clearly felt that their participation in mediation was voluntary, an earlier study by Coates and Gehm (1989) found that many offenders did not experience their involvement in mediation as voluntary. Particularly because of the highly coercive nature of any justice system's inter-action with an offender, one would expect that many offenders in mediation would feel coerced into it. Yet eight out of ten offenders from the combined sites in the present study experienced their involvement in mediation as voluntary. There was, however, a sta-tistically significant difference found between program sites. The Minneapolis program site had the highest rating of voluntary par-ticipation for offenders (90 percent), and the Albuquerque program site had the lowest rating (71 percent). There was no similar sig-nificant difference for victims across the four sites.

The Mediation Process

The three primary victim offender mediation programs employ a similar four-phase process: intake, preparation for mediation, medi-ation, and follow-up. During the preparation phase, the mediator usually met separately with both parties to hear to their version of what happened, to explain the program, and to schedule a date for mediation.

The agenda of the mediation session with victim and offender in the present study focuses first on the facts and feelings related to the crime. Offenders are put in the often uncomfortable position of having to face the person they victimized. They are given the opportunity to become known as a person and even to express remorse in a very personal fashion. Through open discussion of their feelings, both victim and offender have the opportunity to deal with each other as people, often neighbors who live in the same neighborhood, rather than as stereotypes. The second part of the session focuses on victim losses and negotiation of a mutually satisfying restitution agreement. Mediation sessions tend to last about an hour.

The follow-up phase consists of monitoring completion of the restitution agreement, intervening if additional conflict develops, and scheduling a follow-up victim offender meeting when appro-priate.

The three primary program sites accept referrals of juvenile offenders from probation officials, at both the preadjudication (diversion) and postadjudication stage. Both staff and community volunteers serve as mediators. Each mediator receives twenty to twenty-five hours of initial training in mediation skills and program procedures.

From the twenty-eight observations of mediation sessions conducted at the three primary sites, it was found that the process was usually applied as just described, though not always in strict sequence (opening statement, telling of stories, transition to restitution discussion and agreement). Also, there were a number of notable examples in which the mediation process appeared to be applied in a very routinized fashion, with unclear leadership and guidance by the mediator, including missed opportunities for facilitating the mediation in such a way that both victim and offender received the maximum possible emotional benefit.

Both parties in the mediation ranked the importance of specific tasks performed by mediators. Victims ranked leadership most important in a mediator. This was followed by making participants feel comfortable, helping with the restitution plan, and allowing participants to talk. Offenders had a slightly different ranking, beginning with the ability of the mediator to make them feel comfortable, followed by allowing talk, helping with the restitution plan, and being a good listener.

Immediate Outcomes

The most obvious immediate outcome for the victims and offenders who chose to participate in mediation was the high probability of a successful negotiation of a restitution agreement. These agreements consisted of a variety of elements (see Table 10.4), but most focused on payment of financial restitution by the offender to the victim. It was not unusual for agreements to include personal service to the victim or community service, both of which were likely to result from conversion of a specific dollar amount of loss into

Table 10.4 Immediate Outcomes, 1990–1991

Variable	Albuquerque	Austin	Minneapolis	Oakland	Total
Number of mediations	158	300	468	205	1,131
Successfully negotiated restitution agreements	99%	98%	93%	91%	95%
Substance of agreement					
Financial restitution	82	171	279	111	603
Personal service	57	21	31	36	145
Community service	29	130	107	39	305
Total financial restitution	$23,542	$41,536	$32,301	$23,227	$120,606
Average financial restitution	$287	$243	$135	$209	$200
Total personal service	1,028 hrs.	439 hrs.	508 hrs.	585 hrs.	2,560 hrs.
Average personal service	18 hrs.	21 hrs.	16 hrs.	16 hrs.	18 hrs.
Total community service	1,073 hrs.	4,064 hrs.	1,937 hrs.	588 hrs.	7,662 hrs.
Average community service	37 hrs.	31 hrs.	18 hrs.	15 hrs.	25 hrs.

hours of work, usually at around the rate of the minimum wage. Some restitution agreements simply required that the offender apologize to the victim. The majority of participants in the current study reported successful negotiation of restitution agreements (ranging from 91 percent in Oakland to 99 percent in Albuquerque).

Restitution contracts were not the only immediate outcome of the mediation program. As indicated in Table 10.5, victims from all the sites were significantly less upset about the crime and less fearful of being revictimized by the same offender after having met in mediation. "It minimized the fear I would have as a result of being a victim because I got to see that the offender was human, too" was a commonly expressed sentiment.

Client Satisfaction with Mediation

Nearly 80 percent of the offenders in the mediation sample and the two comparison group samples indicated satisfaction with how the system handled their case, with no significant differences among groups. For offenders, therefore, participation in mediation appears not to have significantly increased their satisfaction with how the juvenile justice system handled their case.

A significant difference (at the .05 level) was found, however, for victims (see Table 10.6). Whereas 79 percent of victims in the

Table 10.5 Emotional Impact of Mediation on Victims (All Sites)

Victim's Sentiment	Before Mediation		After Mediation		Statistical Significance
Upset about crime	67%	(155)	49%	(162)	$p < .0001*$
Afraid of being revictimized by offender	23%	(154)	10%	(166)	$p < .005*$

*Statistically significant difference.

mediation group indicated satisfaction, only 57 percent in the "referred, no mediation" group and 57 percent of victims in the "nonreferred" group indicated satisfaction. This greater sense of satisfaction among victims in the mediation group was reflected in such statements as "It gave us a chance to see each other face to face and to resolve what happened" and "It reduced my fear as a victim because I was able to see that they were young people."

Nine out of ten victims and offenders at all of the sites combined were satisfied with the actual outcome of the mediation session, which was nearly always a written restitution agreement. A frequent theme expressed among offenders was "It was helpful to see the victim as a person and to have a chance to talk and make up for what I did." No major differences were found between sites.

Client Perceptions of Fairness

Aggregated data from all three sites indicated that the mediation process was significantly more likely to result in victims' perceptions that cases were handled fairly by the juvenile justice system. Eighty-three percent of victims in the mediation group stated they felt the processing of their case was fair, compared to only 53

Table 10.6 Client Satisfaction with Case Processing: Mediation Sample Compared with "Referred, No Mediation" Sample

	Victims		Offenders	
Mediation sample (experimental group)	79%	(204)	87%	(181)
Referred, no-mediation sample (comparison group 1)	57%	(95)	80%	(95)
Statistical significance	$p < .0001*$		$p = .15$ (n.s.)	

*Statistically significant difference; n.s. = not significant.

percent in the "referred, no mediation" group and 62 percent in the "nonreferred" group.

When compared to similar offenders who were never referred to the mediation program, juveniles who met their victim in mediation were also significantly more likely to say that the processing of their case was fair. For offenders in mediation, 89 percent felt it was fair, compared to 78 percent in the "nonreferred" group. When compared to other juveniles who were referred to the mediation program but who did not participate, however, no statistically significant difference was found in their experience of fairness in the processing of their case by the system.

Consistent with a prior study (Umbreit, 1988), when crime victims who participated in mediation were asked to rank their most important concerns related to fairness in the justice system, they identified obtaining help for the offender as the primary concern. This was followed by paying back the victims for their losses and receiving an apology from the offender. Juvenile offenders in mediation indicated that payback was their most important concern related to fairness in the justice system. This was followed by personally making things right and apologizing to the victim.

When the data on perceptions of fairness were examined per program site, no significant differences were found among the offender groups. Victims in mediation were, however, considerably more likely than other victims to say their treatment was fair at each of the three primary sites. Significant differences were found at the Albuquerque site between the mediation sample and "referred, no mediation" sample and at the Minneapolis site between the mediation sample and both comparison groups.

Victim and Offender Attitudes About Mediation

Both victims and offenders identified a number of important issues related to the process of talking about the crime and negotiating restitution. Negotiating restitution was important to nearly nine out of ten victims both before and after mediation. Actually receiving restitution, however, was important to only seven out of ten victims.

The opportunity to participate directly in an interpersonal problem-solving process to establish a fair restitution plan was more important to victims than actually receiving the agreed-on restitution.

Significant differences related to the victims' informational and emotional needs, as well as to the process of negotiating restitution, were found between pre- and postmediation group samples. The importance that victims placed on receiving answers from the offender about what happened and being able to tell the offender how the crime affected them was higher after the mediation session than before it. This was also true of negotiating restitution with the offender during the meeting, even though actually receiving restitution was rated less important.

For offenders, there were no significant differences between the pre- and postmediation samples. Negotiating restitution, paying restitution, telling the victim what happened, and apologizing to the victim were important to nine out of ten offenders in both samples.

This finding does not, however, fully capture the impact that mediation had on the attitude of the offenders. Being held personally accountable for their criminal behavior, through a face-to-face meeting with their victim, can trigger a significant change in the attitude of many juvenile offenders. This change is expressed in statements such as "After meeting the victims, I now realize that I hurt them a lot" and "Through mediation, I was able to understand a lot about what I did. I realized that the victim really got hurt, and that made me feel really bad." The importance of this change in the attitude of many offenders is conveyed by a judge in the Oakland area, who stated that the main impact of victim offender mediation is "a major learning experience for kids about the rights of others, with implications far beyond just the delinquent act."

Juvenile Court Support for Mediation

Juvenile court officials at the three primary research sites uniformly supported the victim offender mediation program in their jurisdiction. Although some people were skeptical of the mediation concept during the early development of the program, most notably at

the Minnesota site, judges and probation staff are now strong supporters and have played an important role in promoting institu-
tionalization of these programs.

Judges at all three sites recognized that the emotional benefits
of the program were even more important than simply the payment
of restitution. A judge in Albuquerque said, "Mediation helps these
kids realize that victims are not just targets, they are real people."
A Minnesota judge noted, "Victim offender mediation humanizes
the process. . . . Victims gain a sense of control and power . . . [and]
offenders learn the real human impact of what they have done."
The importance of young offenders taking responsibility for their
criminal behavior by compensating the victim was highlighted by
a judge in the Oakland area who said, "Victim offender mediation
teaches kids that 'what I did affected real people.' . . . Paying restitution as a consequence for their behavior is part of growing up."

These sentiments were echoed by probation directors and line
staff at the three sites. Probation staff were also often quick to add
that the mediation programs relieved the pressure of their high
caseloads, particularly in cases involving more complex issues of
restitution determination and payment.

Impact of Mediation on Restitution Completion

Restitution is increasingly being required of juvenile offenders in
many courts throughout the United States. Whether or not restitution is actually completed by the offender, however, is a critical
issue, since victims who have their expectations raised by court-
ordered restitution and never receive compensation by the offender
can experience a renewed sense of victimization.

At the Minneapolis and Albuquerque program sites, court
data related to completion of restitution were analyzed. The comparison groups for this analysis represented a sample of similar
offenders from the same jurisdiction who were matched on the
variables of age, race, sex, offense, and amount of restitution. As
Table 10.7 indicates, offenders who negotiated restitution agree-

Table 10.7 Restitution Completion by Offenders

	Minneapolis		Albuquerque		Total	
Mediation sample (experimental group)	77%	(125)	93%	(42)	81%	(167)
Nonreferred matched sample (comparison group 2)	55%	(179)	69%	(42)	58%	(221)
Statistical significance	$p < .0001*$		$p < .005*$		$p < .0001*$	

*Statistically significant difference.

ments with their victims through mediation were significantly more likely to complete their restitution obligation than similar offenders who were ordered by the court to pay a set amount of restitution.

Representing the first study to examine the impact of face-to-face mediation on successful completion of restitution, this finding is critical. At a time when concern for serving the needs of crime victims continues to grow, the fact that victim offender mediation can significantly increase the likelihood of victims being compensated, in some form, for their losses has very important implications for juvenile justice policymakers.

Impact of Mediation on Recidivism

The question of whether the victim offender mediation process reduced further criminal behavior (recidivism) by offenders participating in mediation was examined at each of the three primary sites. The comparison group at each site consisted of similar offenders from the same jurisdiction who were matched with offenders in mediation on the variables of age, sex, race, offense, and restitution amount.

Juvenile offenders in the three mediation programs committed significantly fewer additional crimes (18 percent recidivism) within a one-year period following the mediation than similar offenders in the court-administered restitution program (27 percent recidivism). They also tended to commit crimes that were less serious than the offense that was referred to the mediation program. The largest reduction in recidivism occurred at the Minneapolis program site, with a recidivism rate of 22 percent for the mediation sample compared to 34 percent for the comparison group. These findings were statistically significant and bode well for broader public policy support for victim offender mediation.

Implications

Substantial quantitative and qualitative data were collected from a total of 1,153 interviews with crime victims and juvenile offenders in four states, reviews of program and court records, interviews with court officials and program staff, and observations of twenty-eight mediation sessions. Although this multisite analysis of juvenile victim offender mediation programs represented the largest study of its kind in North America, it also had a number of important limitations. First, the necessity of using a quasi-experimental design, without random assignment of subjects into an experimental and control group, eliminated the ability to generalize its conclusions to all victims and offenders in these four or similar mediation programs. Also, early in the study, it became evident that the premediation interviews were conducted too far into the case management process. At the point of the premediation interview, subjects had already agreed to mediation, and their expectations were quite high. This resulted in considerably less change between the pre- and postmediation measurements than initially anticipated. Yet no acceptable earlier point for conducting the premediation interview could be determined without significantly contaminating the normal case management process.

Although caution must be exercised in generalizing these conclusions to other subjects or programs, they nevertheless provide important insight into the growing international field of justice reform.

The victim offender mediation programs in the four states examined in this study enjoyed strong support from local juvenile justice officials. No significant differences in outcomes were found between the three private community-based programs and the one probation-administered program. Together they made a significant contribution to enhancing the quality of justice experienced by juvenile offenders and victims. This conclusion is consistent with a number of previous studies (Coates & Gehm, 1989; Dignan, 1990; Marshall & Merry, 1990; Umbreit, 1988, 1990, 1991).

The mediation process is meant to increase the active participation of crime victims in the justice process, as well as encourage offenders to "make amends" and be held accountable directly to the person they victimized, not just to the state. The vast majority of offender participants indicated that they chose to participant voluntarily. Programs in this study appear to have done a better job of presenting mediation as a voluntary choice to the offender (81 percent of offenders) than has been indicated in some prior research (Coates & Gehm, 1989). Mediation was perceived as voluntary by the vast majority of victims (91 percent) who participated in it. Still, a small number of victims (9 percent) felt that they were coerced into participating in the VOM program. Whether this perception of coercion was a function of the program staff, mediators, court officials, or even parents (of juvenile victims) is unclear.

The mediation process resulted in very high levels of satisfaction with the juvenile justice system for both parties. The vast majority of crime victims and juvenile offenders in mediation also felt that the manner in which their case was disposed of by the court was fair. For victims, an even greater differential impact was found related to satisfaction and perceptions of fairness when compared to victims who did not enter mediation.

Victims and offenders consistently indicated, at all four sites, that the mediation process had a strong impact on humanizing the justice system response to the crime and allowed them more active involvement in resolving the issues related to compensating victims for their losses. After meeting and talking with the young offender in the presence of a mediator, victims indicated a significant reduction in their sense of vulnerability and anger.

Juvenile offenders did not perceive victim offender mediation to be a significantly less demanding response to their criminal behavior than other options available to the court. The use of mediation was consistent with the concern to hold young offenders accountable for their criminal behavior.

Victim offender mediation had a significant impact on the likelihood of offenders' completing their restitution obligation to victims (81 percent), when compared to similar offenders who completed their restitution in a court-administered structured restitution program without mediation (58 percent). This study is the first in North America or Europe to examine the impact of mediation on restitution completion.

Juvenile offenders who participated in a mediation session with their specific victim were significantly less likely to commit a new offense within the year following the mediation.

Although this multisite analysis of victim offender mediation identified a number of outcomes that enhanced the quality of justice for both victims and offenders, several limitations of the intervention also emerged. Mediation is clearly not a "quick fix" for reducing delinquency.

A small amount of data suggest that the mediation process could eventually become so routinized that it might be done in an impersonal atmosphere that could become dehumanizing for participants. The spontaneity, vitality, and creativity of the mediation process must be preserved by effective training of mediators and monitoring of mediator performance and program outcomes. As the field of victim offender mediation expands and becomes more institutionalized, a danger exists that it might alter its model to accommodate the dominant system of retributive justice, rather than influence the present system to alter its model to incorporate the more restorative vision of justice on which victim offender mediation is based.

Chapter Eleven

Victim Offender Mediation in Canada

A Multisite Assessment

This chapter reports on the first cross-national replication of the U.S. study described in Chapter Ten. Four victim offender mediation programs in Canada were studied between 1991 and 1993 (Umbreit, 1995b), using the research design and instrumentation of the U.S. study as much as possible. Limited resources, however, necessitated important design adaptations for the Canadian component of the study. One major difference is that it was not possible to develop and follow a "nonreferred" comparison group; the Canadian data reported here therefore compare participants who were referred and did participate in mediation with those who were referred and did not participate.

Program Sites

Community-based nonprofit organizations providing mediation services for referrals from the criminal justice systems in cities in four provinces were examined. Three of these programs (Langley, British Columbia; Calgary, Alberta; and Winnipeg, Manitoba) specifically identify themselves as victim offender mediation programs, whereas the program in Ottawa-Carleton, Ontario, identifies itself as a criminal court mediation program. Both staff and community volunteers serve as mediators. Because of differences in

---

Note: This chapter is based on Umbreit (1996). Reprinted with permission of Criminal Justice Press.

the point of referral, the programs in Winnipeg and Ottawa-Carleton refer to "the accused" since no formal admissions of guilt have been obtained, whereas programs in Langley and Calgary refer to "offenders." Similarly, Winnipeg and Ottawa-Carleton refer to "complainants" rather than "victims," the term used in Langley and Calgary. When discussing results across all sites, I will therefore refer to participants as "complainants/victims" and "accused/offenders."

Calgary

The Youth Advocacy and Mediation Services (YAMS) Program in Calgary was initiated in 1985 by the Calgary John Howard Society as a program under the Young Offenders Act proclaimed by the Canadian Parliament in 1984. The YAMS Youth Alternative Disposition Program is directly associated with the Youth Court System. In this program, youth who plead guilty to breaking and entering, shoplifting, or similar offenses are given an opportunity to participate in mediation with their victim in order to negotiate a restitution agreement. In this program, a mediated agreement serves as the core condition of the proposed disposition for consideration by the judge. The most common point of case referral is after conviction but before sentencing, although cases may be referred to mediation by anyone at any point in the criminal justice process. Most often the crown prosecutor or defense attorney screens the youth and refers the case to YAMS. If at any stage in the referral, premediation, or mediation process the victim or the offender wishes not to be involved further in the program or if no agreement is reached through mediation, the youth is referred back to the Crown Prosecutor's Office for standard court procedures.

From 1991 through 1993, some 258 cases were referred to this victim offender mediation program, primarily by the local probation department. The most frequent offense referred to the program was breaking and entering.

Langley

The Victim Offender Reconciliation Program (VORP) in Langley was initially developed in 1982 by the Langley Mennonite Fellowship and later became one of several programs of the Fraser Region Community Justice Initiatives Association, which was founded in 1985. As indicated in its program flyer, the Langley VORP is a community-based alternative that empowers participants to devise their own solutions in face-to-face encounters, guided by trained community mediators. Mediation in the Langley VORP is carried out as a four-step process, consisting of referral and screening, individual premediation meetings to prepare participants, the mediation session, and report and monitoring of the agreement. The report is written by the mediator and given to the VORP office case manager, who is responsible for postmediation follow-up of agreements.

This program serves courts in both Langley and Surrey. Referral sources are probation officers, crown counsel, and the courts. Case referral is either pretrial (diversion) or court-ordered. From 1991 through 1993, a total of 851 cases were referred to the Langley VORP, primarily by the local probation department. The most common offense referred was criminal mischief.

Ottawa-Carleton

The Criminal Pretrial Mediation Programme of the Dispute Resolution Centre (the Centre) for Ottawa-Carleton was established in 1986 as a community-based nonprofit agency with the mandate to demonstrate and facilitate the practice of conflict resolution techniques in the Ottawa-Carleton community. An initial goal was in part to help reduce the backlog of pending "minor" criminal cases. Mediations are conducted in selected cases after a charge has been laid by the police but generally before the case has been set for trial.

Referrals of both youth and adult accused are received from police, assistant crown attorneys, defense counsel, accused, complainants, outside agencies, and the Centre itself. Final authority for deciding whether cases are suitable for the mediation options rests with the Centre's executive director. The accused is not required to admit to committing the act that led to the criminal charges. The likelihood that an accused will honor an agreement based on the parties' common understanding is the primary consideration in determining whether a case is suitable for mediation. From 1991 through 1993, a total of 689 cases were referred to the Dispute Resolution Centre for Ottawa-Carleton.

After the case is deemed suitable for mediation, a representative of the Centre contacts the accused on behalf of the crown attorney and offers the mediation option. Once the accused has agreed, a date is finalized, and all parties, including the defense counsel, are notified. Legal counselors do not attend any of the mediation sessions. Mediation is conducted by a trained volunteer mediator who has had no prior contact with any of the parties. When required, language interpreters are provided through the Office of the Crown for participants whose first language is neither English nor French. This has proved necessary in nearly 20 percent of the Centre's mediations, reflecting the cultural diversity of the Ottawa-Carleton region. In mediation, the parties agree to attempt to settle their disagreement, knowing that the final decision on disposition of the case rests with the crown attorney, who receives a copy of the negotiated agreement.

Winnipeg

The Criminal Court Program of the Mediation Services agency in Winnipeg was initially established in 1979 as a victim offender mediation project of the Mennonite Central Committee (MCC) of Manitoba. In 1992, Mediation Services: A Community Resource for Conflict Resolution was born, growing out of the MCC's desire to establish a broader base of community support and involvement in the organization. The purpose of Mediation

Services is to "promote peace and restorative justice within the community by empowering people, through education and mediation, to resolve conflict using non-violent conflict resolution processes."

Referrals are initiated from a variety of sources, including staff, crown, defense counsel, complainants/victims, accused/offenders, and rural locations. Cases are referred after charges are brought but before trial. Typical cases mediated include assault (most common), assault causing bodily harm, mischief, possession of a weapon dangerous to public peace, and theft under $1,000, although others, including five cases involving sexual assault, have also been handled. In most instances, participants are contacted and arrangements for the mediation are made by telephone, but in some situations, a face-to-face meeting may be conducted with a victim who is elderly or is particularly frightened. The Winnipeg program is the only one of the four that routinely uses co-mediation. From 1991 through 1993, a total of 2,647 cases were referred by the crown prosecutor to the Criminal Court Program of Mediation Services in Winnipeg, representing the largest volume of case referrals to a single victim offender mediation program in Canada.

All four program sites have developed individual variations on the generic victim offender mediation model described in Part One. The most significant difference is evident in the process of preparing participants for mediation. Following the practice of the vast majority of VORP/VOM programs in North America, the Calgary and Langley programs consistently have the assigned mediator meet with both parties separately before the mediation session. The program in Winnipeg only occasionally has its mediators meet with the involved parties prior to the joint session. More routinely, it has a staff person conducting the case preparation over the phone, and mediators first meet the parties in person at the scheduled mediation session. Mediators in the Ottawa-Carleton program have no prior contact with the involved parties.

Methodology

A quasi-experimental design was employed in this cross-site assessment of VOM programs. Phone interviews with complainants/victims and accused/offenders were conducted approximately two months following either the mediation session (experimental group) or the date that the prosecutor, court, or related agency otherwise disposed of the case (comparison group). Observations of actual mediation sessions at program sites in different provinces provided extensive qualitative data and were particularly important in gaining insight into the mediation process itself.

A total of 610 interviews were conducted with participants in mediation, involving 323 complainants/victims and 287 accused/offenders. In addition, the study conducted 45 interviews with criminal justice system officials, 24 observations of actual mediation sessions, multiple interviews with program staff in the four provinces, and review of program records.

Fifty-nine percent of the complainants/victims were male, with an average age of thirty-three; 86 percent were white and 14 percent minorities. Eighty percent of accused/offenders were male, with an average age of twenty-four; 80 percent were white and 20 percent minorities. The largest minority race for both complainants/victims and accused/offenders was First Nation peoples. The most common offense referred was assault, followed by property crimes such as vandalism, theft, and burglary. There were no significant differences between the mediation and no-mediation samples for complainants/victims or accused/offenders. The subsamples per program site are identified in Table 11.1.

The study was guided by the following questions:

1. What are the immediate outcomes of the mediation process?
2. Were crime victims and offenders satisfied with the mediation process?
3. Did victims and offenders experience the mediation process and outcome as fair?

Table 11.1 Canadian Cross-Site Program Subsamples

Program	Experimental Groups (Participating in Mediation)		Comparison Groups (Not Participating in Mediation)		Total Sample
	Complainants/ Victims	Accused/ Offenders	Complainants/ Victims	Accused/ Offenders	
Calgary	7	7	2	5	21
Langley	42	41	37	42	162
Ottawa-Carleton	42	16	22	12	92
Winnipeg	92	95	79	69	335
Totals	183	159	140	128	610

4. Was the fear of revictimization reduced for crime victims who participated in mediation?

Findings

Program descriptions and variations, participant perceptions, outcomes, and justice system perceptions are reported.

Program Description

A total of twenty-four observations of mediation sessions were completed at three of the four program sites (Winnipeg, Langley, and Ottawa-Carleton). From these data emerge the following picture of the differences between the two primary models. As clarified earlier, Langley and Ottawa-Carleton primarily follow the VOM model described in Part One, referred to in this discussion as the U.S. VOM model. Winnipeg departs sufficiently from the U.S. VOM model to be given its own title; it will be referred to as the Winnipeg model.

Both models use an opening statement by the mediator that is designed to set the participants at ease and let them know what is happening. Mediators in the U.S. VOM model tend to provide a more structured description of the process, while mediators in the Winnipeg model basically suggest that each participant should begin by telling his or her story.

In the U.S. VOM model, mediators nearly always sat at the end of the table, with the complainant/victim and accused/offender sitting across from each other, allowing for easy and natural direct eye contact. In the Winnipeg model, the co-mediators sat directly across from the participants. This made eye contact between mediator and participants easy but between participants and between co-mediators difficult. Mediators in this model did not emphasize the importance of the participants' speaking directly to each other. In the U.S. VOM model, direct communication between the involved parties was often emphasized and facilitated by the mediator. This would often result in a process of dialogue and sharing, rather than simply discussion and debate.

In the U.S. VOM model, mediators followed a fairly consistent pattern of encouraging the parties first to tell what happened, then to express how they felt about it, to ask each other any relevant questions they may have, and finally to explore a possible resolution to the conflict. The Winnipeg mediator instructions were more loosely structured, with co-mediators simply asking first one and then the other participant to tell his or her story. One result of this difference was that the co-mediators in the Winnipeg model became more involved in directing the process and were more often the primary speakers in the observed mediation sessions. Winnipeg mediators also made frequent use of timeouts to confer with participant, perhaps made more necessary because of the lack of premediation preparation sessions. This opportunity for breaks adds a lot to victim offender mediation, providing an opportunity to step out of the intensity for a bit and reflect. It also provided a unique perspective on what participants were thinking midway through the mediation process. Though some seemed pleased with what was happening, many more used this private conversation with the mediators to complain and blow off steam; impressively, these same participants consistently returned to the sessions and successfully negotiated agreements.

Immediate Outcomes

Case referrals to the four program sites during 1991 through 1993 totaled 4,445 (primarily adult cases). Mediation Services in Winnipeg is by far the largest and best-established program providing mediation in criminal cases, with a total of 2,647 cases during this three-year period. The Victim Offender Reconciliation Program in Langley had the next largest number of cases referred (851), followed by the Dispute Resolution Centre for Ottawa-Carleton (689) and the Victim Young Offender Reconciliation Program in Calgary (258). In Winnipeg and Ottawa, nearly all referrals were adult cases, while in Langley and Calgary, most referrals were youth.

Mediation sessions between the involved parties were held in 39 percent of the cases referred to the four program sites during 1991 through 1993. Mediation rates were 35 percent in Calgary, 38 percent in Ottawa, 39 percent in Langley, and 40 percent in Winnipeg. It should be noted that for referred cases that did not result in a joint mediation session, a number of services were still usually provided, including supportive listening, conflict assessment, presentation of options for resolution, or referral to another agency.

Successfully negotiated agreements that were acceptable to both parties were reached in 92 percent of the cases that were mediated at the four program sites from 1991 through 1993 (90 percent in Winnipeg, 91 percent in Calgary, 94 percent in Ottawa, 99 percent in Langley). Outcomes are summarized in Table 11.2.

Client Perception of Voluntary Participation

Client perception of participating voluntarily in mediation was indicated by 90 percent of complainants/victims and 83 percent of accused/offenders at the combined sites. At the individual sites, voluntary participation in mediation by complainants/victims ranged from 87 percent in Ottawa ($N = 33$) to 100 percent in Calgary ($N = 7$). For accused/offenders, voluntary participation ranged from 68 percent in Langley ($N = 40$) to 100 percent in Calgary ($N = 6$).

Client Satisfaction

Overall, clients' satisfaction with the manner in which the justice system responded to their case was significantly more likely to be found among complainants/victims (78 percent) and accused/offenders (74 percent) who participated in mediation, at the

Table 11.2 Canadian Program Outcomes

	Calgary	Langley	Ottawa-Carleton	Winnipeg	Combined
Case referrals, 1991	40	317	178	725	1,260
Case referrals, 1992	79	349	200	963	1,591
Case referrals, 1993	139	185	311	959	1,594
Total case referrals, 1991–1993	258	851	689	2,647	4,445
Mediations, 1991	12	142	60	335	549
Mediations, 1992	28	107	85	393	613
Mediations, 1993	51	82	114	327	574
Total mediations, 1991–1993	91	331	259	1,055	1,736
Successfully negotiated agreements, 1991	11 (92%)	141 (99%)	53 (88%)	299 (89%)	504 (92%)
Successfully negotiated agreements, 1992	24 (86%)	105 (98%)	79 (93%)	358 (91%)	566 (92%)
Successfully negotiated agreements, 1993	48 (94%)	81 (99%)	111 (97%)	290 (89%)	530 (94%)
Successfully negotiated agreements, 1991–1993	83 (91%)	327 (99%)	243 (94%)	947 (90%)	1,600 (93%)
Proportion of mediations to case referrals, 1991	33%	45%	34%	46%	44%
Proportion of mediations to case referrals, 1992	36%	31%	43%	41%	39%
Proportion of mediations to case referrals, 1993	37%	44%	37%	34%	36%
Proportion of mediations to case referrals, 1991–1993	35%	39%	38%	40%	39%

combined sites, than among similar complainants/victims(48 percent) and accused/offenders (53 percent) who were referred to mediation but never participated in mediation. At the individual sites, significant differences between mediation participants and nonparticipants in complainant/victim satisfaction with the justice system were found in Ottawa and Winnipeg. Significant differences in accused/offender satisfaction were found in Langley and Winnipeg.

Overall, the vast majority of complainants/victims (89 percent) and accused/offenders (91 percent) at the combined sites were satisfied with the outcome of the mediation session they participated in. At the individual sites, complainant/victim satisfaction with the mediation outcome ranged from 82 percent in Langley (N = 38) to 100 percent in Calgary (N = 7). Accused/offender satisfaction with the mediation outcome ranged from 88 percent in Winnipeg (N = 93) to 100 percent in Calgary (N = 6).

An additional index of participants' overall satisfaction was the willingness they expressed to mediate again should they find themselves in similar circumstances. Among mediation participants across all sites, 93.2 percent of the complainants/victims and 92.6 percent of the accused/offenders said that should the need arise, they would choose to participate in the mediation process again. Among complainant/victims who participated, 92.8 percent said they would recommend the process to others; for accused/offender participants, this figure was 97 percent.

Perceptions of Fairness

Being fairly treated by the justice system was significantly more likely to be expressed among complainants/victims (80 percent) and accused/offenders (80 percent) who participated in mediation, at the combined sites, than similar complainants/victims (43 percent) and accused/offenders (56 percent) who were referred to mediation but never participated in mediation.

Significant differences in complainant/victim perceptions of fairness were found at two of the four program sites (Ottawa and Winnipeg). A significant difference in accused/offender perceptions of fairness was found only at Winnipeg.

The mediated agreement was viewed as fair to the victim by 92 percent of complainants/victims at the combined sites and fair to the offender by 93 percent of accused/offenders. At specific sites, complainant/victim perceptions of the fairness of the mediated agreement to the victim ranged from 80 percent in Calgary (N = 5) to 98 percent in Ottawa (N = 42). Complainant/victim perceptions of the fairness of the agreement to the accused/offender ranged from 82 percent in Langley (N = 34) to 100 percent in Ottawa (N = 40). At specific sites, accused/offender perceptions of the fairness of the mediated agreement to the accused/offender ranged from 87 percent in Winnipeg (N = 87) to 100 percent in Ottawa (N = 14). Accused/offender perceptions of fairness of the agreement to the complainant/victim ranged from 85 percent in Ottawa (N = 13) to 100 percent in Langley (N = 37).

Fear of Revictimization

Overall, fear of being revictimized by the same offender was significantly less likely to be expressed among complainants/victims (11 percent) who participated in a mediation session with the offender, at the combined sites, than similar complainants/victims(31 percent) who were referred to mediation but never participated in mediation. This was particularly true at two of the program sites, Ottawa and Winnipeg.

Remaining upset about the crime was significantly less likely to be expressed by complainants/victims (53 percent) who participated in a mediation session with the offender, at the combined sites, than similar complainants/victims (66 percent) who were referred to mediation but never participated in mediation. At the program sites, this was found to be true only at Winnipeg.

Participant Perspective on Preparation

A high proportion of participants across all four program sites felt they were sufficiently prepared for the mediation session. For complainants/victims, this figure was 87.2 percent. Among accused/offenders, 82.6 percent felt preparation was sufficient. Both complainants/victims and accused/offenders reported that being informed of what happens in mediation was the most helpful component in getting them prepared. Rated second was feeling that they were being listened to by the mediator, and rated third was having the benefits of mediation explained.

Participant Perspective on the Mediation Process

As part of the open-ended portion of the interview, participants were asked what three things they found most and least satisfying about the victim offender mediation experience. The following analysis focuses on their primary response to each of these questions. For complainant/victims who participated in mediation, the most frequently mentioned positive aspect of the process was the opportunity for face-to-face contact ($N = 51$), represented in such comments as the following:

"I believe in face to face problem solving."

"I got to see the individual in a different light, when he wasn't as hostile as he was at the time of the offense. We were able to speak one on one."

"It was helpful to look at his face and tell him how I felt."

"We worked things out because we got to sit down and talk together, which we had never done before. We resolved it."

An additional category of positive comments centered around viewing mediation as a good alternative to court ($N = 30$); often these comments were coupled with the comments on the benefits of face-to-face contact, in comparison to which courts were viewed as impersonal and cold. Complainants/victims also felt that mediation was a way to prevent future crime ($N = 25$); some had chosen it for precisely this reason:

"I chose it to teach him a lesson."

"It was an education opportunity to help the offender."

The remaining positive reasons offered as primary by complainant/victims were to obtain a restitution or compensation agreement ($N = 23$) and that mediation is a system that is responsive to complainant/victims ($N = 11$).

Negative comments by complainants/victims were far fewer in number and centered around the perceived lack of accountability ($N = 12$), the fact that mediation was uncomfortable ($N = 5$), that mediation had been too slow or time-consuming ($N = 3$), and that some participants felt coerced into mediation ($N = 3$).

Accused/offenders who participated in mediation similarly confirmed the face-to-face nature of the encounter as the most important positive aspect ($N = 61$), evident in such comments as the following:

"[It] lifted the weight off my back. I was able to apologize and talk and have my story heard."

"Mediation is more personal."

"[The complainant] turned out to be a very nice person, far more reasonable than had appeared at the time of the incident."

"You can express yourself. It's more private and more informal than the court."

As expected, many accused/offenders liked mediation for avoiding court or criminal charges ($N = 24$). Thirteen accused/offenders said that mediation helped them learn something. They expressed that they had violated a person, and they should be responsible for controlling their own behavior. Comments included these:

> "It made me think a lot. Mediation made me see what I did was wrong."

> "You are made responsible for what you did, not just a charge."

> "I have changed how I react to stressful situations. [The experience] made me think twice about future crime."

Finally, seven of the accused/offenders emphasized obtaining a sense of closure as their primary benefit from mediation.

Accused/offender negative comments numbered even fewer than those by complainants/victims. Six accused/offenders felt in some way uncomfortable with going through mediation. Four said mediation was not effective in their cases, and four felt they had been coerced into participating. Three felt inadequately prepared, and three found mediation to be too slow.

Justice System Perceptions

A total of forty-five criminal justice officials—judges, police officers, probation officers, crown attorneys, and defense attorneys—at the four sites were interviewed to ascertain their perceptions and level of support for victim offender mediation as a concept and for the particular program in their jurisdiction. Interviews included a number of fixed, closed-ended items and several open-ended, qualitative questions. Not all interviewees answered all questions. Slightly under two-thirds (60 percent) of the justice system officials interviewed had themselves referred cases into their local mediation programs. The following observations therefore reflect both direct experience and more general perceptions about the role of the program in the local community.

The initial response of justice system officials to the idea of mediation upon first learning about it was moderately positive: 71

percent (N = 30) of those interviewed were supportive of the concept from the beginning. Comments included the "We criminalize far too much behavior" and "I couldn't imagine anything that would be more of a learning experience for both the victim and the young person." Results of subsequent analysis show that generally, as time passed and mediation programs were given the opportunity to develop a track record, the majority of officials who were initially reluctant to endorse the value of mediation became supportive.

Respondents were asked about their perceptions regarding whether or not the accused/offender was held accountable. Fully 93 percent (N = 38) believed that accused/offenders are held accountable, and 95 percent (N = 36) further reported that they thought the level of accountability was appropriate. Comments included "Yes, there is very little real accountability in the revolving door of our criminal justice system [as compared to mediation]" and "It's harder to face the victim than to get shuffled through the criminal justice system."

Eighty one percent (N = 35) of the officials responding to the satisfaction question said that they were either satisfied or very satisfied about the performance of the mediation program in their city. Cross-site differences were more marked on this question, with five of the six officials who were either mixed or dissatisfied coming from Calgary. It should be noted that the Calgary program is also the smallest of the four and may not have developed as much of an impact in its criminal justice community as the other three programs. In general, officials felt that their local programs were doing good-quality work. Many felt that the major need was for more resources to expand the programs and give them a stronger role in the criminal justice system and in society as a whole. Comments included the following:

"[The program staff] are doing their job well. The crown needs a more enlightened attitude about mediation. Most defense lawyers don't know much about it."

"I have heard very good things about [the VOM program]

from lawyers. The dialogue that goes on in mediation is far more effective and desirable than court."

Respondents were asked whether, if they themselves were a victim of a crime, they would elect to participate in mediation. Interestingly, this was the only question to which all forty-five participants gave an answer. Thirty-two (71 percent) said that they would do so; three more (7 percent) said that it would depend on the circumstances and nature of the crime. Reasons expressed by those who would choose to participate echo themes from victims across all the studies: "to express anger, make them realize they affected my life"; "I would hope I could deter them. I would want a genuine apology, some remorse"; "I would want to unload, let them know how upset I am."

Respondents who had referred cases into mediation were asked about the short-term and long-term outcomes they perceived. Short-term benefits cited included promoting complainant/victim healing ($N = 10$), communicating the impact of the crime to the accused/defendant ($N = 9$), facilitating greater victim/complainant input ($N = 5$), helping the victim/complainant understand why it happened ($N = 4$), saving resources and time ($N = 3$), and demonstrating caring for the accused/defendant ($N = 2$). Longer-term outcomes perceived by these officials included rehabilitating or "straightening" the accused/offender ($N = 23$) and the fact that the parties were able to solve the underlying problem ($N = 6$). In addition, when asked what benefits they perceived for the criminal justice system in general, respondents highlighted the following outcomes: that mediation saves resources ($N = 16$), that it reduces caseloads ($N = 8$), that it lowers recidivism ($N = 6$), and that it improves public satisfaction with the criminal justice system ($N = 4$).

Summary

The results of this first cross-national replication of the U.S. study confirm the same major findings. Both complainants/victims and accused/offenders are very satisfied with the outcome of their mediation sessions and feel that the process was fair, participants generally feel that their participation was voluntary, satisfactory agreements are negotiated and honored in most cases, and the justice systems in the jurisdictions under study were largely supportive. Two important differences in service delivery underscore the significance of these similar findings: (1) in the Canadian programs, many referrals take place before the accused has either admitted guilt or been tried and found guilty; and (2) the extent of preparation of both parties prior to mediation varies widely across programs. That outcomes remain positive in the face of these differences suggests that there are many variations to the generic mediation model and that in spite of its many differences, it meets a strongly felt need among individuals who participate. Further research is needed to explore these differences and discover any potential impact they may have on the outcome of victim offender mediation programs.

Chapter Twelve

Victim Offender Mediation in England

A Multisite Assessment

The third component of the cross-national assessment of victim offender mediation took place in Great Britain (Umbreit & Roberts, 1996). In England, experimentation with the concept of mediation in a small number of cases (prior to any major initiative) actually began in the early 1970s. By 1986, there were twelve projects in England, and this number had grown to twenty by the mid-1990s.

The process of victim offender mediation in England is similar in most ways to the process being followed in the United States, with a few differences. In England, the mediation phase consists of two distinct subcategories: direct and indirect mediation. In direct mediation, a face-to-face meeting is facilitated between the victim and the offender; in indirect mediation, the mediator meets with both parties separately and exchanges information and needs between the parties while never facilitating a face-to-face session. In some cases, this may require quite a few meetings with the involved individuals before a final resolution of the conflict emerges. Only a small portion of referred cases in England involve direct mediation. In the United States, the process of indirect mediation is often called "conciliation." Others sometimes refer to the process as "shuttle diplomacy."

Note: This chapter is based on Umbreit and Roberts (1996). Adapted with permission.

Methodology

With extremely limited resources available to support the English component of this cross-national study, only two sites could be included. Coventry and Leeds were selected because they represent two of the best-developed projects in England and both were interested in participating in the cross-national study. Also in view of the limited resources, the need for a valid and reliable design had to be balanced with practical issues related to administering a low-budget study. Despite the limited resources, the use of a comparison group was critical. Employing a true experimental design, however, was not feasible given the limited number of referred cases available for random assignment and the time and complexity of negotiating such arrangements. Therefore, the study used a quasi-experimental design including quantitative and qualitative data collection and analysis.

An additional limitation imposed by available resources was the small size of the sample of individuals who could be interviewed (123 participants, compared to 610 in Canada and 948 in the United States). The major impact of this reduction in sample size was a concomitant reduction in significant differences between the mediation participants and the two comparison groups. Most of the comparisons that were examined corroborated the direction of findings in the United States and Canada, but very few reached statistical significance.

Research Design

Telephone and in-person interviews with victims and offenders were conducted following either direct or indirect mediation or the disposal of a case by a prosecutor, court, or related agency. Three groups were obtained for a comparative study approach: individuals who went through a direct mediation experience, individuals who went through an indirect mediation experience, and individuals who were referred to mediation but did not go through mediation.

The language in the interview schedules was adapted to fit the context of Great Britain. Interviews with key criminal justice officials and organizations were conducted, along with extensive review of program materials. Several Likert scales were used, as well as open-ended questions with probes. Descriptive statistics related to respondent characteristics were also used.

Samples

Participants in the study were from the Coventry Reparation Scheme and the Leeds Mediation and Reparation Service. A total of 123 interviews were conducted, involving 70 victims and 53 offenders. Thirty-four interviews were done in Coventry and 89 in Leeds, as noted in Table 12.1.

Sixty percent of the victims studied were male. They accounted for 52 percent of the indirect mediation group, 58 percent of the direct mediation group, and 70 percent of the no-mediation group of victims. The average age of victims was forty. Those who went through direct mediation had an average age of thirty-five. Those who went through indirect mediation had an average age of forty-six. Those who did not go through the mediation experience averaged thirty-eight years old.

Ninety-four percent of offenders studied were male. All three female offenders were part of the no-mediation subsample. The average age of offenders was twenty-four. Those who went through direct mediation averaged nineteen years of age, those who went through indirect mediation averaged twenty-seven; and those who did not go through mediation were an average of twenty-five years old.

Research Questions

The study was guided by the following questions:

1. How does the mediation process work in the two British projects?

Table 12.1 English Subsamples

Project	Direct Mediation		Indirect Mediation		No Mediation		Total Victims	Total Offenders	Combined Total (Victims and Offenders)
	Victims	Offenders	Victims	Offenders	Victims	Offenders			
Coventry	8	7	9	4	4	2	21	13	34
Leeds	11	9	16	10	22	21	49	40	89
Total	19	16	25	14	26	23	70	53	123

2. How do mediation participants evaluate the mediation process?

3. What are the immediate outcomes of the mediation process?

4. What do criminal justice system officials think about the mediation process?

Research Sites

The two sites examined in this study were probation-based victim offender mediation programs in Leeds and Coventry. Most projects in Europe and the United States use trained volunteer mediators from the community, along with staff. While the Leeds project follows this pattern, in the Coventry project only staff serve as mediators.

Coventry

The Coventry Reparation Scheme was established by the West Midlands Probation Service (WMPS) in 1985 as part of an experiment involving four projects and funded by the Home Office (the government agency in charge of domestic affairs, elections, and the police). Serving a population of three hundred thousand, the project in Coventry was initially designed to work with less serious offenders (following a guilty plea) referred by the Magistrates Court. Both the offender and the victim are given the choice of participating in the project. Within a year, the Coventry Reparation Scheme began working with the local Juvenile/Youth Liaison Panel. By 1987, the project was also accepting referrals from the Crown Court.

During the first two years of operation (1986–1987), the Coventry Reparation Scheme had a total of 196 referrals, representing 158 cases from the Magistrates Court, 26 cases from Juvenile Court, and 12 cases from Crown Court. The 196 referrals involved 196 offenders and 223 victims. The types of cases referred were primarily property offenses (burglary and theft) and minor assaults. Approximately 50 percent of these referred cases ended up with some type of action being taken by the project: 58 cases in direct mediation and 41 cases in indirect mediation. During this initial two-year period, only sixteen agreements for practical reparation or voluntary compensation resulted from the mediated cases. The project had the full-time equivalent of 2.75 staff to manage its services.

The project continued to refine its policies and procedures following review of its first years of operation. During the two-year period 1992–1993, the Coventry Reparation Scheme had a total of 170 referrals, representing: 75 cases from the Magistrates Court; 22 cases from Juvenile Court; and 73 cases from Crown Court. The 170 referrals involved 171 offenders and 179 victims. The types of cases referred continued to be primarily property offenses (burglary and theft) and minor assaults, although a number of more serious cases were also referred. As during its first two years of operation, approximately 50 percent of these referred cases ended up with some type of action being taken by the project: 17 cases went to direct mediation; and 70 cases were handled in indirect mediation. During this two-year period, seventy agreements for practical reparation or voluntary compensation resulted from the mediated cases. It is particularly worth noting the changes that occurred between its first two years of operation and the two-year period of 1992–1993, total case referrals decreased by 13 percent; referrals from the Crown Court increased by more than 500 percent, from 12 to 73; referrals from the Magistrates Court decreased from 81 percent (1986–1987) to 44 percent (1992–1993); direct mediation conducted decreased from 58 percent of all mediations in the first two years to only 20 percent in 1992–1993; and agreements reached in mediation for practical reparation or voluntary compensation increased from only 16 percent in the first two years to 80 percent in 1992–1993. Additional details about the operation of the Coventry Reparation Scheme are summarized in Table 12.2.

Table 12.2 Coventry Reparation Scheme, 1991–1993

	1991	1992	1993	Combined 1991– 1993
Total referrals to mediation project	106	91	79	276
Juvenile Court	17	14	8	39
Magistrates Court	40	44	31	115
Crown Court	49	33	40	122
Total cases in mediation	59	55	32	146
(percentage of total cases referred)	(56%)	(60%)	(41%)	(53%)
Direct mediation (percentage of mediated cases)	19 (32%)	12 (22%)	5 (16%)	36 (25%)
Indirect mediation (percentage of mediated cases)	40 (68%)	43 (78%)	27 (84%)	110 (75%)
Number of offenders referred	106	91	80	277
Number of victims referred	114	98	81	293
Number of agreements for practical reparation or voluntary compensation	41	47	23	111
Number of referrals by source				
Probation officers				128 (48%)
Solicitors				68 (26%)
Police, court	n.a.	n.a.	n.a.	15 (6%)
Offender, other				12 (4%)
Unknown				43 (16%)
Number of offenses by type				
Burglary, robbery, theft	55 (50%)	45 (50%)	37 (47%)	137 (49%)
Assault	26 (24%)	21 (23%)	25 (32%)	72 (26%)
Property damage	4 (4%)	6 (7%)	4 (5%)	14 (5%)
Other	15 (13%)	17 (19%)	9 (11%)	41 (15%)
Unknown	10 (9%)	2 (1%)	3 (4%)	16 (5%)

Note: Percentages may not sum to 100 due to rounding; n.a.= not available.

Leeds

The Leeds Mediation and Reparation Service was initiated by the West Yorkshire Probation Service (WYPS) in 1985 as one of the four experimental projects funded by the Home Office. The project was initially referred to as the Leeds Reparation Project and changed to its current name in 1987. Serving a population of five hundred thousand, the project in Leeds was designed to work with more serious and persistent criminal offenders in the Crown Court. Participation in the Leeds Mediation and Reparation Service is voluntary for both the victim and the offender. Today, the project also receives referrals from the Juvenile/Youth Liaison Panel and Magistrates Court.

A total of 272 cases were referred to the project during the first two years, representing 201 cases from Crown Court; 62 cases from Magistrates Court; and 9 cases from Juvenile Court. Burglary was the most frequent offense referred to the project, representing nearly half of all referrals. Theft and assault were the other two most frequently referred cases. One-third of the referred cases (N = 95) resulted in mediation: 35 in direct mediation (37 percent of mediated cases) and 60 in indirect mediation (63 percent of mediated cases). A total of forty-two agreements for practical reparation or voluntary compensation resulted from the mediated cases during this initial two-year period (1985–1986). Agreements were far more likely to occur in direct mediation (80 percent of the total) than in indirect mediation (20 percent of the total). The Leeds Mediation and Reparation Scheme had a staff of four.

After the first two years of funding from the Home Office, a plan was developed to expand the mediation and reparation services throughout the county of West Yorkshire. By late 1995, mediation services were operating in all five divisions of the West Yorkshire probation area.

During the two-year period 1992–1993, the Leeds Mediation and Reparation Service had a total of 358 referrals, representing 187 from Crown Court, 63 from Magistrates Court, 31 from Juvenile Court, 32 cautions, 32 postsentence, and 13 from either an unknown source or a victim referral. Burglary, assault, and robbery were the most frequently referred cases. The number of referred cases that resulted in mediation increased from about a third in the initial two years of the project to nearly half of all cases during 1992 and 1993. The number of direct mediations, however, decreased from 37 percent during the first two years to 13 percent during 1992–1993. Of the 174 cases involved in mediation in 1992–1993, 87 percent (N = 151) employed indirect mediation. In 1993 alone, 172 cases were referred, and 84 of them (49 percent) participated in mediation. The referrals were primarily from probation officers and occurred at all stages: caution, before sentencing, and after sentencing. The proportion in direct mediation increased slightly, from 11 percent in 1992 to 16 percent in 1993. Further details about the activity of the Leeds project are summarized in Table 12.3.

In 1993, the Leeds Mediation and Reparation Service, in conjunction with the Save the Children organization, published a very comprehensive and practical victim offender mediation training manual. The *Victim and Offender Mediation Handbook* (Quill & Wynne, 1993) provides a helpful resource to other communities as the practice of victim offender mediation develops in England.

Findings

The findings from both sites have been combined for the purposes of the following discussion. Participant perceptions are compared for both victims and offenders, for mediation versus no-mediation groups, and where data were available, for direct versus indirect mediation.

Participant Satisfaction with the Criminal Justice System

In both Leeds and Coventry, the majority of victims in both samples (mediation, 62 percent; no-mediation, 58 percent) expressed overall satisfaction with the criminal justice system. The experience of

Table 12.3 Leeds Mediation and Reparation Service, 1991–1993

	1991	1992	1993	Combined 1991– 1993
Total referrals to mediation project	177	186	172	535
Juvenile Court	14	8	23	45
Magistrates Court	33	35	28	96
Crown Court	74	106	81	261
Caution	31	15	· 17	63
After sentencing	23	16	16	· 55
Unknown, victim referral	2	6	7	15
Total cases in mediation	90	90	84	264
(percentage of referred cases)	(51%)	(48%)	(49%)	(49%)
Direct mediation	18	10	13	41
(percentage of referred cases)	(20%)	(11%)	(16%)	(16%)
Indirect mediation	72	80	71	223
(percentage of referred cases)	(80%)	(89%)	(84%)	(84%)
Number of offenders referred	177	186	172	535
Number of victims referred	n.a.	n.a.	n.a.	n.a.
Number of referrals by source				
Probation officers	116 (66%)	143 (77%)	126 (73%)	385 (72%)
Social services	5 (3%)	2 (1%)	6 (3%)	13 (2%)
Case referral panels	39 (22%)	20 (11%)	23 (13%)	82 (15%)
Other	14 7%)	10 (5%)	7 (4%)	31 (6%)
Victim	3 (2%)	11 (6%)	10 (6%)	24 (5%)
Number of offenses by type				
Burglary	49 (28%)	66 (36%)	54 (31%)	169 (31%)
Assault	30 (17%)	31 (17%)	39 (23%)	100 (19%)
Theft	27 (15%)	24 (13%)	17 (10%)	68 (13%)
Robbery	27 (15%)	28 (15%)	30 (17%)	85 (16%)
Other	44 (25%)	37 (19%)	32 (19%)	113 (21%)

Note: n.a.= not available.

satisfaction from participation in mediation is well expressed by a victim who said, "Most helpful was to talk about the offense. . . My viewpoint was listened to, and I felt less like a crime statistic."

Differences were also examined between participants in direct mediation and indirect mediation. Although no significant differences were found in satisfaction among victims, those who went through direct mediation showed consistently greater satisfaction and less dissatisfaction than those who went through indirect mediation. For the two sites, 68 percent of victims in direct mediation were satisfied, compared to 57 percent of victims in indirect mediation.

Among offenders, there were no significant differences between mediation and no-mediation groups in the expression of satisfaction with the justice system's response to their case. Overall, offender satisfaction was somewhat greater among the offenders who went through mediation (79 percent) than among those who did not (55 percent).

Offender satisfaction with mediation is captured by the following statement: "Mediation made me feel better. . . . I was able to apologize and reimburse the victim. . . . [Mediation] helped me come to terms with [what I had done] and put the crime behind me."

Whereas English victims reported slightly greater satisfaction with direct than with indirect mediation, offenders showed the opposite result. This finding clearly suggests that a face-to-face meeting with the person they victimized is not an easy or preferred response for offenders. A direct mediation session is likely to be an uncomfortable experience for many offenders, even though they are quite satisfied with the process when it is completed.

According to the combined statistics, 86 percent of offenders who went through indirect mediation and 73 percent of those who went through direct mediation expressed satisfaction with the criminal justice system. In Leeds, those differences were quite pronounced, although not statistically significant: 90 percent of the offenders who went through indirect mediation and only 62 percent of those who went through direct mediation expressed satisfaction with the criminal justice system's response to their case. In Coventry, more offenders who went through direct mediation (86 percent) expressed satisfaction than those who went through indirect mediation (75 percent). However, the Coventry sample was quite small.

Client Satisfaction with the Outcome of Mediation

A clear majority of victims in direct and indirect mediation were satisfied with the outcome of their mediation sessions. Direct mediation resulted in considerably higher satisfaction with the outcome among victims than indirect mediation. Overall, victims participating in direct face-to-face mediation were satisfied in 84 percent of the cases, while those participating in indirect mediation were satisfied in 74 percent of the cases. This difference was not statistically significant.

Offenders expressed an even stronger sense of satisfaction with mediation outcomes than victims in mediation did. Every single offender who participated in direct mediation reported being satisfied with its outcome (100 percent), compared to 79 percent of offenders who were involved in indirect mediation. The 21 percent who said they were dissatisfied all came from Leeds.

Perceptions of Fairness in the Justice System

Victims at both sites who participated in mediation were somewhat more likely to express a perception of fairness in the justice system's response to their case (59 percent) than similar victims who were referred to mediation but never participated in it (50 percent). This difference was not statistically significant. Victims' sense of fairness in the mediation process was expressed in the following typical statement: "Fairness to me means that the offender gets the opportunity to make amends."

Victims who took part in direct mediation were more likely to have a perception of fairness in the criminal justice system

(71 percent at the two sites) than victims who took part in indirect mediation (50 percent). This difference did not reach statistical significance, although it approached significance more than the difference between the mediation and no-mediation groups.

Offenders who participated in mediation were significantly more likely to express a perception of fairness in the justice system (89 percent at the two sites) than similar offenders who did not participate in mediation (56 percent; see Table 12.4). The offenders' experience of fairness is represented by the following statement: "Mediation is a good thing: it helps the offender understand how the victim feels. . . . The agreement was fair to both."

Offenders who participated in indirect mediation seemed to perceive the justice system as somewhat more fair (100 percent of all participants) than those who participated in direct mediation (80 percent at the two sites). This difference, however, was not statistically significant.

Victim Fear of Revictimization

Victims who participated in mediation were less likely to remain afraid of revictimization by the same offender (16 percent at the two sites) than similar victims who did not participate in mediation (33 percent). Victims who participated in direct mediation were less likely to remain afraid of revictimization by the same

Table 12.4 Offender Perceptions of Criminal Justice System
Fairness, Mediated Versus Nonmediated Cases
(Coventry and Leeds Combined)

Perception	Mediated (N = 27)	Nonmediated (N = 23)
Fair	24 (89%)	13 (57%)
Unfair	3 (11%)	10 (43%)

Note: p < .05.

offender (11 percent) than similar victims who participated in indirect mediation (21 percent).

Criminal Justice System Support

A total of thirteen criminal justice system officials were interviewed at the two sites examined in this study. In Leeds, seven individuals were interviewed: one Crown Court judge, one magistrate, three probation officers, one police inspector, and one attorney. The four women and three men interviewed ranged in age from thirty-one to sixty-two years, and their experience in the criminal justice system ranged from three to forty years.

In Coventry, six individuals were interviewed: a magistrate, the chief clerk to justices in Magistrate Court, a senior probation officer, a probation officer, a police sergeant and youth liaison officer, and a social worker. The two women and four men interviewed ranged in age from thirty-five to sixty-three years old. Their experience in the criminal justice field ranged from four to forty-seven years.

Eighty-three percent of those interviewed at both sites indicated that they supported the development of the project from the very beginning. Only one person at each site admitted not supporting the mediation program from the beginning. One of these nonsupportive individuals remained essentially nonsupportive at the time of these interviews, many years later, while the other expressed a change of attitude and is now quite supportive. When certain criminal cases are referred to mediation, virtually all of the respondents indicated that their hope that it will have a positive impact on offenders by holding them accountable and forcing them to face the reality of their crime. Over half of the respondents expressed hope that the mediation process would benefit victims by allowing them to express their feelings, affording them a better understanding of the criminal event, and humanizing the entire criminal justice process. The voluntariness of the mediation process for both victim and offender and the sincerity of the offender's motivation for participating was identified, respectively, as the most important factors in having cases referred to victim offender mediation.

Victim Participation

These officials identified two reasons as the most likely ones for a victim's electing to participate in mediation: the need to get answers to questions about the crime and the need to express feelings of anger and frustration to the offender.

With respect to the most important immediate outcomes of the mediation process for victims, the two themes identified most frequently by interviewees were a sense of relief and reassurance and greater understanding of what actually happened and why it happened. For offenders, the themes most frequently identified by these criminal justice officials were holding the offender directly accountable to the victim and helping the offender understand the full impact of the crime on the specific victim. When asked about hoped-for longer-term impacts of the mediation process, the most common themes expressed were the ability for the victim to resolve the incident and obtain closure and the reduction of recidivism among offenders who participate in the program.

Offender Participation

The officials cited the most likely reasons for offender participation in mediation as mitigation, diversion, and self-interest. All are related to offenders' perception that they would get a "better deal" or a lesser punishment. These reasons were followed by the need to express remorse and the need to make amends. The magistrate in Leeds observed, "Whatever the motives are to start, there is value once [offenders] are in mediation. They will face the consequences of what they have done." The probation officer in Coventry commented, "Some know they may get a lesser sentence . . . [but] at the end of the day, mediation is one of the toughest 'sentences' you could do."

The issue of holding offenders accountable in a meaningful way was expressed throughout the interviews, with 85 percent of the respondents indicating their belief that victim offender mediation was effective in holding offenders accountable for their criminal behavior. Seventy-five percent of those interviewed indicated their satisfaction with the performance of the mediation project they related to, with the highest level of satisfaction found at the Coventry site (100 percent). None of the respondents indicated dissatisfaction with the performance of the project, although 50 percent of those interviewed in Leeds indicated some mixed feelings, with one person specifically mentioning external pressures in the justice system, a likely source of his mixed feelings about the project.

Implications

A number of conclusions and implications emerged from this study. They must, however, be viewed as only suggestive and cannot be generalized to all victim offender mediation projects in England. Because of the limited resources available to conduct the study and, particularly, the quasi-experimental design and small sample sizes, this study was largely descriptive and exploratory in nature. Nonetheless, the following trends were observed.

• Victims and offenders who participated in mediation at the Coventry and Leeds projects were more likely to have expressed satisfaction and a perception of fairness in the justice system's response to their case than victims and offenders who were referred to the projects but never participated in mediation.

• Victims who participated in mediation at the two sites were less fearful of being revictimized by the same offender than similar victims who were referred to the project but did not participate in mediation. Victims in direct mediation were even less fearful of revictimization than those in indirect mediation.

• Direct face-to-face mediation is not very frequently practiced at the two projects. During 1993, only 16 percent of the cases using mediation of any kind involved direct mediation. When compared to the total number of cases referred to both projects in 1993, only 7 percent featured direct mediation. Whether this low participation in direct mediation is related to the traditional British reserve is not clear. Some observers in England have suggested that it has little to do with the culture and is more likely related to case management and preparation procedures that do not assertively encourage participation in direct mediation for fear of compromising the individual's freedom of choice. A number of other factors may also be related to the low rate of direct mediation. For example, offenders in England are generally adults (high rates of direct mediation in the United States reflect the large numbers of juveniles referred to mediation programs), many cases involve parties with a prior relationship (most programs in the United States involve strangers), and more serious cases enter the process in England after sentencing (many of the U.S. programs accept case referrals at the diversion stage).

• Victims of crime who participated in the study of the Coventry and Leeds projects were considerably more likely to benefit from direct face-to-face mediation with the offender than from indirect mediation. Victims in direct mediation were more likely to feel they participated voluntarily, to express satisfaction with the justice system's response to their case, to be satisfied with the outcome of mediation, to be less fearful, and to indicate that the justice system's handling of their case was fair.

• Offenders who participated in the study of the Coventry and Leeds projects were more likely to benefit from direct face-to-face mediation with the victim related to certain issues examined than from indirect mediation. Offenders in direct mediation were more likely to feel they participated voluntarily and to express satisfaction with the outcome of the mediation. But offenders in indirect mediation were more likely to express satisfaction and a perception of fairness in the justice system's response to their case.

• Strong consideration should be given to providing more opportunities and encouragement for victims and offenders to participate in direct face-to-face mediation at the Coventry and Leeds projects, particularly since victims were consistently more likely to indicate positive benefits from direct mediation. A more assertive, encouraging, and supportive approach to victims and offenders during the premediation phase may be required, while still respecting each party's right to make an informed and voluntary choice. This is not, however, recommending a "hard sell" approach in which either victim or offender would feel coerced into the mediation process, which would violate the basic principles of the process as a restorative justice intervention.

• Participation in the victim offender mediation projects in Coventry and Leeds increased the quality of justice experienced by both victims and offenders.

• Consistent with similar studies of victim offender mediation at four sites in the United States (Chapter Ten) and four sites in Canada (Chapter Eleven), victims and offenders who participated in mediation in Coventry and Leeds indicated very high levels of satisfaction with the process and outcome of mediation, and victims also indicated less fear of revictimization by the same offender. Victims at the two English projects, however, indicated lower levels of satisfaction and perceptions of fairness with the criminal justice system's response to their case when compared to the North American studies.

• During the course of conducting this study, it became increasingly clear that the leadership and support provided by Mediation U.K., the national mediation association, was vital to the development of victim offender mediation in England. The high quality of the association's journal, *Mediation*, and its initiative in developing standards for development of victim offender mediation projects are particularly outstanding contributions to the field. Other related nationwide mediation associations in North America could greatly benefit from the model of supportive leadership and networking exemplified by Mediation U.K.

Part Three

Emerging Issues

Part Three explores future directions in the practice of victim offender mediation. Chapter Thirteen presents a preliminary look at the application of VOM in cases of severe violence. Chapter Fourteen provides an overview of emerging trends, opportunities, and hazards the field faces as it continues to develop throughout the world.

Chapter Thirteen

Advanced Mediation and Dialogue in Crimes of Severe Violence

Both restorative justice in general and victim offender mediation specifically continue to be identified as primarily, if not exclusively, addressing nonviolent property crimes and perhaps even minor assaults. This chapter will challenge such assumptions by providing empirical evidence that suggests that many of the principles of restorative justice can be applied in crimes of severe violence, including murder. Some would even suggest that the deepest healing impact of restorative justice is to be found in addressing and responding to such violent crime.

As victim offender mediation has become more widely known and accepted, an increasing number of victims of severely violent crimes have expressed interest in meeting the offender, most often an inmate in a correctional facility. These victims want to meet the offender to express the full impact of the crime on their lives, to get answers to questions they have, and to gain a greater sense of closure so that they can move on with their lives. In most cases, this occurs many years after the crime occurred, and the actual mediation or dialogue session is typically held in a secure institution where the offender is incarcerated.

In the mid-1980s, the opportunity for a mediated dialogue was available to only a handful of victims of sexual assault and attempted homicide and survivors of murder victims at scattered

Note: This chapter is based on Umbreit and Bradshaw (1995) and Coates and Umbreit (1999). Adapted with permission.

locations throughout the United States. Currently, correctional departments and victim services units in seven states are at various stages in developing a statewide protocol for allowing such encounters between the victim or survivor of a severely violent crime and the offender. In Texas, there is a waiting list of nearly 150 victims of severe violence, including many parents of murdered children, who have requested a meeting with the offender through the Victim Offender Mediation/Dialogue Program of the Victim Services Unit, Texas Department of Criminal Justice. A growing number of victims of severe violence in Canada and Europe have also expressed interest in a mediated dialogue session with the offender. Since 1991, the Canadian Ministry of Justice has supported the development of these services through the pioneering work of the Victim Offender Mediation Program of the Fraser Region Community Justice Initiatives Association in Langley, British Columbia.

Victim-Sensitive Offender Dialogue: The VSOD Model

When responding to the expressed needs of victims of severe violence who desire to meet the offender, it is important to recognize a number of distinguishing characteristics of such cases. These typically include heightened emotional intensity, extreme need for a nonjudgmental attitude toward all parties, longer case preparation by the mediator (six to eighteen months), the need for multiple separate meetings prior to the joint session (two to four or even more), multiple phone conversations, negotiating with correctional officials to secure access to the inmate and to conduct a mediated dialogue in prison, coaching of participants in the communication of intense feelings, and boundary clarification (mediation/dialogue versus therapy). The field of restorative justice and victim offender mediation is only beginning to come to grips with how the basic mediation model must be adapted to serve the more intense needs of parties involved in serious and violent criminal conflict.

Persons who are interested in mediating a dialogue between victims and offenders in crimes of severe violence need far more advanced training than typically received in basic mediation training. Because of the intense nature of these cases, there are a number of clear implications for advanced training for any person who chooses to work in this area. For example, mediators will need special knowledge and skills related to working with severely violent crimes, in addition to the normal mediation skills. Advanced training would not focus on the mechanics of negotiation or mediation. Instead, it would emphasize an experiential understanding of the painful journey of the participants. Such advanced training would need to focus on the process of facilitating a direct and frank dialogue between the parties related to the violent crime that occurred, the journey of grieving being experienced by the victim or surviving family members, and the possibilities for some degree of closure and healing through a process of mutual aid.

To work effectively with victims of severe violence, it will be important for the mediator to have a thorough understanding of the victimization experience and its phases, the capacity to understand and deal with grief and loss (our own and that of others), an understanding of posttraumatic stress and its impact, and the ability to collaborate with psychotherapists.

Work with offenders involved in such cases requires a thorough understanding of the criminal justice and corrections system, familiarity with the offender and prisoner experience, the ability to relate to offenders convicted of heinous crimes in a nonjudgmental manner, and the ability to negotiate with high-level correctional officials to gain access to the offender-inmate.

Communication and dialogue between interested victims of severe violence and the offenders can occur in a number of forms, ranging from highly therapeutic models developed and used by Dave Gustafson in Langley, British Columbia, and by David Doerfler in Austin, Texas, to nontherapeutic dialogue models developed and used in the early pioneering work of Dennis Wittman in Genesee County, New York; by Mark Umbreit in St. Paul, Minnesota;

and by Karen Ho in Columbus, Ohio. This chapter presents the victim-sensitive offender dialogue (VSOD) model (Umbreit & Bradshaw, 1995), which uses humanistic "dialogue-driven" mediation (Umbreit, 1997). The basic elements of the VSOD model, in one form or another, tend to serve as a foundation for many practitioners. However, programs are characterized by considerable diversity and creativity.

Victim-sensitive offender dialogue should be understood more as a process than as a rigid model. It requires a tremendous amount of compassionate listening, patience, and self-care for the practitioner throughout the entire work on the case, in addition to the specific phases and tasks identified.

VSOD in crimes of severe violence relies on a two-dimensional integrated model for facilitating healing and growth following violent crime. The first dimension focuses on spirituality and peace-making. Spirituality may be synonymous with religion for some people, but for the purposes of the VSOD model, spirituality is understood as the search for a deeper meaning and purpose in life and the circumstances that we now face, an honoring of the sacred gift of life, and a yearning for a greater connectedness with other beings and, for some, a higher being and all of creation. The spiritual is profoundly nonjudgmental and nonseparative. Rachel Naomi Remen (1998) points out that for many people, religion is a bridge to the spiritual, but the spiritual lies beyond the dogma of religion. Unfortunately, in seeking the spiritual, many get stuck on the bridge. Recognizing and honoring the importance that spirituality and religion may play in the lives of those affected by violent crime is central to the healing process offered through victim-sensitive offender dialogue. Recognizing and honoring the journey of those for whom spirituality and religion have virtually no meaning is also very important. Of tremendous importance is the recognition that any discussion of or action related to the spiritual needs of the involved parties must be anchored in their expressed needs, their culture, and their mutual agreement. Issues related to spirituality must never be imposed by the mediator, based on the mediator's own needs, beliefs, or assumptions.

Peacemaking goes far beyond typical conflict resolution. Peacemaking requires a different set of skills and abilities. The humanistic model of mediation described in Chapter One is focused on peacemaking by maximizing the opportunity for offering the parties a safe place in which they feel prepared and comfortable enough to engage in a direct dialogue. Whereas typical conflict resolution and mediation follow a problem-solving model, peacemaking and humanistic mediation are grounded in a paradigm of healing. Qualities of the mediator that are central to peacemaking through humanistic mediation include being fully present and centered on the needs of the involved parties; feeling compassion and empathy—right-brain functions—for all, in addition to having the more rational, analytical qualities of left-brain functions; being comfortable with silence, with ambiguity, and with intuition; maintaining a spirit of humility about one's own contribution to the healing process; and bearing witness to the enormous courage, strength, and capacity of the parties to help each other and honoring the meanings they place on the encounter.

The second dimension of the VSOD model focuses on the actual case development process. Where the first dimension draws heavily on right-brain functions—expression of feelings, empathy, compassion, connectedness, trusting intuition, honoring the sacred—the second dimension of the VSOD model require the more rational, analytical, logical, compartmentalized, problem-solving skills of left-brain thinking. Both dimensions typically occur simultaneously rather than sequentially. Case development skills are very necessary but not sufficient for the full impact of the VSOD model on the parties involved. A balance needs to be found between the spirituality and peacemaking dimension and the case development dimension.

Phase One: Case Development

The following overview of the case development phases of VSOD as practiced in cases of severe violence highlights some specific ways in which the model is often adapted for work in these intense situations. It draws on my own experience conducting such mediations, on numerous conversations with other mediators involved in similar work, and on preliminary qualitative data from an exploratory study of mediation and dialogue in violent crimes in Ohio and Texas.

Assessment

The goal of assessment is to determine if victim offender dialogue is an appropriate and possible eventuality for the parties involved. Note that referral source and point of referral in violent crimes are consistently different than in most other VOM programs. Almost always, the request for an opportunity to meet with the violent offender has come from the victims themselves; and almost always, the offender is already convicted and incarcerated for the crime. In some instances, the offender may have admitted guilt or accepted a plea bargain; in others, there has been no admission of guilt but the offender has been tried and found guilty.

Multidimensional assessments are done on the critical elements essential for mediation of a violent offense. These include assessment of the legal status of the case, opportunities in the correctional system for mediation, and assessment of the motivation and capacity of the victim and offender for dialogue. Case development assessment for mediation of violent offenses involves four major tasks.

Preliminary Assessment. After an inquiry about mediation, the worker does an initial review of the legal status of the case and contacts each party to assess their motivation for and expectations of mediation.

Engagement with Participants. In most programs, numerous individual meetings with each participant are held in order to build a working relationship with each party, to clarify and reality-test their expectations of the potential mediation, and to help them understand the potential risks along with the benefits of mediation. The specific number of individual meetings varies with each case, based on the needs of the parties and the circumstances of the case. It is not uncommon to have four or five separate preparation meetings with each person prior to the mediation/dialogue session. Many cases have far more, and in most programs it is rare to have fewer than two separate preparation meetings.

Individual Assessment.   Each participant is assessed in a number of areas: needs for mediation, feelings, attitudes, and capacity for expressing oneself in mediation, available support systems, and any safety or risk factors. Currently, there are no standardized assessment tools or instruments that are used in all cases.

Engagement and Assessment of Associated Systems.   These may include family and friends of the victim and offender, a victim advocate, a prison counselor, attorneys, psychotherapists, and the correctional system. It is critical to engage and assess these support systems and negotiate any conflicts related to the potential mediation between support persons and the participants.

Contracting

The goal of the contracting phase is to develop an agreement with the participants about the process of victim offender dialogue, the time involvement, roles, expectations, and risk factors.

Several tasks need to be accomplished in the contracting phase. The correctional facility will have to be approached to secure necessary support and agreement as to the time and location of the mediation. The mediator must confirm participants' goals and expectations for mediation and their capacity and willingness to express themselves in ways that won't harm the other party. Other relevant support systems will need to be mobilized. This may involve working out conflicts between people regarding the mediation or working with the psychotherapist of the victim to ensure safety, appropriateness, and timing of mediation.

Preparation of Parties

The goal is to prepare the clients for the victim offender dialogue so they can know what they want and can express themselves in the process as well as possible. Numerous tasks in this area are critical to maximizing successful dialogue. Mediators will conduct ongoing review of client expectations and reality checks of them and obtain in-depth information regarding the perspective of each client on the offense. Often clients will need coaching on communication issues so that they will be clear about what they want to say and the skills to say it without "pushing the buttons" of the other person. Helping participants acknowledge their feelings rather than projecting them in an attacking manner is a crucial task of the mediator during the preparation phase. And the mediator will begin to communicate to each client information gained in meetings with the other (if permission is granted by each person to do so) to help each participant begin to see the other as a human being and to prepare both for the mediated dialogue session.

Phase Two: Victim Offender Dialogue

Facilitating victim offender dialogue in crimes of severe violence involves three discrete phases: a final predialogue briefing, the dialogue itself, and a postdialogue debriefing for both victim and offender.

Predialogue Briefing

The purpose of the predialogue briefing is to put the clients at ease so that they can engage in the dialogue. This usually involves individual check-ins with all parties the day before the dialogue as well as a few minutes prior to the actual encounter. Mediators will need to find out how the participants are feeling and any last minute concerns they may have. It is important to affirm participants' strengths and encourage them to use the special opportunity of the encounter in the victim offender dialogue. The briefing is also a good time to discuss how they will want to greet each other and handle introductions and to help clients refocus on what they want to say.

Victim Offender Dialogue

The goal for the mediator is to facilitate the encounter between the victim and the offender. This involves putting the participants at ease, setting the tone for the dialogue, and clarifying the process in the opening statement so that the clients can quickly engage in dialogue with minimal intervention by the mediator.

Several major tasks must be accomplished to facilitate the dialogue. Mediators tend to open with a brief introductory statement that welcomes the participants, explains the process and ground rules, and clarifies the roles of any support people who may be present. Effort is made to connect with both parties and ground them in their feelings so that they can tell their story and engage with one another. Throughout the dialogue, the mediator maintains a safe environment; monitors the process, making sure to not intervene too quickly in silences; and provides for breaks as needed by either participant. When the dialogue is reaching a stopping point, the mediator offers a closing statement that includes a brief summary, discussion of any needed follow-up, clarification of any agreements, and thanks to both parties.

Postdialogue Debriefing

The purpose of the debriefing is to evaluate the dialogue experience by checking in with the participants as soon as possible immediately following the dialogue. The major task of this debriefing is to review the dialogue experience with each client, learning how each client is feeling, how each felt the process went, and how it fit with their expectations. This is also an important time to explore any unresolved issues or new issues or questions that have emerged in the dialogue.

Phase Three: Follow-Up

Follow-up includes contact with all involved parties and ultimate closure of the case. The purpose of follow-up contact is to evaluate the mediation process further and to discuss any unmet needs. Follow-up is done separately with each client and may also involve joint follow-up sessions. It may occur over several months to a year following the mediation or dialogue session. It should focus on the impact of the dialogue on the participants and how they are doing, emotionally and in terms of expectations. It is also important to identify any unmet needs, arrange for any further services, and begin to plan for termination.

Following the conclusion of all follow-up meetings and discussion of any lingering issues, the case is closed and the mediator has no further contact with either party in connection with mediation but may provide referrals to other services that may be of help to one or both parties.

What We Are Learning from Research

Victims and offenders often speak of their participation in a mediated dialogue as a powerful and transformative experience that helped them in their healing process. Parents of murdered children have expressed a sense of relief after meeting the incarcerated offender and expressing their pain as well as being able to reconstruct what actually happened and why. One mother whose son was murdered said, "I just needed to let him see the pain he has caused in my life and to find out why he pulled the trigger." A schoolteacher who was assaulted and nearly killed commented after meeting the young man in prison, "It helped me end this ordeal. For me, it has made a difference in my life, though this type of meeting is not for everyone." An offender who met at his prison with the mother of the man he killed stated, "It felt good to be able to bring her some relief and to express my remorse to her." A doctor in California whose sister was killed by a drunk driver and who had initially been very skeptical about meeting the offender reported after the mediation session, "I couldn't begin to heal until I let go of my hatred. . . . After the mediation, I felt a great sense of relief. I was now ready to find enjoyment in life again."

Only three studies of victim offender mediation in crimes of severe violence have been conducted in the United States. Two were small exploratory initiatives, each of which examined four case studies. The third study, begun only recently, is the first major initiative in the United States involving multiple sites.

The first study (Umbreit, 1989b) found that offering a mediated dialogue session in several very violent cases, including a sniper shooting case, was very beneficial to the victims, offenders, and community members or family members that were involved in the process. Three of these four cases (all adult offenders) were handled by a police department in upstate New York (Genesee County) that operates a comprehensive restorative justice program. The second study (Flaten, 1996) involved four cases of severely violent crime committed by juvenile offenders and found very high levels of satisfaction with the process and outcomes, among both victims and offenders. The offenders were inmates in a juvenile correctional facility in Alaska.

A third study (Umbreit, 1998) is a multisite, multiyear study that represents the largest initiative in the United States to examine the impact of victim offender mediation and dialogue in crimes of severe violence. Programs in Texas and Ohio are being examined, along with a number of cases in other states. Preliminary data from eleven completed postmediation victim interviews indicated that all eleven were very satisfied with the case preparation; all felt the meeting with the offender was very helpful; all were very satisfied with their overall involvement in the program;

ten said their overall outlook on life had changed since meeting the offender, becoming more positive and at peace with their life circumstances; ten said that meeting the offender had helped a great deal with their healing process; and ten said that meeting the offender had a positive effect on their religious or spiritual life and definitely enriched their religious or spiritual perspective.

Preliminary data from nine completed postmediation offender interviews indicated that all nine were very satisfied with the case preparation; eight reported that meeting the victim was very helpful; all were very satisfied with their overall involvement in the program; seven indicated that their outlook on life had changed since meeting the victim, that they were more positive and content with their life circumstances; all nine said that meeting the victim greatly changed their understanding of how the crime affected others; and seven said that meeting the victim had a positive effect on their religious or spiritual life.

The only completed study (T. Roberts, 1995) that has examined a larger number of cases examined the Victim Offender Mediation Project in Langley, British Columbia. This community-based Canadian program, having pioneered the early development of victim offender mediation and reconciliation with property offenses and minor assaults many years ago, initiated in 1991 a new project to apply the mediation process to crimes of severe violence involving incarcerated inmates. Prior to initiating this project, the VOMP conducted a small study (Gustafson & Smidstra, 1989) to assess whether victims and offenders involved in severely violent crime would be interested in meeting with each other in a safe and structured manner, after intensive preparation, if such a service were available. A very high level of interest in such meetings was found.

In the 1995 study (T. Roberts, 1995), virtually all of the twenty-two offenders and twenty-four victims who participated indicated support for the program. This support included their belief that they found considerable specific and overall value in the program, felt it was ethically and professionally run, and would not hesitate to recommend it to others. Victims reported that they experienced relief at having finally been heard; the offender now no longer exercised control over them; they could see the offender as a person rather than a monster; they felt more trusting in their relationships with others; they felt less fear; they weren't preoccupied with the offender anymore; they felt at peace; they would not feel suicidal again; and they had no more anger.

For offenders, the overall effects of a mediated dialogue with the victim included discovering emotions; feelings of empathy; increasing awareness of the impact of their acts; increasing self-awareness; opening their eyes to the outside world, rather than closed institutional thinking; feeling good about having tried the process; and achieving peace of mind in knowing one has helped a former victim.

Three Case Studies: Parents of Murdered Children Meet the Offender

Let us examine the courageous stories of parents of murdered children who initiated the process of eventually meeting the incarcerated offender responsible for their child's death. For the purposes of these case studies, the names and personal details of all the parties have been changed. A brief overview of each case will be followed by an analysis of themes that emerged; specific implications for the practice of mediated dialogue in similar cases will then be offered.

Case One: Jan Ellison—Allen Jones

Twenty-year-old Mark Ellison was simply in the wrong place at the wrong time. Though details remain elusive, he was driving in his car just before dawn on September 14, 1984, when Allen Jones stopped him, pulled a gun on him, and told him it was a robbery. Mark responded by speeding off, and the gun discharged as the car pulled away. Mark was shot in the head. Allen then ran to where Mark's car had hit a guard rail and took what he could quickly find—a $15 watch and a $20 silver chain. Police were rapidly on the scene and transported Mark to a nearby hospital, where he lingered in a coma for three more days.

Allen Jones was in his mid-twenties at the time, a high school dropout, divorced custodial father of twin daughters, and small-time drug dealer with a cocaine addiction. He reported that he was high on both drugs and alcohol at the time of the crime and does not remember many details. Allen was convicted and sentenced to a maximum-security prison for twenty-seven years with the possibility of parole in nine years.

Mark's mother, Jan Ellison, felt that her life had been shattered; she grieved her loss deeply. In time, she reached out to other families in her home state who suffered the loss of a murdered family member and became active in the victims' rights movement. It was surprising and disconcerting to some of her friends and colleagues when several years later she expressed a desire to meet with the man who killed her son. She was advised not to do so but began exploring how to accomplish her goal nonetheless.

Many members of Allen's family did not want him to meet with Jan Ellison face to face. Nevertheless, mother and murderer agreed to meet, with a mediator present. The out-of-state mediator worked for months, by means of in-person meetings and telephone conversations, to help Jan and Allen understand the purposes and the process of victim offender mediation or dialogue, as well as to clarify their own needs and expectations. He also coordinated with Jan's psychotherapist, obtaining a release stating that mediation would not interfere with Jan's long-term psychotherapy goals and even eventually enlisting the therapist's participation in the dialogue session as a support person for Jan.

In July 1991, nearly seven years after the murder of her son, Jan Ellison met with the man who held the gun to Mark's head. She wanted him to feel and see her pain, to have a glimpse of Mark, and to answer many lingering questions. Their meeting lasted two and a half hours. Jan told Allen her experience at the hospital after the police had called to tell her there had been an accident: "I went to the nurse and I asked where my son was and she said that he was in the other room. . . . I said, 'But I don't even know what's wrong with Mark.' She took me to behind the nurses' station and she sat me down and she said Mark was shot in the head and he's not going to live."

Allen was subdued and tearful as Jan told her story. Then Jan began asking questions, appealing to Allen for total honesty: "I have a lot of questions. Even though whatever you have to say may hurt me and it may hurt you to say it, I want to know. I need to know. I know that you are very afraid to hurt me because you feel that you have hurt me enough. But there are so many things I need to know and only you can answer them. I'm not here as your enemy. I'm here because I want to understand. I want to understand why."

Allen shared his own experience. "I just took too many [hits] and went out that night and partied with my friends. How I ended up down in that area where Mark was I don't know. . . . I don't know what I was doing down there. I know now what happened, and I can never forgive myself for what I done. I only hope I can get forgiveness here today."

As their dialogue continued, they found areas of common ground. Allen had lost custody of his two daughters as a result of his actions; he and Jan talked together about what it was like to miss loved ones at holidays and birthdays. They described how the murder changed all their family relationships. Jan continued to ask questions about the events and about Allen's life, past and present. Allen had questions about Mark's life and his hopes. And they shared their pain. Jan asked him about what he planned to do when he was released, and she encouraged him to take advantage of the self-help programs like Alcoholics Anonymous and Narcotics Anonymous available to him in the prison.

Part of the mediator's closing comments included the potential for a second meeting if the participants so desired, and Jan in fact requested to meet with Allen again nearly two years later. She had further questions about exactly how the gun went off, which Allen was still unable to answer clearly. She wanted to let him know her own plans for moving on, leaving the state, and looking forward rather than back. And she wanted him to know that she would no longer actively block his eventual release from prison, even though it was still in the indefinite future. She told him, "Last April, before we left, you asked if I forgave you and I told you I would have to think about it. This is really hard for me to say. I guess we each want something from one another. I want you to give me Mark, and you can't do that. You want me to give you forgiveness, and I can't do that. But not giving you forgiveness doesn't mean that I don't want to help. I just can't. I tried."

Jan was very grateful for the opportunity to meet with Allen and felt that the meeting was pivotal in her healing process. "Now I know that for me there is life after murder. So many doors have opened; so many other doors have closed. There is nothing more I need to know about what happened to Mark. Allen understands the pain he caused me now and what he took away from me."

Case Two: Jim and Sue Manley—Gary Evans

On the morning of June 20, 1991, the parents of Carol Manley discovered that their daughter, barely home two weeks from her freshman year in college, had not returned to the house from an evening with friends. Knowing that she always called if she was not going to be home at a normal hour, they became concerned quickly and reported her as missing. The police and a great many neighbors in their small town searched for Carol for five days.

On the fifth day of the search, two young men turned themselves in to the police, each attempting to incriminate the other. They led the police to Carol's body, in a shallow grave in a wooded area. She had been abducted, raped, and murdered.

The Manley family and the rest of the small rural community felt repeatedly victimized by the abduction, rape, and murder, by not knowing what happened, and by the conflicting stories presented at the offenders' separate trials. Around the time of the trials in late 1991, Jim Manley became aware of restorative justice concepts and specifically about victim offender mediation. He saw this approach as a possible way of getting answers to questions about Carol's death that continued to plague him and his family. It would also be an opportunity to share their own story of pain.

After much preparatory work by a mediator, one of the two offenders agreed to meet with the Manleys. Over the course of eighteen months, the mediator met separately with the Manleys and their offender seven times each. Jim and Sue Manley met with Gary Evans initially on November 4, 1992, less than a year and a half after the murder of their daughter. The meeting lasted three hours. The Manleys began by recounting their experience. They spoke of the agony of not knowing, the fear, and then the pain of knowing and the resulting grief and anger. Even after finding out that Carol was dead and throughout the trial process, they received only bits and pieces of details about what happened on that terrible night. As Jim explained to Gary in the session, "Carol is gone, and that whole emptiness is there. And what can be done to see that it doesn't happen again? I think to answer that we have to know what happened—just the facts."

They held nothing back in describing to Gary who their daughter was, what she had been like, and what her hopes and plans were for the future. In Sue's words, "She was like sunshine. And there is a huge hole which can never be filled, not just in our family but [in] our extended family. And another part—think of what she was going to become, what she would have offered the world." Sue went on to describe Carol's studies at the university and her plans to work with young children. Finally, they turned to Gary and asked for his account of the evening their daughter was murdered.

Gary Evans walked them through that night in graphic detail. He claimed not to have planned or participated in the rape and murder. He reported that he was driving the car for his friend, the other offender, who was high on drugs and who pulled a gun on him. He saw himself as a victim who didn't know how to stop what

was happening. Dialogue began to show that the Manleys appreciated learning of some things that they had not previously known,
but neither did they immediately accept Gary's version of the
events.

Gary became most empathic during a discussion with Jim about
losing contact with his son. Tearfully, Gary said, "I think about my
son. If anything happened to him, I couldn't take it. I think I know
how you guys are feeling. 'Cause if it happened to me, I don't think
I could take it." Silently, he struggled with his emotions, finally saying, "You don't have a Kleenex around here, do you?" Sliding him
a packet of hers, Sue replied between sobs, "It is extremely hard
when something happens to your child."

There were subsequent meetings. Jim met with Gary three
times with a mediator present before Jim and Sue met with him
together in June 1995. And Jim and the mediator were able to hold
one meeting with the other offender, who was incarcerated in
another state. Even at the last meeting, there were continued
efforts to clarify the story of what happened. The Manleys realized
that the "truth" would never be known. Gary was presenting them
with what he could recall, and that may have been true or flawed.
There would be no certainty. But more important to them at that
time was working with Gary to try to have something good come
out of tragedy. They saw in him remorse, empathy, and a desire to
help. Toward that end, the Manleys and Gary Evans attempted to
come up with ways to share their stories so that others, particularly
young people, would be able to say no before being dragged into
violent situations beyond their control.

Both the Manleys and Gary felt that their meetings affected
their lives greatly. Jim summed up his changed perspective on the
offenders: "They're not throwaways, these two guys. I think each
has the capacity to contribute." Sue added, "If forgiveness is defined
as letting go of the anger and not letting the bitterness and anger
and grief define me, then indeed I have forgiven them. I don't
spend a lot of time thinking about it—or about them." And Gary
stated, "I'm glad I went and did it. My family is all pleased that I

went ahead and did it. I guess it kind of gets something off both our shoulders."

Case Three: Betsy Lee Hanks—William Greene

On a late March night in 1986, twenty-year-old college student Craig Hanks was finishing a video game at the arcade when he was approached by seventeen-year-old William Greene. William asked Craig for a ride across town, telling him, "My mother is dying." But once they were on the road, William demanded the car keys, planning to steal the car and drive out of state to avoid warrants already out on him for two counts of burglary and missing his court date. When Craig refused to give him the keys, William shot him.

Betsy Lee Hanks was a single mother who had sacrificed greatly to send her only child to college. Sometime before dawn the next morning, she received a phone call from a police officer in Craig's college town, 250 miles away. "Do you know a Craig Hanks?" she was asked. When she replied in the affirmative, the voice continued, "He was murdered a couple of hours ago. Is he related to you?"

William was apprehended and agreed to a plea bargain. Betsy Lee was gradually introduced to her state victim services program and became active in People Against Violent Crime. She also campaigned before the parole board every six months to prevent William's release; she described her level of rage at that time, saying she would come into their office asking, "Is he dead yet? Does he have AIDS? Has somebody killed him? Well, this is a violent prison, why can't we put him there?"

When presented with the option of meeting with William if that would be helpful for her, Betsy Lee was opposed to the notion of ever seeking to meet her son's murderer. But victim services staff offered her the opportunity to view excerpts of other similar mediations, and she was deeply moved by the healing she saw taking place, even though she recognized that there could be no ultimate resolution. Gradually, she came to have a different view of what justice would mean: "If he could feel the pain in my heart, if he could feel the hole that he left in my life, then that would be justice." She worried that such a confrontation might be harmful to offenders: "What if they can't deal with it and they go commit suicide?" Eventually it was her concern for the offender that prompted her decision to meet with him. "I wanted to talk to that guy and see if I could make a change in his life."

William was at first also opposed to the idea of meeting his victim's mother. He was afraid she might attack him physically; the mediator showed excerpts from videos of other mediations, assured him there had never been an attack during such a mediation session, and explained what safeguards would be in place. It was ultimately the videos that moved William to change his mind. "I grown to trust him [the mediator]; I seen him in the videos."

In late winter 1997, after several months of intensive preparation work individually with their mediator, Betsy Lee and William met together for an eight-hour mediation/dialogue session in the visiting room of the prison. Betsy Lee had planned very carefully what she wanted to say and the impact she hoped she would have. She had researched William's life, seeking to understand "how do you get to be a murderer at seventeen?" She knew of his lengthy rap sheet—148 disciplinary cases in the prison over eleven years. And she brought with her a copy of a book about rising out of the ghetto written by someone who had grown up in the same public housing project where William once lived.

It took William a full ten minutes after he was seated to raise his eyes and meet Betsy Lee's gaze. When he did so, tears welled up and flowed out over his cheeks, and Betsy Lee reached for a tissue and wiped them off. Betsy Lee then told her story, asking for and receiving details about her son's last night. She told William who Craig was and showed pictures from his baby book that she had brought with her.

The exchange was deeply emotional. William was shocked to learn just how much what he had done had affected his victim's mother: "The whole thing was really hard for me. I damn near took *her* life—she tried [suicide] a couple of times, too." Betsy Lee cried heavily throughout, and William returned her earlier gesture of kindness: "I hate that she was cryin'—I grabbed some Kleenex from her and I was wipin' the tears from her face." Betsy Lee commented later that she hoped when their video was edited, this incident would be included.

Toward the end of their session, Betsy Lee handed William the book about life in the housing projects: "He just clutched this book, he was just cradling it in his arms, and he said 'I never had no book come to me before. You can get 'em, but I ain't never had no book.'" She challenged him to change his life even though there was no one there to help him.

In interviews conducted after their mediation session, both Betsy Lee and William offered the interviewers evidence that their mediation session had had an impact on William. Betsy Lee reported that her letters from William indicated he wasn't getting in trouble anymore. She worried that he was merely skimming the surface and not really examining himself but recognized that for an inmate with such a long history of in-prison infractions, this was at least a start. William's words suggested that more may be going on: "We can change our lives—because if you don't try to change your life in here you just waste your time going back out there, so if you got somebody out there tryin' to help you, you'd be a fool not to take up on it."

Case Analysis: Implications for Mediation Practice

The practice implications that can be drawn from these three case vignettes highlight additional areas of focus for mediators during preparation, the mediation session itself, and follow up.

Preparation

The importance of preparing participants for mediation or dialogue cannot be overstated. This is the most time-consuming part of the work for the mediator. Preparation will involve developing relationships, listening to the needs stated verbally and non-verbally, articulating the scope and purpose of the mediation or dialogue, and shuttling back and forth between victim and offender to clarify broad agendas and expectations. The mediator has a huge responsibility for setting the stage for the initial and any future encounters. The message the mediator brings—whether about the process of mediation or about the needs and mannerisms of the victim or offender—must be stated clearly while being sensitive to the emotional overload that so often characterizes these cases. Four specific implications for the preparation phase arise from these case studies.

Don't Oversell Expectations. Victims typically want to meet the offender because they have many unanswered questions, want the offender to see and feel the pain he or she caused, or desire to help the offender so that the same kind of crime will not happen again. However, expectations about obtaining answers, sensing offender remorse, and helping the offender should be modest. The mediator must not oversell the program. The results of these encounters, as with any human interaction, are likely to be mixed. This was explicitly true for the Manleys; and given that Jan Ellison fought against Allen's parole at his first hearing, which occurred after their first mediation, it can be assumed that she experienced mixed results also. Sue Manley told her mediator that she had changed her expectations: "I don't think we could have done it [mediation/dialogue] without you and without all the preparation. I remember when we first started talking about it when my expectations were here (*gesturing high*). As we talked, I said, 'Oh, I better lower my expectations or I'm going to be very disappointed.'" Betsy Lee felt that viewing excerpts of actual mediations especially helped her have realistic expectations. Overselling would not only be misleading, it would entail revictimizing people who are already suffering enormously.

Emphasize at Each Step the Choice to Participate. Individuals—victims or offenders—can refuse to participate at any point in the process. Any such refusal must be honored by the mediator.

Refusal might occur at the point of initial contact. It might occur after seven contacts and much work on the part of many people. It might simply be a refusal to answer a particular question or to delve into an area of questioning during the course of a mediation/dialogue session. The mediator must be prepared to honor the refusal while allowing the individual to feel good about the decision made. This is part of creating a safe place for all participants to deal as openly as they can with difficult, emotionally charged questions and concerns.

Prepare Participants for Meeting the Other.   The victims and offenders may or may not have seen each other during trials, but it is likely, in many cases, that they have never actually met or talked to each other. The mediator will carry considerable responsibility for sharing and shaping first impressions. Again, the questions and concerns of participants can be shared broadly. Sometimes participants have requested and received recent photographs of one another prior to the meeting.

If there are areas that one or the other participant has declared off limits, that information needs to be known by all participants. It may be important to make it known that a particular offender, for example, is very slow of speech. In such cases, it will be necessary to be extra careful to allow the offender to complete his or her thoughts without interruption. Victims would likely find this information helpful in reducing their own frustration at the pace of the meeting.

Visit the Prison in Advance.   Most citizens are not familiar with the sights and smells of a maximum-security prison. First exposure to metal detectors, searches, clanging heavy doors, disinfectant smells, blank faces of prisoners and guards, and the air of hopelessness that often permeates such places can be distressing and overwhelming. Coming to grips with the setting may be quite demanding emotionally and intellectually. As the Manleys indicated, the opportunity to tour the prison earlier helped them stay focused on the day of the initial meeting with Gary Evans rather than be caught up in the whirlwind of feelings caused by the foreign nature of the prison setting.

The Meeting

Videotapes of victim offender mediation/dialogue sessions belie the work of the mediator. A mediator who is working effectively may appear to be part of the background, almost extraneous. That is not the case. If the preparation work requires the proactive involvement of the mediator, the session requires the active and mostly nonverbal presence of the mediator. The extent of direct verbal involvement will depend on the dynamics of the meeting. Five implications for the mediator are apparent as we consider the three cases.

Breaking the Ice. In light of all the one-on-one preparation meetings, it may seem surprising that the opening comments of the mediator must serve both to provide information and to break the ice for the encounter. The mediator basically tells the participants things they already know—the purpose of the meeting and the ground rules governing their interaction, to which they have already agreed. This is, however, not just a reminder for participants; it serves to make it clear that the mediator is on neither side and has shared all relevant information with all participants. It is one thing to be told the ground rules in private; it is another to be informed of them and agree to them in the presence of the other party. A more subtle effect of the opening statement by the mediator is that it gives all participants a chance to catch their breath, to compose themselves, to "take in" the other participant, and to become more comfortable with the space and the task at hand. If this icebreaking function is given short shrift by the mediator, the opening statement becomes merely a string of words. The opening sets the tone, at least for the early stages of the meeting, as well as reinforces the mediator's role as responsible for maintaining a safe setting for difficult exchange.

Honoring Silence. Silence may indicate that participants are reflecting on what has been said or formulating a new line of inquiry. To rush to fill the gaps of silence may cut off the flow of dialogue. Silence may be uncomfortable for some people, but few expect this kind of exchange to be easy. That said, it is equally important to sense when silence has gone on too long or has become detrimental to the dialogue. Gary Evans, for example, encouraged the mediator during a premediation meeting before the last taped session to step in if things "get into a lull." Gary often referred to "pulling a blank" at times. Leaving him to spin in his blankness would not be helpful for the overall movement of the meeting, and it would likely be experienced as punishing.

Tolerating Repetition. The mediator should expect and develop a tolerance for repetition. Victims will ask the offender the same question in a variety of ways. The same questions may be asked in the same ways in follow-up sessions. It may be that the victim must listen to the answer several times to hear and integrate it, or it may be that the victim is trying to determine if the offender has changed the story. In either case, this repetition is part of the dialogue. One could imagine an overbearing mediator saying, "We've covered that. Let's move on." However, repetition by either party may become so annoying that it will be necessary for the mediator to interject a comment along the lines of "You've been pursuing this line of questioning now in a variety of ways. Do you want to continue, or do you want to move on?" or "This part of the story has been covered several times. Do you want to hear it again, or do you want to move on?" What the mediator may experience as repetitive may not be experienced in the same way by the participants, who should be the only parties to determine when to move on. The mediator must expect and accept much more repetition of questions and descriptions than occurs in standard conversation.

Presiding Attentively yet Unobtrusively. The mediator must be attentive at all times yet out of the way, allowing dialogue to occur between victim and offender. A mediator who takes a nondirective humanistic approach to mediation, in which the mediator does not talk much, is by no means passive. The mediator must be prepared to intervene in a split second to head off an inappropriate line of inquiry, to respond to a verbal or nonverbal request, and to send nonverbal signals that what the participants are doing is appropriate, respected, and honored. If the mediator tunes out or seems uninvolved, it won't take long for that absence of mind to be noticed. Participant responses may range from feeling brushed aside and betrayed to having one party begin to exercise excessive control. The mediator's active presence thus serves several functions, none perhaps more important than symbolically (and occasionally literally) preserving a balance of control and participation among the participants.

The need to help strike a balance between the participants can require an immediate response. During the second taped session between the Manleys and Gary Evans, Jim Manley posed a question about Gary's juvenile record. The mediator immediately broke in: "Excuse me a second. Do you feel comfortable responding to that? Because that is protected by privacy laws. But if you choose to talk about it, you have a right to." Quick intervention empowered the offender to make an informed choice.

In the Ellison case, Allen was hopeful that Jan would be able to forgive him. Jan said, "I don't know if I can forgive you right now. I need some time." Sobbing, she added, "I'm gonna try." The mediator did not interrupt the flow of the dialogue at this time but made a point to come back to this issue at a later moment: "I want to make a comment on something you brought up, Jan. It is important for both of you to realize that the purpose of this mediation session is not to talk about forgiveness. If that happens, that's your choice, Jan. Whatever your decision is, that's OK. I think you realize that, Allen. The purpose is really to talk about what happened and to try to get some kind of closure, and that may or may not involve forgiveness. Forgiveness does take time, even when a person chooses to forgive." The mediator thus clarified the purpose of the session, placing forgiveness in the overall context, and underscored the individual's right to forgive or not to forgive.

Being Affirming and Nonjudgmental. Regardless of individuals' ability to articulate their concerns or viewpoints and despite the level of emotional affect displayed, it takes a lot of courage as victim or offender to enter into face-to-face dialogue with the other. The mediator will likely have several opportunities to affirm the choices each person has made to be at the table. There may be things said that could press the mediator's own judgment buttons. This must be avoided at all costs. The mediator is human and is certainly subject to being overly engaged in an issue or a question or even overidentifying with an individual. During the preparatory work, the mediator should be in a position to flag issues and questions that might lead to becoming overly directive or overly involved. Knowing ahead of time what is likely to arise should help the mediator deal with such potential pitfalls. If after assessing the situation, it appears that the mediator cannot be affirming or nonjudgmental with a particular set of individuals, a replacement must be found who can be both affirming and nonjudgmental. A mediator who cannot withhold judgment will create a situation in which chances are greatly increased of participants feeling further victimized.

Follow-Up Debriefing

Debriefing after the session is as integral to the process as preparation and the meeting itself. Debriefing may occur immediately after the session or some time later.

Evaluating the Experience. Whether immediately or later, this is an opportunity for the victim or offender to review the meeting—its content and emotions—without the other being present. Here it is OK for the participant to express disbelief and ventilate. It is OK to acknowledge the pain experienced during the session and the pain that remains. It is OK to blame or shame. It is OK to express what needs to be expressed about the experience.

Accepting the Results. This is also an opportunity for the mediator to work with participants to identify and accept the mixed results of the session. It is unlikely that all questions will be answered to one's satisfaction or that what one hopes to happen will indeed occur. The Manleys acknowledged quite clearly that they were not satisfied with all the answers they received. There remained differences of opinion regarding Gary's story, his understanding, and his level of willingness to accept responsibility in the abduction, rape, and murder of their daughter. Still, they found something human in Gary Evans, as well as remorse and a desire to help make things better somehow. Even with the mixed experience, they stated that they would have joined in the mediation dialogue again knowing what they then knew. Likewise, Jan Ellison did not receive all the information or comfort she was looking for, yet she wants other survivors to know that such potentially beneficial opportunities of mediation and dialogue exist. In this regard, by accepting the mixed results, the mediator is helping the victim and the offender leave with a realistic assessment of individual and shared outcomes.

Moving Toward Integration. Participants, particularly victims, take the opportunity during debriefing to retell portions of their story now with new information or differing shades of interpretation. By asking questions of the victims, such as their feelings about the mediation session, the mediator prompts them to integrate the mediation into their story of victimization. This may be a necessary step for letting go of some of the rage, the sense of being out of control, or the feeling of being crippled. Without ever suggesting that this mediation-dialogue resolves all the hurt and anger resulting from being victimized, the mediator's activity at this debriefing stage may prompt some degree of letting go and moving on. In the case studies, this was a theme for all participants either at the close of the mediation session or during the debriefing meetings.

Overarching Themes

In addition to practical implications for mediators, these three case studies also share common themes. It behooves the mediator to be prepared to observe and support participants as they attempt to work through issues at this more global level.

Finding Common Ground. There is an apparent strong need to find common ground between victim and offender. This was true in all three case studies. The Manleys worked hard with Gary to come up with some kind of shared understanding of the events surrounding the death of their daughter. Ultimately, they must accept that not all their questions will be answered. They accept Gary's remorse and move on to try to "make something good come of all of this." Gary and Jim are able to touch one another as fathers. Gary misses his son and recognizes the pain of a father whose child was murdered. Gary speaks of holidays as the hardest times for being in the prison and away from family. The Manleys admit that holidays are hardest for them also. Jim and Sue try to work with Gary to tell his story so that other youth might not make the same mistakes. Gary wants to please the Manleys and works with them, seeking and finding common ground.

The same phenomenon is present in the Ellison-Jones case. Jan shares the pain and loss at the death of her son. Allen identifies with her by speaking of the loss of his mother and daughters. They each speak of holidays as the hardest times for feeling their losses. They discover similarities in the fact that some of Allen's family were highly critical of his participating in the mediation and some of Jan's friends took the same position. Jan shows a picture of her son. Allen holds the picture and says, "God bless him." They discuss the common struggles of starting new lives—Allen as he hopes to leave prison and Jan as she leaves the state. Allen says, "I'm a little scared of that. It's gonna be hard to start over." And Jan responds, "I'll be starting over, too. That's gonna be tough. It's gonna be hard."

Betsy Lee found common ground in an eerie reversal: she could see that William had never had any of the care or opportunities she had been able to give her own son, and she poured her energies into providing whatever she could for William during the eight hours of their meeting. In her words, "I was the mother to him that day that he never had . . . because nobody else was gonna do it. He hadn't had a visitor in two years." They also found common ground in their shared tears and in their shared human gesture of wiping them off each other's faces.

This mirroring of one another, this search for common ground, may be a part of what draws the participants together in the first place. As the result of a heinous, inhuman event, there is a quest for humanity. When they find it, there is a desire to grasp on to it and build on it. As strange as it may seem to observers and mediators, one fact binds the offender and victim in a very elemental way: the offender was among the last persons to have seen their child alive or to have heard their child's last words. This unnerving bond should not be minimized by anyone who has not sat at the table as victim or offender.

Helping Each Other Heal. In part, victims are seeking some kind of closure that allows them to integrate the events of the murder and the grief of loss somehow so that they can move on with their lives in more healthy ways. This in no way means that they seek to forget the loss but rather that they seek to manage the loss so that it does not paralyze. To create something good out of the tragedy is one way for this closure to happen. In all three featured cases, the hope of helping rehabilitate the offender was part of the healing for the victim. In the Manley case, the focus was on helping Gary Evans experience remorse, feel empathy, and do something good for community youth by telling his story. In the Ellison case, Jan was very concerned about Allen's well-being and about what he would be like when he returns to the community. She praised him for completing his GED and pressed him on why he was not attending Alcoholics Anonymous or Narcotics Anonymous meetings. And Betsy Lee commented afterward, "William didn't see a reward for any positive behavior. Now he sees the reward because I expect better of him." In all of these cases, the victims had a desire to help the good part of the human being who had somehow participated in the death of their child.

Similarly, the offenders, too, are seeking healing. All three of them made clear that they wanted to help the victims, and in fact they did make concrete efforts to do so. Gary, particularly in the preparatory and debriefing meetings with the mediator, said quite clearly that he participated and continues to participate in order to help the Manleys. He also desires to help the community, but that is a rather more abstract idea for him. His relationship is with the Manleys, and for them he will try his best. Is this desire to help driven by guilt? That cannot be known for sure. But an empathic relationship does exist, particularly between Gary and Jim—perhaps as a result of their both being fathers who have lost a relationship with a child.

Allen is resolute as he listens to Jan's pain. Not only does he listen to what she expresses voluntarily, but he actually elicits more. When the mediator turns to ask whether he has more questions to ask, unlike what we might expect of the offender who simply wants to get this over, Allen asks probing, sensitive questions. For example, he wanted to know about Mark's goals, which led to a lengthy discussion of the man he killed—and renewed tears. When Jan asks, "Can you tell me how I can get on with my life?" Allen does not hesitate. His response: "Well, have you tried praying?" A discussion of God and prayer ensued.

William felt initially that the only thing he could give Betsy Lee was "answers to why her son was murdered. . . . There's a lot of questions, mysteries that were haunting her all these years." He wrote her after the mediation and was relieved that when she wrote back, she spoke of feeling better because of the information she had received from him. He also found during the session that he could help her in one other important way—by finishing his education, trying to stay out of further trouble, and making something of himself.

There are moments watching these taped sessions when one is struck by the fact that one could be observing an intense, emotional exchange between any two or three persons. Little about the exchange would suggest animosity or the enormity of the events that brought these people together. The human dialogue of telling, listening, and sharing appears to have tremendous potential for healing even in the most conflictual of circumstances.

Forgiveness. Although forgiveness may be an outcome of the dialogue for some, it is not the goal of the program. Even if it is a goal of participants, there are limits as to how far such dialogues can move victim and offender. To recognize the humanity of the person who took the life of your child is not easy but can be done. To want that person as well as yourself to heal and therefore to become better at living nonviolently is understandable and attainable. But to forgive the individual for what he or she has done requires an almost superhuman effort.

Mediators must be prepared for this question to arise explicitly or implicitly. In the Manley case, it was present only implicitly. Gary Evans does not ask for forgiveness from the Manleys. Perhaps it is enough for him to feel somewhat understood and at least be somewhat respected. It is clear that he senses both those things. Jim Manley readily admits both but also points out that this in no way mitigates the loss. Nor does it reduce Gary's responsibility for contributing to the death of Jim's daughter. Their differences in perception of Gary's role in some ways doesn't matter. "The differences remain, but so does the conviction. . . . Justice is being served from my perspective." Perhaps Sue Manley spoke to the dilemma that makes forgiveness unlikely, if not unreachable: "As good as this is that we're trying to make [some good] come of it, she asked him to help her [escape], and he didn't. And that makes me very angry. . . . It's just the pain, and it hurts. We try, we're trying to have something good come of this—but that's always underneath there."

In the Ellison case, the forgiveness issue surfaced quite explicitly. Allen stated in the mediation that he was hoping for forgiveness. Jan acknowledged his hope but could not forgive him. Clearly, she was torn, perhaps because of her faith tradition, about her inability to forgive. She believes her son has forgiven Allen, but she cannot.

Forgiveness did not surface explicitly in the Hanks-Greene case, but several elements of the participants' reactions and perspectives shed light on related issues. William was keenly conscious that Betsy Lee had changed her opinion of him: "She said at one time she was prayin' that I got killed down here. . . . But after knowin' me, she said I'm a different person." Betsy Lee spoke of the transformation that has resulted from her experience: "I have no idea, not only William's, but how many lives have been positively changed because of Craig's murder. . . . I very consciously every day work at doing what I can to change this planet to a more peaceful, loving, gentle, caring place." For her, though forgiveness is not named, bitterness and resentment have been transformed into compassion.

The mediator must be prepared, as occurred in the Ellison case, to address the question of forgiveness. It may be a possible outcome of mediation or dialogue, but it is not at all an appropriate goal or expectation. In preparatory work, it may be useful to listen for the issue of forgiveness either as an expectation of the offender or perhaps as a fear from the victim—a fear that he or she may be expected to forgive. If forgiveness is to occur, it must be genuine and not contrived or done because someone thought the mediator expected it.

Implications for Policy and Practice

It is of course neither possible nor wise to generalize from a sample of only three case studies. However, reflection on these three cases in the context of what is known more generally about VOM and preliminary data emerging from the two-state study described earlier in the chapter leads to a number of tentative recommendations that will ultimately be fleshed out as additional information becomes available from ongoing research on VOM in cases of violent crime. As additional states consider developing policies to provide opportunities for interested victims of severe violence to meet with the offender-inmate, the following preliminary recommendations are offered for consideration.

Policy

1. Departments of corrections should consider developing specific procedures for responding to the requests of victims who request a mediation/dialogue session with the offender-inmate.

2. Public funding should be obtained to support the development and management of victim-sensitive offender dialogue services in crimes of severe violence.

3. Consideration should be given to amending current state crime victim compensation laws to allow reimbursement for the cost of victim-initiated mediation/dialogue services with offender-inmates when such encounters are clearly related to the healing process and when such services are provided only by mediators who can document that they have received advanced training in providing victim-sensitive offender dialogue services in crimes of severe violence.

Practice

1. Only persons who can document that they have received advanced training in victim-sensitive offender dialogue in crimes of severe violence and who are under the supervision and support of a mentor should be allowed to provide such services.

2. When providing victim-sensitive offender dialogue services in crimes of severe violence, a minimum of two or three in-

person preparation meetings with each party should be held. In most cases, even more are required.

3. The process of victim-sensitive offender dialogue in crimes of severe violence should be entirely voluntary for all parties.

4. Victim-sensitive offender dialogue in crimes of severe violence should be victim-initiated. When inmates initiate the process, their letter should be kept on file in case their victims later request a mediation/dialogue session.

5. The planning, development, and implementation of victim-sensitive offender dialogue services should be conducted with the active involvement of victim services providers along with correctional staff and other persons familiar with the VSOD process, preferably one who has completed advanced VSOD training.

Summary

It is clear that the principles of restorative justice can be applied in selected cases of severe violence, particularly through the practice of victim offender mediation and dialogue. Preliminary data indicate exceptionally high levels of client satisfaction with the process and the outcomes of victim offender mediation and dialogue in crimes of severe violence. This bodes well for the future development of this emerging restorative justice intervention. Although these studies provide important preliminary data related to the impact of the mediation/dialogue process in crimes of severe violence, particularly homicide, they are suggestive at best. Far more rigorous studies involving larger samples are required before any conclusions can be drawn. A great deal of caution, however, must be exercised in applying restorative justice principles in such cases. There have already been numerous examples of well-intentioned criminal justice officials and individual mediators who are too quick to refer or facilitate the use of mediation and dialogue in crimes of severe violence without having first secured advanced training and mentoring. Many unintended negative consequences could result from such initiatives, including significant revictimization of the victim.

There remain many unanswered questions as well. For whom, under what circumstances, and when is the use of victim offender mediation in crimes of severe violence most appropriate? How extensive should the case development process be? Is there significant variance in the degree and length of premediation case preparation based on characteristics of individual cases? What type of crime victim and offender respond best to such an intervention? How can victim offender mediation/dialogue services, in crimes of severe violence, be offered as a voluntary restorative justice intervention on a larger scale and in a cost-effective manner? How extensive should advanced training be? To what extent should families and other support persons be routinely involved in the process, at what points, and to what degree? Can state victim compensation laws cover the cost related to victims of severe violence who request this intervention? Although nearly all cases to date are victim-initiated, is there a place for offender-initiated cases without triggering the unintended consequence of revictimizing the victim?

At its core, the process of victim offender mediation and dialogue in crimes of severe violence is about engaging the individuals most affected by the horror of violent crime in the process of holding the offender truly accountable; helping victims gain a greater sense of meaning, if not closure, concerning the severe harm resulting from the crime; and helping all parties develop a greater capacity to move on with their lives in a positive fashion. This emerging restorative justice practice warrants further development and analysis, underpinned by an attitude of cautious and informed support.

Chapter Fourteen

Potential Hazards and Opportunities

Victim offender mediation is the most widely implemented restorative justice practice in North America and Europe. Its more than a quarter century of experience and recent trends offer important pointers regarding potential threats to core principles and emergent opportunities that can deepen the impact of restorative justice for victims, offenders, family members, and other members of the community who choose to engage the process.

Potential Hazards

The VOM field faces a threat common to many reform movements: the tendency as a reform becomes institutionalized to abandon in favor of efficiency and standardization the unique features that originally helped it improve on the status quo. Several related hazards stem from this phenomenon.

Loss of Vision

As with many reform movements, the greatest threat to restorative justice is that of loss of vision. Programs developed to implement reforms often become preoccupied with securing more stable funding sources and developing more routine day-to-day operating procedures. As mediation professionals seek to collaborate with system professionals, it becomes easy to lose sight of the underlying values and principles that motivated the individuals who initiated the program and on which the program was built. The importance of providing opportunities for addressing the emotional issues surrounding crime and victimization, including the possibility of genuine forgiveness and reconciliation for interested parties who initiate such actions, is a core principle of victim offender mediation. Data from a growing number of studies continue to document high levels of victim and offender satisfaction with the mediation process and outcome. There is no evidence that large numbers of VOM programs have veered from this principle. However, a number of developments suggest that maintaining the vision may require increasing diligence.

The "McDonaldization" of Mediation

In some parts of the United States (and perhaps in other parts of the world), the expression "victim offender mediation" is used quite loosely to describe quickly arranged and executed negotiations between victims and offenders, often not face to face, held for the sole purpose of negotiating a restitution agreement to include in a diversion or dispositional order. A probation department in a large urban jurisdiction, for example, conducts its mediations in the probation officer's office, with no prior separate meeting with victim and offender. These sessions last around fifteen to twenty minutes and focus exclusively on developing a restitution plan. Inadequate follow-up on cases and failure to monitor the offender's completion of restitution have also been common complaints heard from a small number of victims in VOM programs.

In one mediation program, a victim reported feeling coerced to participate, receiving the strong impression that participation was required in order to obtain restitution. Some victims in another program reported feeling revictimized by the process, primarily because of the attitude of offenders and the inability of some mediators to facilitate sessions effectively. In yet another program in which offenders and their parents are required to participate in mediation, an offender and parent were quite resistant and displayed a hostile attitude in the session, which had a predictably adverse effect on the victim and his parent. Finally, perhaps the most disturbing story involves a program in which a mediator reportedly shouted at a victim, who later filed a complaint with the local victim services agency.

Isolated and anecdotal as these reports may be, a recent evaluation of a probation-based initiative found a lower level of victim satisfaction with the mediation process than in previous studies, which have almost always found extraordinarily high victim satisfaction. The most distinguishing characteristic of this otherwise well-developed and thoughtful program is that offenders have no choice about participating in mediation.

The requirement for involuntary participation flies in the face of what has been learned to date from research. Across all the range of sites where VOM has been investigated by research, self-selection has been an indispensable part of the process of determining who ends up proceeding with mediation. The consistently high satisfaction rates seen until now reflect the fact that the specific set of people who participate in mediation are enabled to carry out something they have chosen and desire to do. This phenomenon is not a "research bias"; it is simple human nature: people who want to participate in mediation tend to be very satisfied. People who don't want to participate will almost certainly not be quite so satisfied. It would be a mistake to require mediation of victims or offenders just because satisfaction rates are high. The research supports offering VOM more widely as an option, but it equally supports continuing to allow participation to be voluntary.

The rush of some programs to process cases quickly, with little or no preparation, focusing entirely on determining a restitution agreement and having little patience with hearing the full story of the involved parties, can lead to a "fast-food" version of mediation, the sort of "McDonaldization" that has affected so many aspects of Western European culture in recent years. This is a disturbing trend among a still small number of programs that moves far away from the core principles of restorative justice.

Elimination of Separate Premediation Meetings

A small but growing trend among some victim offender mediation programs is to bypass individual meetings with victim and offender prior to the session. This development is disturbing to many restorative justice advocates. Although originally a major element of the initial victim offender mediation and reconciliation model, a recent national survey in the United States (see Chapter Six) found that 37 percent of programs do not require mediators to meet with the parties separately before the mediation session. Mediation by itself, with little preparation of the parties, is far less likely to tap into the major empirically validated restorative benefit of victim offender mediation, that of humanizing the process for both victim and offender so that they feel safe enough to engage in a genuine conversation or dialogue with each other about what happened and how it affected their lives.

In fact, the large four-state study reported in Chapter Ten had an important unintended finding related to the impact of face-to-face premediation sessions. As the study progressed, it became clear that the in-person separate premediation session with the victim and the offender constituted a major intervention in itself, whether or not the parties proceeded to actual mediation. Simply taking the time to listen to the impact of the crime on their lives, to validate their experience, and to offer the choice of mediation appeared to offer a level of respect and support that both victims and offenders valued greatly, even if their choice was to not proceed any further. This finding was particularly significant for victims, who receive minimal attention and support from the criminal and juvenile justice systems.

Agreement-Driven Mediation

Another consequence of losing sight of the restorative vision could be a utilitarian and exclusive focus on restitution determination and payment. Allowing little time for the sharing of facts and feelings related to the crime, the mediation session could become agreement-driven rather than dialogue-driven. This is not to say that such mediation is of no value, but healing and true peace-making require more time and patience. The temptation to focus the mediation process primarily on securing a mutually satisfactory restitution agreement is great, and it is understandable. As courts seek more options for handling cases in a more "efficient" manner and mediation programs seek to justify their existence with large numbers of case referrals, program staff may be tempted to down-play the dialogue phase of the mediation encounter.

If efficiency, rather than creating a safe place for the victim and offender to talk with each other about the full impact of the crime, becomes the primary value driving the program, the time allotted for mediation sessions will dramatically decrease. As a result, rather than facilitating a restorative process of dialogue, mutual aid, and healing, the mediator will serve more as an arbitrator who directs the process toward an agreement, leaving the victim and offender limited input and little, if any, time to talk with each other about the impact of the crime.

Although restitution agreements nearly always result from dia-logue-driven mediation sessions, these agreements are secondary to the opportunity to talk about what happened and how it affected both victim and offender and any support people or parents that are present. Some practitioners would even maintain that far more realistic and creative restitution agreements are likely to emerge following a dialogue about what actually happened and how peo-ple felt about the incident.

Taking Fewer Risks

As programs become preoccupied with acceptance into the main-stream of court services, there is often a tendency to take fewer risks, particularly related to the types of cases being referred to the program. In an eagerness to negotiate new referral arrangements, programs may be too quick to accept cases that the prosecutor's office might refer due simply to lack of sufficient evidence for a court petition. The likelihood that mediation will be taken seriously is decreased if the process is identified with only the "easy" cases, those that the system would have otherwise dismissed.

Programs that place sole emphasis on the efficient negotiation of restitution agreements are often also likely to take few risks in regard to the types of cases they will handle. If the goal is to meet the needs of the individuals most directly affected by the crime, the victim and the offender, rather than system interests only, the key issue is one of balance, between so-called easy cases and more serious cases (based on victim needs). Programs must also strike a balance between facilitating a process of meaningful dialogue between the victim and the offender and developing feasible restitution agreements as a program outcome.

Lack of Victim Sensitivity and Involvement

Finally, as a growing number of probation departments in the United States and related agencies in other countries sponsor victim offender mediation programs, there is a clear hazard that these historically offender-driven criminal justice agencies will lose sight of the central role of crime victims in any restorative process. A few probation-based programs in the United States, for example, frequently ask probation officers to represent the views of victims rather than having the victim present. Such a practice is, at best, a weak alternative that undercuts the fundamental goal of giving the crime victim the opportunity to confront and enter into a dialogue with the person who harmed them, including the development of a plan to compensate them for their losses. For offenders, hearing about the harm their crimes have caused from the mouth of a probation officer rather than actual victims will do little to reinforce true accountability and victim empathy.

Another hazard is that probation-based programs operating in isolation will be unlikely to develop the basic sensitivity among staff to serve victims effectively and address their needs. Victim service providers can help remedy this and other program problems by providing the training for mediators and other juvenile justice staff on the victimization experience and the range of needs victims face. However, a recent national survey of victim offender mediation programs in the United States (see Chapter Six) found that 61 percent of mediation programs do not take advantage of this resource and the opportunity to increase staff sensitivity and effectiveness. From a broader restorative justice perspective, the concern for victim sensitivity should go far beyond just focusing on mediators. Many observers would maintain that all correctional staff should receive victim awareness training in order to be better prepared to understand the needs of crime victims and to invite their participation in the justice process.

Opportunities

With the increasing recognition of the value of victim offender mediation and restorative justice, the movement faces a number of important opportunities. In the twenty-five-year history of victim offender mediation and reconciliation programs, there has never been a greater opportunity than now for having a significant impact on criminal and juvenile justice systems in the United States and certain parts of Europe. Although it is likely that smaller programs continue to have a minimal effect on local justice systems, other programs—including several in North America that receive a thousand or more referrals a year—are having an increasingly important influence.

As more probation departments in the United States begin to sponsor victim offender mediation programs and mainstream professional organizations such as the American Bar Association, a former critic, endorse the practice and recommend its use in all courts throughout the country, the VOM movement is likely to grow considerably. Recent changes in German law, which now allows for greater use of victim offender mediation, have resulted in a large number of new programs, and related developments in other countries bode well for continued growth internationally.

However, despite its growth and increasing acceptance, victim offender mediation, as part of the larger vision of restorative justice, continues to operate in many communities as a kind of sideshow to the mainstream pursuit of justice in modern industrialized Western democracies. The basic principles of restorative justice require a fundamental shift in power related to who controls and "owns" crime in society—a shift from the state to the individual citizen and local communities. Although restorative justice has significant popular appeal, the principles of retributive justice continue to drive juvenile and criminal justice systems. Moving the principles of restorative justice theory and the practice of victim offender mediation from the margins to the mainstream of how we do justice in our society represents a major opportunity and presents several challenges.

Working with Severely Violent Cases

Many programs have worked with simple assault cases from their inception, even while focusing their main effort on nonviolent property crime. The small but growing trend to apply the VOM process in more serious, violent cases represents a major opportunity to expand the impact and credibility of restorative justice. As discussed in Chapter Thirteen, this trend has been brought about by requests from individuals victimized by such crimes as aggravated assault, armed robbery, sexual assault, and attempted homicide and by family members of homicide victims.

Over the past decade, the response to such requests has evolved from individual case-by-case adaptations of VOM to more thoroughly developed and organizationally supported programs aimed specifically at meeting the needs of these victims. Most encouraging is the recognition by a growing number of representatives of major victim advocacy organizations in the United States of the value of mediation for those victims of violence who express a need for it. As they directly confront the very source of terror in their lives through mediation, many victims of violence are able to obtain a greater sense of healing and closure.

The VOM field faces an exciting opportunity to stretch its original vision and significantly alter its original model to address the needs of parties affected by severely violent criminal conflict in an appropriate way. This can happen only if there is a serious commitment to reexamine the basic model and to understanding its limitations; an increased awareness of the victimization experience, including posttraumatic stress and grieving; and a willingness to apply tighter boundaries to when mediation is appropriate, what kind of advanced training is required, and who should serve as mediators. Far more extensive networking and coalition building with victim advocacy groups is also required.

Working with the Media

From the moment of birth, most of us are socialized in the belief that criminal conflict is, in the words of Christie (1977), the property of the state. From a very early age, we are bombarded with media images of cops and robbers. Many children's cartoons have themes of crime, violence, and good conquering evil. Each year the prime-time television schedule includes police shows with intense action, adventure, and violence. More recently, television programs based on realistic re-creations of actual crime incidents have emerged. These shows further promote an adversarial perspective on crime and victimization and reinforce commonly held stereotypes and images of criminals.

Restorative justice is based on very different principles than those that drive our current criminal justice system. In fact, restorative justice values run counter to dominant legal culture, which rests on the foundation of an adversarial process and the need for professional dispute resolvers (for example, lawyers). In order for the victim offender mediation process to move beyond marginalization, it must become better known and more accurately understood in the world of popular culture. The mass media, and television in particular, are crucial to the development of such a strategy.

Although care must be taken to avoid allowing the media to exploit victims and offenders—for example, by conducting live mediations on television entertainment shows in front of an audience—collaborating with credible television documentaries or newsmagazine shows that respect the needs of mediation participants, including the private filming of mediation sessions if the parties approve, can be an effective educational tool. Mediation programs must negotiate with the media so that their underlying interests and needs are met as much as possible.

For example, programs must coach journalists in a clear and credible manner so that the message of the program comes across effectively to the general public, and programs must always assume an active rather than passive role in working with the media.

Increasing Access

While working with the media is a critical strategy in moving mediation beyond its frequent marginalization, other long-term policy initiatives and strategies that yield immediate short-term impact in expanding access also need to be considered. The most obvious need is to address the fact that many victim offender mediation programs receive only a small number of referrals. Even programs that handle three hundred to five hundred cases a year often have a small impact on the local juvenile justice system when compared to the total number of cases in that jurisdiction.

For the VOM process to be taken seriously, it must be able to demonstrate that it can work with a substantial volume and range of cases in a cost-effective manner through the use of trained community volunteers. Far more cases need to be referred to mediation as a true diversion from prosecution. In addition, more postadjudication cases need to be referred either as a condition of probation or as a sole sanction alternative to traditional probation supervision. In the short term, a presumptive referral-to-mediation strategy could be developed in most jurisdictions. Such a referral procedure would assume, for example, that all property offenses involving a restitution requirement would first be given the opportunity to participate in victim offender mediation, rather than selecting only certain cases for referral.

Another short-term strategy already taking place in the United States is including mediation in victims' rights legislation. Because such an approach tends to link mediation with only one side of the conflict, this strategy would not be preferable. Mediation is intended to serve both parties in a fair and impartial manner; promoting wider access in this manner would therefore seem to be biased toward victims' concerns alone.

Given the reality of criminal justice policy and public attitudes in most North American and European communities, however, no other strategy is more likely to expand access to the mediation process for both crime victims and offenders. A recently passed victims' bill of rights in Indiana became the first act of public policy to include these provisions.

Whereas strategies that lead to these short-run advancements must be weighed carefully against the aforementioned disadvantages, a longer-term alternative solution might ultimately involve systematic advocacy for mediation as a basic *right* of any crime victim in any community, conditioned on the availability of a competent mediator, the willingness of the parties, the absence of any major mental health issues, and other relevant considerations.

Achieving Balance Through an Integrated Multimethod Approach

When victim offender mediation first appeared in the late 1970s and early 1980s, many advocates of this intervention viewed it as a "one size fits all" template involving primarily the individual victim, the offender, and the mediator. Family members and other support people were not frequently involved in the mediation process in most communities. In recent years, this has changed dramatically.

In the national survey reported in Chapter Six, only 8 percent of the more than 116 VOM programs reported that they never had parents or other support persons present. The current norm in VOM practice is to have parents of juveniles and, at times, other support persons present.

Emerging Models

One recent and promising restorative justice intervention to emerge is family group conferencing (FGC), a process that facilitates a dialogue among the victim, offender, families of both, and support people of both. Family group conferencing in correctional settings is widely used in New Zealand and is based on a traditional process of its indigenous people, the Maori. FGC is also used quite a bit in Australia, although the models are somewhat different (Umbreit & Stacey, 1995; Umbreit & Zehr, 1996). In some ways similar to the early years of victim offender mediation, family group conferencing is most frequently presented and marketed in North America as an entirely "new" program with a very prescriptive, script-driven, "one size fits all" perspective. Although the exact number of FGC programs is unknown, many hundreds of people have been trained to run them, and programs are developing in numerous communities in the United States and Canada.

An even more recent development in the United States is the use of peacemaking or sentencing circles in a small but growing number of communities. Circles are based largely on explicit traditions from Native American culture, although their use has been widespread in many other cultural and religious traditions as well. Sentencing circles have been used in many communities in the Yukon Territory of Canada, particularly among aboriginal and First Nation people.

Judge Barry Stuart has been conducting sentencing circles for many years in Canada and has been training an increasing number of criminal justice officials and community activists in the United States. The circle process represents a deeper, more spirituality grounded (though not necessarily religious), and community-involved form of restorative justice through victim, offender, family, and community dialogue.

Comparisons Across Models

During the early development of any new program initiative, it is quite understandable that models are presented as unique and distinct from other programs. As the field of restorative justice continues to develop around the world, however, it becomes increasingly important to find the common ground among all restorative justice policies and practices and to ensure that such initiatives are victim-sensitive and adaptable to diverse people, communities, and cultures.

Programs in a number of communities in the United States and England are already beginning to deemphasize the program model and highlight the underlying process in such a way that it can be adapted to meet the needs of specific people. By doing so, these programs are maximizing the strengths of each model while compensating for the limitations of each, based on the expressed needs of the specific victim and offender.

Exhibit 14.1 identifies some of the advantages and disadvantages of one-on-one mediation between the victim and offender versus a larger group conference including family members, other support people, or interested members of the community. As can be seen, traditional one-on-one victim offender mediation (as opposed to current practice) and larger group conferencing (such as family group conferencing) complement each other quite well.

From our perspective, they are all a form of victim offender "dialogue" or "conferencing," rather than three entirely distinct interventions. Use of a circle seating arrangement and even a talking piece that is passed around the circle, with larger groups, can often enhance the conferencing process. In fact, in more serious cases, blending both can be the most effective intervention, beginning with a one-on-one or small group conference and then

Exhibit 14.1 Advantages and Disadvantages of One-on-One Mediation Versus Larger Group Conferencing

Approach	Potential Advantages	Potential Disadvantages
One-on-one mediation (conference) • Conversation is between the crime victim and the offender. • One or more family members or other support people may be present but are not actively involved in the conversation.	• Setting is more private, reducing victim and offender anxiety. • Victim and offender are more likely to feel safe enough to be vulnerable and open. • Victim and offender are more likely to speak frankly rather than be influenced by what others might think. • Victim and offender are more likely to engage in genuine dialogue. • There is a greater focus on the needs of the direct crime victim. • Offender is less likely to "clam up" or feel shamed by others.	• Offender is unlikely to understand the full impact of his or her behavior on other people affected by the crime. • Participation of others who are part of the victim and offender's community of support, including family, is limited. • Conflict that affects the entire community is moved behind closed doors. • Approach is less likely to engage a network of people who can offer follow-up support to the victim or offender. • Community is less involved in holding the offender accountable.

Larger group conference

- Conversation is among all present, although the victim and offender are likely to begin by telling their stories.
- Meeting is likely to involve six to eight people and may occasionally involve twenty or more.

- Many other people affected by the crime are likely to be involved.
- Community is more involved in the process of holding the offender accountable.
- Offender is more likely to understand the full impact of his or her behavior on both primary and secondary victims.
- Family members and others who can offer support to the victim and offender are more likely to be involved.
- Network of people is available to offer follow-up support to victim and offender.

- Young offenders are likely to feel intimidated by so many adults present.
- Primary victim's needs may not receive as much attention as those of other family and community members.
- Some victims are likely to prefer a less public forum.
- Some offenders may not feel safe enough to talk openly and may even feel pressured by the group to respond in certain ways.
- One or more people may dominate the conversation, giving the victim and offender little time to talk with each other.

following this by enlarging the circle to include family members and other support people or other options or combinations.

It is easy to assume either that a one-on-one victim offender dialogue is most effective or, the more common current assumption, that more is better, that having family members and support people is far more effective. The truth is that the most appropriate form of a conversation between victims and offenders needs to be grounded in the expressed needs of the specific crime victim and offender, their cultural context, and practical realities in terms of time and other resources.

Toward an Integrative Framework

A broader, more inclusive, and more flexible conceptualization of the process for facilitating a direct conversation among crime victims, offenders, family members, and other support people in the community is needed. Such a broader conceptualization of victim, offender, family, and community dialogue needs to be grounded in the importance of adapting the process selected to the unique characteristics of the people, their communities, and their cultures.

The conceptual framework presented here is grounded in the actual practice of a growing number of programs in different parts of North America and Europe that are blending the strengths of victim offender mediation, family group conferences, and peacemaking circles in order to compensate for their weaknesses, thereby resulting in a stronger overall intervention that is more flexible and more adaptable.

For the purposes of this discussion, "restorative justice conferencing" is an overarching process (Bazemore & Umbreit, 1999), not a specific program model, that includes such program initiatives as victim offender mediation, victim offender reconciliation, victim offender meetings, family group conferencing, victim offender conferencing, community justice conferencing, and peacemaking circles. The process of facilitating a conversation among victims, offenders, and their families or support people in the community will be referred to as "mediation" since the skills of mediation (particularly humanistic dialogue-driven mediation) are used in all forms of victim offender conferencing whether or not the program itself uses the term *mediation*.

A multimethod approach involves adapting the practice wisdom and techniques of various methods, most notably victim offender mediation, family group conferencing, and circles, to the specific context of each case referral. Using a multimethod approach moves far beyond the "one size fits all" perspective of many programs and offers a more flexible intervention to respond to the unique needs of individuals, based on their communities and cultures. The choice of which method or combination of methods to use is grounded in the expressed needs of the specific victim and offender, rather than the assumptions of program staff about what is best.

For the sake of clarity, we are highlighting the importance of blending the strengths of traditional victim offender mediation and the more recent family group conferencing and peacemaking or sentencing circles based on the needs of each case since these are the most widely used venues for victim offender dialogue. The central issue is how to create a safe place for people to engage in a genuine dialogue based on their needs. Neither the needs of the program advocates nor the desire to compete with another program for increased referrals should be allowed to obscure this central focus.

Two examples of actual cases are offered to illustrate the meaning of a multimethod approach to restorative justice conferencing.

Case One: Sniper Shooting

A young suicidal man who lived in an apartment above the main street in a small rural community pulled out a rifle and started firing. He shot two other young men, nearly killing one of them, and then shot himself but survived the wound. The case was referred to a local conferencing-type program administered by the sheriff's department. After extensive preparatory and in-person meetings, the mediator first brought the offender, the two victims, and a parent of one of the victims together. The conference was convened in a circle format, and all present had an opportunity to speak. A second session was convened on the same day, after a lunch break. The circle was enlarged to include the police officer who investigated the case, the minister whose church the conference was held in, a community activist on an antidrug crusade, another interested community member, and a local politician.

Both sessions were powerful but different. This was the first known effort to use a two-phase approach to conferencing, blending the strengths of victim offender mediation and family group conferencing, as well as peacemaking circles. The smaller first session was similar to many VOM sessions. It provided a safe place for an intimate sharing of the impact of the crime on all parties. However, this first session did not provide a format to address the effect of the crime on others in the community. The second session allowed for that, and although the victim and offenders spoke far less, many of their needs had already been met in the earlier, more intimate setting. Such a serious case was referred to this program because the program had an exceptionally credible track record in the community and a sensitive and well-trained mediator-facilitator. A highly trained co-mediator was also present at both sessions.

Case Two: Pipe Bombing of School Official

Several high school students placed a CO_2 cartridge between the screen door and main front door of the assistant principal's home in a midwestern community. The "bomb" exploded and tremendously frightened the family, including two young children. In the press, the case was hyped up as a "pipe bombing" incident, leading many residents to construe it as a terrorist act. In reality, the CO_2 cartridge did very little property damage, though the emotional impact on the family was huge.

Upon referral of this case to a local community justice program operated by a county court services department, the mediator-facilitator conducted a number of in-person preparation sessions with each party directly affected by the crime. These combined the standard VOM approach with separate "healing circles" conducted with the victims and offenders and their support people before ever bringing them together.

Two group conferences of around twenty people each were eventually convened, adapting techniques from victim offender mediation, family group conferencing, and sentencing circles to the specific needs of these people and their community and culture. These group conferences each lasted nearly two and a half hours and involved intense expressions of feelings by most participants.

Finally, a large group conference resembling a sentencing circle and numbering nearly seventy people was held. Every person present spoke, and the session concluded with a discussion of specific recommendations for how to hold these juveniles accountable. The judge altered only one recommendation when the juveniles appeared in court for sentencing. All other recommendations were honored as determined in the circle.

Program Examples

A growing number of programs throughout the United States are beginning to use a multimethod approach. Rather than referring to their program as either "victim offender mediation" or "family group conferencing," they are beginning to use the expression "victim offender conferencing" or "restorative justice conferencing." Two specific programs in Minnesota that now routinely use a multimethod approach are offered as examples. Both began as victim offender mediation programs and later, after many years of experience, broadened their approach to victim, offender, family and community dialogue. Rather than initiating an entirely new model, they built their newer and more inclusive efforts upon the practice wisdom they had accumulated over the years with the initial victim offender mediation model.

Program One: Victim Offender Conferencing Program, Washington County (Minnesota) Court Services

The program in Washington County, Minnesota, was one of the first in the country to use a multimethod approach. Working with about 250 cases a year, this juvenile probation–based program trains community volunteers and probation officers to serve as comediators in small and large group conferences involving primarily property crimes but also some types of violent crime. It has mounted several very large conferences with as many as 150 people in a school setting involving a racial incident. The basic principles of traditional victim offender mediation, which focus on the importance of in-person preparation and developing a safe place for direct dialogue between the parties with limited intervention by the mediator, are emphasized in this program. To learn more about this program, contact Carolyn McLeod, Community Justice Program, Washington County Department of Court Services, 14900 Sixty-First Street N., P.O. Box 6, Stillwater, MN 55082.

Program Two: Restorative Conferencing Program, Dakota County (Minnesota) Community Corrections

The juvenile probation department in Dakota County, Minnesota, initiated one of the first probation-based victim offender mediation programs in 1980. Although the mediation initiative was inactive for a number of years, in the early 1990s, the county began a renewed effort to offer VOM services. The county administered the program, but actual mediation services were delivered by trained community volunteers. In more recent years, Dakota County has been experimenting with family group conferencing as well. Because of the similarities and the obvious advantages of blending the wisdom that has been learned from both "models," Dakota County has restructured its initiative to accommodate a multi-method approach. For more information about this program, contact Stephanie Haider, Restorative Conferencing Program, Dakota County Community Corrections, Western Service Center, 14955 Galaxie Avenue, Apple Valley, MN 55124.

Summary

Many observers would argue that these are the best of times and the most precarious of times for the restorative justice movement. On the one hand, the growing acceptance of various forms of victim, offender, family, and community dialogue through a mediated process bodes well for the future of this social reform movement. On the other hand, restorative justice and conferencing or circles are becoming so popular in some communities that it is now "politically correct" to talk the talk of restorative justice. Many grants cannot be obtained unless the applications are couched in restorative justice language. A big gulf often exists, however, between talking the talk and walking the walk.

As the field of victim offender mediation moves increasingly from the margins to the mainstream, there will be inevitable pressure to eliminate many of its fundamental principles, in the name of "efficiency" or in terms of other bureaucratic needs. Practitioners need continually to reflect on how their efforts relate to the core principles of restorative justice.

The future of this movement must never lose site of the most basic value: that dialogue of any sort among victims, offenders, family members, and community folk can have a profound restorative impact. As noted in Chapter One, the practice of restorative justice conferencing needs to be anchored in two bedrock principles: (1) creating a safe place through appropriate preparation and flexibility that maximizes the opportunity of the involved parties to enter into a direct dialogue about the impact of the crime on their lives and their community and (2) repairing the harm caused to the greatest possible extent. The experience of restorative justice through mediation and dialogue should heighten understanding, accountability, repair, and healing so that all of the involved parties experience a greater sense of connectedness, community safety, closure, and the ability to move on with their lives.

Appendixes

Appendix A

Resources:
Organizations, Publications, Videotapes

Organizations

Center for Peacemaking and Conflict Studies
Fresno Pacific University
1717 South Chestnut Avenue
Fresno, CA 93702
Phone: (209) 455-5840
Fax: (209) 252-4800
Internet: www.fresno.edu/pacs

Center for Restorative Justice & Peacemaking
University of Minnesota
School of Social Work
1404 Gortner Avenue, 105 Peters Hall
St. Paul, MN 55108
Phone: (612) 624-4923
Fax: (612) 625-8224
E-mail: rjp@tlcmail.che.umn.edu
Internet: http://ssw.che.umn.edu/rjp

Church Council on Justice and Corrections
507 Bank Street
Ottawa, Ontario K2P 1Z5
Canada
Phone: (613) 563-1688

Conflict Transformation Program
Eastern Mennonite University
1200 Park Road
Harrisonburg, VA 22802
Phone: (504) 432-4490
E-mail: ctprogram@emu.edu
Internet: http://narnia.emu.edu/ctp/ctp.htm

Genesee Justice Program/Victim Assistance Program
Genesee County Sheriff's Department
County Building 1
Batavia, NY 14020
Phone: (716) 344-2550 ext 2216

Justice Fellowship
P.O. Box 16069
Washington, DC 20041
Phone: (703) 904-7312
Newsletter: *Justice Report*

Mennonite Central Committee, Canada
Victim Offender Ministries
P.O. Box 2038
Abbotsford, British Columbia V2T 3T8
Canada
Phone: (604) 850-6639
Fax: (604) 850-8734
E-mail: mccbcvom@web.apc.org
Newsletter: *Accord*

Mennonite Central Committee, US
Office of Community Justice
P.O. Box 500
21 South Twelfth Street
Akron, PA 17501
Phone: (717) 859-3889
E-mail: mailbox@mcc.org
Internet: http://www.mcc.org
Journal: *Conciliation Quarterly*

National Organization for Victim Assistance (NOVA)
1757 Park Road N.W.
Washington, DC 20010
Phone: (800) 879-6682; (202) 232-6682
Fax: (202) 462-2255
E-mail: nova@try-nova.org
Internet: http://www.try-nova.org
Newsletter: *NOVA Newsletter*

National Resource Center for Youth Mediation
New Mexico Center for Dispute Resolution
800 Park Avenue S.W.
Albuquerque, NM 87102
Phone: (800) 249-6884); (505) 247-0571
Fax: (505) 242-5966
E-mail: nmcdr@igc.apc.org
Newsletter: *Dispute Resolution News*

National Victim Center
2111 Wilson Boulevard, Suite 300
Arlington, VA 22201
Phone: (703) 276-2880
Infolink: (800) 394-2255
E-mail: nvc@mail.nvc.org
Internet: http://www.nvc.org/
Newsletter: *NetWorks*

Neighbors Who Care
P.O. Box 16079
Washington, DC 20041
Phone: (703) 904-7311
E-mail: llampman@neighborswhocare.org
Internet: http://www.neighborswhocare.org

The Network: Interaction for Conflict Resolution
Conrad Grebel College
Waterloo, Ontario N2L 3G6
Canada
Phone: (519) 885-0880
Fax: (519) 885-0806
E-mail: nicr@watserv1.uwaterloo.ca
Internet: http://watserv1.uwaterloo.ca/~nicr
Newsletter: *Interaction*

Office for Victims of Crime (OVC)
U.S. Department of Justice
810 Seventh Street N.W.
Washington, DC 20531
Phone: (202) 616-3573; (202) 307-5983
Clearinghouse: (800) 627-6872
Internet: http://www.ojp.usdoj.gov/ovc
Newsletter: OVC *Advocate*

Office of Juvenile Justice and Delinquency Prevention (OJJDP)
810 Seventh Street N.W.
Washington, DC 20531
Phone: (202) 307-5911
Juvenile Justice Clearinghouse: (800) 638-8736
Fax: (301) 251-5212
Fax-on-demand: (800) 638-8736 (select 1 for automated ordering,
2 for fax-on-demand instructions)
Internet: http://www.ncjrs.org/ojjhome.htm
Journal: *Juvenile Justice*
Listserv: JUVJUST

Presbyterian Criminal Justice Program
100 Witherspoon Street
Louisville, KY 40202
Phone: (502) 569-5810
E-mail: parti@pcusa.org
Newsletter: *Justice Jottings*

REALJUSTICE
P.O. Box 229
Bethlehem, PA 18016
Phone: (610) 807-9221
E-mail: usa@realjustice.org; canada@realjustice.org
Internet: http://www.realjustice.org
Newsletter: REALJUSTICE *Forum*

Restorative Justice Initiative
Minnesota Department of Corrections
1450 Energy Park Drive, Suite 200
St. Paul, MN 55108
Phone: (651) 642-0329
Fax: (651) 642-0457
Internet: http://www.corr.state.mn.us
Newsletter: *Restorative Justice Newsletter*

Restorative Justice Institute
P.O. Box 16301
Washington, DC 20041
Phone: (703) 404-1246
Fax: (703) 404-4213
E-mail: grichardjd@aol.com
Newsletter: *Full Circle*

Restorative Justice Project
Fresno Pacific University
1717 South Chestnut Avenue
Fresno, CA 93702
Phone: (209) 455-5840
Fax: (209) 252-4800
E-mail: pacs@fresno.edu
Internet: http://www.fresno.edu/pacs/rjp.html

Victim Offender Mediation Association (VOMA)
c/o Restorative Justice Institute
4624 Van Kleeck Drive
New Smyrna Beach, FL 32169
Phone: (904) 424-9200
Fax: (904) 423-8099
E-mail: voma@voma.org
Internet: http://www.voma.org
Newsletter: VOMA Connections

VORP Information and Resource Center
19813 N.E. Thirteenth Street
Camas, WA 98607
Phone: (360) 260-1551
Fax: (360) 260-1563
E-mail: martyprice@vorp.com
Internet: http://www.vorp.com

Books and Monographs

Adler, C., & Wundersitz, J. (Eds.). (1994). *Family conferencing and juvenile justice: The way forward or misplaced optimism?* Canberra: Australian Institute of Criminology.

Barajas, E. (Ed.). (1996). *Community justice: Striving for safe, secure, and just communities.* Washington, DC: U.S. Department of Justice, National Institute of Corrections.

Bard, M., & Sangrey, D. (1986). *The crime victim's book.* Secaucus, NJ: Citadel Press.

Bazemore, G., Pranis, K., & Umbreit, M. S. (1997). *Balanced and restorative justice for juveniles: A framework for juvenile justice in the 21st century.* St. Paul: University of Minnesota, Center for Restorative Justice & Peacemaking.

Bazemore, G., & Umbreit, M. S. (1994). *Balanced and restorative justice program summary.* Washington, DC: Office of Juvenile Justice and Delinquency Prevention.

Bazemore, G., & Walgrave, L. (1999). *Restorative juvenile justice: Repairing the harm of youth crime.* Monsey, NY: Criminal Justice Press.

Boles, A. B., & Patterson, J. C. (1997). *Improving community response to crime victims: An eight-step model for developing protocol.* Thousand Oaks, CA: Sage.

Braithewaite, J. (1989). *Crime, shame and reintegration*. New York: Cambridge University Press.

Burnside, J., & Baker, N. (1994). *Relational justice: Repairing the breach*. Winchester, England: Waterside Press.

Butts, J. A., & Snyder, H. N. (1991). *Restitution and juvenile recidivism*. Pittsburgh, PA: National Center for Juvenile Justice.

Davis, R. C., Lurigio, A. J., & Skogan, W. G. (1997). *Victims of crime*. Thousand Oaks, CA: Sage.

Finn, P., & Lee, B. (1987). *Serving crime victims and witnesses*. Washington, DC: National Institute of Justice.

Galaway, B., & Hudson, J. (Eds.). (1990). *Criminal justice restitution and reconciliation*. Monsey, NY: Criminal Justice Press.

Galaway, B., & Hudson, J. (Eds.). (1996). *Restorative justice: An international perspective*. Monsey, NY: Criminal Justice Press.

Gilligan, J. (1996). *Violence*. New York: Putnam.

Hudson, J., Morris A., Maxwell G., & Galaway, B. (Eds.). (1996). *Family group conferences: Perspectives on policy and practice*. Monsey, NY: Criminal Justice Press.

Immarigeon, R. (1994). *Reconciliation between victims and imprisoned offenders: Program models and issues*. Akron, PA: Mennonite Central Committee, U.S.

Klein, A. (1996). *Alternative sentencing: A practitioner's guide*. Cincinnati, OH: Anderson.

Lampman, L.(Ed.). (1996). *Helping a neighbor in crisis*. Washington, DC: Neighbors Who Care.

McKnight, J. (1995). *The careless society: Community and its counterfeits*. New York: Basic Books.

Messmer, H., & Otto, H. U. (Eds.). (1992). *Restorative justice on trial: Pitfalls and potentials of victim-offender mediation: International research perspectives*. Norwell, MA: Kluwer.

Pennsylvania Coalition Against Rape. (1996). *Victim empowerment: Bridging the systems of mental health and victim service providers*. Washington, DC: Office of Victims of Crime.

Schneider, A. L. (1985). *Guide to juvenile restitution*. Washington, DC: Office of Juvenile Justice and Delinquency Prevention.

Schneider, A. L. (1990). *Deterrence and juvenile crime: Results from a national policy experiment*. New York: Springer-Verlag.

Spungen, D. (1997). *Homicide: The hidden victims: A guide for professionals*. Thousand Oaks, CA: Sage.

Stoneman, D., & Calvert, J. (1990). *Youthbuild: A manual for the implementation of the Housing-Related Enhanced Work Experience Program*. New York: Coalition for Twenty Million Dollars.

Umbreit, M. S. (1994). *Victim meets offender: The impact of restorative justice and mediation*. Monsey, NY: Criminal Justice Press.

Umbreit, M. S. (1995). *Mediating interpersonal conflicts: A pathway to peace*. West Concord, MN: CPI.

Umbreit, M. S., & Greenwood, J. (1997). *Guidelines for victim-sensitive victim offender mediation*. St. Paul: University of Minnesota, Center for Restorative Justice & Peacemaking.

Van Ness, D. W. (1986). *Crime and its victims*. Downers Grove, IL: Intervarsity Press.

Van Ness, D. W., & Strong, K. (1997). *Restoring justice*. Cincinnati, OH: Anderson.

Viano, E. C. (1990). *The victimology handbook*. New York: Garland.

Wright, M. (1996). *Justice for victims and offenders: A restorative response to crime* (2nd ed.). Winchester, England: Waterside Press.

Wright, M., & Galaway, B. (1989). *Mediation and criminal justice*. Thousand Oaks, CA: Sage.

Young, M. (1995). *Restorative community justice: A call to action*. Washington, DC: National Organization for Victim Assistance.

Zehr, H. (1985). *Retributive justice, restorative justice*. Akron, PA: Mennonite Central Committee, U.S.

Zehr, H. (1990). *Changing lenses: A new focus for crime and justice*. Scottsdale, PA: Herald Press.

Zehr, H., Van Ness, D. W., & Harris, M. K. (1989). *Justice: The restorative vision*. Akron, PA: Mennonite Central Committee, U.S.

Training Manuals

Claasen, R., & Zehr, H. (1989). *VORP organizing: A foundation in the church*. Akron, PA: Mennonite Central Committee, U.S.

Community Justice Initiatives Association. *Victim offender mediation training package*. Langley, British Columbia: Author.

McLeod, C. (1997). *Conferencing: Victim offender, small and large group*. Stillwater, MN: Washington County Community Justice Project.

Quill, D., & Wynne J. (1993). *Victim and offender mediation handbook*. London: Save the Children.

Stuart, B. (1997). *Building community justice partnerships: Community peacemaking circles*. Ottawa: Department of Justice of Canada.

Umbreit, M. S. (1996). *Advanced victim-sensitive mediation in crimes of severe violence: Training manual*. St. Paul: University of Minnesota, Center for Restorative Justice & Peacemaking.

Umbreit, M. S., & Greenwood, J. (1997). *Guidelines for victim-sensitive victim offender mediation*. St. Paul: University of Minnesota, Center for Restorative Justice & Peacemaking.

Umbreit, M. S., Greenwood, J., & Lipkin, R. (1996). *Introductory training manual: victim offender mediation and dialogue in property crimes and minor assaults*. St. Paul: University of Minnesota, Center for Restorative Justice & Peacemaking.

Training Resources

Bazemore, G., et al. (1988). *Restitution by juveniles: Information and operating guide for restitution programs*. Washington, DC: U.S. Department of Justice, Office of Justice Programs, Bureau of Justice Assistance.

Bazemore, G., & Umbreit, M. S. (1995). Rethinking the sanctioning function in juvenile court: Retributive or restorative responses to youth crime. *Crime & Delinquency, 41*(3), 296–316.

Beers, S (1994). *Overcoming loss: The other victims of homicide*. Allentown, PA: Crime Victims Council of the Lehigh Valley.

Lord, J. H. (1990). *Victim impact panels: A creative sentencing opportunity*. Fort Worth, TX: Mothers Against Drunk Driving.

Mackey, V. (1990). *Restorative justice: Toward nonviolence*. Louisville, KY: Presbyterian Church U.S.A., Presbyterian Justice Program.

Umbreit, M. S. (1993). *How to increase referrals to victim-offender mediation programs*. Winnipeg, Manitoba, Canada: Fund for Dispute Resolution.

Umbreit, M. S. (1995). *Mediation of criminal conflict: An assessment of programs in four Canadian provinces*. St. Paul: University of Minnesota, Center for Restorative Justice & Peacemaking.

Umbreit, M. S., & Coates, R. B. (1992). *Victim offender mediation: An analysis of programs in four states of the U.S.* St. Paul: University of Minnesota, Center for Restorative Justice & Peacemaking.

Umbreit, M. S., & Roberts, A. W. (1996). *Mediation of criminal conflict in England: An assessment of services in Coventry and Leeds*. St. Paul: University of Minnesota, Center for Restorative Justice & Peacemaking.

Young, M. (1993). *Victim assistance: Frontiers and fundamentals*. Washington, DC: National Organization for Victim Assistance.

Videotapes

The following videotapes are available through Center for Restorative Justice & Peacemaking, School of Social Work, University of Minnesota, 1404 Gortner, 105 Peters Hall, St. Paul, MN 55108; phone: (612) 624-4923; fax: (612) 625-4288; e-mail: rjp@tlcmail.che.umn.edu

Dakota County Victim Offender Meeting Program. Presents the victim offender mediation process used by the Victim Offender Meeting Program at Dakota County, Minnesota's Community Corrections Department, which uses trained community volunteers as mediators. Role-plays of premediation meetings with the offender and victim are presented, along with the actual mediation session. (60 minutes)

Model of Entire Victim Offender Mediation Process. Mark Umbreit models the entire victim offender mediation process, including calling and meeting the offender; calling and meeting the victim; and conducting a follow-up victim offender meeting. An excellent core training tape for role-playing the entire process. (80 minutes)

Restorative Justice: A Victim Awareness Resource: "The Importance of Listening to Crime Victims." Features the personal stories of three victim-survivors of crime that reveal how the crime affected the victims and their families. Stories involve a home burglary, a car theft, and a violent assault. Marlene A. Young, executive director of the National Organization for Victim Assistance, shares her thoughts on the importance of listening to victims of crime. An excellent resource for victim offender dialogue and victim awareness training. (32 minutes)

Victim Offender Mediation Simulation. This simulation of a mediation session models an empowering nondirective-style of mediation. The tape has proved effective for presentations to groups or funding sources interested in learning more about victim offender mediation. (28 minutes)

Victim Offender Mediation Overview. This brief video explains the victim offender mediation concept and process. Produced by the Center for Victim Offender Mediation of the Minnesota Citizens Council on Crime and Justice. Written by Mark Umbreit, the video follows a burglary case through the victim offender mediation process and places local program efforts in the context of the growing network of victim offender programs throughout the country. A basic resource for public presentations. (6 minutes)

The following videotapes were produced by the Center for Restorative Justice & Peacemaking and are available through the College of Continuing Education, 77 Pleasant Street S.E., 202 Wesbrook Hall, Minneapolis, MN 55455; phone: (612) 624-9898; Internet: http://www.cce.umn.edu

Restorative Justice: For Victims, Communities, and Offenders.
Abridged version of the Presbyterian Church U.S.A.'s video *Restoring Justice* that includes an updated presentation of what we have learned about the impact of restorative justice on victims, communities, and offenders. Specific program models are presented. An excellent resource for illustrating how restorative justice values and practices benefit crime victims, communities, and offenders. (25 minutes)

Restorative Justice: Victim Empowerment Through Mediation and Dialogue. Mark Umbreit briefly describes victim offender mediation, with an emphasis on the benefits for those victims who voluntarily chose to meet the offender. Comments by a diverse group of victims who have participated in mediation are presented, including their initial needs, what occurred in the mediation session, and their description of the benefits. Several key research findings are briefly highlighted. An excellent resource for gaining support from individual victims and victim advocates. (20 minutes)

The following videos give additional information on victim offender mediation and restorative justice.

Circle Sentencing: Yukon Justice Experiment. Judge Barry Stuart leads the application of circle sentencing practice based on the traditions of First Nation peoples in Canada's Yukon. (30 minutes) For a copy, contact Northern Native

Broadcasting Yukon, 4228A Fourth Avenue, Whitehorse, Yukon Y1A 1K1, Canada; phone: (403) 668-6332.

Glimmer of Hope. Documentary produced by the National Film Board of Canada about the journey toward healing of a family in Minnesota whose young daughter was brutally kidnapped, raped, and killed. It portrays many expressions of restorative justice, including several mediated dialogue sessions with the offenders involved. An excellent resource to show how restorative justice principles were applied in the most serious crime imaginable. (51 minutes) Distributed through Films for the Humanities and Sciences, P.O. Box 2053, Princeton, NJ 08543; phone: (800) 257-5126; fax: (609) 275-3767; e-mail: custserve@films.com; Internet: www.films.com

Portrait of a Reconciliation. Victim offender training video. (55 minutes) Available, with manual series and training package, from Community Justice Initiatives Association, 20678 Eastleigh Crescent, Suite 101, Langley, British Columbia V3A 4C4, Canada; phone: (604) 534-5515 or 534-6773; fax: (604) 534-6989; e-mail: cjibc@axionet.com

RealJustice Introduction to Family Group Conferencing. This video presents the basic family group conferencing model with youth offenders. The purpose of the conference is described, an actual case involved in a conference is presented, and postconference interviews with various participants are highlighted. In some ways similar to victim offender mdeiation, family group conferencing typically involves a larger number of family members or support people in an active discussion and review of the impact of the crime. (17 minutes) Available from *RealJustice*, P.O. Box 229, Bethlehem, PA 18016; phone: (610) 807-9221.

Restoring Justice. Produced in 1996 by the National Council of Churches for broadcast on national television, *Restoring Justice* is one of the best videos available for explaining what restorative justice is and what it can mean for victims, community, and offenders. Program examples are excellent. (50 minutes) Available from Presbyterian Criminal Justice Program, 100 Witherspoon Street, Louisville, KY 40202; phone: (800) 524-2612 or (502) 569-5810; fax: (502) 569-8030; contact Kathy Lancaster.

Victim Impact Panel Program. Video explains the concept of the victim impact panel for use in cases of drunk driving crashes. Provides good material on how the panels work, how to set them up, and the effects they have on participants. (13 minutes) Available from: Mothers Against Drunk Driving (MADD), P.O. Box 541688, Dallas, TX 75354; phone: (800) 438-6233.

Pamphlets

The following pamphlets are available through Mennonite Central Committee, Office of Community Justice, P.O. Box 500, 21 South Twelfth Street, Akron, PA 17501; phone: (717) 859-3889.

Justice: The Restorative Vision by Howard Zehr, Dan Van Ness, and M. Kay Harris (1989).

Mediating the Victim Offender Conflict by Howard Zehr (1982).

Retributive Justice, Restorative Justice by Howard Zehr (1985).

VORP Organizing: A Foundation in the Church by Ron Claassen and Howard Zehr with Duane Ruth-Heffelbower (1989).

Bibliographic Resources

McCold, P. (1997). *Restorative Justice: An Annotated Bibliography.* Monsey, NY: Criminal Justice Press. Prepared for the Alliance of NGOs on Crime Prevention and Criminal Justice.

National Criminal Justice Reference Service. (1996). *Restorative/Community Justice: A Programmatic Perspective (Topical Bibliography)*. Publication No. TB010629. Up to two hundred citations from the NCJRS Abstract Database. Available through the National Criminal Justice Reference Service, (800) 851-3420.

National Criminal Justice Reference Service. (1996). *Restorative/Community Justice: A Theoretical Perspective (Topical Search)*. Publication No. TS011686. Thirty bibliographic citations from the NCJRS Abstract Database. Available through the National Criminal Justice Reference Service, (800) 851-3420.

Appendix B

Directory of VOM Programs in the United States

Programs are alphabetized first by state, then by city, and finally by program name. If a state is not listed, it means that the Center for Restorative Justice & Peacemaking does not have any record of a victim offender mediation program in that state. It does not necessarily mean that there are no programs in that state. Readers who are aware of additional programs are invited to contact the center with the relevant program information: Center for Restorative Justice & Peacemaking, 1404 Gortner Avenue, 105 Peters Hall, St. Paul, MN 55108.

Alabama

Victim Offender Reconciliation Program (VORP)
Reconciliation and Justice Ministries, Inc.
102 South Powell Street
Union Springs, AL 36089
Phone: (334) 738-3282
Fax: (334) 738-3282

Alaska

Victim Offender Mediation Program
Resolution Center
Community Dispute Resolution Center, Inc.

505 West Northern Lights Boulevard, Suite 210
Anchorage, AK 99503
Phone: (907) 274-1542
Fax: (907) 274-0332
E-mail: CDRC1@juno.com

Juneau Community Mediation Center, Inc.
114 South Franklin Street, Suite 201
Juneau, AK 99801
Phone: (907) 586-4958
Fax: (907) 463-5858
E-mail: mreges@aol.com

Note: This directory was compiled by Mark S. Umbreit and Robert Schug, with assistance from Jean Greenwood, Claudia Fercello, and Jenni Umbreit, at the Center for Restorative Justice & Peacemaking, School of Social Work, University of Minnesota. The most current version of this directory, including additional details about each program, may be viewed at the center's Web site: http://ssw.che.umn.edu/rjp

Arizona

Conflict Resolution Section
Arizona Attorney General's Office
1275 West Washington Street
Phoenix, AZ 85007
Phone: (602) 542-4192
Fax: (602) 542-8899

Attorney General's Victim Offender
    Mediation Program
920 South Placita Cona Lea
Tucson, AZ 85748
Phone: (520) 628-6783

Victim Offender Mediation Program
11600 North Oracle Road
Tucson, AZ 85737

California

Victim Offender Reconciliation Program
    (VORP)
Youth Mediation Interface, Children
    Family Services
1305 Del Norte Road, Suite 130
Camarillo, CA 93010
Phone: (805) 485-0788
Fax: (805) 983-0789

Mediation Center of the North Valley
341 Broadway Street, Suite 200
Chico, CA 95928
Phone: (916) 899-2277
Fax: (916) 899-2270
E-mail: mcnv@shocking.com

Victim Offender Reconciliation Program
    (VORP) of the Central Valley, Inc.
2529 Willow Avenue
Clovis, CA 93612
Phone: (559) 291-1120
Fax: (559) 291-8214
E-mail: vorp@fresno.edu
Internet: http://www.vorp.org

Victim Offender Mediation Program
Restorative Justice Program
643 Blackburn Avenue
Corning, CA 96021
Phone: (530) 824-4408
Fax: (530) 824-4709
E-mail: research7@snowcrest.net

The Mediation Center
Access to Justice
2133 Fairview Road, Suite 100
Costa Mesa, CA 92627
Phone: (714) 574-5990
Fax: (714) 574-5999

South Valley Dinuba Victim Offender
    Reconciliation Program (VORP)
P.O. Box 401
Dinuba, CA 93618
Phone: (559) 897-0110

Victim Offender Reconciliation Program
    (VORP) of Sacramento County
P.O. Box 276629
Fair Oaks, CA 95827
Phone: (916) 364-1010
Fax: (916) 364-1037
E-mail: admin@ygc.org

Center for Peacemaking and Conflict
    Studies
Fresno Pacific College
1717 South Chestnut Avenue
Fresno, CA 93702
Phone: (559) 455-5840
Fax: (559) 252-4800
E-mail: rlclaass@fresno.edu
Internet: http://www.vorp.org;
    http://fresno.edu/pacs/

Centinela Valley Juvenile Diversion
    Project (CVJDP)
Inglewood City Hall
1 Manchester Boulevard, Suite 880
Inglewood, CA 90301
Phone: (310) 412-5578
Fax: (310) 330-5705
E-mail: cvjdp@cityofinglewood.org

CSP—Dispute Resolution Services
16842 Von Karman Street, Suite 425
Irvine, CA 92606
Phone: (949) 851-3168
Fax: (949) 251-1659
E-mail: disputeresolution@CSPinc.org
Internet: http://cspinc.org/

Placer Dispute Resolution Service
4191 Godley Lane
Lincoln, CA 95648
Phone: (916) 645-9260
Fax: (916) 645-9260

Asian Pacific American Dispute
  Resolution Center
1010 South Flower Street, Suite 301
Los Angeles, CA 90015
Phone: (213) 747-9943
Fax: (213) 748-0679

Martin Luther King Dispute Resolution
  Center
4182 South Western Avenue
Los Angeles, CA 90062
Phone: (213) 290-4126
Fax: (213) 296-4742

Los Angeles Victim Offender Reconcilia-
  tion Program (VORP), Pasadena Pilot
Archdiocesean Catholic Center
3424 Wilshire Boulevard
Los Angeles, CA 90010
Phone: (213) 637-7486
Fax: (213) 637-6161

Madera County Victim Offender Reconciliation Program (VORP)
3270 Tragon Street
Madera, CA 93637
Phone: (209) 675-8373

Community Violence Prevention
  Program
Catholic Charities of the East Bay
433 Jefferson Street
Oakland, CA 94607
Phone: (510) 768-3151
Fax: (510) 451-6998

Mediatrix
P.O. Box 3955
Quincy, CA 95971
Phone: (916) 283-2156
Fax: (916) 283-2156

Victim Offender Reconciliation Program
  (VORP) of San Diego County
1984 Sunset Cliffs Boulevard
San Diego, CA 92107
Phone: (619) 223-2544
Fax: (619) 223-4794
E-mail: sdvorp@att.net
Internet: http://www.vorp.org/sandiego/

Community Board of San Francisco
1540 Market Street, Suite 490
San Francisco, CA 94102
Phone: (415) 552-1250
Fax: (415) 626-0595

Dispute Resolution Program Services
Santa Clara County Probation Depart-
  ment, Juvenile Division
70 West Hedding Street, West Wing
San Jose, CA 95110
Phone: (408) 299-2206
Fax: (408) 297-2463
E-mail: chere.montgomery@co.scl.ca.us

Victim Offender Mediation Program
840 Guadalupe Parkway
San Jose, CA 95110
Phone: (408) 278-6057
Fax: (408) 294-1872
E-mail:
  jeanne_lucchesi@mail.jpd.co.santa-
  clara.ca.us

Victim Offender Reconciliation Program
  (VORP)
Conflict Resolution Program of the
  Central Coast
265 South Street, Suite B
San Luis Obispo, CA 93401
Phone: (805) 549-0442
Fax: (805) 549-0654
E-mail: crpcc@lgc.org

Victim Offender Mediation Program
Peninsula Conflict Resolution Center
520 South El Camino Real, Suite 640
San Mateo, CA 94402
Phone: (650) 373-3490
Fax: (650) 373-3495
E-mail: marshalljs@earthlink.net
Internet: http://pcrcweb.org/

Victim Offender Reconciliation Program
  (VORP)
Institute for Conflict Management
2525 North Grand Avenue, Suite N
Santa Ana, CA 92705
Phone: (714) 288-5600
Fax: (714) 836-8585
E-mail: vorpoc@igc.org

Restorative Justice Project
Community Mediation Program
330 East Carrillo Street
Santa Barbara, CA 93101
Phone: (805) 963-6765
Fax: (805) 963-81651
E-mail: humanity96@aol.com

RE-VORP~RE-COURSE
Victim Offender Reconciliation Program
(VORP)
Redwood Empire Conflict Resolution Services (RE-COURSE)
520 Mendocino Avenue, Suite 233
Santa Rosa, CA 95401
Phone: (707) 538-7827
Fax: (707) 538-7827
E-mail: revorp@aol.com

Victim Offender Reconciliation Program
(VORP) of San Joaquin County
1020 West Lincoln Road
Stockton, CA 95207
Phone: (209) 369-7121
Fax: (209) 473-2314
E-mail: waldol@lodinet.com

Victim Offender Reconciliation Program
(VORP) of Mendocino County
205 North Bush Street, Room 6
P.O. Box 355
Ukiah, CA 95482
Phone: (707) 462-6160

Victims/Offenders Learning Together
(VOLT)
CA Medical Facility—Vacaville
P.O. Box 2000
Vacaville, CA 95696
Phone: (707) 453-7056
Fax: (707) 448-1467

Colorado

San Luis Valley Victim Offender
Reconciliation Program (VORP)
P.O. Box 1775
Alamosa, CO 81101
Phone: (719) 589-5255
Fax: (719) 589-5255
E-mail: SLV-VORP@juno.com

Face-to-Face
Community Alternatives, Inc.
2600 South Parker Road,
Suite 5-250
Aurora, CO 80014
Phone: (303) 794-4890 ext. 119
Fax: (303) 794-9560

City of Boulder Community Mediation
Service
P.O. Box 791
Boulder, CO 80306

Phone: (303) 441-4344
Fax: (303) 441-4348

Victim Offender Reconciliation Program
(VORP) of Boulder County
1520 Euclid Avenue
Boulder, CO 80302
Phone: (303) 442-6040
Fax: (303) 444-6523
E-mail: vorp@bcn.boulder.co.us

Center for Conflict Resolution in the
Roaring Fork Valley
P.O. Box 292
Carbondale, CO 81623
Phone: (970) 945-7364
Fax: (970) 945-6424

Office of the District Attorney
Neighborhood Justice Center
105 East Vermijo Avenue, Suite 600
Colorado Springs, CO 80903
Phone: (719) 520-6016
Fax: (719) 520-6006

Denver District Attorney's Juvenile
Diversion Program
303 West Colfax Avenue, Suite 1000
Denver, CO 80204
Phone: (720) 913-9013
Fax: (720) 913-9263

Victim Offender Reconciliation Program
(VORP) of Denver
430 West Ninth Avenue
Denver, CO 80204
Phone: (303) 534-6167
Fax: (303) 796-9593
E-mail: aschrade@ix.netcom.com

Larimer County Youth Services Bureau
419 West Mountain Street
Fort Collins, CO 80522
Phone: (970) 498-7470

Jefferson County Victim Offender
Reconciliation Program (VORP)
Jeffereson County Mediation Services
700 Jefferson County Parkway, Suite 220
Golden, CO 80401
Phone: (303) 271-5062
Fax: (303) 271-5064
E-mail: mloye@co.jefferson.co.us

Mesa County Partners, Inc.
735 South Avenue
Grand Junction, CO 81501
Phone: (970) 245-5555
Fax: (970) 245-7411

Garfield Youth Services
136 East Twelfth Street
Rifle, CO 81650
Phone: (970) 625-3141
Fax: (970) 625-9532

Connecticut

Hartford Area Mediation Program
151 Farmington Avenue, Suite 13
Hartford CT 06156
Phone: (860) 280-1184
Fax: (860) 280-1186

Dispute Settlement Center, Inc.
5 Mott Avenue
Norwalk, CT 06850
Phone: (203) 831-8012
Fax: (203) 831-8025

Delaware

Center for Community Justice
111 West Loockerman Street,
    Suite R
Dover, DE 19904
Phone: (302) 674-4015
Fax: (302) 674-4599

Center for Community Justice, Sussex
    Office
132 East Market Street, Suite B
Georgetown, DE 19947
Phone: (302) 854-9311
Fax: (302) 856-2620

Citizen Dispute Settlement (CDS)
City of Wilmington Law Department
Louis L. Redding City/County Building
800 French Street, Ninth Floor
Wilmington, DE 19801
Phone: (302) 571-4122
Fax:(302) 429-6815

Delaware Center for Justice/Community
    Mediation Initiative
501 Shipley Street
Willmington, DE 19801
Phone: (302) 658-7273
Fax: (302) 658-7170
E-mail: memical@aol.com

District of Columbia

Ubuntu: The Community Victim
    Offender Program

5100 Connecticut Avenue N.W., Suite 204
Washington, DC 20008
Phone: (202) 364-0992
Fax: (202) 737-0844
E-mail: ucvop@starpower.net

Florida

Juvenile Alternative
2600 Southeast Fourth Avenue
Fort Lauderdale, FL 33301
Phone: (954) 467-4592
Fax: (954) 467-4699

Neighborhood Justice Center
918 Railroad Avenue
Tallahassee, FL 32310
Phone: (850) 921-6980
Fax: (850) 414-0166
E-mail: mwnjc@juno.com

Georgia

Bartow County Juvenile Court Mediation
    Program
135 West Cherokee Avenue, Suite 333
Cartersville, GA 30120
Phone: (770) 387-5039
Fax: (770) 387-5044

Office of Dispute Resolution
216 Tenth Street
Columbus, GA 31901
Phone: (706) 649-1414
Fax: (706) 649-1413
E-mail: thirdodr@leo.infi.net

Association of Registered Mediators
301 West Crawford Street
Dalton, GA 30720
Phone: (706) 278-6558
Fax: (706) 272-7018

De Kalb Juvenile Court Mediation
    Program
3631 Camp Circle
Decatur, GA 30032
Phone: (404) 294-2756
Fax: (404) 297-3834

Office of Dispute Resolution
Ninth Judicial Administrative District
311 Green Street, Suite 409
Gainesville, GA 30501
Phone: (770) 535-6909
Fax: (770) 531-4072
E-mail: adr9th@mindspring.com

Mediation Diversion Program
Clayton County Juvenile Court
Annex 3, Second Floor
Jonesboro, GA 30236
Phone: (770) 477-3270
Fax: (770) 477-3255

Mediation Center
114 Church Street
La Grange, GA 30240
Phone: (706) 883-2168
Fax: (706) 883-2169

Juvenile Court of Cobb County
Mediation Program
Administrative Annex
1738 County Services Parkway S.W.
Marietta, GA 30060
Phone: (770) 528-2275
Fax: (770) 528-2561

Mediation Center, Inc.
23 East Charlton Street, Suite 1A
Savannah, GA 31401
Phone: (912) 236-0918
Fax: (912) 232-9510

Mediation Program
Juvenile Court of Houston County
202 Carl Vinson Parkway
Warner Robins, GA 31088
Phone: (912) 542-2011
Fax: (912) 922-4279

Hawaii

Ku'ikahi Mediation Center
300 West Lanikaula Street
Hilo, HI 96720
Phone: (808) 935-7844
Fax: (808) 969-1772

Neighborhood Justice Center
Juvenile Restitution and Adult Victim
Offender Mediation
200 North Vineyard Boulevard, Suite 320
Honolulu, HI 96817
Phone: (808) 521-6767
Fax: (808) 538-1454

Idaho

Victim Impact Program (VIP)
Ada County Juvenile Court Services
6300 West Denton Street
Boise, ID 83704

Phone: (208) 364-3000
Fax: (208) 364-3010
E-mail: jvpooljl@ac1.co.ada.id.us

Victim Impact Program (VIP)
Kootenai County Juvenile Services
501 Government Way
P.O. Box 9000
Coeur d'Alene, ID 83816
Phone: (208) 666-2414
Fax: (208) 666-2416
E-mail: jcrowley@co.kootenai.id.us

Illinois

Victim Offender Reconciliation Program
(VORP) of McLean County, Inc.
207 West Jefferson Street, Suite 304
P.O. Box 1445
Bloomington, IL 61702
Phone: (309) 829-7177

Victim Offender Reconciliation Program
(VORP) of Champaign County
404 West Church Street
Champaign, IL 61820
Phone: (217) 352-9287
Fax: (217) 352-6494

Woodford County Victim Offender
Reconciliation Program (VORP)
504 Crestwood Street
Eureka, IL 61530
Phone: (309) 467-2194

Indiana

Madison City Community Justice
123 East Tenth Street
Anderson, IN 46016
Phone: (765) 649-7341
Fax: (765) 649-7354

Victim Offender Reconciliation Program
(VORP) of Bloomington
233 South Pete Ellis Drive, Suite 11
P.O. Box 6282
Bloomington, IN 47407
Phone: (812) 336-8677
Fax: (812) 336-8679
E-mail: vorp@bloomington.in.us
Internet: http://www.bloomington.in.us/
~vorp/

Victim Offender Reconciliation Program
(VORP)
Center for Community Justice
121 South Third Street
Elkhart, IN 46516
Phone: (219) 295-6149
Fax: (219) 522-6685
E-mail: ccjfolks@aol.com

Victim Offender Reconciliation Program
(VORP)
Mediation Services of Tippecanoe
County, Inc.
1107 South Eighteenth Street
Lafayette, IN 47905
Phone: (765) 474-0501
Fax: (765) 474-0501
E-mail: mstc123@aol.com
Internet:
http://members.aol.com/mstc123

Hoosier Hills Prisoner and Community
Together (PACT) Victim Offender
Reconciliation Program (VORP)
108 South Main Street
Salem. IN 47167
Phone: (812) 883-1959
Fax: (812) 883-0358

United Religious Community of St.
Joseph County Victim Offender Rec-
onciliation Program (VORP)
2015 Wern Avenue
South Bend, IN 46629
Phone: (219) 282-2397

Porter County Prisoner and Community
Together (PACT) Victim Offender
Reconciliation Program (VORP)
254 Morgan Boulevard
Valparaiso, IN 46383
Phone: (219) 465-1100
Fax: (219) 464-0128

Iowa

Center for Creative Justice
210 Lynn Avenue
Ames, IA 50014
Phone: (515) 292-3820
Fax: (515) 292-1223

Victim Offender Mediation
1202 West Third Street
Davenport, IA 52804
Phone: (319) 326-5090
Fax: (319) 326-1154
E-mail: mediation@qconline.com

Victim Offender Reconciliation Program
(VORP)
Polk County Attorney's Office
206 Sixth Avenue, Suite 500
Des Moines, IA 50309
Phone: (515) 286-3057
Fax: (515) 323-5254

Juvenile Court Services
350 West Sixth Street, Suite 215
Dubuque, IA 52001
Phone: (319) 589-7831
Fax: (319) 589-7842

Victim Offender Mediation Program
Office of Dubuque County Attorney
Dubuque County Courthouse
720 Central Avenue
Dubuque, IA 52001
Phone: (319) 589-4470
Fax: (319) 589-4477
E-mail: Barbswork@aol.com

Iowa Mediation Service
6200 Aurora Avenue, Suite 608W
Urbandale, IA 50322
Phone: (515) 331-8081
Fax: (515) 331-8085
E-mail: iamed8@netins.net

Kansas

Victim Offender Reconciliation Program
(VORP) of Central Kansas
2015 Lakin Street
Great Bend, KS 67530
Phone: (316) 793-3668

Victim Offender Reconciliation Program
(VORP) of Reno County
1 East Ninth Avenue, Suite 205
Hutchinson, KS 67501
Phone: (316) 669-9944
E-mail: renovorp@southwind.net

Victim Offender Reconciliation Program
(VORP) of Douglas County
United Way Center for Human Services
2518 Ridge Court, Room 213
Lawrence, KS 66046
Phone: (785) 843-9969

Victim Offender Reconciliation Program
(VORP)
Offender/Victim Ministries, Inc.
900 North Poplar Street, Suite 200
Newton, KS 67114
Phone: (316) 283-2038
Fax: (316) 283-2039
E-mail: ovm@southwind.net

Dispute Resolution Services of Kansas
Legal Services
465 South Parker Street
Olathe, KS 66061
Phone: (913) 764-8585
Fax: (913) 764-8588

KINnections Program
Kansas Children's Service League
1365 North Custer Street
Wichita, KS 67203
Phone: (316) 942-4261 ext. 248
Fax: (316) 943-9995

Kentucky

Mediation Center of Kentucky
271 West Short Street, Suite 200
Lexington, KY 40517
Phone: (606) 255-6056

Transformation House, Inc.
121 Walton Avenue
Lexington, KY 40508
Phone: (606) 231-1282
Fax: (606) 255-8143
E-mail: lharvey@igc.org

Mediation First
101 Cresent Avenue
Louisville, KY 40206
Phone: (502) 897-3020
Fax: (502) 899-1545
E-mail: mstein@mediationfirst.com
Internet: http://mediationfirst.com

Louisiana

Family Mediation Council of Louisiana
6031 Perrier Street
New Orleans, LA 70118
Phone: (504) 558-9080
Fax: (504) 895-4355
E-mail: quadrapro@aol.com

Maine

Community Mediation Center
222 St. John Street, Suite 254
Portland, ME 04102
Phone: (207) 772-4070
Fax: (207) 874-7402
E-mail: cmc@neis.net

Maryland

Anne Arundel Conflict Resolution
Center
2666 Riva Road, Suite 130
Annapolis, MD 21401
Phone: (410) 266-9033
Fax: (410) 573-5391

Massachusetts

Mediation Examines Negative Dialogue
and Conflicts (MEND Conflicts)
P.O. Box 185
Amherst, MA 01004
Phone: (413) 253-4602
Fax: (413) 253-4602

Brockton District Court Mediation
Project
155 West Elm Street
Brockton, MA 02401
Phone: (508) 587-8000
Fax: (508) 587-6663

Metropolitan Mediation Services
43 Garrison Road
Brookline, MA 02146
Phone: (617) 277-8107
Fax: (617) 734-6385
E-mail: jacks@vmbsky.cc.umb.edu

Cambridge Dispute Settlement Center,
Inc.
872 Massachusetts Avenue, Suite 2-9
Cambridge, MA 02146

Phone: (617) 876-5376
Fax: (617) 876-6663

North Central Court Services, Inc.
Fitchburg District Court
100 Elm Street
Fitchburg, MA 01420
Phone: (978) 345-2111 ext. 242
Fax: (978) 342-2524
E-mail: mlpersons@aol.com

Framingham Court Mediation Services
600 Concord Street
P.O. Box 1969
Framingham, MA 01701
Phone: (508) 872-9495
Fax: (508) 872-9764

Mediation and Training Collaborative
Franklin Community Action Corpora-
    tion
277 Main Street, Fourth Floor
Greenfield, MA 01301
Phone: (413) 774-7469
Fax: (413) 774-7460
E-mail: mediation@fcac.net

Mediation Works, Inc.
169 Summer Street
Kingston, MA 02364
Phone: (617) 582-1494
Fax: (617) 585-7483
E-mail: MWI@mwi.org
Internet: http://www.mwi.org

Middlesex Community College Law
    Center
33 Kearney Square
Lowell, MA 01852
Phone: (508) 656-3340
Fax: (508) 656-3339

Juvenile Probation Department
Quincy District Court
1 Dennis Ryan Parkway
Quincy, MA 02169
Phone: (617) 471-1650 ext. 212
Fax: (617) 471-8429
E-mail: beef99@ziplink.net

Dispute Resolution Services, Inc.
115 State Street, Suite 200
Springfield, MA 01103
Phone: (413) 787-6480
Fax: (413) 788-9685

Community Mediation Center
Worcester Community Action Council
484 Main Street, Second Floor
Worcester, MA 01608
Phone: (508) 754-1176
Fax: (508) 754-0203

Michigan

Sunrise Mediation Service
2284 Diamond Point Road
Alpena, MI 49707
Phone: (517) 356-0586
Fax: (517) 354-6939

Dispute Resolution Center
1100 North Main Street, Suite 217
Ann Arbor, MI 48104
Phone: (313) 741-0603
Fax: (313) 998-0163

Citizens Mediation Service, Inc.
292 Bellview Street
Benton Harbor, MI 49022
Phone: (616) 925-5884
Fax: (616) 925.5514
E-mail: citizen@parrett.net
Internet: http://citizensmediation.org

Cadillac Area Oasis/Family Resource
    Center
P.O. Box 955
230 East Cass Street
Cadillac, MI 49601
Phone: (616) 775-7299
Fax: (616) 775-4074

Human Development Commission
    Center for Dispute Resolution
429 Montague Avenue
Caro, MI 48723
Phone: (517) 672-4044
Fax: (517) 673-2031
E-mail: peggyg@hdc-caro.org

Victim Offender Restitution Program
Wayne County Neighborhood Legal
    Services
3400 Cadillac Tower
Detroit, MI 48226
Phone: (313) 962-0466 ext. 251
Fax: (313) 962-6374
E-mail: LDBernard@wcnls.org

Resolution Services Program
Upper Peninsula Commission for Area
 Progress
2501 Fourteenth Avenue South
P.O. Box 606
Escanaba, MI 49829
Phone: (906) 789-9580
Fax: (906) 786-5853

Community Dispute Resolution Center
 of Genesee County, Inc.
631 Beach Street
Flint, MI 48502
Phone: (810) 232-2185
Fax: (810) 768-4667

Dispute Resolution Center of Western
 Michigan
701 Fourth Street N.W.
Grand Rapids, MI 49504
Phone: (616) 774-0121
Fax: (616) 774-0323

Center for Dispute Resolution
272 East Eighth Street
Holland, MI 49423
Phone: (616) 494-3800
Fax: (616) 494-3802

Victim Offender Reconciliation Program
 (VORP)
Center for Dispute Resolution
13565 Port Sheldon Road
Holland, MI 49424
Phone: (616) 399-6940 ext. 318
Fax: (616) 399-8263

Superior Resolution Service
Michigan State University Extension
P.O. Box 717
Houghton, MI 49931
Phone: (906) 482-4524
Fax: (906) 482-1385

Livingston Community Dispute
 Resolution Services
P.O. Box 138
Howell, MI 48843
Phone: (517) 546-6007
Fax: (517) 546-4115

Western Upper Peninsula Mediators
115 East Ayer Street
Ironwood, MI 49938
Phone: (906) 932-0010
Fax: (906) 932-0230

Southeastern Dispute Resolution Services
Community Action Agency
1214 Greenwood Street
P.O. Drawer 1107
Jackson, MI 49204
Phone: (517) 784-4800
Fax: (517) 784-5188

Dispute Resolution Center of Central
 Michigan
1609 East Kalamazoo Street, Suite 9
Lansing, MI 48912
Phone: (800) 873-7658 or
 (517) 485-2274
Fax: (517) 485-1183
E-mail: crccmi710@aol.com

Marquette-Alger Resolution Service
200 West Spring Street
Marquette, MI 49855
Phone: (906) 226-4372
Fax: (906) 226-4369

Resolution Center
18 Market Street
Mount Clemens, MI 48043
Phone: (810) 469-4714
Fax: (810) 469-0078
E-mail:
 theresolutioncenter@mediate.com

Victim Offender Reconciliation Program
 (VORP)
Isabella County Trial Court
200 North Main Street
Mount Pleasant, MI 48858
Phone: (517) 772-0911 ext. 279
Fax: (517) 773-2419

Juvenile Court Program
Westshore Dispute Resolution Center,
 Inc.
1218 Jefferson Street
Muskegon, MI 49441
Phone: (616) 727-6001
Fax: (616)727-6011

Victim Offender Reconciliation Program
 (VORP) of Charlevoix and Emmit
 Counties
912 Lindell Avenue
Petoskey, MI 49770
Phone: (616) 348-3406

Mid-Michigan Dispute Resolution Center
116 South Michigan Avenue
Saginaw, MI 48602

Phone: (517) 797-4188
Fax: (517) 797-4185
E-mail: mmdrc@juno.com

Minnesota

Anoka Police Department
2015 First Avenue North
Anoka, MN 55303
Phone: (612) 576-2813
Fax: (612) 422-2092

Dakota County Community Corrections
Western Service Center
14955 Galaxie Avenue
Apple Valley, MN 55124
Phone: (612) 891-7206
Fax: (612) 891-7282
E-mail:
    stephanie.haider@co.dakota.mn.us

Mower County Community Conferencing
Cooperative Solutions
110 North Main Street
Austin, MN 55912
Phone: (507) 433-3663
Fax: (507) 433-3990
E-mail: csi@smig.net

Ninth Judicial District Mediation
    Program
Department of Corrections
P.O. Box 397
Bemidji, MN 56619
Phone: (218) 755-4034
Fax: (218) 755-4186

North Hennepin Mediation Program,
    Inc.
3300 County Road 10, Suite 212
Brooklyn Center, MN 55429
Phone: (612) 561-0033
Fax: (612) 561-0266
E-mail: nhmp@pclink.com

Houston County Mediation and Victim
    Services
Houston County Courthouse, Room 210
304 South Marshall Street
Caledonia, MN 55921
Phone: (507) 725-5831
Fax: (507) 725-5550
E-mail: hcvicsrv@means.net

Victim Offender Mediation Program
Mediation Services for Anoka County
2520 Coon Rapids Boulevard, Suite 100
Coon Rapids, MN 55433
Phone: (612) 422-8878 or 755-6905
Fax: (612) 422-0808

Victim Offender Dialogue/Family Group
    Conferencing
Peaceful Solutions
4B East Drive
Fergus Falls, MN 56537
Phone: (218) 739-4340
Fax: (218) 736-2772
E-mail:
    peacefulsolutionsltd@netscape.net

Cooperative Solutions, Inc.
Grand Rapids Mediation Center
3 Northwest Fifth Street
P.O. Box 146
Grand Rapids, MN 55744
Phone: (218) 327-4908
Fax: (218) 327-9215
E-mail: coopsolu@uslink.net

West Suburban Mediation Center
1011 First Street South, Suite 200
Hopkins, MN 55343
Phone: (612) 933-0005
Fax: (612) 933-6046
E-mail: wsmc@juno.com

State Probation
Meeker County Courthouse
325 North Sibley Street
Litchfield, MN 55355
Phone: (320) 693-5260

Hennepin County Bureau of Community
    Corrections
Family Conferencing
822 South Third Street, Suite B5
Minneapolis, MN 55415
Phone: (612) 348-3470
Fax: (612) 348-4790
E-mail: jill.stricker@co.hennepin.mn.us

Minneapolis Mediation Program
1300 Nicollet Avenue, Suite 3046
Minneapolis, MN 55403
Phone: (612) 359-9883
Fax: (612) 359-9906
E-mail: mplsmediation@cs.com

Juvenile Victim/Offender Conferencing
Program
Hennepin County Home School
14300 County Highway 62
Minnetonka, MN 55345

Restorative Justice Program
Oakdale Police Department
1584 Hadley Avenue North
Oakdale, MN 55128
Phone: (612) 730-2763
Fax: (612) 730-2828

Victim Offender Interactive
Conferencing
Dodge Fillmore Olmsted County
Community Corrections
Government Center
151 Fourth Street S.E., Fourth Floor
Rochester, MN 55904
Phone: (507) 287-2164
Fax: (507) 287-2673
E-mail: Ryan.Cindy@co.olmsted.mn.us

Project Remand
50 West Kellogg Boulevard, Suite 510A
St. Paul, MN 55102
Phone: (651) 298-4932

Juvenile Diversion Mediation Program
St. Paul Youth Services
1167 Arcade Street
St. Paul, MN 55106
Phone: (651) 771-1301
Fax: (651) 771-2542
E-mail: dsilberstein@spys.org

Victim Offender Conferencing,
Community Justice Project
Washington County Court Services
14900 Sixty-First Street, Fifth Floor
P.O. Box 6
Stillwater, MN 55082
Phone: (612) 430-6948
Fax: (612) 430-6947
E-mail: wacovoc@igc.apc.org

Todd-Wadena Victim/Offender Dialogue
Program
Wadena County Courthouse, Room 115
Wadena, MN 56482
Phone: (218) 631-4773
Fax: (218) 631-2103

Kandiyohi County Community
Corrections
1900 Highway 294 N.E., Suite 2060
Willmar, MN 56201
Phone: (320) 231-7072
Fax: (320) 231-6292
E-mail: katherine_s@co.kandiyohi.mn.us

Restorative Justice Program
Woodbury Police Department
2100 Radio Drive
Woodbury, MN 55125
Phone: (651) 714-3600
Fax: (651) 714-3708
E-mail: dhines@cl.woodbury.mn.us

Missouri

Victim Offender Dialogue
Family Court of St. Louis County
501 South Brentwood Boulevard
Clayton, MO 63105
Phone: (314) 962-6866 ext. 17
Fax: (314) 961-6102

RESPECT Restorative Justice Project
Northland Community Conciliation
Center, Inc.
9 Victory Drive, Suite 202
P.O. Box 67
Liberty, MO 64069
Phone: (816) 415-0005
Fax: (816) 415-8904
E-mail: khlbird@aol.com

Montana

Dispute Resolution Center of Central
Montana
321 East Main Street, Suite 410
Bozeman, MT 59715
Phone: (406) 522-8442
E-mail: drc@montana.com

Montana Conservation Corps/
Corps LINK
1404 Gold Avenue, Suite 3
Bozeman, MT 59715
Phone: (406) 587-4475
Fax: (406) 587-2606

Nebraska

Southeast Nebraska Mediation Center
5109 West Scott Road, Suite 414
Beatrice, NE 68310
Phone: (402) 223-6061
Fax: (402) 223-6043
E-mail: jonkrutz@aol.com

Central Mediation Center
1419 Central Avenue
P.O. Box 838
Kearney, NE 68848
Phone: (800) 203-3452 or
    (308) 237-4692
Fax: (308) 236-7780

Lincoln Lancaster Mediation Center
1033 O Street, Suite 316
Lincoln, NE 68508
Phone: (402) 441-5740
Fax: (402) 441-5749

Center for Conflict Resolution
P.O. Box 427
Scottsbluff, NE 69363
Phone: (308) 635-2002
Fax: (308) 635-2420

Nebraska Justice Center Mediation
    Services
315 Main Street
P.O. Box 475
Walthill, NE 68067
Phone: (402) 846-5576
Fax: (402) 846-5105
E-mail: nejustice@huntel.net

Nevada

ASPEN
P.O. Box 810
Minden, NV 89423
Phone: (775) 588-7171
Fax: (775) 782-1942

New Hampshire

Victim Offender Mediation Program
New Hampshire Mediation Program, Inc.
10 Ferry Street, Suite 425
Concord, NH 03301
Phone: (603) 224-8043
Fax: (603) 224-8388
E-mail: mediate@totalnetnh.net

Carroll County Victim-Offender
    Mediation Services
Carroll County Mediation Services, Inc.
P.O. Box 1997
Conway, NH 03818
Phone: (603) 447-3003
Fax: (603) 447-5719
E-mail: mediate@landmarket.net

Nashua Mediation Program
18 Mulberry Street
Nashua, NH 03060
Phone: (603) 594-3330
Fax: (603) 594-3452

Lake Sunapee Area Mediation Program
87 Sunapee Street
Newport, NH 03773
Phone: (603) 863-1905
Fax: (603) 863-3992

New Jersey

Community Justice Institute
1201 Bacharach Boulevard
Atlantic City, NJ 08401
Phone: (609) 345-7267
Fax: (609) 343-2238

Victim Offender Mediation Program
Bergen County Justice Center
10 Main Street, Room 332D
Hackensack, NJ 07601
Phone: (201) 646-3141
Fax: (201) 646-3490

New Mexico

Victim Offender Mediation Program
New Mexico Center for Dispute
    Resolution
5100 Second Street N.W.
Albuquerque, NM 87107
Phone: (505) 841-7641
Fax: (505) 841-7601

Victim Offender Mediation Program
New Mexico Center for Dispute
    Resolution
811 St. Michaels Drive, Suite 107
Santa Fe, NM 87505

New York

Center for Alternative Dispute
Resolution
30 Watervliet Avenue
Albany, NY 12206
Phone: (518) 463-3686
Fax: (518) 463-3680

Tri-County Mediation Center
1 Kimball Street
Amsterdam, NY 12010
Phone: (518) 842-4202
Fax: (518) 842-4245
E-mail: tricomed@midtel.net

Orange/Putnam Dispute Resolution
Center
180 Main Street
Goshen, NY 10924
Phone: (914) 294-8082 ext. 3
Fax: (914) 294-7428
E-mail: rozm@pioneeris.net

Community Mediation Center
Education and Assistance Corp. (EAC)
P.O. Box 6100
Hauppauge, NY 11788
Phone: (516) 265-0490
Fax: (516) 265-0831
E-mail: epsteineac@aol.com

Mediation Alternative Project
Education and Assistance Corp. (EAC)
50 Clinton Street, Suite 102
Hempstead, NY 11550
Phone: (516) 489-7733
Fax: (516) 489-7532

Ulster-Sullivan Mediation, Inc.
150 Kisor Road
Highland, NY 12528
Phone: (914) 691-6944
Fax: (914) 691-2888
E-mail: clare@ulster.net

Community Dispute Resolution Center
Inc.
120 West State Street
Ithaca, NY 14850
Phone: (607) 273-9347
Fax: (607) 275-9225
E-mail: cdrc@cdrc.org

Community Mediation Services, Inc.
89-64 163rd Street
Jamaica, NY 11432
Phone: (718) 523-6868
Fax: (718) 523-8204

Volunteer Counseling Service of
Rockland County, Inc.
Center for Conflict Resolution
77 South Main Street
New City, NY 10956
Phone: (914) 634-5729
Fax: (914) 634-7839

Institute for Mediation and Conflict
Resolution
505 Eighth Avenue, Second Floor
New York, NY 10018
Phone: (212) 643-0711
Fax: (212) 643-0405

Manhattan Mediation Project—
Victim Services
346 Broadway, Suite 400W
New York, NY 10013
Phone: (212) 577-1742
Fax: (212) 577-1748

Mediation Program
346 Broadway, Fourth Floor
New York, NY 10013
Phone: (212) 577-1743
Fax: (212) 577-1748
E-mail: dshime@victimservices.org

Northern New York Center for Conflict
Resolution
127 Water Street North
Ogdensburg, NY 13669
Phone: (315) 393-7079
Fax: (315) 393-7081

Mediation Services, Inc.
48 Dietz Street, Suite 1
Oneonta, NY 13820
Phone: (607) 433-1672
Fax: (607) 433-0361
E-mail: potterbj@oneonta.edu

Mediation Center of Dutchess County
29 North Hamilton Street
Poughkeepsie, NY 12601
Phone: (914) 471-7213

Center for Dispute Settlement
300 State Street, Suite 301
Rochester, NY 14614
Phone: (716) 546-5110
Fax: (716) 546-4391
E-mail: Carolyn@cdsadr.org
Internet: http://cdsadr.org/

You Participate in Solutions (YPIS) of
Staten Island, Inc.
Staten Island Community Dispute
Resolution Center
42 Richmond Terrace, Fourth Floor
Staten Island, NY 10301
Phone: (718) 720-9410
Fax: (718) 876-6068
E-mail: bornstein@ypis.com

Justice Center of Oneida County, Inc.
250 Genesee Street, Suite 103
Utica, NY 13502
Phone: (315) 797-5335
Fax: (315) 793-0818

Westchester Mediation Center of Cluster
20 South Broadway, Suite 501
P.O. Box 1248
Yonkers, NY 10702
Phone: (914) 963-6500
Fax: (914) 963-4566

North Carolina

Mediation Center
189 College Street
Asheville, NC 28801
Phone: (704) 251-6089
Fax: (704) 232-5140
E-mail: tmc@buncombe.main.nc.us

Blue Ridge Dispute Settlement Center
133 North Water Street, Suite B
Boone, NC 28607
Phone: (704) 264-3040
Fax: (704) 265-3041
E-mail: brdsc@boone.net

Transylvania Dispute Settlement Center
P.O. Box 1205
Brevard, NC 28712
Phone: (828) 877-3815
Fax: (828) 877-5060

Restorative Justice for Youth
Orange County Dispute Settlement
Center
302 Weaver Street
Carrboro, NC 27510
Phone: (919) 929-8800
Fax: (919) 942-6931
E-mail: dscyouth@aol.com
Internet:
http://www.disputesettlement.org/

Charlotte-Mecklenburg Dispute Settle-
ment Program
600 East Trade Street
Charlotte, NC 28202
Phone: (704) 336-3057
Fax: (704) 336-5176
E-mail: sjennings@ci.charlotte.nc.us

Dispute Settlement Center of Durham,
Inc.
P.O. Box 2321
Durham, NC 27702
Phone: (919) 490-6777
Fax: (919) 490-6364

Cumberland County Dispute Resolution
Center
155 Gillespie Street
Fayetteville, NC 28301
Phone: (910) 486-9465
Fax: (910) 486-9465
E-mail: Bpeaceful@aol.com

Mediation Center of the Southern
Piedmont
401 North Highland Street
Gastonia, NC 28052
Phone: (704) 868-9576
Fax: (704) 865-6436
E-mail: med_so_pied@hotmail.com

Victim/Offender Restitution Program
Mediation Services of Guilford County
621 Eugene Court, Suite 101
Greensboro, NC 27401
Phone: (910) 273-5667
Fax: (910) 378-0959
E-mail: mediationservicesofguilford@
yahoo.com

Henderson County Dispute Settlement
Center
101 South Grove Street
Hendersonville, NC 28792
Phone: (828) 697-7055
Fax: (828) 697-8528
E-mail: hcdsc@henderson.lib.nc.us

Piedmont Mediation Center, Inc.
P.O. Box 462
Lexington, NC 27293
Phone: (336) 238-5041
Fax: (336) 871-9794
E-mail: lexdir@piedmediate.org

Chatham County Dispute Settlement
Center
P.O. Box 1151
Pittsboro, NC 27312
Phone: (919) 542-4075
Fax: (919) 542-2360
E-mail: chathamdsc@mindspring.com

Carolina Dispute Settlement Services
P.O. Box 1462
Raleigh, NC 27602
Phone: (919) 508-0700
Fax: (919) 508-0752
E-mail: msw@ipass.net

ReEntry Youth Development
P.O. Box 724
Raleigh, NC 27602
Phone: (919) 664-5507
Fax: (919) 856-5673
E-mail: asummers@co.wake.nc.us

Mountain Dispute Settlement Center
P.O. Box 651
Waynesville, NC 28786
Phone: (828) 452-0240
Fax: (828) 452-0585
E-mail: mtndsc@dnet.net

Mediation Services of Forsyth County
P.O. Box 436
801 Martin Luther King Jr. Drive
Winston-Salem, NC 27102
Phone: (910) 724-2870
Fax: (910) 724-9883

Ohio

Talbert House
Victim Service Center
830 Main Street, Suite 711
Cincinnati, OH 45202

Phone: (513) 241-4484
Fax: (513) 684-7955

Cleveland Mediation Center
3000 Bridge Avenue
Cleveland, OH 44113
Phone: (216) 771-7297
Fax: (216) 771-0620

Community Mediation Services of
Central Ohio
80 Jefferson Avenue
Columbus, OH 43215
Phone: (614) 228-7191
Fax: (614) 228-7213

Office of Victim Services
Ohio Department of Rehabilitation and
Correction
1050 Freeway Drive North
Columbus, OH 43229
Phone: (614) 728-1976
Fax: (614) 728-1980

Juvenile Court Diversion Program
Dayton Mediation Center
330 South Ludlow Street
Dayton, OH 45402
Phone: (937) 333-2345
Fax: (937) 333-2366

Delaware County Juvenile Court
88 North Sandusky Street
Delaware, OH 43015
Phone: (614) 368-1865
Fax: (614) 368-1879

Brown County Juvenile Court Media-
tions
P.O. Box 379
Georgetown, OH 45121
Phone: (513) 378-6726
Fax: (513) 378-4729

Victim Offender Mediation Program
Butler County Juvenile Court
280 North Fair Avenue
Hamilton, OH 45011
Phone: (513) 887-3830
Fax: (513) 887-3698

Crime Victim Services
116 West North Street
Lima, OH 45801
Phone: (419) 222-8666
Fax: (419) 227-7478
E-mail: victim@wcoil.com
Internet: http://crimevictimservices.org

Face 2 Face
Richland County Court of Common
    Pleas
50 Park Avenue East
Mansfield, OH 44902
Phone: (419) 774-5659

Conflict Resolution Associates
P.O. Box 636
Marysville, OH 43040
Phone: (937) 645-3051
Fax: (937) 645-3149
E-mail: cra@midohio.net

Holmes County Victim Offender
    Reconciliation Program (VORP)
United Church of Christ
5395 Township Road, Room 336
Millersburg, OH 44654
Phone: (330) 674-0943
Fax: (330) 674-1112

Erie County Mediation Program, Juvenile
    Division
Erie County Juvenile Court
323 Columbus Avenue
Sandusky, OH 44870
Phone: (419) 627-7782
Fax: (419) 627-6600

Victim Offender Reconciliation Program
    (VORP) of Meduria County
185 Franks Avenue
Wadsworth, OH 44281
Phone: (330) 336-1654
Fax: (330) 336-1654
E-mail: stroudm@akron.infi.net

Fayette County Mediation
110 East Court Street
Washington, OH 43160
Phone: (614) 333-3501
Fax: (614) 333-3530

Conflict Resolution Center of the
    West Shore
24700 Center Ridge Road, Suite 6
Westlake, OH 44145
Phone: (216) 808-1111
Fax: (216) 808-1112

Village Mediation Program
100 Dayton Street
Yellow Springs, OH 45387
Phone: (937) 767-7701
Fax: (937) 767-7701
E-mail: mediation@yso.com

Oklahoma

Center on Alternative Dispute
    Resolution
Early Settlement Mediation Program
Oklahoma City University Law School
2501 North Blackwelder Avenue
Oklahoma City, OK 73106
Phone: (405) 557-1796
Fax: (405) 557-2546

Oklahoma Victim Restitution
Juvenile Offender Responsibility Program
Department of Juvenile Justice
P.O. Box 268812
Oklahoma City, OK 73126
Phone: (405) 530-2800

Post-Conviction Mediation Program
Department of Corrections
3400 Martin Luther King Avenue
Oklahoma City, OK 73136
Phone: (405) 425-2688

Oregon

Victim Offender Reconciliation Program
    (VORP)
Mediation Services of Linn County
330 Southwest Fifth Avenue
P.O. Box 861
Albany, OR 97321
Phone: (541) 928-5323
Fax: (541) 967-1029
E-mail: vorplc@proaxis.com

Community Dispute Resolution Program
City of Beaverton
P.O. Box 4755
Beaverton, OR 97076
Phone: (503) 526-2523
Fax: (503) 526-2572
E-mail: mharrold@ci.beaverton.or.us

Deschutes County Department of
    Community Justice
63333 Highway 20 West
Bend, OR 97701
Phone: (541) 385-1723
Fax: (541) 383-0165
E-mail: debg@deschutes.com

Mediation Services
Community Outreach, Inc.
128 Southwest Ninth Street
Corvallis, OR 97333
Phone: (541) 758-3000
Fax: (541) 758-3481
E-mail: cmdrs@igc.apc.org

Victim Offender Reconciliation Program
(VORP)
Community Mediation Services of Polk
County
976 Southwest Hayter Street
Dallas, OR 97338
Phone: (503) 623-3111
Fax: (503) 623-7772
E-mail: vorp@open.org

Restorative Justice Program
Lane County Community Mediation
Services
44 West Broadway, Suite 202
Eugene, OR 97401
Phone: (541) 344-5366
Fax: (541) 687-8392
E-mail: mediate@efn.org

Yamhill County Mediators
P.O. Box 444
McMinnville, OR 97128
Phone: (503) 435-2835
Voice mail: (503) 550-2343

Victim Offender Program
Mediation Works
33 North Central Avenue, Suite 306
Medford, OR 97501
Phone: (541) 770-2468
Fax: (541) 770-6022

Community Dispute Resolution Services,
Inc.
c/o Juvenile Court Services
Juvenile Justice Department
P.O. Box 610
Ontario, OR 97914
Phone: (541) 889-8802
Fax: (541) 889-6212

Victim Offender Mediation Program,
Clackamas County Juvenile
Department
2121 Kaen Road
Oregon City, OR 97045
Phone: (503) 655-8342
Fax: (503) 655-8448
E-mail: warrenos@co.clackamas.or.us

Resolutions Northwest
1401 Northeast Sixty-Eighth Avenue
Portland, OR 97213
Phone: (503) 306-5609
Fax: (503) 736-6050

Douglas County Neighbor-to-Neighbor
P.O. Box 2328
Roseburg, OR 97470
Phone: (888) 890-8282 or
(541) 957-8282
Fax: (541) 957-9042

Neighbor-to-Neighbor, Inc.
P.O. Box 2362
Salem, OR 97308
Phone: (503) 585-0651

Pennsylvania

Neighborhood Dispute Settlement
315 Peffer Street
Harrisburg, PA 17102
Phone: (717) 233-8255
Fax: (717) 233-3261
E-mail: mediator@ezonline.com
Internet:
http://www.geocities.com/Eureka/
Plaza/6502/

Lancaster Area Victim Offender
Reconciliation Program (LAVORP)
44 East Orange Street
Lancaster, PA 17602
Phone: (717) 397-2404
Fax: (717) 397-5140

Lancaster Mediation Center
225 West King Street
Lancaster, PA 17603
Phone: (717) 293-7231
Fax: (717) 390-7783
E-mail: info@lancmed.org
Internet: http://www.lancmed.org

Victim Services, Inc.
211 North Edgewood Avenue
Somerset, PA 15501
Phone: (814) 443-1555
Fax: (814) 443-6807
E-mail: kwalters_barj@yahoo.com

Victim Offender Mediation Program
Mediation Services for Conflict
Resolution, Inc.
P.O. Box 2912
York, PA 17405
Phone: (717) 854-6727
Fax: (717) 854-6585
E-mail: janeriese@juno.com

South Carolina

Juvenile Arbitration Program
Eleventh Judicial Circuit
139 East Main Street, Suite 6
Lexington, SC 29072
Phone: (803) 359-8355
Fax: (803) 359-8229

South Dakota

Western South Dakota Center for
Community Justice
2323 Lance Street
Rapid City, SD 57702

Victim Offender Reconciliation Program
(VORP) of Southeastern South Dakota
119 South Van Eps Avenue
Sioux Falls, SD 57103
Phone: (605) 338-6020
Fax: (605) 338-6020
E-mail: loisjp@qwtc.net

Tennessee

Mediation Center
104 West Seventh Street, Suite B
Columbia, TN 38401
Phone: (615) 840-5583
Fax: (615) 840-0269

Victim Offender Reconciliation Program
(VORP)
Community Mediation Center (CMC)
15 Division Drive
Crossville, TN 38555
Phone: (615) 484-0972
Fax: (615) 484-0972
E-mail: cmcvorpxville@multipor.com

Community Mediation Center (CMC)
Andrew Johnson Building
912 South Gay Street, Suite L300
Knoxville, TN 37902
Phone: (423) 594-1879
Fax: (423) 594-1890
E-mail: mediate@korrnet.org
Internet: http://www.korrnet.org/mediate

Mediation and Restitution/
Reconciliation Services (MARRS)
4488 Poplar Avenue
Memphis, TN 38117
Phone: (901) 761-7028
Fax: (901) 261-4393
Internet:
http://cumcmemphis.org/marrs.htm

Neighborhood Justice Center
1310 Jefferson Street, Suite 200
Nashville, TN 37208
Phone: (615) 321-4114
Fax: (615) 321-0313

Victim Offender Reconciliation Program
(VORP) of Nashville
522 Russell Street
Nashville, TN 37206
Phone: (615) 256-2206
Fax: (615) 256-2962

Victim Offender Reconciliation Program
(VORP) of Anderson County
Community Mediation Services
P.O. Box 4081
Oak Ridge, TN 37831
Phone: (423) 457-5400 ext. 888
Fax: (423) 457-7208
E-mail: cms@korrnet.org
Internet: http://www.korrnet.org/cms/

Texas

Dispute Resolution Center
415 West Eighth Street
Amarillo, TX 79101
Phone: (806) 372-3381
Fax: (806) 373-3268

Dispute Resolution Center
5407 North Interstate Highway 35,
Suite 410
Austin, TX 78723
Phone: (512) 371-0033
Fax: (512) 371-7411
E-mail: drc@realtime.net
Internet: http://www.realtime.net/drc

Travis County Juvenile Court
2515 South Congress Street
Austin, TX 78704
Phone: (512) 448-7000
Fax: (512) 448-7097

Dispute Resolution Center—Jefferson
County
1149 Pearl Street, Third Floor
Beaumont, TX 77701
Phone: (409) 835-8747
Fax: (409) 835-8718

Dispute Resolution Center of
Montgomery County, Inc.
P.O. Box 3609
Conroe, TX 77305
Phone: (409) 760-6914
Fax: (409) 788-8364

Dispute Resolution Services
901 Leopard Street, Suite 401.2
Corpus Christi, TX 78401
Phone: (361) 888-0650
Fax: (361) 888-0754
E-mail: drscctex@igc.org

Dallas County Mediation Department
2600 Lone Star Drive, Box 5
Dallas, TX 75212
Phone: (214) 698-4223
Fax: (214) 698-5563

Dispute Mediation Services, Inc.
3400 Carlisle Avenue, Suite 240, LB9
Dallas, TX 75204
Phone: (214) 754-0022
Fax: (214) 754-0378

Dispute Resolution Services
1 Summit Avenue, Suite 210
Fort Worth, TX 76102
Phone: (817) 877-4554
Fax: (817) 877-4557
E-mail: mediate@startext.net
Internet: http://startext.net/homes/
    mediate

Dispute Resolution Center
49 San Jacinto Street, Suite 220
Houston, TX 77002
Phone: (713) 755-8274
Fax: (713) 755-8885

Victim Offender Restitution Program
Harris County Community Supervision
    and Correction Department
49 San Jacinto Street, Suite 516
Houston TX 77002
Phone: (713) 755-2126
Fax: (713) 755-2776
E-mail:
    Stephanie_Pecora@csc.co.harris.tx.us

Victim Offender Restitution Program
Innovative Alternatives, Inc.
1300A Bay Area Boulevard, Suite 218
Houston, TX 77058
Phone: (713) 222-2525
Fax: (281) 282-6002

Victim Services
Llano County Courthouse, Room 108
Llano, TX 78643
Phone: (915) 247-5640
Fax: (915) 247-3455

Victim Offender Mediation Program
Bexar County Dispute Resolution Center
300 Dolorosa Street, Suite 1102
San Antonio, TX 78205
Phone: (210) 335-2128
Fax: (210) 335-2941

Utah

Victim Offender Mediation
Administrative Office of the Court
P.O. Box 140241
Salt Lake City, UT 84114
Phone: (801) 578-3800
Fax: (801) 578-3843
E-mail: kathye@e-mail.utcourts.gov
Internet: http://courtlink.utcourts.gov/

Vermont

Vermont Reparative Probation Program
Court and Reparative Services
32 Cherry Street, Suite 315
South Burlington, VT 05401
Phone: (802) 651-1793
Fax: (802) 651-1798

Virginia

Key Bridge Therapy and Mediation
    Center
1925 North Lynn Street, Suite 700
Arlington, VA 22209
Phone: (703) 528-3900
Fax: (703) 524-5666
E-mail: key-bridge-center@erols.com

Mediation Center at Focus
1508 Grady Avenue
Charlottesville, VA 22903
Phone: (804) 977-2926
Fax: (804) 984-0249

Northern Virginia Mediation Service
Institute for Conflict Analysis and
    Resolution
George Mason University, MS 4D3
4260 Chain Bridge Road, Suite A2
Fairfax, VA 22030
Phone: (703) 993-3656
Fax: (703) 993-3070

Dispute Settlement Center
586 Virginian Drive
Norfolk, VA 23505
Phone: (757) 480-2777

Washington

Victims and Offenders in Creating
  Effective Solutions (VOICES)
Dispute Resolution Center of Kitsap
  County
P.O. Box 555
Bremerton, WA 98337
Phone: (360) 377-8179
Fax: (360) 377-7305
E-mail: mediator@tscnet.com

Dispute Resolution Center of Lewis
  County
P.O. Box 117
462 Northwest Park Street
Chehalis, WA 98532
Phone: (360) 748-0492
Fax: (360) 748-9884

Victim Offender Mediation Project for
  Kittitas County
507 North Nanum Street, Room 16
Ellensburg, WA 98926
Phone: (509) 933-2150
Fax: (509) 963-3941
E-mail: mediation@ellensburg.com

Dispute Resolution Center, Snohomish
  and Island Counties
Volunteers of America
P.O. Box 839
Everett, WA 98206
Phone: (800) 280-4770 or
  (206) 339-1335
Fax: (425) 259-2110

Common Ground Dispute Resolution
  Center of Skagit County
811 Cleveland Street
Mount Vernon, WA 98273
Phone: (360) 336-9494
Fax: (360) 336-9323
E-mail: cground@cnw.com
Internet: http://www.cnw.com/~cground

Mediation Services for Victims and
  Offenders
Northwest Institute for Restorative
  Justice
1305 Fourth Avenue, Suite 606
Seattle, WA 98101
Phone: (206) 621-8874
Fax: (206) 621-7192
E-mail: ronein@restorejustice.org
Internet: http://restorejustice.org

Inland Mediation Center
Volunteers of America Building, Lower
  Level
525 West Second Avenue
Spokane, WA 99201
Phone: (509) 456-0103
Fax: (509) 624-2275
E-mail: inmedctr@aol.com

Pierce County Center for Dispute
  Resolution
705 South Ninth Street, Suite 207
Tacoma, WA 98405
Phone: (206) 572-3657
Fax: (206) 572-3579

Victim Offender Mediation Program
City of Vancouver
P.O. Box 1995
Vancouver, WA 98668
Phone: (360) 735-8873 ext. 8304
Fax: (360) 696-8073

Dispute Resolution Center of Yakima and
  Kittitas Counties
1106B West Lincoln Avenue
Yakima, WA 98902
Phone: (509) 453-8949
Fax: (509) 453-0910

Wisconsin

Fond du Lac County Victim Offender
  Services
Juvenile Resource Unit
160 South Mary Street
Fond du Lac, WI 54935
Phone: (920) 929-3303
Fax: (920) 929-6826

Coulee Region Mediation and
  Restorative Justice Services
400 North Fourth Street, Room B01
La Crosse, WI 54601
Phone: (608) 784-7322
Fax: (608) 784-5910

Restorative Justice Project
Frank J. Remington Center
University of Wisconsin Law School
975 Bascom Mall, Room 4318
Madison, WI 53706
Phone: (608) 262-1002
Fax: (608) 263-3380

Victim Offender Mediation Program
Lakeshore Community Action
540 North Eighth Street
Manitowoc, WI 54220
Phone: (920) 686-8708

Juvenile Victim Offender Mediation
P.O. Box 67
Whitehall, WI 54773
Phone: (715) 538-2311 ext. 322
Fax: (715) 538-4123

Winnebago Conflict Resolution Center,
   Inc.
Winnebago County Courthouse,
   Room 412
415 Jackson Street
Oshkosh, WI 54901
Phone: (920) 236-4711
Fax: (920) 236-4799
E-mail: KBradish@co.winnebago.wi.us

Youth and Family Project, Inc.
314 North Franklin Street, Suite A
Port Washington, WI 53074
Phone: (414) 284-7188
Fax: (414) 338-7761

Mediation Center of Waukesha County
Wisconsin Correctional Service
414 West Moreland Boulevard,
   Room 200
Waukesha, WI 53188
Phone: (414) 544-5431
Fax: (414) 544-9456
E-mail: mcwc@wiscs.org

Project Payback Program
NOVA
702 Elm Street
West Bend, WI 53095
Phone: (414) 338-8842
Fax: (414) 338-3724
E-mail: payback@novaservices.org

Appendix C

Program Profiles

Seven programs were selected as representative of established programs, large and small, operating in a variety of settings. Highlighted in addition to basic program information are special features and initial ideas about victim sensitivity ascertained in response to two telephone interview questions: "In what ways do you feel your program is currently sensitive to the needs of victims?" and "Do you have other ideas of things that could be done to make your program more sensitive to the needs of victims?"

Victim Offender Reconciliation Program of the Central Valley, Inc. (Fresno County, California)

The Fresno County program conducted its first victim offender meeting in 1983. Mediations are conducted at several points in the justice process: at diversion, after adjudication but before disposition, and after disposition. Of cases referred in a recent year, 55 percent were mediated, and agreements were written in 60 percent of those cases.

Type of agency: Church-based

Primary sources of funding: Local government and individual contributions

Staff: 6

Volunteers: 250

Current annual budget: $110,000

Juvenile cases referred in 1996: 598

Adult cases referred in 1996: 2

Felony referrals: 1 percent

Misdemeanor referrals: 99 percent

Primary source of referrals: Probation officers

Most common offenses referred: Vandalism, theft, battery

Serious offenses mediated: Assault with a deadly weapon, assault with bodily injury, involuntary manslaughter

Special Features

- Training of mediators includes a guest speaker from Victim Services and crime victims who have been through mediation describing their experiences.

- Outdated videos are used in training to illustrate ineffective practices in mediation.

- Experienced volunteer mediators are used in training to coach role-playing groups, assisting them to debrief the process.

- Mediators work with juvenile offenders to help them understand the experience of mediation, providing support for them through a process that they typically find much harder than treatment or incarceration. Offenders comment, "I get it now—it made me think about the victim. I didn't think about the victim's wants—I just thought about me."

- When possible, the program helps offenders find jobs to earn money to pay restitution.

- During the mediation session, victims and offenders are invited to restate or summarize what the other party has said.

- Additional participants may be present during the mediation session. These may include representatives of the school system, the community, or the faith community.

Victim Sensitivity Principles

- Devote an hour to active listening with the victim.
- On the first visit with victims, help them feel heard and understood; validate their experience.
- Ensure that the entire mediation process allows the victim to feel heard and validated.
- Consult first with the victim regarding the site for mediation.
- Conduct a follow-up meeting after three months.

Victim Offender Reconciliation Program, Institute for Conflict Management (Orange County, California)

The Orange County VORP began in 1989. Mediations are conducted at several points in the judicial process: before filing from local law enforcement, at diversion, and after adjudication but before disposition. Approximately 50 percent of the referred cases are mediated. Of the cases mediated in a recent year, 60 percent resulted in written agreements, 95 percent of which were successfully completed.

Type of agency: Private community-based

Primary source of funding: Local government

Staff: 9

Volunteers: 150

Current annual budget: $265,000

Juvenile cases referred in 1996: 900

Adult cases referred in 1996: 100

Felony referrals: 0 percent

Misdemeanor referrals: 100 percent

Primary sources of referrals: Probation officers, police officers, prosecutors, defense attorneys, victim advocates, community members

Most common offenses referred: assault and battery, vandalism, petty theft

Special Features

- Mediators initially receive twenty-five hours of classroom training, after which they observe two cases facilitated by an experienced mediator. Then they are observed while co-mediating cases.
- Actual case experiences are presented during the training of mediators.
- Occasionally, volunteer mediators will use their own professional offices as the site for the mediation session.
- Intake staff contact the victim first to confirm basic data before the mediator calls.
- Plans are made for volunteers to do face-to-face interviews with participants four to six weeks following the mediation.
- Staff members work closely with a lobbyist to procure legislation supportive of victim offender mediation.

Victim Sensitivity Guidelines

- Meet the offender first, even before contacting the victim.
- Provide victims with some degree of control over the process.
- Offer the victim the opportunity to talk first in the mediation session and to have questions answered.
- Make sure the process addresses the victims' needs.

Victim Offender Reconciliation Program, Center for Community Justice (Elkhart, Indiana)

The Elkhart VORP was established in 1978 as the first replication in the United States of a model developed in Kitchener, Ontario, in 1974. Mediations are presently conducted at the following stages in the justice process: diversion, after adjudication but before disposition, and after disposition. Of the cases referred in a recent year, 26 percent were mediated. Written agreements were reached in 100 percent of those cases, and 95 percent of the agreements were successfully completed.

Type of agency: Private community-based

Primary sources of funding: Local government, foundations

Staff: 2

Volunteers: 15

Current annual budget: $110,000

Juvenile cases referred in 1996: 330

Adult cases referred in 1996: 50

Felony referrals: 70 percent

Misdemeanor referrals: 30 percent

Primary sources of referrals: Probation officers, judges, prosecutors

Most common offenses referred: Theft, burglary, auto theft

Serious offenses mediated: Assault with deadly weapon, assault with bodily injury

Special Features

- The victim assistance program makes the first contact with the victim, before mediation is explored.
- Guest speakers for training sessions include judges, probation officers, and representatives of the victim assistance program.
- Assumptions about victims are discussed during training; stereotypes of vindictiveness are challenged by sharing actual victim stories.
- In the training of mediators, emphasis is placed on the ways in which victim offender mediation differs from classical forms of mediation.

- Mediations are typically held in the program office to ensure safety, privacy, and confidentiality.

Victim Sensitivity Guidelines

- Take time with each victim.
- Discuss various options with the victim.
- Inform victims of their rights.
- Assist victims in getting their questions answered.
- Coach offenders to consider what they might say to the victim—if they were the victim, what might they want to hear?

Victim Offender Reconciliation Program, Polk County Attorney's Office (Des Moines, Iowa)

The Polk County VORP has been in operation since 1971. Mediations are conducted at diversion, postadjudication but predisposition, and postdisposition stages in the justice process.

Type of agency: Prosecuting attorney

Primary sources of funding: Local and federal government

Staff: 2

Volunteers: 9

Current annual budget: $356,649 (including community mediation program)

Juvenile cases referred in 1996: 20

Adult cases referred in 1996: 1,300

Felony referrals: 90 percent

Misdemeanor referrals: 10 percent

Primary sources of referrals: Judges, prosecutors, defense attorneys

Most common offenses referred: Theft, assault, drunk driving, criminal mischief

Serious offenses mediated: Assault with deadly weapon, assault with bodily injury, negligent homicide

Special Features

- Mediators, known as "facilitators," are trained in victim sensitivity by Polk County Victim Services personnel and by crime victims themselves who present a victim impact panel. Trainees also visit a local prison.

- Training consists of thirty hours of basic mediation training, followed by ten hours specific to victim offender mediation. Mediators then observe cases for two to three months before they are prepared to conduct sessions themselves.

- Before mediators are considered for victim offender mediation training, they must have six months to one year of intensive experience conducting community mediations.

- All mediators are paid a modest standard sum per case.

- If intake staff become aware that there are additional issues, they may offer to contact victim services, probation, or a therapist to offer immediate assistance to the parties.

- Probation officers, conducting final evaluations with offenders, ask them what they believe will most help them avoid reoffending. Offenders who have experienced mediation often respond, "The one thing that helped me see what crime really does was meeting the victim; I had no idea it hurt an individual."

Victim Sensitivity Guidelines

- Provide victims of all crimes with an advocate who offers support through the victim offender mediation process and is present at the mediation session.

- Prepare victims well for the victim offender process.

- Work closely with Victim Services.

- Provide the safest place possible for the mediation, making sure there is security.

- To enhance victim sensitivity, spend more time with victims before the mediation, develop educational videos to describe the program, provide community education using victim impact panels, spend more time with judges and county attorneys, and have them experience a mediation.

Houston County Mediation and Victim Services (Caledonia, Minnesota)

In the Houston County VOM program, mediations are done as diversions and after disposition. Approximately 45 percent of the cases referred are mediated. In a recent year, 95 percent of those resulted in a written agreement, and 100 percent of those agreements were successfully completed.

Type of agency: Victim services

Primary source of funding: State government

Staff: 3

Volunteers: 10

Current annual budget: $30,000

Juvenile and adult cases referred in 1996: 122

Felony referrals: 1 percent

Misdemeanor referrals: 99 percent

Primary source of referrals: Prosecutors

Most common offenses referred: Criminal damage to property, theft, tampering with a motor vehicle

Special Features

- Mediators receive forty hours of classroom training, followed by observation and then co-mediation of at least five sessions.

- Victims' advocates, as well as crime victims themselves, are invited to speak during the training sessions for mediators.

- Because the program is part of the county court system, parties are occasionally sent directly over from the courthouse, and mediation is done at that time.

- The program has also added a family group conferencing component, which is used when a case has a significant impact on a neighborhood.

Victim Sensitivity Guidelines

- Explore victims' questions.

- Never try to talk a victim into participating in mediation.

- When it is helpful, reframe what the victim is saying.

- Learn by listening.

- Encourage victims to be empowered. "As victim advocates, we have learned through this process that having someone in your corner is not always the best for the victim. How do victims heal? By taking their power back, by claiming some control. Victims face their fear and tremendous sense of loss. If you can put a face to it and a process, it helps victims come to terms with the fear, so that it doesn't own them."

Victim Offender Conferencing, Community Justice Project, Washington County Court Services (Stillwater, Minnesota)

The Washington County Community Justice Project is a relatively new program, begun in 1995. The Victim Offender Conferencing program conducts conferences at both diversion and postdisposition stages in the justice process. Approximately 70 percent of the cases referred are mediated. Of those mediated in a recent year, 99 percent resulted in written agreements, and 99 percent of the agreements were successfully completed.

Type of agency: Probation

Primary source of funding: Local government

Staff: 1

Volunteers: 37

Current annual budget: $61,000

Juvenile cases referred in 1996: 175

Adult cases referred in 1996: 25

Felony referrals: 40 percent

Misdemeanor referrals: 60 percent

Primary sources of referrals: Probation officers, judges, prosecutors, victim advocates

Most common offenses referred: Burglary, theft, assault, harassment

Serious offenses mediated: Assault with bodily injury, negligent homicide

Special Features

- Mediators are given twenty-four to thirty hours of classroom training, followed by apprenticeship on up to three cases. During training, participants are given a folder with a mock case, which they use in role playing.

- Training of mediators includes guest speakers from the Victim Witness Advocate Program, the Probation Department, and the Youth Services Bureau, working with juvenile offenders. In addition, probation officers, judges, and the sheriff participate in a skit illustrating law enforcement and court procedures.

- Additional ongoing training is provided for mediators on communication skills, community resources, diversity training, and victim sensitivity.

- Probation officers team with community volunteers to co-mediate cases beyond their caseload. Juvenile probation officers mediate adult cases, and officers working with adult probation mediate in juvenile cases. Probation officers do not mediate cases in their own immediate communities.

- In addition to victim offender conferencing done between individual parties, large and small group conferences are also conducted. These conferences may include siblings, interested parties, or primary and secondary victims, who may participate in a small group conference or may be invited to attend but not necessarily participate in a large group conference.

- The Community Justice Project also sponsors community forums on restorative justice and issues of concern to specific neighborhoods and facilitates dialogue in schools experiencing tensions around issues such as race or ethnicity.

Victim Sensitivity Guidelines

- Meet with victims at their request and convenience.
- Listen.
- Provide structure and a safe environment.
- Assist where indicated with referrals for other kinds of help victims may want.
- Follow up on contracts, and notify the victim upon completion.
- Provide training and ongoing education on victim sensitivity.
- To enhance victim sensitivity, make follow-up phone contact with victims one week and two months after mediation.

Restorative Justice Program, Lane County Community Mediation Services (Eugene, Oregon)

The Restorative Justice Program has been in operation since 1981. Victim offender mediations are done as a diversion from the justice process. Of the cases referred to the program in a recent year, 74 percent were actually mediated. Of those, 100 percent resulted in written agreements, which were successfully completed in 80 percent of the cases.

Type of agency: Nonprofit community

Primary source of funding: County government

Staff: 1

Volunteers: 15

Current annual budget: $26,000

Juvenile cases referred in 1996: 146

Adult cases referred in 1996: 0

Felony referrals: 25–40 percent

Misdemeanor referrals: 60–75 percent

Primary source of referrals: Juvenile intake counselors

Most common offenses referred: burglary, assault, criminal mischief

Special Features

- Training of mediators involves thirty hours of basic mediation training and six hours on the Restorative Justice Program. Following classroom work, trainees complete two observations with a supervisor-mediator, after which they co-mediate sessions.
- Guest speakers during training include juvenile counselors

from the Department of Youth Services and representatives from the Victim Advocacy Office.

- Classroom training of mediators includes a component on communicating with victims—what to say and what not to say.

- The program is exploring the possibility that if the victim does not wish to mediate, the offender could meet with a victim panel instead. In addition, mediators might work with the offender to construct a plan (an "offender-only restitution agreement") or conduct shuttle negotiations between the parties.

- Evaluations are conducted by volunteers from the Department of Youth Services.

Victim Sensitivity Guidelines

- Listen to the victim.
- Provide input into the criminal justice process.
- Encourage victims in mediation to begin telling their story first.
- Offer the opportunity to process their experiences with staff, to normalize what has happened.

Appendix D

Promising Practices and Innovations

As the field of victim offender mediation continues to develop in numerous communities, local programs are increasingly engaging in new and creative innovations. This appendix highlights a number of promising practices and innovations.

Program Innovations

- The goals of mediation are included in the agreement: recognition of injustice, some kind of restitution, plans for the future—for example, how the parties will treat each other. (Placer Dispute Resolution Service, Lincoln, California)
- As part of the sentence, the offender pays $40 for mediation. (Placer Dispute Resolution Service, Lincoln, California)
- If the initial introductory letter does not reach the parties, intake staff seek to locate the parties by phoning or driving to see them. (Community Violence Prevention Program, Oakland, California)
- Approximately twenty-five to forty hours of volunteer time are devoted to each case, with mediators spending two to three hours with each party separately and also meeting with the co-mediator for an hour before and after the mediation

---

Note: This list of promising practices was originally drafted by Jean Greenwood (Umbreit & Greenwood, 1997). Adapted with permission.

session. In tough cases, mediators meet with staff to brainstorm ideas and then debrief also with staff following the mediation. (Community Violence Prevention Program, Oakland, California)

- A thirty-six-hour course has been developed for offenders and their parents, covering the conflict management, empathy, communication, esteem building, and developing skills for peer support. (Victim Offender Reconciliation Program, San Luis Obispo, California)

- In addition to mediation, a broad spectrum of programs is provided for offenders, including jail screening, host homes, electronic home monitoring, public works programs, training in conflict resolution skills, and recreation, which serves as the last eight hours of community service. (Larimer County Youth Service Bureau, Fort Collins, Colorado)

- Offenders are given the victim's questions in advance to assist in preparing for the mediation. (Victim Offender Reconciliation Program of McLean County, Bloomington, Illinois)

- Conflict resolution training is conducted in a local detention center using a juvenile ex-offender as co-trainer. (Victim Offender Reconciliation Program of McLean County, Bloomington, Illinois)

- Mediations are occasionally held near the site where the crime was committed to enhance realism and impact. (Woodford County Victim Offender Reconciliation Program, Eureka, Illinois)

- Mediators are trained to avoid using *don'ts* as ground rules, which may feel demeaning to the parties, and to model respect and frame the goals carefully, affirming the parties' choice to speak honestly and work together to see what can be done about the situation. If the conversation becomes disrespectful, the mediator is to stop the process, nonjudgmentally, ask the parties how it feels ("Did it help you feel open to talking and listening?"), and offer feedback if relevant to what is happening (for example, "It would make it hard for me to listen."). (Victim Offender Reconciliation Program, Lafayette, Indiana)

- If the victim chooses not to participate, the offender sends a letter of apology. (Center for Creative Justice, Ames, Iowa)

- The offender pays a fee to participate in mediation. (Center for Creative Justice, Ames, Iowa)

- Important qualifications for mediators include attitude and perspective. (Victim Offender Mediation, Davenport, Iowa)

- Victims are notified by phone as soon as restitution is completed. (Victim Offender Reconciliation Program of Reno County, Hutchinson, Kansas)

- Teenage offenders are provided with information about drugs, mental health issues, and other relevant matters. (Victim Offender Reconciliation Program, Offender/Victim Ministries, Newton, Kansas)

- "Mini-VORP" to be used with shoplifters involves a relationship with a mentor and a letter of apology written and delivered by the juvenile offender. (Victim Offender Reconciliation Program, Offender/Victim Ministries, Newton, Kansas)

- When offenders are young and somewhat inarticulate, probation officers work with them before mediation to develop a tentative script of what they might choose to express. (Mid-Michigan Dispute Resolution Center, Saginaw, Michigan)

- The program uses the term *meeting* instead of *mediation* to avoid the possible impression that the parties are involved in a mutual dispute rather than a crime. (Dakota County Community Corrections, Apple Valley, Minnesota)

- Mediators offer to role-play the mediation session with offenders, to help them prepare for the kinds of questions victims often ask. (MOVR Program, Rochester, Minnesota)

- The goals of mediation are framed as "gaining understanding" and "being able to move on," which are considered more realistic than "making things right." (Restorative Justice for Youth, Orange County Dispute Settlement Center, Carrboro, North Carolina)

- An advisory council, consisting of victims, offenders, and youth workers, assists the board in its work. (Restorative Justice for Youth, Orange County Dispute Settlement Center, Carrboro, North Carolina)

- Offenders are given job training and attend a life skills class. A work-study program is offered following the mediation process. (One Step Further, Greensboro, North Carolina)

- Mediations are conducted at the program office, where a typist is available to draft an agreement on the spot and to provide copies of the completed agreement (Monroe County Community Mediation Program, Rochester, New York)

- Mediations are held at the site of the crime whenever possible to make it more real to the parties and "help victims take their power back." (Crime Victim Services, Lima, Ohio)

- A program on victimization is provided for juvenile offenders and their parents. Victim impact panels are used in cases where victims choose not to mediate. Offenders also attend assault class, which teaches them other ways to deal with anger. (Victim Offender Reconciliation Program/Mediation Services of Linn County, Albany, Oregon)

- A desired outcome of mediation is that the parties achieve a "sense of understanding." (Lancaster Area Victim Offender Reconciliation Program, Lancaster, Pennsylvania)

- One of the goals of mediation, as it is framed in this program, is to assist the victim in finding "some measure of peace." (Victim Offender Reconciliation Program of Southeastern South Dakota, Sioux Falls, South Dakota)

- Mediation is part of a three-phase program that consists of recreational activities for offenders, relationship building with adults through program-supervised community service, and ultimately housing facilities for youthful offenders. (Mediation and Restitution/Reconciliation Services, Memphis; Tennessee)

- Victims are added to the program's mailing list. Some victims have sent in contributions to support the operating expenses of the program. (Victim Offender Reconciliation Program of Anderson County, Oak Ridge, Tennessee)

- Juvenile offenders, averaging fifteen years of age, are trained as mediators and currently co-facilitate cases. (Travis County Juvenile Court, Austin, Texas)

- Volunteers are used to promote the program by speaking to juvenile court personnel about their experiences in mediation. (Dispute Mediation Service, Dallas, Texas)

- Mediation programs are funded through a $10 surcharge on civil court filing fees. (Dispute Resolution Services, Fort Worth, Texas)

- Victims and offenders are given self-guided workbooks that assist them in preparing for the mediation session. The workbook invites participants to reflect on their experiences and the impact and to consider thoughts they would like to share and questions they would like to ask. (Dispute Resolution Center, Fort Worth, Texas)

- Victims and offenders determine the goals of the mediation session. (Mediation Services for Victims and Offenders, Seattle, Washington)

- Mediations are being done in schools in cases where it is uncertain whether the parties are identifiably victims or offenders. The cases are initiated prior to any charges being filed or an admission of guilt being recorded, and the labels "victim" and "offender" are dropped in order to acknowledge the nature of the case and to assist with the peacemaking effort. (Mediation Services for Victims and Offenders, Seattle, Washington)

- An advisory board for the mediation program consists of representatives from the court administration, health care, media, victim witness, probation and parole, diversion, and police fields. The program itself was developed by this advisory board. (Victim Offender Reconciliation Program, La Crosse, Wisconsin)

- Volunteer mediators keep office hours at the program office. (Victim Offender Reconciliation Program, La Crosse, Wisconsin)

- The program has found that by reducing the number of volunteers and providing them with more cases, the level of commitment on the part of volunteer mediators has increased and cases are completed more promptly. (Victim Offender Reconciliation Program, La Crosse, Wisconsin)

- Long-term services are provided for victims even when they choose not to participate in mediation. (Victim Offender Mediation Program, Manitowoc, Wisconsin)

- Mediators follow up with juvenile offenders, monitoring the restitution, taking them on job search excursions, encouraging and reminding them, and meeting them when they bring restitution payment into the office. (Victim Offender Mediation Program, Manitowoc, Wisconsin)

- Forums are conducted with victims in order to get their input about the process and their experiences. (Youth and Family Project, Port Washington, Wisconsin)

- In the mediation session, parents of the offender are seated by the mediator, to avoid having "too many eyes staring at the victim." (Mediation Center of Waukesha County, Waukesha, Wisconsin)

- In discussing possible outcomes of mediation with the parties, mediators are careful not to "oversell" the process—for instance, by making it clear that closure is not guaranteed. (Mediation Center of Waukesha County, Waukesha, Wisconsin)

Training Ideas

- Mediators are trained to know the community's resources and structure and to understand how the program and the use of volunteers relates to community building. (Victim Offender Mediation Program, Anchorage, Alaska)

- Training is designed as a short lecture on a small segment of the process, followed by group practice and then role-play. (Conflict Resolution Section, Arizona Attorney General's Office, Phoenix, Arizona)

- Local high school freshmen who are committed to helping their peers find a better way are trained as mediators who then serve on a panel of three, facilitating mediations. (Placer Dispute Resolution Service, Lincoln, California)

- Systemic and societal inequities that underlie anger are explored in training. (Victim Offender Reconciliation Program, San Luis Obispo, California)

- An actual offender helps with role-plays, playing the part of the offender. (San Luis Valley Victim Offender Reconciliation Program, Alamosa, Colorado)

- To assist mediators in understanding their own responses to conflict, the training explores with trainees how conflict was handled when they were growing up. (Victim Offender Reconciliation Program of Boulder County, Boulder, Colorado)

- One component of mediator training seeks to sensitize mediators to their own needs and their own style of communication. (Victim Offender Reconciliation Program of McLean County, Bloomington, Illinois)

- Training is organized with worksheets, verbal practice, interaction with trainer, and role-plays for each skill being taught. (Victim Offender Mediation, Davenport, Iowa)

- Trainees are invited to reflect on their own experiences of victimization and on what others said that was helpful or not helpful. They also reflect on their experiences of offending. (Offender/Victim Ministries, Newton, Kansas)

- During mediation training, a probation officer and a judge participate in a skit illustrating the offender's movement through the system. (Dakota County Community Corrections, Apple Valley, Minnesota)

- Efforts have been made over a period of years to cultivate a healthy working relationship with the county's victim services program, including suggestions that joint training be conducted and that portions of the mediation training be held in the offices of the victim services unit. (Victim Offender Mediation Program, Coon Rapids, Minnesota)

- Training of mediators includes a segment on juvenile culture. (Victim Offender Mediation Services, Coon Rapids, Minnesota)

- To enhance the effectiveness of role playing, participants are educated to be realistic in their portrayal of victim and offender behavior. (Restorative Justice Program, Woodbury, Minnesota)

- Experienced mediators visit training sessions to discuss mediation experiences with trainees. (Restorative Justice for Youth, Orange County Dispute Settlement Center, Carrboro, North Carolina)

- A panel of young people is presented during mediation training to educate mediators about adolescence. (Community Dispute Resolution Center, Ashland, Oregon)

- To prepare mediators for parent-adolescent mediations, additional training is given on family systems and adolescent development. (Victim Offender Reconciliation Program, Dallas, Oregon)

- Role-plays are designed with "kinks" that elicit discussion about particular issues mediators find challenging—for example, youthful offender chooses not to participate in mediation but the parents insist; restitution amount is deemed unrealistic or unfair by the mediator; cultural tensions. (Lancaster Area Victim Offender Reconciliation Program, Lancaster, Pennsylvania)

- Mediators are trained and encouraged in supervision to provide timely contact with the parties and follow-up that is efficient, dependable, and accurate re court proceedings or referrals. (Lancaster Area Victim Offender Reconciliation Program, Lancaster, Pennsylvania)

- The trainer participates in the role-plays in order to "even the ground" between trainer and trainee and give the trainer a better sense of where mediators might become stuck. (Victim Offender Reconciliation Program of Southeastern South Dakota, Sioux Falls, South Dakota)

- During mediation training, participants unknowingly receive the actual case for role-playing that they will in reality be given to mediate. (Mediation and Restitution/Reconciliation Services, Memphis; Tennessee)

- During training, each participant is videotaped as the mediator in a role-play. The tapes are then made available to be checked out. (Victim Offender Reconciliation Program of Anderson County, Oak Ridge, Tennessee)

- Community members are brought in to play the roles of victim, offender, and parent in the role-plays. (Victim Offender Reconciliation Program of Anderson County, Oak Ridge, Tennessee)

- Trainees are given information about the victim experience and then urged not to prejudge what might be important to a particular victim. (Victim Offender Reconciliation Program of Anderson County, Oak Ridge, Tennessee)

- Excerpts from movies and newspapers are used in training to explore the nature of conflict and what could be done differently. (Dispute Mediation Service, Dallas, Texas)

- Speakers from the judiciary are included in mediation training so that trainees realize the system appreciates and supports mediation. (Mediation Services for Victims and Offenders, Seattle, Washington)

- Trainees are given the opportunity to practice thinking on their feet in an exercise that simulates meeting the victim and offender in the hallway on the day of the mediation. (Mediation Services for Victims and Offenders, Seattle, Washington)

- As part of the training, mediators attend court proceedings to observe victims and offenders in the actual court process. (Victim Offender Reconciliation Program, La Crosse, Wisconsin)

Appendix E

Summary of Forty VOM Empirical Studies

Exhibit E.1 was compiled by Mark S. Umbreit and Robert B. Coates. It describes and summarizes the forty available victim offender mediation outcome studies that could be located. The complete reference for each study cited is given below the exhibit.

Exhibit E.1 Empirical Studies of Victim Offender Mediation Outcomes

Author, Date, Location	Design	Population Sample	Data	Key Findings
1. Davis et al. (1980). New York City.	Random assignment of those eligible for mediation. Postintervention measures.	Disputants known to each other; conflict resulted in felony arrest.	(No information provided.)	Participants believed they had more opportunity to participate in mediation than in court. Believed outcome more fair. No evidence that mediation reduced levels of future conflict.
2. Collins (1984). Grand Prairie, Alberta, Canada.	Purposive sample. Postintervention measures.	About 30% of youth with charged offenses in jurisdiction referred to reconciliation project. Typical offender: age 15, male, one offense, theft.	Interviews: staff, 18; victims, 19; offenders, 22; parents, 16; community workers, 6.	Process perceived as working extremely well. Most participants had more positive view of justice system. Most believed agreements to be fair and reasonable. Program more costly than other diversion projects.
3. Coates & Gehm (1985, 1989). Three programs in Indiana and one in Ohio.	1983—matched sample of VORP and non-VORP cases from three programs. 1984—availability sample in four programs. Postintervention.	1983—73 VORP offenders: age 16; 78% juvenile; 92% white; 93% male; 93% no prior incarceration postconviction; 54% convicted on burglary charges.	1983 sample—record data. 1984—interviews: victim, 37; offender, 23; staff, 22; justice system personnel, 27; victim refusals, 26; observations, 9.	1983 sample—60% of eligible case resulted in meetings; 98% meetings yielded contracts; 87% contracts included restitution; VORP offender got less jail time. 1984 sample—high levels of satisfaction reported; complaints regarding time delay.

4. Schneider (1986). Washington, D.C.	Random assignment. Postintervention measures.	Typical offender: full-time student, black, male, repeat offender, referred for felony, average age 15.4. VOM, 143; referred but refused, 131; probation, 137.	Record data.	40% referred to VOM refused on advice of lawyers. Offenders referred have statistically significant lower recidivism than those in probation group. VOM participants have lower rates than offenders on probation.
5. Perry, Lajeunesse, & Woods (1987). Winnipeg, Manitoba, Canada.	Postintervention measures. 465 of the 1,021 referred in 1984 and 1985 resulted in mediation. Purposive sample: 45 respondents, 67 complainants.	Types of cases: community disputes, 20%; diversion, 65%; after plea, 15%; first-time offender; summary conviction type cases, identifiable victim, relationship between complainant and respondent.	Record data on those referred to mediation. Telephone interviews with 112 participants.	77% increase in cases referred between 1984 and 1985. 65% in both years were for diversion. 45% referrals reached mediation. In nearly 40% of cases, victims were not willing to meet. 88% of mediations reach agreements. Subsample: good to excellent service: 84% offenders and 91% victims.

(Continued)

Exhibit E.1 Empirical Studies of Victim Offender Mediation Outcomes, cont'd

Author, Date, Location	Design	Population Sample	Data	Key Findings
6. Umbreit (1988). Minneapolis and St. Paul, Minnesota.	Availability sample: all referred to program in 1985 and 1986. Purposive sample: subsample of participants for interviewing. Postintervention measures.	183 offenders and 179 victims referred to VOM in 1985 and 1986. Most referred after adjudication; some diversion. Typical offense: burglary.	Records. Interviews: victims, 31; offenders, 11.	54% of victims and 64% of offenders went to mediation. 79% of restitution agreements were completed: total monetary compensation, $11,376; total personal service, 127 hours; total community service, 489 hours. Client satisfaction (interviews): restitution agreement fair: 93% victims, 100% offenders.
7. Umbreit (1989). Minneapolis, Minnesota.	Purposive sample. Postintervention measures.	50 victims of burglary; 62% in VOM.	Face-to-face interviews.	Attempting to understand victims' sense of fairness, three dimensions were discovered: rehabilitation, compensation, punishment. Victim participation was regarded as critical across all types of victims. 80% of VOM participants experienced fairness, compared to 38% of nonparticipants.

Study	Sampling/Design	Sample	Data Source	Findings
8. Umbreit (1989). Genesee County, New York, and southern Wisconsin.	Purposive sample of four individual cases studies.	Cases: armed robbery, assault of a police officer, negligent homicide, sniper shooting.	Interviews with victims, offenders, mediators. Referral sources.	Victims of violent crimes have needs that can be addressed, with considerable sensitive care, through face-to-face mediation. The traditional VORP model developed for property crimes can be expanded as a framework for cases involving violent crime.
9. Galaway (1989). Minneapolis and St. Paul, Minnesota.	Purposive sample. Postintervention measures.	87 VORP participants over a two-year period.	Records. High number of agreements for participants.	54% of those referred participated. 128 agreements were reached: 44% monetary restitution, 17% personal service, 16% a combination of the two, 10% community service. 79% of agreements were fulfilled.
10. Gehm (1990). Six VORPs in Indiana, Wisconsin, and Oregon.	Availability sample. Postintervention measures.	All individuals referred from July 1, 1985, through Oct. 1, 1987. Eligible cases: 555.	Records.	Of 555 eligible, 250 meetings were held, 228 contracts agreed to, and 203 successfully completed. 53% of victims were unwilling to participate. More likely to meet if offender was white, offense was misdemeanor, and victim was representing an institution.

(Continued)

Exhibit E.1 Empirical Studies of Victim Offender Mediation Outcomes, cont'd

Author, Date, Location	Design	Population Sample	Data	Key Findings
11. Marshall (1990). Four sites in England: Coventry, Leeds, North East Essex, and Wolverhampton.	Availability and purposive sample. Postintervention measures.	Little descriptive sample information. Coventry, 30% violent cases; Leeds, 35% burglary; North East Essex (not reported); Wolverhampton, most minor offense referrals and 55% corporate victims.	Records on all participants. Samples interviewed.	Police-based programs are more perfunctory than court-based programs. Corporate victims seemed less willing to meet and to reach agreement. Mediation has moderate influence on sentencing. Majority of participating victims would do it again.
12. Dignan (1990). Kettering, England.	Availability and purposive samples. Matched subsample. Pre- and postintervention measures.	1987–1989—291 referrals, primarily from police. 74% accepted. Typical participant: age 17+, no court record, admission of guilt, eligible for prosecution.	Record. Sample interviewed: 50 offenders, 45 individual victims, 45 corporate victims.	Comparing matched samples: 60% diversion, 13% net-widening effect, recidivism slightly lower for Kettering than for comparison group. 15.4% for face-to-face mediation versus 21.6% for go-between. Face-to-face mediations increased from 32% to 43% from year 1 to year 3.

Study	Sampling/Design	Data Sources	Findings
13. Hughes & Schneider (1990). Various U.S. restitution sites.	Purposive and random sampling. Postintervention measures.	Surveys sent to 342 organizations; 240 responded; 79 of those had VOMPs.	Record. Surveys.	Mediation programs were found in counties with 3,000 to 2 million population. Most often governed by the private sector, with referrals from the courts. VOM was regarded as functioning well, with most respondents favorably disposed.
14. Umbreit (1991). Minneapolis and St. Paul, Minnesota.	Availability sample for record data. Purposive sample for interview. Postintervention measures.	379 cases referred to VOM in 1989. 228 victims, 257 offenders (56% were misdemeanor offenses). Vandalism most frequent.	Record data. Interviews: 51 victims and 66 juvenile offenders.	50% of referred cases led to face-to-face meetings. These resulted in restitution agreement 96% of the time. 81% of agreements were completed. 86% of victims and 94% of offenders said it was helpful to meet the other party.
15. Umbreit & Coates (1992). Albuquerque, New Mexico; Minneapolis, Minnesota; Oakland, California; and Austin, Texas.	Availability and purposive samples. Two comparison groups. Pre- and postintervention measures.	2,799 victims and 2,659 offenders referred; average age, 15; 86% male; 54% Caucasian; most frequent offense, burglary.	Records. Preliminary interviews by telephone; postmediation interviews in person. Observations.	High levels of client satisfaction: 79% offenders and 87% victims. VOM offenders more likely (81%) to complete agreements than similar youth in program without mediation (58%). Both offenders and victims said meeting, sharing pain, hearing stories was important.

(Continued)

Exhibit E.1 Empirical Studies of Victim Offender Mediation Outcomes, cont'd

Author, Date, Location	Design	Population Sample	Data	Key Findings
16. Warner (1992). Glasgow and Edinburgh, Scotland.	Availability sample. Randomly assigned comparison group. Postintervention measures.	175 referrals between October 1989 and February 1990. 87% accepted; 174 victims and 185 accused; 77% individual victims; 67% involving violence or criminal damage; average age of accused: 30.2.	Record data. Interview or questionnaires with 33% of victims and 22% of offenders. Observations of decision-making process.	33% of cases accepted were sent back primarily because of victim. Of 103 cases, 84 reached agreement. Respondents were highly satisfied. Few victims met face to face with accused, and most did not want to. Mediation was deemed a fair and just alternative to prosecution for minor offenders.
17. Clarke, Valente, & Mace (1992). Three counties in North Carolina.	Availability and purposive sampling. Comparison counties. Postintervention measures.	Court record data: sample of 1,421 eligible clusters. Mediation program data set: 544 clusters sent to the three mediation programs. Related party misdemeanor cases.	Record data. Telephone interviews: 354 complainants randomly selected, 32 defendants.	58% of clusters received for mediation were mediated. Agreements were arrived at in over 90% of mediated cases. None of those reaching agreement went to trial. In one county (Henderson), number of trials resulting from these was reduced by two-thirds. Length of process increased in two of the three counties.

18. Roy (1993). Elkhart, Indiana, and Kalamazoo, Michigan.	Random sample of participants in each program. Postintervention measures.	Youth in face-to-face VOM compared to youth in court-based restitution program. Over half involved felonies.	Record data: 218 youth representing 50% of those participating in both programs.	No difference in rate of completion of restitution contracts. No difference in rate of recidivism.
19. Galaway (1995). New Zealand.	Availability sample of six sites.	1,455 offenders, 1,672 cases involving monetary penalties, 22 district court judges, 341 probation officers.	Record data. Interviews. Survey questionnaires.	Reparation appropriate as sole sentence for offenders with minor or no prior criminal history who committed minor property offenses.
20. Nugent & Paddock (1995). Anderson County, Tennessee.	Random sample of participants. Matched sample of time period preceding. Postintervention measures.	125 VORP and 150 matched from prior time period; all pleaded guilty to property offenses.	Records.	VORP offenders were less likely to offend than non-VORP: 19.8 versus 33.1; VORP offenders' reoffenses were less severe than youth processed through traditional approaches.

(Continued)

Exhibit E.1 Empirical Studies of Victim Offender Mediation Outcomes, cont'd

Author, Date, Location	Design	Population Sample	Data	Key Findings
21. Roberts (1995). Langley, British Columbia, Canada.	Availability sample. Pre- and postintervention measures.	130 referrals; 39 total cases accepted. Violent offenders: 46% sexual assault; 18% murder; 23% armed robbery. Average time from sentence to referral: 3.7 years.	Record data. Personal or telephone interviews: 22 offenders; 24 victims; 23 justice system personnel. Videos of some interviews and 15 mediations.	Involved showing victim and offender interviews to victim and offender counterparts before meeting. 56% of cases had met face to face by end of study. Two VOM staff were present; mediations lasted 3 to 5 hours. Unanimous support of program from all participants.
22. Umbreit (1995). Four Canadian sites: Langley, British Columbia; Calgary, Alberta; Winnipeg, Manitoba; and Ottawa, Ontario.	Purposive samples: mediation and nonmediation. Postintervention measures.	4,445 referred to mediation. 39% met face to face. Offenders: 59% male; average age, 33; 86% Caucasian.	Records. Phone interviews: 323 victims and 287 offenders. Observation: 24 sessions. Interviews with staff and officials.	93% of face-to-face mediations led to agreements. Victims who participated in mediation were significantly more likely to be satisfied (78%) than those who did not (48%). Offenders in mediation were also significantly more satisfied (74%) than those not in mediation (53%). Mediation contributes to an enhanced sense of justice.

Study		Data Source	Findings
23. Umbreit & Roberts (1996); Robert & Umbreit (1996). Coventry and Leeds, England.	Availability sample. Postintervention measures.	70 victims and 53 offenders. Groups: direct mediation; indirect mediation; referred but did not participate.	Record data. Phone and in-person interviews. System officials also interviewed.	Majority of mediations were indirect, not face to face. Participants in mediation were more likely to express satisfaction and a sense of fairness than nonparticipants. More benefits with face-to-face mediation.
24. Flaten (1996). Anchorage, Alaska.	Purposive sample. Postintervention measures.	In-depth study of seven serious offense mediations including manslaughter.	Interviews with offenders, victims, victims advocates, offender counselors, and mediators.	Mediation can be helpful with very serious cases. Six of seven victims believed mediation was successful. Offender felt meeting victim personalized the crime event. Preparation key to success.
25. Wynne (1996). Leeds, England.	Availability and purposive samples. Postintervention measures.	For cases closed 1988–1992: most offenders male and 21 or younger; most frequent offenses: burglary and theft.	Record data.	48% of referred cases resulted in direct or indirect mediation. Two cohorts followed for reconviction: 1985–1987—75% no conviction after one year; 1989—78% no conviction after one year.

(Continued)

Exhibit E.1 Empirical Studies of Victim Offender Mediation Outcomes, cont'd

Author, Date, Location	Design	Population Sample	Data	Key Findings
26. Niemeyer & Shichor (1996). Orange County, California.	Availability sample and systematic random sample for recidivism comparisons. Postintervention measures.	35% of juvenile cases referred for graffiti or tagging, 24% for serious personal injury, 16% for serious property damage.	Record data. Questionnaire.	Over 70% of victims and offenders chose face-to-face mediation. Victims refusing stated that incident was not important enough to warrant participation. Agreements reached in 99% of mediated cases. Recidivism results were mixed.
27. Wiinamaki (1997). Anderson, Putnam, and Cumberland Counties, Tennessee.	Random sample of participants. Matched sample of time period preceding. Postintervention measures.	203 VORP and 217 matched sample from prior time period; all pleaded guilty to property offenses.	Records.	VORP offenders were less likely to offend than non-VORP: 38.4% reduction was associated with VORP participation.
28. Umbreit & Bradshaw (1997). Minneapolis, Minnesota, and Winnipeg, Manitoba, Canada.	Purposive sample. Postintervention measures.	Minneapolis: 89 victims in juvenile VOM program; Winnipeg: 92 victims in adult VOM program.	Record data. Face-to-face interviews.	Victims in juvenile programs were more likely to feel that mediation helped them participate in the justice system than victims in adult programs. Both groups were very satisfied with mediation. Victims of adults were more fearful that the offender would reoffend.

29. Carr (1998). Los Angeles County, California.	Availability and purposive samples. Postintervention measures.	632 juvenile referrals; 279 mediations from July 1997 to July 1998.	Record data. Postmediation interviews: 138 offenders, 135 victims, 133 parents or guardians. Three-month follow-up interviews: 51 youth; 49 parents or guardians.	Offenders, parents, and victims were highly satisfied with the mediation results and felt that the mediators were fair. Nearly all were pleased that they chose to take part and would recommend the program to others. A minimum six-month follow-up indicated that 89% had not recidivated.
30. Roberts (1998). Tucson, Arizona.	Availability sample. Postintervention measures.	483 juvenile referrals for fiscal 1996 and 1997: 196 mediations, 189 agreements.	Record data. Phone interviews: 53 offenders (number of victims not given).	Nearly 90% of offenders and victims felt it was helpful to meet the other party. Nearly all participants felt the mediator was fair to all parties. 79% did not recidivate within a year following mediation.

(Continued)

Exhibit E.1 Empirical Studies of Victim Offender Mediation Outcomes, cont'd

Author, Date, Location	Design	Population Sample	Data	Key Findings
31. Umbreit & Greenwood (1999). United States.	Nationwide survey. Availability sample.	289 VOM programs; 116 interviewed: 43% private, 23% church-based, 16% probation. Referral sources: 29% probation, 23% judges, 15% prosecutors. Offenses: vandalism, minor assaults, thefts, burglaries. Mediation: 34% as diversion, 56% after adjudication. 81% of programs work with juvenile cases.	Phone interviews.	Half of referred cases resulted in mediation. 87% of mediated cases resulted in written agreement.
32. Stone, Helms, & Edgeworth (1998). Cobb County, Georgia.	Availability sample; matched comparison sample. Post-intervention measures.	799 court-based mediated cases, 1993–1996; 1,045 comparison cases, 1990–1992. Mediation sample: average age 13.9; 71% male, 72% white; average prior court contacts: 16.	Court record data.	No difference in return-to-court rates between mediated and nonmediated youth. Mediated cases required one-third the time to process. 75% of the returns to court involved violation of conditions of mediated agreements. More experienced mediators tended to get better results.

33. Bradshaw & Umbreit (1998).	(As in study 15.)		Secondary analysis.	Stepwise multiple regressions shows feeling good about mediator, believing restitution agreement fair, and having a strong desire to meet offender explains much of victim satisfaction.
34. Umbreit, Coates, & Roberts (1998). United States, Canada, and England.	(As in studies 15, 22, and 23.)	(As in studies 15, 22, and 23.)	Secondary analysis.	Comparing victim offender satisfaction rates across countries shows high levels of satisfaction. Lowest level were found in England, where the majority of case are processed using indirect mediation.
35. Fercello & Umbreit (1999). Dakota County, Minnesota.	Availability sample. Postintervention measures.	33 juvenile offenders, 37 crime victims.	Phone interviews.	High level of satisfaction with the victim offender meeting process and outcomes.
36. Umbreit, Bradshaw, & Coates (1999). United States.	Purposive selection. Postintervention data.	Two case studies resulting from mediation with survivors of violent crime and their offender-inmates.	In-person interviews. Videotapes of meetings.	Description of the process of mediation or dialogue with participants in two murder cases. Participants expressed various reasons for being very satisfied with the process.

(Continued)

Exhibit E.1 Empirical Studies of Victim Offender Mediation Outcomes, cont'd

Author, Date, Location	Design	Population Sample	Data	Key Findings
37. Umbreit & Brown (1999). Ohio.	Purposive selection. Postintervention data.	Two case studies resulting from mediation with survivors of violent crime and their offender-inmates.	In-person interviews.	Description of the process of mediation or dialogue with participants in violent cases. Participants expressed reasons for being very satisfied with the process.
38. Umbreit & Vos (2000). Texas.	Purposive selection. Postintervention data.	Two case studies resulting from mediation with survivors of capital murder and offender-inmates.	In-person interviews.	Description of the process of mediation or dialogue with participants in two death row cases. Participants expressed reasons for being very satisfied with the process.

| 39. Nugent, Umbreit, Wiinamaki, & Paddock (in press). United States. | Reanalysis of recidivism data from studies 15, 20, 26, and 27. | Samples of juveniles VOM and non-VOM in four Tennessee counties; Minneapolis, Minnesota; Austin, Texas; Albuquerque, New Mexico; and Oakland, California. Total sample: 1,298 juveniles. | Record data. | Youth participating in VOM are significantly less likely to recidivate than non-VOM youth: a 32% reduction. VOM youth who recidivate do so at significantly less serious level than comparable non-VOM youth. |
| 40. Umbreit & Bradshaw (in press). Winnipeg, Manitoba, Canada. | (As in study 22.) | (As in study 22.) | Secondary analysis. | Regression analysis suggests that feeling good about the mediator, having a sense of fairness about the restitution agreement, and desiring to meet the offender explain much of victim satisfaction. |

Source: Mark S. Umbreit and Robert B. Coates.

1. Davis, R., Tichane, M., & Grayson, D. (1980). *Mediation and arbitration as alternatives to prosecution in felony arrest cases. An evaluation of the Brooklyn Dispute Resolution Center.* New York: VERA Institute of Justice.

2. Collins, J. P. (1984). *Final evaluation report on the Grande Prairie Community Reconciliation Project for Young Offenders.* Ottawa, Ontario: Ministry of the Solicitor General of Canada, Consultation Centre (Prairies).

3. Coates, R. B., & Gehm, J. (1985). *Victim meets offender: An evaluation of victim-offender reconciliation programs.* Valparaiso, IN: PACT Institute of Justice; Coates, R. B., & Gehm, J. (1989). An empirical assessment. In M. Wright & B. Galaway (Eds.), *Mediation and criminal justice* (pp. 251–263). London: Sage.

4. Schneider, A. L. (1986). Restitution and recidivism rates of juvenile offenders: Results from four experimental studies. *Criminology, 24,* 533–552.

5. Perry, L., Lajeunesse, T., & Woods, A. (1987). *Mediation services: An evaluation.* Winnipeg, Manitoba, Canada: Office of the Attorney General, Department of Research, Planning and Evaluation.

6. Umbreit, M. S. (1988). Mediation of victim offender conflict. *Journal of Dispute Resolution, 1988,* 85–105.

7. Umbreit, M. S. (1989). Crime victims seeking fairness, not revenge: Towards restorative justice. *Federal Probation, 53*(3), 52–57.

8. Umbreit, M. S. (1989). Violent offenders and their victims. In M. Wright & B. Galaway (Eds.), *Mediation and criminal justice* (pp. 99–112). London: Sage.

9. Galaway, B. (1989). Informal justice: Mediation between offenders and victims. In P. A. Albrecht & O. Backes (Eds.), *Crime prevention and intervention: Legal and ethical problems* (pp. 103–116). New York: Aldine de Gruyter.

10. Gehm, J. (1990). Mediated victim-offender restitution agreements: An exploratory analysis of factors related to victim participation. In B. Galaway & J. Hudson (Eds.), *Criminal justice, restitution, and reconciliation* (pp. 177–182). Monsey, NY: Criminal Justice Press.

11. Marshall, T. (1990). Results of research from British experiments in restorative justice. In B. Galaway & J. Hudson (Eds.), *Criminal justice, restitution, and reconciliation* (pp. 83–107). Monsey, NY: Criminal Justice Press.

12. Dignan, J. (1990). *Repairing the damage: An evaluation of an experimental adult reparation scheme in Kettering, Northamptonshire.* Sheffield, England: University of Sheffield, Centre for Criminological and Legal Research.

13. Hughes, S., & Schneider, A. (1990). *Victim-offender mediation in the juvenile justice system.* Washington, D.C.: Office of Juvenile Justice and Delinquency Prevention.

14. Umbreit, M. S. (1991, August). Minnesota mediation center produces positive results. *Corrections Today,* pp. 194–197.

15. Umbreit, M. S., & Coates, R. B. (1992). *Victim offender mediation: An analysis of programs in four states of the U.S.* Minneapolis: Minnesota Citizens

Council on Crime and Justice. Other publications related to this study: Umbreit, M. S., & Coates, R. B. (1992). The impact of mediating victim offender conflict: An analysis of programs in three states. *Juvenile and Family Court Journal, 43,* 1–8; Umbreit, M. S., & Coates, R. B. (1993). Cross-site analysis of victim-offender mediation in four states. *Crime and Delinquency, 39,* 565–585; Umbreit, M. S. (1993). Juvenile offenders meet their victims: The impact of mediation in Albuquerque, New Mexico. *Family and Conciliation Courts Review, 31,* 90–100; Umbreit, M. S. (1994). *Victim meets offender: The impact of restorative justice and mediation.* Monsey, NY: Criminal Justice Press; Umbreit, M. S. (1994). Crime victims confront their offenders: The impact of a Minneapolis mediation program. *Research on Social Work Practice, 4,* 436–447; Umbreit, M. S. (1995). Restorative justice through mediation: The impact of offenders facing their victims in Oakland. *Journal of Law and Social Work, 5,* 1–13; Umbreit, M. S. (1998). Restorative justice through victim-offender mediation: A multi-site assessment. *Western Criminology Review, 1,* 1–29.

16. Warner, S. (1992). *Making amends: Justice for victims and offenders.* Aldershot, England: Avebury.

17. Clarke, S. H., Valente, E., & Mace, R. R. (1992). *Mediation of interpersonal disputes: An evaluation of North Carolina's programs.* Chapel Hill: University of North Carolina, Institute of Government.

18. Roy, S. (1993). Two types of juvenile restitution programs in two midwestern counties: A comparative study. *Federal Probation 57*(4), 48–53.

19. Galaway, B. (1995). Victim-offender mediation by New Zealand probation officers: The possibilities and the reality. *Mediation Quarterly, 12,* 249–262.

20. Nugent, W. R., & Paddock, J. B. (1995). The effect of victim-offender mediation on severity of reoffense. *Mediation Quarterly, 12,* 353–367.

21. Roberts, T. (1995). *Evaluation of the Victim Offender Mediation Project, Langley, BC: Final Report* Victoria, British Columbia, Canada: Focus Consultants.

22. Umbreit, M. S. (1995). *Mediation of criminal conflict: An assessment of programs in four Canadian provinces.* St. Paul: University of Minnesota, Center for Restorative Justice and Peacemaking. Other publications related to this study: Umbreit, M. S. (1996). Restorative justice through mediation: The impact of programs in four Canadian provinces. In B. Galaway & J. Hudson (Eds.), *Restorative justice: International perspectives* (pp. 373–385). Monsey, NY: Criminal Justice Press; Umbreit, M. S. (1999). Victim offender mediation in Canada: The impact of an emerging social work intervention. *International Journal of Social Work, 42,* 215–227.

23. Umbreit, M. S., & Roberts, A. W. (1996). *Mediation of criminal conflict in England: An assessment of services in Coventry and Leeds.* St. Paul: University of Minnesota, Center for Restorative Justice and Peacemaking.; Roberts, A. W., & Umbreit, M. S. (1996). Victim-offender mediation: The English experience. *Mediation UK, 12*(3).

24. Flaten, C. (1996). Victim-offender mediation: Application with serious offenses committed by juveniles. In B. Galaway & J. Hudson (Eds.), *Restorative justice: International perspectives* (pp. 387–402). Monsey, NY: Criminal Justice Press.

25. Wynne, J. (1996). Leeds Mediation and Reparation Service: Ten years' experience of victim-offender mediation. In B. Galaway & J. Hudson (Eds.), *Restorative justice: International perspectives* (pp. 442–461). Monsey, NY: Criminal Justice Press.

26. Niemeyer, M., & Shichor, D. (1996). A preliminary study of a large victim/offender reconciliation program. *Federal Probation, 60*(3), 30–34.

27. Wiinamaki, L. (1997) *Victim-offender reconciliation programs: Juvenile property offender recidivism and severity of reoffense in three Tennessee counties.* Doctoral dissertation, University of Tennessee, Knoxville.

28. Umbreit, M. S., & Bradshaw, W. (1997). Victim experience of meeting adult versus juvenile offenders: A cross-national comparison. *Federal Probation, 61*(4), 33–39.

29. Carr, C. (1998). *VORS Program evaluation report.* Inglewood, CA: Centenela Valley Juvenile Diversion Project.

30. Roberts, L. (1998). *Victim offender mediation: An evaluation of the Pima County Juvenile Court Center's victim offender mediation program (VOMP).* Masters thesis, University of Arizona, Tucson.

31. Umbreit, M. S., & Greenwood, J. (1999). National survey of victim-offender mediation programs in the United States. *Mediation Quarterly, 16,* 235–251.

32. Stone, S., Helms, W., & Edgeworth, P. (1998). *Cobb County [Georgia] Juvenile Court mediation program evaluation.* Carrolton: State University of West Georgia.

33. Bradshaw, W., & Umbreit, M. S. (1998). Crime victims meet juvenile offenders: Contributing factors to victim satisfaction with mediated dialogue in Minneapolis. *Juvenile and Family Court Journal, 49*(3), 17–25.

34. Umbreit, M. S., Coates, R. B., & Roberts, A. W. (1998). Impact of victim-offender mediation in Canada, England, and the United States. *Crime Victims Report, 2*(1), 83, 90–92.

35. Fercello, C., & Umbreit, M. S.(1999). *Client satisfaction with victim offender conferences in Dakota County, Minnesota.* St. Paul: University of Minnesota, Center for Restorative Justice and Peacemaking.

36. Umbreit, M. S., Bradshaw, W., & Coates, R. B. (1999). Victims of severe violence meet the offender: Restorative justice through dialogue. *International Review of Victimology, 6,* 321–344.

37. Umbreit, M. S., & Brown, K. (1999). Victims of severe violence meet the offender in Ohio. *Crime Victims Report, 3*(3), 35–36.

38. Umbreit, M. S., & Vos, B. (2000). Homicide survivors meet the offender prior to execution: Restorative justice through dialogue. *Homicide Studies, 4,* 63–87.

39. Nugent, W. R., Umbreit, M. S., Wiinamaki, L., & Paddock, J. B. (in press). Participation in victim-offender mediation and reoffense: Successful replications? *Journal of Research on Social Work Practice*.
40. Umbreit, M. S., & Bradshaw, W. (in press). Factors that contribute to victim satisfaction with mediated offender dialogue in Winnipeg: An emerging area of social work practice. *Journal of Law and Social Work*.

Appendix F

Assessing Participant Satisfaction with VOM

This appendix describes the development of participant satisfaction scales for use in evaluating VOM programs. The complete Victim Satisfaction with Offender Meeting (VSOM) Scale is provided in a format that may be easily copied for use in program evaluation.

Why should restorative justice programs assess victim satisfaction? Demand for accountability, increased funding, and improved services from such programs is growing. Essential to justifying the existence of restorative justice programs is the satisfaction of the individuals they are intended to benefit. When participants' perspectives are not considered, the evaluation of service effectiveness is incomplete and may be biased toward the provider's point of view. In many areas, the law now requires that consumer input be included. Incorporation of consumer views can be used to modify services and make systems more responsive to client needs. Also, in developing areas like restorative justice, satisfaction is an important indicator of the acceptability of innovative programs.

Although consumer satisfaction has frequently been assessed in health and mental health settings, only recently have criminal justice systems begun systematically assessing the satisfaction of victims and offenders receiving restorative justice services (Umbreit & Coates, 1999). Typically, most programs that assess consumer satisfaction develop their own satisfaction scales. This is problematic for three reasons. First, very few of these scales have been psychometrically tested, so their reliability is unknown. Second, because agencies have developed their own unique measures, it is impossible to compare differences in satisfaction between programs and types of services. Data in isolation are difficult to interpret meaningfully, and the lack of comparability restricts the development of knowledge from the consumer perspective that might improve services. Third, most satisfaction measures are not comprehensive and do not assess the multidimensional aspects of satisfaction and the services provided.

Development of the Victim Satisfaction with Offender Meeting Scale

Currently, we have no standardized measure of victim satisfaction and little knowledge of the various aspects of victim offender dialogue services delivery processes and their differential effects on satisfaction with services. For example, a client might be satisfied with the mediator but dissatisfied with the restitution plan. Because a standard measure of victim satisfaction is needed, we sought to develop a simple scale that could be used in a variety of victim offender dialogue services such as victim offender mediation and family group conferencing. In addition, we attempted to develop a scale that can differentiate between victim satisfaction components across multiple dimensions.

Initial Scale Development

The first step in developing the VSOM Scale was to consult published sources in order to identify the potential determinants of satisfaction with services. We identified seven areas of possible determinants in the literature. For each category, we created four scale questions. Each question had a four-point anchored answer without a neutral position. Exhibit F.1 lists the seven areas and gives an example of a question in each.

A panel of six national experts in the field of restorative justice reviewed the twenty-eight items to evaluate how well they tapped each category. After reviewing the scale, nine additional items were

Exhibit F.1   Victim Satisfaction with Offender Meeting (VSOM) Scale Content Categories and Sample Items

Category	Sample Item
Mediator skills	Were you treated respectfully by the mediator?
Preparation for mediation	Was it made clear to you that participation was voluntary on your part?
Restitution	Was the restitution agreement fair to you?
Meeting the offender	Did you have sufficient time to talk with the offender?
Experience of the criminal justice system	Have you ever felt that our program was more concerned with procedures than with helping you?
Experience of the victim-offender dialogue session	While participating in the session, did you feel safe?
Subjective experience of the victim	Did the meeting with the offender reduce how upset you were about the crime?

added by the panel. The preliminary version of the scale consisted of thirty-seven items, with a minimum of five items in each category.

The preliminary scale was administered to 194 victims of criminal offenses who participated in victim offender mediation in four service settings in Orange County and Los Angeles, California, and Washington and Dakota Counties, Minnesota. The satisfaction scale was to be mailed to subjects two weeks following the mediation. The response rate was 59 percent. The sample is described in Table F.1.

As in previous research in consumer satisfaction, the distribution of scores was positively skewed, with a large number of satisfied clients and small numbers of dissatisfied clients. The data from the preliminary study were analyzed with principal-components factor analysis. The first factor derived from this solution accounted for 38 percent of the total variance and roughly 70 percent of the

Table F.1 Sample Used for Testing the Preliminary
VSOM Scale

Gender	
Male	63%
Female	37%
Type of offense	
Person	11%
Property	89%
Age	mean, 39; SD, 13
Education	mean, 15 years; SD, 4

common variance. In the main analysis, the second factor accounted for less than 8 percent of the common variance. When items with high first-factor loading were removed and the analysis was repeated, no other factor accounted for as much as 6 percent of the total variance. These findings suggest only one significant dimension from the responses to the preliminary scale.

Final Scale Development

To construct a briefer scale for assessing victim satisfaction with services, the factor loadings and item-total correlations were examined. Selected were eleven items that loaded highly on the unrotated first factor and exhibited good interitem and item-total correlations. Coefficient alpha for the final VSOM Scale was .87. This indicates a high degree of internal consistency of the scale, indicating that the scale can provide a reliable overall estimate of victim satisfaction with victim offender mediation and dialogue services. The VSOM score is computed by adding the scores of each item on the scale. Scores range from 11 to 44, with higher numbers indicating higher levels of victim satisfaction. In general, scores between 11 and 19 indicate dissatisfaction with services. Scores from 20 to 27 indicate that respondents were somewhat dissatisfied. Scores from 28 to 36 indicate satisfaction with services. Scores from 37 to 44 indicate high levels of satisfaction. A copy of the VSOM Scale is presented in Exhibit F.2.

Guidelines for Use of the VSOM Scale

Use of the VSOM Scale should be based on the unique needs, goals, and resources of each program. Such use might include doing a survey of satisfaction once a year or quarterly and using a random sample or sampling all participants in a specific limited time frame. The VSOM Scale can be used to assess the satisfaction of special subgroups of clients or to compare different types of victim services. Victim satisfaction surveys should be done on a regular basis using a fixed method (same format, timing, method, follow-up procedures) in order to enhance the interpretation of results. If different methods are used, it will prove impossible to distinguish changes in satisfaction from changes due to method.

The following suggestions are offered to assist VOM programs in incorporating the VSOM Scale into ongoing program evaluation:

- Integrate victim satisfaction into all program evaluation activities.
- Communicate victim satisfaction results to funding sources, staff, and community and in victim information brochures.
- Describe the sample (age, gender, race, type of offense) from which the victim satisfaction data are drawn, and note the rate of response. This will provide a better sense of how strongly the results can be generalized to a particular program population.
- Report satisfaction data by total mean scale score with standard deviation as a general measure of level of victim satisfaction. Means for each scale question and the percentages of levels of satisfaction for each question can also be reported.

Exhibit F.2 Victim Satisfaction with Offender Mediation (VSOM) Scale

Please help us improve the services we provide to people who have been victimized by crime in our community by answering the following questions about the services you have received. We are interested in your honest opinions, whether they are positive or negative. Please answer all of the questions by circling the number of your response. We also welcome your comments and suggestions. If a restitution agreement was not developed in your meeting with the offender, please ignore question 4. Thank you very much. We really appreciate your help.

	1	2	3	4
1. How satisfied were you with the manner in which the mediator prepared you for the eventual meeting with the offender?	Quite Dissatisfied	Indifferent or mildly dissatisfied	Mostly satisfied	Very satisfied
2. Was the mediator a good listener?	No, definitely not	No, not really	Yes, generally	Yes, definitely
3. Would you recommend to other victims of similar crimes that they should consider the option of meeting the offender in this type of program?	No, definitely not	No, not really	Yes, generally	Yes, definitely
4. How satisfied were you with the restitution agreement that was made during the meeting?	Quite Dissatisfied	Indifferent or mildly dissatisfied	Mostly satisfied	Very satisfied
5. Did the mediator seem genuinely interested in your expressed needs?	No, definitely not	No, not really	Yes, generally	Yes, definitely
6. Was it helpful to be able to talk directly with the offender about the impact of the crime?	Yes, it helped a great deal (4)	Yes, it helped somewhat (3)	No, it really didn't help (2)	No, it seemed to make things worse (1)

7. Did meeting the offender help reduce any fear that he/she would commit another crime against you?

4	3	2	1
Yes, definitely	Yes, generally	No, not really	No, definitely not

8. During the meeting with the offender, did he/she show any understanding, even the beginnings of understanding, about the real personal impact of the crime upon your life?

4	3	2	1
Yes, definitely	Yes, generally	No, not really	No, definitely not

9. Did the victim offender mediation (conferencing) program allow you to express your feelings about being victimized?

1	2	3	4
No, definitely not	No, not really	Yes, generally	Yes, definitely

10. After participating in a meeting with the offender, do you have a better understanding of why the crime was committed against you?

4	3	2	1
Yes, definitely	Yes, generally	No, not really	No, definitely not

11. Did participation in the victim offender mediation (conferencing) program make the criminal justice process more responsive to your needs as a victim?

4	3	2	1
Yes, definitely	Yes, generally	No, not really	No, definitely not

COMMENTS:

It would be very helpful to our agency if you provided the following information about yourself. *Your identity is confidential, and none of the information in this survey will ever be reported in any way that can be connected to your name.* Please do not feel obligated to provide the following information if you feel uncomfortable doing so.

Type of crime _____

Your age _____ Your sex _____ Your race _____

Highest grade of education you completed _____

Was an agreement reached in the meeting with the offender? _____

Source: Copyright © 2000, Mark S. Umbreit and William Bradshaw, Center for Restorative Justice & Peacemaking, University of Minnesota.

- Use the satisfaction data to examine components of satisfaction, such as mediator skills, experience of meeting the offender, and satisfaction with the restitution plan.
- Explore differences in victim satisfaction for different groups of clients (African American, Hispanic, Caucasian; male, female; mandatory offender participation, voluntary offender participation; and so on).
- Focus on dissatisfied victims, and explore the problems.
- Set quality control limits for acceptable victim satisfaction scores for the program, and monitor routinely for meeting satisfaction goals.
- Collate comments offered on the VSOM Scale form, or routinely have a small number of brief follow-up telephone discussions with victims to hear their experience of restorative justice services in their own words. This use of qualitative data in conjunction with VSOM scores can enrich understanding of critical issues in victim satisfaction.
- Use the VSOM Scale as a part of training and monitoring new staff.
- Integrate victim satisfaction information into continuous improvement activities.

Contact the Center for Restorative Justice & Peacemaking at the University of Minnesota for technical assistance and consultation if needed.

Development of the Offender Satisfaction with Victim Meeting (OSVM) Scale

Work is currently under way on the development of the Offender Satisfaction with Victim Meeting (OSVM) Scale. This scale will be developed in three phases similar to the development of the VSOM Scale. First, a review of the literature on offender satisfaction will be done to identify key aspects of offender satisfaction, and a list of initial scale items will then be generated and reviewed by experts in the field. Second, the preliminary scale will be administered to offenders who have participated in victim offender mediated dialogue. Third, the results will be analyzed by principal-components factor analysis, and the resultant scale will be tested for reliability. When the OSVM Scale is available, it will be placed on the center's Web site, http://ssw.che.umn.edu/rjp

The VSOM Scale appears to be a useful measure of general satisfaction with victim offender mediated dialogue services. It has a high degree of internal consistency and has been used in a four-site U.S. victim satisfaction study.

The VSOM Scale can be easily supplemented by the addition of open-ended questions or items of special interest to particular programs. The scale is easy to administer and score and takes no more than three to five minutes for clients to complete. The VSOM Scale can be used to compare satisfaction between programs and between specific samples. The scale data with comments and any added open-ended questions can increase the richness of the information obtained. Finally, the use of VSOM Scale can encourage more specific feedback from participants in mediated dialogue that can be used to maintain and improve the quality of program services. The VSOM and OSVM scales, when completed, will provide a brief and useful set of consumer satisfaction scales for use in restorative justice programs that offer a mediated dialogue between interested victims and offenders.

References

Bae, I. (1992). A survey on public acceptance of restitution as an alternative to incarceration for property offenders in Hennepin County, Minnesota, U.S.A. In H. Messmer & H. U. Otto (Eds.), *Restorative justice on trial: Pitfalls and potentials of victim-offender mediation—international research perspectives* (pp. 291–308). Dordrecht, Netherlands: Kluwer Academic.

Bazemore, G., & Umbreit, M. S. (1999). *Conferences, circles, boards, and mediations: Restorative justice and citizen involvement.* Ft. Lauderdale, FL: BARJ Project, Florida Atlantic University.

Bradshaw, W., & Umbreit, M. S. (1998). Crime victims meet juvenile offenders: Contributing factors to victim satisfaction with mediated dialogue in Minneapolis. *Juvenile and Family Court Journal, 49*(3), 17–25.

Braithwaite, J. (1989). *Crime, shame and reintegration.* New York: Cambridge University Press.

Bush, R.A.B., & Folger, J. P. (1994). *The promise of mediation: Responding to conflict through empowerment and recognition.* San Francisco: Jossey-Bass.

Carr, C. (1998). *VORS program evaluation report.* Inglewood, CA: Centenela Valley Juvenile Diversion Project.

Christie, N. (1977). Conflicts as property. *British Journal of Criminology, 17,* 1–15.

Clarke, S. H., Valente, E., & Mace, R. R. (1992). *Mediation of interpersonal disputes: An evaluation of North Carolina's programs.* Chapel Hill: University of North Carolina, Institute of Government.

Coates, R. B., & Gehm, J. (1985). *Victim meets offender: An evaluation of victim-offender reconciliation programs.* Valparaiso, IN: PACT Institute of Justice.

Coates, R. B., & Gehm, J. (1989). An empirical assessment. In M. Wright & B. Galaway (Eds.), *Mediation and criminal justice* (pp. 251–263). London: Sage.

Coates, R. B., & Umbreit, M. S. (1999). *Parents of murdered children meet the offender: An analysis of two cases.* St. Paul: University of Minnesota, Center for Restorative Justice & Peacemaking.

Collins, J. P. (1984). *Final evaluation report on the Grande Prairie Community Reconciliation Project for Young Offenders.* Ottawa, Ontario: Ministry of the Solicitor General of Canada, Consultation Centre (Prairies).

Cook, T. D., & Campbell, D. T. (1979). *Quasi-experimental design and analysis issues in field settings.* Boston: Houghton Mifflin.

Davis, R., Tichane, M., & Grayson, D. (1980). *Mediation and arbitration as alternatives to prosecution in felony arrest cases: An evaluation of the Brooklyn Dispute Resolution Center.* New York: VERA Institute of Justice.

Dignan, J. (1990). *Repairing the damage: An evaluation of an experimental adult reparation scheme in Kettering, Northamptonshire.* Sheffield, England: University of Sheffield, Centre for Criminological and Legal Research.

Duryea, M. L. (1994). *Conflict analysis and resolution as education.* Victoria, British Columbia, Canada: University of Victoria, Institute for Dispute Resolution.

Fercello, C., & Umbreit, M. S. (1998). *Client evaluation of family group conferencing in 12 sites in First Judicial District of Minnesota.* St. Paul: University of Minnesota, Center for Restorative Justice & Peacemaking.

Flaten, C. (1996). Victim-offender mediation: Application with serious offenses committed by juveniles. In B. Galaway & J. Hudson (Eds.), *Restorative justice: International perspectives* (pp. 387–402). Monsey, NY: Criminal Justice Press.

Galaway, B. (1984). *Public acceptance of restitution as an alternative to imprisonment for property offenders: A survey.* Wellington: New Zealand Department of Justice.

Galaway, B. (1989). Informal justice: Mediation between offenders and victims. In P. A. Albrecht & O. Backes (Eds.), *Crime prevention and intervention: Legal and ethical problems* (pp. 103–116). New York: Aldine de Gruyter.

Gehm, J. (1990). Mediated victim-offender restitution agreements: An exploratory analysis of factors related to victim participation. In B. Galaway & J. Hudson (Eds.), *Criminal justice, restitution, and reconciliation* (pp. 177–182). Monsey, NY: Criminal Justice Press.

Gold, L. (1993). Influencing unconscious influences: The healing dimension of mediation. *Mediation Quarterly, 11,* 55–66.

Gottfredson, S. D., & Taylor, R. B. (1983). *The correctional crisis: Prison overcrowding and public policy.* Washington, DC: U.S. Department of Justice and National Institute of Justice.

Gustafson, D. L., & Smidstra, H. (1989). *Victim offender reconciliation in serious crime: A report on the feasibility study undertaken for the Ministry of the Solicitor General.* Langley, British Columbia, Canada: Fraser Region Community Justice Initiatives Association.

Huber, M. (1993). Mediation around the medicine wheel. *Mediation Quarterly, 10,* 355–366.

Hughes, S., & Schneider, A. (1990). *Victim-offender mediation in the juvenile justice system.* Washington, DC: Office of Juvenile Justice and Delinquency Prevention.

Le Resche, D. (1993). Native American perspectives on peacemaking [Editor's notes]. *Mediation Quarterly, 10,* 321–325.

Marshall, T. (1990). Results of research from British experiments in restorative justice. In B. Galaway & J. Hudson (Eds.), *Criminal justice, restitution, and reconciliation* (pp. 83–107). Monsey, NY: Criminal Justice Press.

Marshall, T., & Merry, S. (1990). *Crime and accountability: Victim/offender mediation in practice*. London: Home Office.

McCold, P., & Wachtel, B. (1998). *Restorative policing experiment: The Bethlehem, Pennsylvania, Family Group Conferencing Project*. Pipersville, PA: Community Service Foundation.

Myers, S., & Filner, B. (1993). *Mediation across cultures*.San Diego, CA: Authors.

Niemeyer, M., & Shichor, D. (1996). A preliminary study of a large victim/ offender reconciliation program. *Federal Probation, 60*(3), 30–34.

Nugent, W. R., & Paddock, J. B. (1995). The effect of victim-offender mediation on severity of reoffense. *Mediation Quarterly, 12*, 353–367.

Nugent, W. R., Umbreit, M. S., Wiinamaki, L., & Paddock, J. B. (in press). Participation in victim-offender mediation and reoffense: Successful replications? *Journal of Research on Social Work Practice*.

Perry, L., Lajeunesse, T., & Woods, A. (1987). *Mediation services: An evaluation*. Winnipeg, Manitoba, Canada: Office of the Attorney General, Department of Research, Planning and Evaluation.

Pranis K., & Umbreit, M. S. (1992). *Public opinion research challenges perception of widespread public demand for harsher punishment*. Minneapolis, MN: Citizens Council.

Public Agenda Foundation. (1987). *Crime and punishment: The public's view*. New York: Edna McConnell Clark Foundation.

Public Opinion Research. (1986). *Report prepared for the North Carolina Center on crime and punishment*.Washington, DC: Author.

Quill, D., & Wynne, J. (1993). *Victim and offender mediation handbook*. London: Save the Children.

Remen, R. N. (1998). On defining spirit. *Noetic Sciences Review, 47*, 64.

Ridley, C. R. (1995). *Overcoming unintentional racism in counseling and therapy*. Thousand Oaks, CA: Sage.

Roberts, L. (1998). *Victim offender mediation: An evaluation of the Pima County Juvenile Court Center's victim offender mediation program (VOMP)*. Masters thesis, University of Arizona, Tucson.

Roberts, T. (1995). *Evaluation of the Victim Offender Mediation Project in Langley, B.C.* Victoria, British Columbia, Canada: Focus Consultants.

Rogers, C. (1961). *On becoming a person*. Boston: Houghton Mifflin.

Roy, S. (1993). Two types of juvenile restitution programs in two midwestern counties: A comparative study. *Federal Probation 57*(4), 48–53.

Satir, V. (1976). *Making contact*. Berkeley, CA: Celestial Arts.

Schneider, A. L. (1986). Restitution and recidivism rates of juvenile offenders: Results from four experimental studies. *Criminology, 24*, 533–552.

Stone, S., Helms, W., & Edgeworth, P. (1998). *Cobb County [Georgia] Juvenile Court mediation program evaluation*. Carrolton: State University of West Georgia.

Sue, D. W., & Sue, D. (1990). *Counseling the culturally different* (2nd ed.). New York: Wiley.

Thomson, D. R., & Ragona, A. J. (1987). Popular moderation versus governmental authoritarianism: An interactionist view of public sentiment toward criminal sanctions. *Crime and Delinquency, 33*, 337–357.

Umbreit, M. S. (1988). Mediation of victim offender conflict. *Journal of Dispute Resolution, 1988*, 85–105.

Umbreit, M. S. (1989a). Crime victims seeking fairness, not revenge: Towards restorative justice. *Federal Probation, 53*(3), 52–57.

Umbreit, M. S. (1989b). Violent offenders and their victims. In M. Wright & B. Galaway (Eds.), *Mediation and criminal justice* (pp. 99–112). London: Sage.

Umbreit, M. S. (1990). The meaning of fairness to burglary victims. In B. Galaway & J. Hudson (Eds.), *Criminal justice, restitution, and reconciliation* (pp. 47–57). Monsey, NY: Criminal Justice Press.

Umbreit, M. S. (1991, August). Minnesota mediation center produces positive results. *Corrections Today*, pp. 194–197.

Umbreit, M. S. (1994). *Victim meets offender: The impact of restorative justice and mediation.* Monsey, NY: Criminal Justice Press.

Umbreit, M. S. (1995a). The development and impact of victim-offender mediation in the United States. *Mediation Quarterly, 12*, 263–276.

Umbreit, M. S. (1995b). *Mediation of criminal conflict: An assessment of programs in four Canadian provinces.* St. Paul: University of Minnesota, Center for Restorative Justice & Peacemaking.

Umbreit, M. S. (1996). Restorative justice through mediation: The impact of programs in four Canadian provinces. In B. Galaway & J. Hudson (Eds.), *Restorative justice: International perspectives* (pp. 373–385). Monsey, NY: Criminal Justice Press.

Umbreit, M. S. (1997). Humanistic mediation: A transformative journey of peacemaking. *Mediation Quarterly, 14*, 201–213.

Umbreit, M. S. (1998). Restorative justice through victim-offender mediation: A multi-site assessment. *Western Criminology Review, 1*, 1–29.

Umbreit, M. S. (1999). Victim offender mediation in Canada: The impact of an emerging social work intervention. *International Journal of Social Work, 42*, 215–227.

Umbreit, M. S., & Bradshaw, W. (1995). *Victim-sensitive offender dialogue in crimes of severe violence.* St. Paul: University of Minnesota, Center for Restorative Justice & Peacemaking.

Umbreit, M. S., & Bradshaw, W. (1997). Victim experience of meeting adult versus juvenile offenders: A cross-national comparison. *Federal Probation, 61*(4), 33–39.

Umbreit, M. S., & Bradshaw, W. (in press). Factors that contribute to victim satisfaction with mediated offender dialogue in Winnipeg: An emerging area of social work practice. *Journal of Law and Social Work.*

Umbreit, M. S., Bradshaw, W., & Coates, R. B. (1999). Victims of severe violence meet the offender: Restorative justice through dialogue. *International Review of Victimology, 6,* 321–344.

Umbreit, M. S., & Brown, K. (1999). Victims of severe violence meet the offender in Ohio. *Crime Victims Report, 3*(3), 35–36.

Umbreit, M. S., & Coates, R. B. (1992). *Victim offender mediation: An analysis of programs in four states of the U.S.* Minneapolis: Minnesota Citizens Council on Crime and Justice.

Umbreit, M. S., & Coates, R. B. (1993). Cross-site analysis of victim-offender mediation in four states. *Crime and Delinquency, 39,* 565–585.

Umbreit, M. S., & Coates, R. B. (1999) Multicultural implications of restorative justice. *Federal Probation, 63*(2) 44–51.

Umbreit, M. S., Coates, R. B., & Roberts, A. W. (1998). Impact of victim-offender mediation in Canada, England, and the United States. *Crime Victims Report, 2*(1), 83, 90–92.

Umbreit, M. S., Coates, R. B., & Roberts, A. W. (2000). Victim-offender mediation: A cross-national perspective. *Mediation Quarterly, 17,* 215–229.

Umbreit, M. S., & Fercello, C. (1998). Family group conferencing program results in client satisfaction. *Juvenile Justice Update, 3*(6), 3–13.

Umbreit, M. S., & Greenwood, J. (1997). *Criteria for victim-sensitive mediation and dialogue with offenders.* St. Paul: University of Minnesota, Center for Restorative Justice & Peacemaking.

Umbreit, M. S., & Greenwood, J. (1999). National survey of victim-offender mediation programs in the United States. *Mediation Quarterly, 16,* 235–251.

Umbreit, M. S., Greenwood, J., & Lipkin, R. (1996). Introductory training manual: Victim offender mediation and dialogue in property crimes and minor assaults. St. Paul: University of Minnesota, Center for Restorative Justice & Peacemaking.

Umbreit, M. S., & Roberts, A. W. (1996). *Mediation of criminal conflict in England: An assessment of services in Coventry and Leeds.* St. Paul: University of Minnesota, Center for Restorative Justice & Peacemaking.

Umbreit, M. S., & Stacey, S. L. (1995). Family group conferencing comes to the U.S.: A comparison with victim offender mediation. *Juvenile and Family Court Journal, 47*(2), 29–38.

Umbreit, M. S., & Vos, B. (2000). Homicide survivors meet the offender prior to execution: Restorative justice through dialogue. *Homicide Studies, 4,* 63–87.

Umbreit, M. S., & Zehr, H. (1996). Restorative family group conferences: Differing models and guidelines for practice. *Federal Probation, 60*(3), 24–29.

Van Ness, D., & Strong, K. H. (1997). *Restoring justice.* Cincinnati: Anderson Publishing.

Warner, S. (1992). *Making amends: Justice for victims and offenders.* Aldershot, England: Avebury.

Young, M. (1995). *Restorative community justice: A call to action.* Washington, DC: National Organization for Victim Assistance.

Zehr, H. (1985). Restorative justice, retributive justice. *New Perspectives on Crime and Justice, 4.* Akron, PA: Mennonite Central Committee, Office of Criminal Justice.

Zehr, H. (1990). *Changing lenses: A new focus for crime and justice.* Scottsdale, PA: Herald Press.

Index

About the Authors

Author

MARK S. UMBREIT, PH.D., is a professor in the School of Social Work, University of Minnesota, and the founder and director of the school's Center for Restorative Justice & Peacemaking and the National Restorative Justice Training Institute. He is an internationally recognized mediation practitioner and scholar with nearly thirty years' experience as a mediator, trainer, lecturer, researcher, and author of three books and more than one hundred articles, book chapters, and monographs in the field of restorative justice and mediation. Umbreit has conducted training seminars and lectures throughout the United States and Canada; in Belgium, Denmark, England, Germany, Italy, Norway, and Sweden; and in Japan and China. As a practicing mediator, he specializes in facilitating a dialogue between surviving family members of homicide victims and the incarcerated offenders. Umbreit recently completed the largest cross-national study of restorative justice through victim offender mediation in multiple sites in Canada, England, and the United States and is finalizing the first multisite study of victim offender mediation in crimes of severe violence in Texas and Ohio prisons. For the past twenty years, he has served as a consultant and trainer for the U.S. Department of Justice.

Contributing Authors

WILLIAM BRADSHAW, PH.D., is a senior research associate at the Center for Restorative Justice & Peacemaking at the University of Minnesota. He began his career in the field of corrections and has lengthy experience in community mental health services, as both a practitioner and a researcher. Bradshaw is an assistant professor in the School of Social Work at the University of Minnesota.

ROBERT B. COATES, PH.D., is a senior research associate at the Center for Restorative Justice & Peacemaking at the University of Minnesota. He has an extensive background in juvenile justice and has written numerous articles, monographs, and book chapters on the subject. He has served on the faculty of the School of Social Service Administration at the University of Chicago, the Graduate School of Social Work at the University of Utah, and the Harvard Criminal Justice Center.

JEAN GREENWOOD, M.DIV., is the former training coordinator for the Center for Restorative Justice & Peacemaking at the University of Minnesota. She is currently a mediator, trainer, and consultant in the field of restorative justice. She is also a community faculty member who periodically teaches a course on mediation and conflict resolution at the University of Minnesota's School of Social Work. An ordained minister, Greenwood heads a Presbyterian congregation in St. Paul, Minnesota, and is currently developing a restorative model for use in religious institutions. She has coauthored a number of works on victim offender mediation published by the Center for Restorative Justice & Peacemaking.

TERRI GROB, B.A., is a consultant, trainer, and mediator for restorative justice projects. She recently developed and managed a grassroots victim offender mediation program in Anoka County, Minnesota, and is currently working with the Minnesota Department of Corrections to develop victim, offender, and community dialogue groups at the women's prison at Shakopee. Actively involved in supporting the restorative justice movement in the state of Minnesota, Grob serves on restorative justice boards at both the local and state levels.

ANN WARNER ROBERTS, M.S., is the community outreach coordinator at the Center for Restorative Justice & Peacemaking at the University of Minnesota. She is a researcher, practitioner, and consultant in the field of restorative justice and works closely with Dakota County (Minnesota) Community Corrections, a nationally recognized leader in systemic change toward implementing restorative policies and practices. Roberts has coauthored several publications on victim offender mediation and group conferencing and has been actively involved in monitoring and supporting the development of restorative justice practices in the United States, England, and other countries.